FIRST TO THE FRONT

FIRST TO
THE FRONT

·························

THE UNTOLD STORY OF
DICKEY CHAPELLE,
TRAILBLAZING FEMALE
WAR CORRESPONDENT

LORISSA RINEHART

ST. MARTIN'S PRESS
NEW YORK

First published in the United States by St. Martin's Press, an imprint of St. Martin's Publishing Group

www.stmartins.com

Library of Congress Cataloging-in-Publication Data

Names: Rinehart, Lorissa, author.
Title: First to the front : the untold story of Dickey Chapelle, trailblazing female war
    correspondent / Lorissa Rinehart.
Description: First edition | New York : St. Martin's Press, 2023. | Includes bibliographical
    references and index.
Identifiers: LCCN 2022058083 | ISBN 9781250276575 (hardcover) |
    ISBN 9781250276582 (ebook)
Subjects: LCSH: Chapelle, Dickey, 1919–1965. | War correspondents—United States—
    Biography. | Photojournalists—United States—Biography. | Women photographers—
    United States—Biography.
Classification: LCC PN4874.C44 R56 2023 | DDC 070.4/333092 [B]—dc23/eng/20230209
LC record available at https://lccn.loc.gov/2022058083

Our books may be purchased in bulk for promotional, educational, or business use. Please contact your local bookseller or the Macmillan Corporate and Premium Sales Department at 1-800-221-7945, extension 5442, or by email at MacmillanSpecialMarkets@macmillan.com.

First Edition: 2023

10 9 8 7 6 5 4 3 2 1

For my mother

CONTENTS

INTRODUCTION

SHE DIDN'T HAVE much time. They would be leaving soon. In the next room over, she heard the names of familiar drop zones as the commanders debated where they should jump after the sun went down. Their tone anticipated enemy resistance. The chop of an incoming helicopter thundered outside as she lit another cigarette at her typewriter. She had to get the story out.

"Dear Hobe," she wrote her editor, "This letter is a try at reporting to you what I've been doing and thinking. Mostly for my sake, I'll try to put down in words a point of view from which I'll be drafting copy later this week. The subject matter of the copy will be some 5,000 people on our side, the Vietnamese Airborne Brigade. I can't imagine that most Americans know they exist; no reporter (man or woman, Viet or US) was ever permitted to go out on their operations before. Yet the five weeks—no it's six now—that I've spent with them have been as unforgettable an adventure as I have ever had in my life."

In the autumn of 1961, Georgette "Dickey" Meyer Chapelle made seven jumps with the Vietnamese Airborne Brigade, slept seventeen nights in the field, came under fire seven times, and marched over two hundred miles through head-high jungles and knee-deep streams. She patrolled the Ho Chi Minh Trail along the Cambodian border with them; photographed them fighting with bravery and valor; watched them die in agony and got up the next day with the survivors to begin their battle again.

Blond, petite, and hailing from a sleepy suburb outside Milwaukee, Wisconsin, Dickey might have seemed an unlikely figure to be making camp with South Vietnam's finest, let alone to be the first reporter of any gender to have the honor of being credentialed with the Airborne. But fighting men had welcomed her since World War II when, with equal parts grit and compassion, she covered America's armed servicemen giving their last full measure of devotion on Iwo Jima and Okinawa.

With her hard-won reputation for being as tough as a Marine with a soft spot for freedom fighters, the Airborne seamlessly integrated Dickey into their ranks. They even designed a special parachute for her with extra pockets to hold her film. But since first touching down in enemy territory she saw with perfect clarity what few Americans were willing to admit for years to come. There was a full-blown war raging in Vietnam and one that America, along with its South Vietnamese allies, was losing. Hampered by conventional tactics and a lack of meaningful support from their American allies, the Vietnamese forces were no match for the Viet Cong guerrillas who gained ground every night.

Even in these early days, Dickey understood Vietnam as a pivotal battleground in the Cold War. But more importantly, she saw it was a moment of monumental consequence for the men and women of Southeast Asia fighting for their independence. More than most, Dickey knew the consequences of defeat at the hands of a brutal communist regime.

During the late 1940s, she witnessed the inception of the Cold War in the rubble pits of postwar Europe. Along with her then husband, Anthony "Tony" Chapelle, she worked as a documentarian for numerous international aid organizations while living out of the back of a retrofitted baby food delivery truck for months at a time. In war-ravaged capitals, she interviewed families who made a home in former bomb shelters. In the countryside, she hiked miles to remote communities that had been all but cut off from desperately needed supplies. Few were willing to go to such lengths to demonstrate the true cost of international peace through international war, and perhaps more than any other single documentarian, Dickey captured a complete portrait of postwar Europe.

It was this unique vantage point that allowed her to analyze the emergent Cold War with an uncommonly nuanced understanding. While her contemporaries often described this conflict in outdated dualistic moralities of good and evil, us and them, the USSR and the USA, Dickey recognized the granular, human element at work within the wider geopolitical landscape. Having lived with the starving, the exhausted, the psychologically traumatized men, women, and children of postwar Europe, she well understood how the Soviets used the promise of peace and prosperity to tighten their vise grip of oppression. She was also one of the few to acknowledge the heroic strength of those who mounted yet another resistance to tyranny, even after so many years of hardship during World War II. It was reporting on this renewed fight for freedom within the context of the wider Cold War that defined Dickey's career.

Yet acting solely as a reporter and documentarian struck Dickey as increasingly insufficient as the Cold War progressed. More and more, she did what she could to directly intervene. Such was the case in revolutionary Hungary where freedom fighters battled a repressive Soviet-backed regime in the streets of Budapest. In the wake of this brutal urban warfare, thousands fled across the frozen tundra by night to Austria, and Dickey was there to cover this humanitarian crisis for *Life* magazine. But for all those fortunate enough to cross over, more were stranded just a few thousand yards from their goal, lost in the icy darkness or pinned down by machine-gun fire and tracer rockets. For weeks, Dickey ventured into Soviet-controlled territory to help guide these refugees that last mile to freedom.

Her bravery came at a cost. While trying to deliver lifesaving penicillin to resistance fighters, Dickey was arrested at gunpoint by Soviet border guards and held in solitary confinement at Budapest's infamous Fö Street Prison for five weeks. She emerged deaf in one ear and suffering from post-traumatic stress disorder. Her devoted family as well as her own will helped her to recover in less than a year. But her experiences had changed her indelibly, and she found the fire that fueled her drive to document the fight for freedom for everyone, everywhere, burned with that much more heat. Simultaneously, the Cold War burst into flame across the globe through limited wars of independence. Dickey did whatever it took to get the story, every time, at any cost.

She became the first Western journalist to gain accreditation with the Algerian National Liberation Front and spent a month covering their campaign against French colonial rule. She was the first Western female reporter to march with the Cuban Revolutionary Army. She was the first woman to be given permission to paratroop with the 82nd and 101st Airborne Divisions. Later, she became the first female reporter to be stationed with covert special forces in Laos.

But it was in Vietnam that she saw the greatest need to bridge the ever-widening gap in empathy and understanding between America and its allies. She became the first correspondent of any gender to live with anticommunist guerrilla forces in the Mekong Delta and the first to jump with the Vietnamese Airborne. Later, she would become the first female reporter to go on patrol with the First and Third Battalions of the Seventh Marines Regiment that were among the initial US combat troops sent to Vietnam. Her numerous on-the-ground experiences led her to believe that more than any other Cold War conflict she had so far covered, the battle for this coastal Southeast Asian nation was a moment of decision not just for the United States, but for the free world whose boundaries were eroding by the day.

Nor was she blind to her own country's complicity and even participation in undermining the cause of liberty. She became one of the first and one of the few to speak out against the rampant anti-Asian racism that ran through US policies from the first days of the Vietnam War. She did so publicly in her writing, privately in confidential memos to top military leadership, and directly to commanding officers in the field.

As colleague and friend Joseph Galloway recalled, he and Dickey were once witnesses to the abuse of suspected Viet Cong soldiers. The Marines who had arrested them tied their hands behind their backs with wire, blindfolded them, gagged them, surrounded them in a pen of razor wire, then had two guards point their rifles at them. As Joseph described it, "Ms. Dickey looked at that and went berserk. The gunnery sergeant who was in charge of this platoon, she drew herself up . . . and she got right in his face and she ate him a new one. Sarcasm was dripping from her. She said are you sure you have good enough control of these dangerous prisoners. Don't you think you should get some camo wire and tie their feet together?" She then photographed these egregious abuses.

When he later asked her why she had reacted so vehemently, Dickey told him that she too had her human rights violated as a prisoner of war and that America would invariably lose if it continued down this dark road. Her insight could not have been more tragic or more prescient.

By EVERY RIGHT, Dickey Chapelle should be a household name. Throughout her career, which spanned the length and breadth of the early Cold War, Dickey's capacity to march beside fighting men regardless of creed or color made her insights singular. Her commitment to human rights, equality, and social justice made her reporting invaluable. The stories she brought back from the last days of World War II to the first days of the Vietnam War continue to shed new light on the evolution and history of the Cold War. Yet while she was alive, and after she died as the first American female journalist to be killed in combat, Dickey's fellow journalists dismissed her uncomfortable relevance. They accused her of being obsessed with military life, of being overly consumed by her career, and of being incapable of objectivity. For decades their arrows stuck, relegating her to obscurity. But it was precisely the criticisms leveled against her that made her such an extraordinary reporter then, and such a relevant voice now.

Dickey was in fact obsessed with military strategies, tactics, deployments, morale, and esprit de corps. Having spent so many years reporting on the Cold War's low-intensity conflicts, her real specialty lay in guerrilla warfare tactics, about which she wrote for some of the world's premier journals, magazines, and newspapers. Because she was an expert in her field, the leadership of numerous branches of the military as well as the Joint Chiefs of Staff often consulted her on their upcoming campaigns and long-term policies.

That she was consumed by her career also rang true, especially after she divorced her husband, Tony Chapelle. Naive, new to New York City and the world of international journalism, Dickey married Tony when she was twenty and he was more than twenty years her senior. From the start, their relationship was far from stable, and Dickey's continued success aggravated Tony, a deeply insecure individual who could not keep up with her ever more frenetic pace as the years passed. When his drinking habit graduated to alcoholism and drug addiction, Tony became verbally and emotionally abusive. At thirty-four, Dickey took legal steps to extricate herself from this increasingly toxic and dangerous relationship. She never had a serious romantic partner again. However lonely, her career flourished in these years of solitude. Besides, she took a lover when she wanted.

But her supposed lack of "objectivity" lies at the heart of Dickey's legacy. During the early days of the Cold War, most journalists were content to receive their information from government sources in hotel bars and press conferences, then print it without question. And this, to a large degree, was what passed as "objectivity." Dickey had no interest in this kind of dispassionate distance that favored the point of view of the powerful and wealthy. In her mind, such journalism couldn't be further from actual objective reporting.

Instead, her instinct led her to be immersed in the story and to prioritize the voices, the lives, and the experiences of those she reported on. Dickey spent days, weeks, sometimes even months pursuing a story in the field. She slept in Bedouin tents in the Algerian desert and in the foxholes she dug herself in the hills overlooking Beirut. She rode in picket boats between battleships off the coast of Iwo Jima and flew in a nuclear-armed jet stationed on an aircraft carrier in the Aegean Sea. On New Year's Eve 1958, she patrolled the Soviet border with the Turkish infantry. On New Year's Day 1959, she photographed Fidel Castro's army as they entered Havana. She jumped out of planes over America, the Dominican Republic, South Korea, Laos, and Vietnam. She heard bullets flying over her head in Asia, North America, Europe, and Africa, and knew that they all sounded the same.

She did this because to Dickey, there was no substitute for seeing the story with her own eyes. Indeed, in letters and lectures to aspiring young journalists, she always extolled the imperative of seeing the story for herself rather than relying on the accounts of others. She had wanted to title her autobiography *With My Eyes Wide Open*.

As the Cold War progressed, Dickey leaned further and further into her unique brand of journalism. Meanwhile, her editors pushed back with increasing frequency, asking her to remove herself from the story or describe those she reported on in easy-to-grasp stereotypes rather than as the complex individuals she encountered. She fought back every time, never straying from her journalistic ethics, never abandoning what she knew to be her job as a correspondent—to report the truth as she saw it firsthand.

The world would catch up to her, eventually.

But in the autumn of 1961, Dickey was too far ahead of her time for most to see. And, from the vantage point of Tan Son Nhut Air Base in Saigon, she knew where history was headed.

The voices from the next room tapered off. Boots thundered down the hallway. She hurriedly finished her letter to Hobe at *Reader's Digest*: "I report my exciting discovery of new allies in the fight, not just with low tones of confidence, but with the shriller voice of Cassandra, and just a little desperation lest the gulfs of geography, skin color and politics that divide my READERS DIGEST-reader friends from my jumping friends will be too wide for my story-telling to span."

It was time to go. She grabbed her parachute. A propeller plane whirred to life at the end of the tarmac. The unit's corporal took her hand and hoisted her in. They took off as the sun slipped beneath the horizon. Below spread Vietnam's lush jungle canopy, and ahead a clearing. The bright lights in the fuselage dimmed to orange, allowing their eyes to adjust to the night. The corporal opened the door, the jump light turned from red to green, the first in their unit disappeared into the dark. Dickey checked the straps on her parachute and took a deep breath. Odds were that one among their number would be wounded or killed. But she could not turn back now, not when she had come so far and when there was still so far yet to go. Besides, she knew no other way of life, no other purpose than reporting on the truth, no matter how deeply buried, no matter how difficult to accept. The corporal motioned for her to stand. Dickey took her place at the door, looked into the unknown, and felt herself enveloped by the slipstream of history once more.

PART I

. . . .

1

A World on the Brink of War

BENEATH A GRAY winter sky, Georgette "Dickey" Meyer watched plane after plane depart the Boston Airfield. They were headed for Worcester, Massachusetts, where a historic flood had cut off every road into the small city. The only way to deliver much-needed supplies was by air. Dickey, a fledgling teen reporter, had pitched the idea of covering the airlift to the *Boston Traveler*, a local newspaper that had given her the tentative green light. But to really get the story, and secure publication, she'd have to make her way aboard one of the supply planes.

Having spent so many hours watching them take off and land, she knew all the pilots by name. Most of them recognized her too since a teenage girl standing on the edge of the tarmac proved a unique sight. Getting a ride to cover the story wouldn't be a problem if she would only ask. But her mother, Edna Meyer, was the kind of woman for whom worry was a religion, and she had made Dickey promise never to set foot in an airplane. Dickey had kept her word until now, when necessity required her to break it.

She glanced at her watch. Her test on flight dynamics at MIT, for which she had failed to study, had undoubtedly begun. She had to get onto one of those planes if she was to keep her place in college. The only way to make up the test was to prove she had been gainfully employed at the time of its proctoring, since at that time, in 1935 at the nadir of the Great Depression, earning money had to take precedence even at this elite institution.

Despite her current predicament, Dickey's start at MIT had been promising. Graduating two years early as valedictorian from her high school in Shorewood, Wisconsin, she had been accepted as one of only three women into the 1934 aeronautical engineering class. Grounded by her promise to her mother, Dickey had figured learning to build planes would be a close second to actually flying in them.

This turned out to be far from true. Blackboard equations of force and lift paled in comparison to the real thing. Almost from the first, Dickey started ditching classes to come to the Boston Airfield. Her grades had slipped a little at first, and then a lot. Now she was in danger of losing her scholarship and, with it, her ability to stay at university.

One of the last planes to depart began to cue up at the end of the airstrip. Dickey took a deep breath, shored up her courage, and ran.

"Captain Wincapaw!" she shouted. "I'm an MIT student trying to sell a story to the *Boston Traveler*. Have you room for me?"

"If you can find room aboard after the bread is loaded, come ahead," he called back.

Dickey hoisted herself through the cargo door and slid between the crates. The engines roared, the wheels started to lift from the ground, then, suddenly, flight. She recorded her first angel's-eye view with the language of a poet. "Green rolling earth, white concrete highways, gray sky and a black rain cloud back Boston-way." Nothing on the ground compared.

Soon thereafter, Dickey flunked out of MIT.

She went home to Shorewood where her parents, Edna and Paul, insisted she get a job. Dickey happily complied, quickly finding employment at the local air circus where she worked as a secretary and took part of her salary in flying lessons. She practiced loops and rolls and spins above green fields dotted with dairy cows. Back in the hangar beneath airplane wings, she practiced French kissing with the pilots.

Displeased with their daughter's maneuvers in the air and on the ground, Edna and Paul soon packed her off to Coral Gables, Florida, to live with her grandparents. They hoped she might settle down in this quiet Miami suburb of sea breezes and citrus trees. But Dickey had no interest in the well-trodden road, or roads at all, really. She soon found employment at the Tenth Annual Miami Airshow as its city editor, in charge of publicizing its events. The job suited her just fine, as did the salary of $15 a week, a princely sum in the doldrums of the Depression to which not even her overprotective mother could object.

Then, as the calendar approached 1939, things in the world began to change. The wheels of the American economy started to turn once again, albeit slowly. Meanwhile, in Europe, Adolf Hitler had undemocratically seized power while his National Socialist German Workers' Party espoused a platform of violence and bigotry. But the machinations of international politics barely crossed Dickey's mind when early in the new year her redheaded, cigar-chomping boss ordered her down to Cuba to help promote Miami's sister airshow in Havana. Being both ambitious and industrious, Dickey also secured an assignment from *The New York Times* to cover the event's flyers for its aeronautical section.

The crowd oohed and aahed as the first pilots executed their tail-slides and stall turns over the Havana Airfield. But Dickey kept her eyes and her pencil trained on the show's star, currently taxiing into takeoff position. Captain Manuel Orta, chief of the Cuban Air Force and the capital city's own hometown hero, would be performing the day's most difficult and dangerous trick: an outside loop, which requires the pilot to successively pass through a dive, inversion, and a climb before returning to normal flight.

The audience waited with both anticipation and confidence as Orta began his dive. Here was Cuba's ace pilot, for whom surely nothing could go wrong. His plane moved into an inverted position, and it seemed nothing would. But, as he began to pull up, his plane began to shake against the sharp blue sky. Orta gunned the engine and it looked for a moment like he might come out of it. Then came a "splintering, thundering, echoing crash," as Dickey wrote. Instinctively, she began to run toward the wreck, her low-slung heels sinking into the soft green grass.

A soldier tried to block her way.

"Prensa!" she shouted. *Press!*, and ran past.

The destruction had been total. As Dickey edged closer, she saw that "Captain Orta's gleaming propeller blade had become his executioner's sword." Back to the edge of the grass, she tried to clear her mind. It was the first death she'd seen in her young life. The romance of flying suddenly became tinged with tragedy. But she knew she had a job to do.

Collecting herself, she began to run toward the terminal's only phone booth, composing his epitaph as she went: "Captain Manuel Orta, 31, chief of the Cuban Air Force, was killed today when his Curtiss *Hawk* fighter plane crashed during an air show in front of 17,000 spectators, including his wife and . . ."

When she arrived, heaving for breath, she found the phone booth already occupied by a man in a white linen suit. She strained to hear him but couldn't make out his words over the pounding rush of blood in her ears. Summoning up all her midwestern manners, Dickey resigned herself to waiting.

Her restraint seemed to pay off when he hung up. He even helped her connect her call. Too distracted to wonder why a stranger would have the number to the *Times*' aeronautics desk, Dickey offered a beleaguered thank-you as the phone rang. Her editor took down her story and sent it to the print shop in time for the deadline. Distracted by a confused mix of pride and grief, Dickey failed to notice that the man was waiting for her until she nearly ran into him.

"I wouldn't have connected you with the competition so quickly except that I'd already scooped you," he said with a kind of stern encouragement.

Dickey blinked, confused.

"I'm with the International News Service. We've had the flash for five minutes now. Next time, girl, I wouldn't depend on the other reporters to put you in communication with your office."

For a moment the air vanished from beneath her wings. But she took it in stride, returning to Miami with a determination to be more self-reliant. In any case, all was not lost. Her article had run in the *Times* and a few weeks later, the other reporter happened to mention the story to a group of friends. One of them turned out to be Theon Wright, the newly appointed publicity chief of Howard Hughes's Transcontinental & Western Air, later known as TWA. Impressed by her pluck, Theon called to offer Dickey a job as his assistant. She was to report to New York in ten short days.

In the summer of 1939, she felt at home in the ceaseless and syncopated rhythm of New York City's streets. She took a room the size of a prison cell in a Brooklyn Heights boarding hotel that suited Dickey just fine. She never was one to stay in.

Weekdays were spent at the TWA offices on Forty-Second Street, where she toiled at typing and addressing thirteen copies of each of the company's many press announcements. But between long stints at the keys, she could glance out of her tiny cubicle's window onto the Chrysler Building, that pinnacle of Art Deco design epitomizing the grace and extravagance of New York City. Besides, the job wasn't all routine. As the publicity director's assistant, Dickey got to accompany Theon at major aviation events. She rode into a pink winter sunrise in an airline limousine. She flew in the first airplane to land at Idlewild Airport on the day Mayor Fiorello La Guardia cut its ribbon. She traveled coast to coast on TWA's famous transcontinental flights without a ticket because she was an airline employee. Not bad for a midwestern girl who'd just turned twenty.

Weekends, Dickey did what she did best—explore. Wandering Manhattan's gridded avenues and streets, she saw the world that called New York City home. Summer breezes and the ring of pushcart bells announced Italian ices on Mott and Mulberry Streets. Cantonese and sandalwood drifted through the air in Chinatown. She dodged clothing racks parading the latest fashions through the Garment District, then grabbed a bite to eat at a corner deli where the pastrami was sliced almost thin enough to see through.

It was a good life for Dickey and she might have gone on living this way indefinitely. But then came the first of September, 1939. The day the world stood still, then doubled the speed of its spin.

As she often did when curious about the news, she walked the few blocks from work to the *Times* building where the day's headlines circled its facade in enormous electrified letters. And there it was, the sentence that veered the course of history onto the path of total war.

HITLER OVERRUNS POLISH FRONTIER WITH FOUR PANZER ARMIES

The war that had long been rumbling in Europe finally erupted.

The US Congress immediately began to debate whether or not to enter the war. Neutrality won the day, but President Franklin Roosevelt appealed to the House for the funds to build 1,700 aircraft that could be sold to the embattled Allied Powers. They granted him twice that much and in so doing sent America's fledgling airplane industry soaring. Dickey knew there had to be an angle in there somewhere, and found it at the Long Island Aviation Country Club.

On an early October Saturday, Dickey held her breath from the ground as Earl T. Converse climbed to 12,000 feet in his Grumman F3F, then dropped into a terminal-velocity dive with his nose pointed directly at his audience. The plane plummeted at 413 miles an hour, about 7 miles a minute. At the last possible second, Converse pulled up. Suddenly reversing such a rapid dive meant the centrifugal force he felt would equal about nine times his ordinary weight, 9 Gs in aviator parlance. Dickey was in awe.

The powerful single-seat F3F was already the aircraft of choice for the US Navy. But with lucrative contracts on the table, Grumman had cut a second seat into this exhibition model for potential foreign buyers to take a ride. No reporter had yet covered it in flight or its groundbreaking maneuverability. When Dickey learned of this, she pitched the story to the *Times* and bought a ticket to the next airshow. Now all she had to do was persuade its pilot to take her up.

Scanning the audience for anyone with the authority to grant her permission to take a ride, her eyes fell on none other than Leroy Grumman himself, founder of the F3F manufacturer. Striding up to him with casual confidence, she inquired if anyone had ever written about the actual experience of a terminal-velocity power dive and threw in a few details about her tenure at MIT and previous experience as an aeronautical journalist.

"I'd like to read your story myself," he replied, impressed with her determination, and led her over to the hangar. "Connie," he said, "I think you'll find this young lady knows something about airplanes. See that she gets a ride."

Less than thrilled to be performing another dive, Converse begrudgingly threw Dickey a parachute. "Don't forget to scream," he said tiredly. "When your eyes black out, it'll be from the G. Give your gut a break. Scream so it'll tighten up."

"Yes, Mr. Converse," replied Dickey, who suddenly had the feeling she might be in over her head. Taking a deep breath, she hoisted herself into the plane.

At a mere 6,000 feet Converse put the plane into a gentle dive that

Dickey could have executed herself. Having completed the kiddy roller-coaster ride, he turned around and shouted over the engines, "Are you all right? Everything okay?"

Dickey replied by putting her thumb on her nose and wiggling the rest of her fingers, a gesture that more or less meant, "Not quite good enough, Jack."

Taking her sarcasm personally, Converse charged up to 12,000 feet and slammed the plane into a vertical power dive. Dickey watched the speedometer's needle push against its limit. As she wrote in her article about the experience, "An irresistible force drives my head into my spine. My legs collapse under me. My back bores into the seat. I try to shout but my cheeks are drawn so tightly that I can't open my mouth."

When the plane leveled out again, Converse turned around once more. "Was that better?" he shouted.

Dickey lifted her hands above her head and grinned. Yes, it was.

On the ground, Converse helped her to her feet. The parachute fell from her shoulders as she made a great effort to exhale the words, "Thank you."

Back in her boardinghouse room, Dickey went to work on her article under the headline A 20-YEAR-OLD GIRL DIVES 10,000 FEET IN A FIGHTING PLANE TO PROVE THAT WOMEN CAN BE COMBAT PILOTS.

Meanwhile, the war in Europe escalated faster than anyone thought possible. Still, Congress refused to join the fight, believing the United States would somehow be spared from the conflict engulfing the globe. Not Dickey, though. Despite her young years, she saw the world teetering on the precipice of a historical moment and knew she had to be a part of it. She also understood that to get in the game, she'd have to become as versatile a reporter as possible. That meant learning how to use a camera.

In the autumn of 1939, Dickey signed up for photography classes with TWA's publicity photographer and World War I veteran Anthony "Tony" Chapelle. Rain, fog, or sun, she and her fellow classmates practiced adjusting their f-stops and shutter speeds to capture the cars humming across the George Washington Bridge. Tony rented a boat launch so his students could capture the bridge's massive caissons and arched suspension towers against the cobalt blue New York City sky. Then he rented a plane and took Dickey, one of his most promising students, flying with her camera.

Dickey leaned out the side of the open cockpit and clicked until all her film was spent. She might as well have been dreaming. And anyway, she was falling in love with the man at the controls. Short, heavy-built, and more than twice her age, Tony was no Prince Charming at first glance. But what he lacked in looks, he made up for in charisma. Gregarious and confident with impassioned brown eyes, he conducted his class with infectious élan. Dickey was not immune, though early on, she came to understand his charisma went hand in hand with a temper she quickly dubbed Tony's "Homeric wrath." He often berated individual students and the class as a whole for their failure to achieve photographic perfection. Nor was Dickey exempt, often finding herself the target of his exacting ire. Still, this proved no barrier.

Tony was no less smitten by this midwestern girl. But rather than love her the way she was, he loved what he might make her and began to sculpt her into his vision of an ideal woman. Young and eager to make it in the man's world of photojournalism, Dickey fell into his hands like clay. She didn't mind when he replaced her horn-rimmed glasses and dowdy dresses with red lipstick and formfitting clothes. He draped her in expensive jewelry and photographed her as if she were a model. To be sure, beneath her Rust Belt patina, she was beautiful. And Tony helped her feel that way.

But he made it clear from the start Dickey would never be his equal. He endlessly criticized her angles and exposures. When she related the story of her report on Captain Orta's tragic death at the Havana Airshow, he ignored her extraordinary audacity as a then teenager and chastised her for not jumping on the fire engine that rushed to the scene. Dickey misread his controlling censures for caring tutelage. When he proposed, she thought she'd hit the lottery. A career, a husband, and an adventurous life all at the age of twenty.

They said "I do" in front of a bank of gladiolas in Dickey's hometown. Though at first skeptical of this much older man, her parents were soon charmed by his boisterous good humor and confidence. By the time the couple departed, Tony had won their enthusiastic blessing. Dickey took Tony's last name, Chapelle, which she kept for the rest of her life. Yet his

temper that often verged on violence and his tendency toward manipu-
lative behavior proved portentous.

For the first few years of their marriage, Dickey remained enamored
of her husband, viewing him as a war hero, a brilliant photographer, and
an experienced lover. In comparison, she felt herself an ingénue, crav-
ing his love and approval. As long as this stayed their dynamic, Tony at
least played the part of a decent husband. But as Dickey began to find
her footing as a journalist and her voice as a woman, Tony began to
change. The more independent Dickey grew, the more controlling Tony
became, going so far as to dictate what she wore, whom she talked to,
and what jobs she took. As Dickey continued to pull away, Tony escalated this abuse into threats of violence, once even brandishing a gun
outside her apartment door.

It is hard to imagine why someone like Dickey would be with someone like Tony at all, let alone for so long. But Tony seized upon Dickey
at a young age, only twenty, barely an adult. For fifteen years he shaped
her experience of the world and her understanding of herself through
his negative psychological conditioning. Simultaneously, he managed
to convince their friends, family, and colleagues that they were happy
and that he was the model doting husband. These antipodal narratives
served only to isolate her further. Who would believe that a man as
charming as Tony actively created a living hell for the woman he so
publicly adored?

But this dark horizon had not yet appeared when they returned to
New York after their wedding. Tony rented a hotel suite with a kitchen
large enough to serve as a darkroom. Dickey quit her job at TWA and
settled into the life of a professional photojournalist. Soon enough, she
landed her first big story, a six-page photo spread in *Look* magazine
picturing the women factory workers building the planes that would
go on to help win the Battle of Britain. Everything seemed peachy keen,
as Dickey might have said. Her career was on the up and up. Things at
home were going well. And America maintained its neutrality.

On December 7, 1941, when the air was crisp with early winter, the
couple took a Sunday drive up to the Hudson River Valley to see the last
of fall's fiery orange and red leaves. Past Inwood, Kingsbridge, Yonkers,
and Hastings, toward the Pocantico Hills. "Green Eyes" came on the

radio, the Tommy Dorsey Orchestra playing behind Helen O'Connell. Blue cigarette smoke curled around their car.

"Your green eyes with their soft lights / Your eyes that promise sweet nights," O'Connell sang, her voice swinging between the notes like a child on the playground. The day, the year, the life felt indelibly perfect at that moment.

The song broke off, a brief silence, and the clipped voice of a newscaster. Three hundred and fifty-three Japanese planes had bombed Pearl Harbor in Honolulu, Hawaii. More than two thousand Americans were dead with another thousand injured.

War had come to America.

2

Trial by Fire,
Reporting from Panama

On an icy January day in 1942, Dickey watched Tony ship out on the Hudson River. The Navy had assigned him as an aerial photography instructor at its base in Panama. Dickey waved him off with regret. While she would miss him, she wished even more that she too could do her part for the war effort. But Navy wives weren't allowed to join their husbands and women weren't allowed to enlist. Still, restrictions rarely stopped Dickey.

As soon as Tony departed, she began pitching articles on American military operations in Panama to every publication she could think of. Takers were not forthcoming. Few editors knew her name and besides, Panama wasn't exactly the most exciting story the war had going. But Dickey kept throwing in the line. Finally, *Look,* the magazine that published her piece on women building war planes, took her up on her angle of reporting on one of the military's lesser known war efforts in this Central American country.

One last hurdle remained in her way: getting credentialed by the Navy. Though Dickey sent the paperwork in immediately after getting her assignment, her zeal wasn't reciprocated by the public relations office. So she waited. And waited.

Winter and spring came and went. At the start of summer 1942, Dickey was still home alone and nowhere closer to getting her story. In a last-ditch effort, Dickey decided to try to cut through the red tape in Washington, DC.

The temperature and humidity intensified as the bus wound past Philadelphia, Wilmington, and Baltimore. Cumulus clouds billowed over the Capitol's cast-iron dome. Heat shimmered off the city's white marble monuments. The Potomac ran smoothly by. As Washington's architects intended, the scene took on mythical proportions. Dickey's eyes filled with the wonder of a patriotic idealist. As a child, she had paused to salute the flag outside of her school each morning, unprompted. Had she been a man, she would have been the first to sign up to serve in the military.

Though Dickey's actual destination—the Coast Guard Headquarters across the Anacostia River—lacked the grandeur of Washington's Mall, it offered something better: a chance to report on the war. Entering the drab bureaucratic building, she rehearsed her interview with its public relations director, Colonel R. Ernest Dupuy, for the thousandth time, trying to anticipate any questions he might ask. But when she sat across from the man who unknowingly held the key to her career, Dupuy only had one question of consequence.

"I see that recognition has been applied for you in part so you may photograph the training of the Fourteenth Infantry Regiment in the jungles of Panama. I presume you realize, Mrs. Dickey, that troops in the field have no facilities for women?"

"Colonel," she said with her usual sincerity, "I'm sure the Fourteenth Infantry Regiment has solved much tougher problems than that, and they'll probably think of a way to lick this one, too."

The colonel's impassive expression did not betray a response. But a few moments later, he slid her signed press credentials across the desk. That afternoon, Dickey booked a ticket to New Orleans where American supply ships were departing for Panama every day.

THE SINGLE CEILING fan did little beyond circulate the humid air in the United Fruit ticketing office. Dickey tried in vain to will herself not to sweat.

"Put her on B deck," said the agent to his clerk before turning back to Dickey. "Now about that stateroom of yours, it's well above the waterline," the agent continued, patting his brow with a well-used handkerchief.

"Torpedoes usually strike well below and the porthole is big enough to get off quickly."

Dickey took her ticket with shaking hands and walked out to the dock to see the ship. Far from the battle-ready vessel its name might suggest, the USS *Santa Marta* was a refitted freighter that had carried vacationers and bananas to and from Central America before the war. Now it ferried food and medical supplies to the US troops defending Panama's vitally important canal and training in its jungles. Since the *Santa Marta*'s route remained the same in war and peace, the Nazi U-boats knew it all too well. Just the day before, two of the line's vessels had been sunk and another was missing.

Waiting for their departure, Dickey tried to walk off her nerves by pacing the decks packed aft to stern with tarp-covered crates. The men who had loaded them dozed on top. The mood on the ship seemed, as Dickey wrote, "so sleepy that the clatter of a cart on the wharf is sort of sacrilegious."

Evening slipped into night. Dickey found her stateroom. The porthole wasn't quite as big as the agent had described. The breeze that moved over the brackish water of Lake Pontchartrain did nothing to dispel the heat. Dickey went up top for some relief and took her typewriter. She found space at a table next to a few sailors playing checkers beneath a bare bulb. To the din of their game, the hum of mosquito wings, and the buzz of the electric light, she added the rhythm of her keystrokes.

"The night is hot as only nights can get hot on a metal ship in a southern port," she wrote to Tony. "I'm the only girl and the only non-government passenger aboard, and all I want to do tonight is breathe in the salt air which masquerades under the name of Adventure."

Crawling to bed at midnight, she woke as the *Santa Marta* slid out of port just before dawn. On deck, Dickey watched the bayou pass, so thick with wiregrass, moss, and cypress that it seemed to roll backward. Grabbing the camera, she captured the first rays of light painting the landscape. But this propitious start to the day didn't last long.

Look had specifically commissioned her for an article on the gun crew aboard the *Santa Marta* and the convoy that would accompany it down to Panama. The Navy, in turn, had assured her the freighter would be armed and accompanied, even asking for copies of her negatives for publicity purposes. So she was particularly flabbergasted when she asked the second mate where the guns were and he replied, "This ship doesn't have any guns."

"Well . . . when do we join the convoy?" she pressed, hoping to salvage at least half of her story.

"Convoy? This ship doesn't need a convoy," he said. "All we've got in the hold is meat, cheese, and scotch. The Navy isn't going to give us a convoy for that."

Her whole reason for being on the *Santa Marta* disappeared. Not to mention she just learned they were effectively sitting ducks for any U-boat that spotted them. Then again, it occurred to her, if they got torpedoed she'd have a real story. In the meantime, she searched for another angle, starting in the mess where she found the chief engineer pouring a second cup of coffee.

"What do you think of the war?" she asked.

"Shipping sure is different than it used to be," he confided. "Now you can tell the boss to go to hell and he can't bar you from the next job there's so much work. Last time they called me I hung up the phone and went fishing for three weeks. The Captain about begged me to come on this one."

"But what about the U-boats?"

"It's always something," he shrugged.

The next afternoon she thought she'd try her luck at the engine room. A few of the crew were taking a break topside. Dickey pulled a pack of cigarettes from her pocket and offered it around before taking one for herself. A sailor telling a joke held his lighter out as a form of benediction. "Come on," he said after they stubbed out their smokes. "I heard you're looking for pictures."

Dickey followed him into the engine room on the lowest level of the ship where it was dark and loud and impossibly hot. Dozens of men, drenched in sweat, worked tirelessly to keep the ship under steam. Dickey arduously positioned her tripod, only to realize she didn't quite have the right angle. But before she could even pick it up off the deck a worker lifted it with one hand.

"Where you want it, hon?" he asked. She pointed and he put it down, carefully, gingerly even, then continued on his way to some other corner of this inferno.

Not once that afternoon was she allowed to move the tripod, or any of her equipment for that matter, since the workers would scoop it up before she could even protest. Somehow, they always had a glass of cold water for her.

Thinking of her own stateroom above the waterline, she asked one of the workers if he was scared of getting hit by a torpedo.

"Honey," he said, "you don't have to worry about anything long's you're down here. You'll never know what hit you. Have a cigarette?"

At night, Dickey paced the ship, breathing in the cool sea air while keeping one eye on the horizon for the glint of a U-boat periscope in the moonlight. One evening the chief mate stopped her on the lower deck, anxious to talk. He spoke at first mostly of women, his wife and various cruise passengers from before the war who had developed undying passions for his curly hair. Maybe he hoped Dickey would share their ardor. She didn't. Eventually, she brought their conversation around to a more serious note.

"You scared?" she asked.

"Do you think I am?" he replied.

"A little bit," she said.

"You're right," he sighed. "You know, a guy in this business gets in the habit of telling the truth. Nobody will trust you if you don't."

Few among this crew of merchant marines had been pleased with the idea of having a woman aboard. Seafaring superstition had long held that a female passenger spelled bad luck and more than one crewman, the captain included, had let her know as much. But as always, Dickey endeared herself to these men who put their lives on the line for their country through her interest in their stories and her willingness to share their risks. After all, if they were torpedoed, she'd be swimming along with the rest of them.

After her late-night talk with the chief mate, word got around that Dickey was all right. The crew grew easy around her and even the curmudgeonly captain let her take pictures of his control room. She gleamed with pride. Beyond personal accomplishment, she was proud of blazing an untrodden path. Few women in history had reported on war. Dickey had to make up her own rules, find her own way. As she put it, "On a war zone story like this, the first girl to try it hasn't much of a formula to go by. She can't become one-of-the-boys for obvious reasons and she is in an even less enviable position if she takes advantage of being a girl. She has to be just a person, a fairly complete entity by herself." She viewed having done so "a victory for feminism."

Unfortunately, her success did not carry ashore.

When she finally arrived in Panama in late June, Tony welcomed her as a lover, but in no way did he acknowledge she too had a job to do in Panama. Instead, Tony expected her to work as his unpaid assistant. She acted as teacher's aide during the days, showing Tony's students how to mount, frame, and retouch their photographs. In the evenings, she made huge portions of spaghetti on a two-burner kerosene stove for his twenty-seven photography students. She had no time to chase her own stories or take her own photographs. For a young woman who had just made it through one of the strongest naval blockades in history while winning over a ship full of merchant marines, being treated as a secretary was an insult, not to mention a rather boring turn of events. It was far from the last time Tony's demands would get in the way of Dickey's career. And it soon proved more than she was willing to put up with.

Less than a month after arriving, Dickey rented an apartment in downtown Colón. Perhaps she wanted to get away from the chores, or maybe she just wanted a room of her own. Though living alone got her off the hook for domestic servitude, it also meant Dickey had to pay her own way.

Hard up for cash, Dickey parlayed her notes and photographs from the *Santa Marta* into an article for *Look* about the U-boat blockade. Chain-smoking in the tropical heat, Dickey labored over her typewriter, affectionately capturing the cast of characters on the United Fruit freighter while placing them within the wider context of global war. Though she finished a draft as soon as humanly possible, before it could be published she had to get it cleared by military censorship, who gave her no indication as to how long that might take. Meanwhile, Dickey's already meager funds dwindled to nothing. She had to beg her editor at *Look* for an advance just to make ends meet.

Then, a little bit of luck broke her way. She received the official go-ahead to photograph the Fourteenth Infantry Regiment "Jungleers," who had joined forces in Panama with the 158th Arizona National Guard Unit, "the Bushmasters," an elite unit named for a venomous pit viper indigenous to Central and South America. More than just a name, the squad honed their trademark style of warfare in Panama's Darién Gap jungle, home to bloodsucking bats, poison dart frogs, jungle scorpions, fire ants, malaria-carrying mosquitoes, and botflies that lay eggs under human skin. Not to mention jaguars. In large part due to a shortage of willing volunteers, the Bushmasters had never been photographed by a journalist.

Clad in fatigues with twenty pounds of camera gear strapped to her back, twenty-three-year-old Dickey followed the military's toughest into one of the most dangerous environments on the planet, smiling ear to ear. Not only an honest-to-goodness scoop, her article on the Bushmasters would be a chance to test her mettle, both against the guys and her own expectations. It was also an experience that would prepare her for the rest of her career.

In the blazing heat and stifling humidity with mosquito clouds swarming at every turn, Dickey more than kept up with the men. She ran ahead, setting up her shots to catch the soldiers midstride, aiming to fire, and crawling through the jungle's primordial mud. When the Bushmasters forded a river with their guns held above their heads, Dickey scurried along the banks, capturing their struggle against the current. She climbed up after them as they built sniper blinds in hundred-year-old mahogany trees. While they macheted their way through otherwise impenetrable foliage in the dead of night, Dickey set off her flashbulb and snapped her shutter.

It would have made for the perfect photo spread. Except almost none of her photos came out. Even at noon, not nearly enough light filtered through the dense canopy for Dickey's action shots. Worse, the intense humidity of the jungle spawned a disastrous explosion of mold in her camera. She saw every unusable frame as a personal failure, and became so down that she even considered resuming her role as Tony's wife-secretary-assistant.

Even so, the Bushmasters were impressed with Dickey's tenacity and courage. Throughout her tour with them, she never expected special dispensation, never asked the soldiers to shoulder her gear, never failed to get where they were going under her own steam. They noticed and welcomed her back day after day for another attempt at getting a decent snap. Finally, their colonel delivered a welcome piece of news. "We'll deploy to the beach tomorrow," he said, "and you'll have more light than you can use." Dickey was ecstatic. It seemed her story was as good as printed.

But on the beach, the soldiers looked different. And it wasn't just the light. Their beards were shaved, their uniforms clean, and their polished guns gleamed in the sun. This was not good. Clearly, the colonel had decided that if his boys were going to appear in print, then they better be regulation. And now they didn't look at all like the most rough-and-tumble outfit in the armed forces that she was supposed to be covering. As Dickey wrote in her autobiography, "Unless everybody crawled a couple of hundred yards on his stomach in the nearest swamp we might just as well be making pictures back at Fort Dix."

Thinking fast, she asked the colonel if the troops could take their shirts off. He replied simply with a command, "Lieutenant, have that platoon strip—to the waist!" Understandably, the soldiers found this order hilarious but did not seem to mind stripping down for the leggy blond reporter who kept up on their marches. Besides, the bit of hijinks endeared her to them all the more. It became an inside joke. The next morning at their jungle bivouac they began to shout, "Here she comes! Strip, men—to the waist!"

Back in Colón, she enlisted Tony to develop her negatives. Even he had to admit they were good, as photo after photo of American soldiers looking fighting fit emerged from the chemical baths. Sure she'd landed the scoop of her young career, Dickey sent the film and story off to the censors.

But all her work, all the days spent in the deadly jungle, all the mosquito bites, all the money spent on flashbulbs and film, came to naught. She received a letter informing her that neither of her articles were approved for print since, as the censor explained, they posed a threat to national security. After all, they didn't want the Nazis to know just how effective their blockade really was or find out where America's fiercest force was training. In effect, Dickey had been too good at her job. Just like that, she was back to square one.

Pressed for cash, Dickey resorted to writing articles about bar fights between sailors and soldiers for *El Panama America,* a small bilingual paper based out of Colón. She almost vomited the first time she saw two men come to blows over what, no one knew. But after seeing a few broken noses and bloody lips, she found herself inured to this kind of violence. Besides, more often than not she'd see the same two men the next night, buying each other rounds and rehashing their fisticuffs in peals of laughter. She came to understand fighting men in this way, their propensity for settling scores with muscle rather than words and their equal ability to let bygones be bygones. Though these relatively benign brushes with violence proved a valuable lesson, the paltry fees she earned for her articles on these dustups were not close to enough to cover her expenses.

Then, the Navy reassigned Tony to a base back in New York. Broke and without an assignment, Dickey didn't stay long after. Besides, Tony kept sending her wires with sweet nothings and reminders of the modern conveniences in New York, like cold milk and an ample supply of American cigarettes. Her defenses depleted, Dickey went home. It had been a long, hard-fought battle, and she finally had to admit she had lost, at least for now.

3

The Way Back

IT HAD BEEN three years since she'd been in the field. Men were fighting and dying. Other journalists were reporting on history. And here she was, playing housewife and churning out title after title of government drivel on not particularly novel ways women could aid the war effort.

She drank whiskey at night. Smoked even more. She and Tony began to fight. She felt trapped. He wanted someone to cook, clean, screw, and be happy about the arrangement. She wanted to cover the war. But both the era and Tony dictated that as long as he was stateside, her wings would remain clipped. Years later Dickey described this period as one that scarred her for life. Even jumping out of planes and skirting the Iron Curtain seemed far less treacherous.

Yet to anyone on the outside looking in, their relationship appeared ideal. Outspoken and charming, Tony collected hangers-on by the dozen who clamored to come to his lavish dinner parties. He shucked oysters for hours, scoured Chinatown for razor clams, and sweated over stewing tomatoes until they were just right. Bottles of fine wine and aged whiskey were opened and emptied. Conversation raged around the table. The dining room chandelier shook with laughter. Even Dickey reveled in these evenings that often turned into early mornings. More than once the sun rose as the last drops were drained from their glasses. These were the times she loved Tony the most, when she basked in the glow of his radiant charm. But even in these moments she could not forget all the stormy tirades that came before and would surely follow.

. . .

DICKEY HEARD TONY come in as she finished yet another chapter on airplane manufacturing one evening. She pressed her bare feet into the white carpet. A steady stream of smoke rose from the ashtray. She paused from hammering the typewriter to take a drag and look out their panoramic windows at the Hudson River idly rolling by their Upper West Side apartment.

He called out, and she let him find her sitting at the table, a new cigarette perched between her lipstickless lips. It was 1944, just before Christmas. Snow began to fall, blanketing the city in a preternatural hush. Tony wrapped his hands around the back of one of the dining room's walnut chairs.

Then he told her.

The Office of War Information had ordered him to Chongqing, China's war capital. He'd had his inoculations and been measured for a uniform. All he needed now was the date of his departure.

Dickey channeled her sheer joy into the appearance of happiness for him.

The next morning, she woke up early, put her makeup on, and walked out the door.

Her first stop was the office of Ralph Daigh, the managing editor of *Woman's Day* and *Popular Mechanics*. He'd published several of her articles on aeronautical innovations and the women riveting them together. While she didn't have particularly high hopes for a positive response, she had to start somewhere. "Short-spoken" was a polite term for his demeanor. "Brusque" was another. He often returned her drafts with more red than black and hung up the phone when she called for clarification.

He didn't let her finish that morning either.

"We need somebody out there right now," he interrupted. "Go ahead. Just be sure you're the first someplace."

Dickey walked out the door, then ran the rest of the way back to her apartment. She cleared the dining room table of her errant notes, crumpled pages, and half-written drafts to spread out a recent map of the war.

His last phrase echoed in her head: *the first someplace.*

There were plenty of women reporters in the European Theater and Dickey found little use in trying to compete. Her gaze ran along the map, over the Western Front, across the Middle East, through the Soviet Union, then out into the Pacific Ocean. Just past Japan's outer archipelago of the Ryukyu Islands, the Allies had begun to amass the largest naval fleet the world had ever seen. Few women were covering this epic sea battle against the Imperial Japanese Army. More importantly, not a single female photographer had made it to the front.

With a rare prayer, Dickey dropped her request for accreditation to the Pacific Ocean Theater in the post. Like a miracle, it was answered ten short days later with her press pass and orders to report aboard on January 20, 1945, less than two weeks away.

She began to pack immediately. While folding rolls of film into her shirts, she made the crucial mistake of thinking Tony would be proud of her achievement, pleased she'd found a way to traverse an ocean and report on the war. But that evening, as ever, Tony proved her wrong. His orders to Chongqing had been delayed without explanation or hint as to when they might be renewed. He would be staying in New York and expected she would as well now that his plans had changed.

Dickey clutched her letter of accreditation, felt the embossed Navy stamp guaranteeing her freedom, her flight, her way out. "No," she replied. "I'm going."

Tony reluctantly accompanied her to Forty-Fourth Street and Fifth Avenue on an icy dawn. A polished blue station wagon swung around the corner, her Navy transport to the Floyd Bennett Airfield in Brooklyn. The young man at the wheel honked. Dickey kissed Tony's lips, curled into the petulant pout of a boy who didn't get his way.

"It won't be long," she promised and slipped into the back of the car, hoping it would.

AMERICA PASSED BY below her window. She'd made this journey before while working for TWA. But nothing compared with the anticipation she felt now. Or the apprehension.

While her credentials granted her passage to the general area of battle, they did not guarantee she'd see any action, get a good story, or make it anywhere near the front. Instead, she'd have to navigate her way through the gauntlet of individual commanders for permission to move forward. She anticipated that few of them would want her there in the first place, and many proved her right.

But for now, she had to strategize and play to her advantage.

Since the combat code prohibited female journalists from being anywhere there were not servicewomen already, Dickey attached herself to the slipstream of Navy air nurses who flew the wounded from the outer Pacific Ocean Theater to US hospitals in Guam, Pearl Harbor, and finally Alameda Hospital in Oakland, California. Dickey landed there first to report on new nurses readying for these air medevac missions in an unpressurized C-3 fuselage that simulated conditions at 12,000 feet.

Dickey took a knee to capture the trainees hanging mock blood bags from the ceiling, practicing their tourniquets, and sewing sutures in subarctic temperatures with minimal oxygen. None complained as the thermometer dropped from freezing to zero to negative ten. Chattering teeth were silenced with the glares of classmates that could have melted the paint off a bomber. Dickey's shutter quit snapping at twenty below. But she kept her pencil moving even as it hit negative thirty, wanting to capture their determination and grit.

Between training sessions, Dickey toured Alameda Hospital, which received dozens of critical cases every day. Though the Nazis were retreating to Berlin in February 1945, the Pacific War was far from over. The Battle of Manila had just begun and no one knew how much longer the Imperial Japanese Army could hold out.

Some of the returning servicemen she interviewed smiled when she approached with her camera, either putting on a brave face or genuinely happy to see a pretty woman. Others were in too much pain to take notice of her. All the while, she took care to keep out from underfoot of nurses and doctors winding their way through the rows of hospital beds. Besides these medical professionals in white uniforms, another woman dressed in bright colors occasionally flitted through the patient wards. She always seemed to be answering or dialing a phone for one of the men. After a few days, Dickey couldn't help but pull her aside.

Esther Carter, as she learned, was the hospital's chief phone attendant. The majority of the patients knew her by her voice if not her face.

She arranged their first calls to their family. Often, mothers started weeping before she even got the boys on the line, half-relieved they were alive, half-heartbroken they were injured, and completely overwhelmed. Sometimes Esther cried right along with them. "I can't help it," she said.

She wrote letters for those whose arms were broken, whose hands had been amputated or mangled. She dispersed nickels from a specially sewn pouch so they could take incoming calls without having to find change. She listened with seemingly endless patience as each told her about the girl that was waiting for him or the one who had not, about the lucky miss or the one that got him, about his dreams of the future or the nightmares that would not stop even when he opened his eyes.

Esther had, as Dickey put it, "a remarkable service record." And that was the thing about Dickey. She always saw how crucial everyone's work really was, even and especially the work of those who were overlooked.

But for all the affinity and reverence she had for the hospital staff, Dickey had no intention of staying so far from the front. She'd paid her dues in Oakland, written two stories on the nurses in training, sent her negatives off to the censorship board for approval, and made nice with the naval press liaisons who sneered at her papers when she arrived. But as she always did, Dickey once again endeared herself to military men.

On Sunday, February 18, the lieutenant in charge of Navy press at the Oakland air base agreed to see her. Eying her credentials once more, he handed them back.

"And just where was it you wanted to go?" he asked.

She had been rehearsing her response ever since her credentials first arrived in the mail.

"As far forward as you'll let me," she replied.

The lieutenant smiled, amused by her brass.

"Be here at 0600, tomorrow," he said.

Dickey arrived early. Her frozen breath mingled with the mist on the edge of the tarmac. Its engines were audible before she saw the Martin JRM Mars emerge from the blanket of dense gray. The largest transport plane ever built, the Mars could fly from Hawaii to the Allied Pacific front, and back, without stopping for fuel. She'd seen this crucial innovation in pictures, even written about these planes once in a government-issued aviation book. But she'd never had the chance to see one up close, let alone fly in one of these behemoths.

A line of smartly dressed and well-coiffed Navy nurses formed a line beside her as the press lieutenant strode up the hallway.

"I'm going to Pearl Harbor?" Dickey guessed as he approached.

"Correct," he said, and handed her the transfer papers. "Good luck."

She said thank you with mixed emotion. True, Oahu was farther forward than Oakland, and Pearl Harbor was a vital base in the Pacific Ocean Theater. But it was thousands of miles from any fighting and besides, several women correspondents had covered the military's operations on this paradisiacal island.

It could not, Dickey vowed to herself, be her last stop.

The engines roared to life. The wheels bounced, then lifted into the air. The earth fell away. Clouds drifted across the bay like spilled paint seeping across a blue canvas. Dickey lost herself in daydreams until the copilot climbed back into the compartment. News had just come in over the radio.

"The Marines just landed on Iwo Jima," he shouted. "It's worse than Tarawa." The horror in his voice was audible even over the plane's roaring engines.

Tarawa had been a well-placed pawn in the Imperial Japanese Army's Pacific Theater strategy and the Japanese army had fortified it accordingly. When the Marines finally took the island, it came at the cost of 3,166 casualties, a full third of their deployed strength. This seemingly unthinkable sacrifice for such a small piece of territory remained in the American imagination as one of the most gruesome battles of the war.

For the copilot to say Iwo Jima was worse than Tarawa meant the Marines were facing an even deeper hell than what had been previously understood as rock bottom.

"THE RAINBOW SHOALS of Oahu overlaid with the pearl light of dawn were sliding beneath us," wrote Dickey in her autobiography. "An hour later, I stood before a racketing teletype in the press room at Navy headquarters."

She watched the endless stream of bad news unfurl in black-and-white for the better part of the next twenty-four hours. "Whole outfits were being committed, macerated, decimated, destroyed," she wrote, knowing full well the Marine Corps couldn't maintain that kind of assault for much longer.

As with Tarawa, Iwo Jima's strategic importance far exceeded its actual size. Only eight square miles, it was nevertheless the location of one of the Imperial Japanese Army's most important remaining air bases. From Iwo Jima, Japan could launch unending aerial assaults on the approaching Allied naval fleet while defending the homeland from bombing raids. Without it, Japan would be rendered that much more defenseless.

Well aware of the stakes, the Imperial Japanese Army leadership had concentrated a significant portion of its remaining manpower and artillery to this lifeless volcanic isle. Still tuned into the teletype at 4 A.M., February 19, Dickey knew Iwo Jima would be the most important story she would ever cover and that she had to get there, somehow.

Flagging down the nearest press agent as the sun began to rise, she requested a transfer. When asked where, she repeated the phrase fast becoming her motto: "As far forward as you'll let me."

Guam came back as the answer. The farthest forward any American woman had managed to make it in the Pacific Ocean Theater. Her transport, a C-47 loaded with Marines, nurses, and ammunition, took off a little after sundown. Exhausted, she fell asleep on the soft mattress of a mail bag for much of the 3,800-mile flight.

A lanky redheaded lieutenant met her at the tarmac. Dickey swung into the front seat of his jeep, he hit the gas, and in a moment, the mud of freshly cut mountain roads caked her trousers. In the distance, she heard what she thought was a waterfall until a rainstorm came crashing down. Not that this lightened the lead foot of the lieutenant, who delighted in skirting the hundred-foot cliff.

Aware he would report how she fared to everyone within earshot, Dickey did her best not to betray her fear, focusing instead on the fact that she, twenty-five-year-old Dickey Chapelle, had done something that no other American woman reporter had. This steadied her as far as the Quonset hut where she was billeted.

"What's your name?" she asked, shakily stepping down from the jeep.

"Joe Magee," he replied. "Find me if you need anything. I'm your man."

Dickey nodded, pleased her faux stoicism had worked.

Exhausted, still muddy, and smelling no better than the soldiers she had traveled with, Dickey threw off her cot's blanket, laid down, and closed her eyes. Sleep enfolded her until hunger woke her at sunrise.

The press aide on duty informed her that she could find food at the officers' club, a short walk down the hill, across the field, around the following three ess turns, and up the next grade. Dickey laced up her boots. It'd been a while since she had been out with the Bushmasters in the jungles of Panama and as her calves began to burn, she promised herself never again to settle in to the sedentary city life.

Inside the commissary, the cook slopped runny eggs and dry potatoes on her plate. She poured herself a cup of coffee and took a seat at a table by the window. The long hike made the food palatable. She ate quickly, then paused to finish her coffee and admire the view of a curving white sand bay below. A gentle valley eased from the ocean, nestling a toy stucco town with perfectly square houses laid out on well-kept dirt roads. The whole scene seemed like a picture postcard until she looked closer. Not one house had a roof and not one of the town's walls remained intact. The church near the top of the valley had completely shattered. Children played in the ruins where even the trees grew at odd angles. "Every structure," Dickey wrote in her notes, "every thing above the muddy ground, is marked with shell holes larger than a man's body. This is Agaña, once Guam's largest city, population 12,000."

Another piece in the Pacific chess match, Guam had been seized from the United States by Japan directly after Pearl Harbor. As reclaiming the island proved essential to the Allied strategy, the United States preempted a ground invasion with heavy bombardment in the summer of 1944. For the residents of Guam, this attack first appeared as a blessing. Under Japanese occupation, nearly fifteen thousand of the island's twenty thousand residents experienced atrocities of war including forced marches and labor, internment, and torture. Over one thousand civilians were killed and untold thousands were injured. But freedom from this repressive regime came at a heavy price as the Allied bombardment left thousands more without shelter.

Dickey had read about incidents of collateral damage, the evacuated villages of the southern Pacific, the cities of Europe reduced to rubble. But she had never seen the atrocities of war firsthand, never witnessed the abject misery that conflict wreaked on innocent bystanders. War had been a distant adventure, abstract and honorable, cleanly divided between good and evil, right and wrong. But she found no morality in the bombed-out town below, no justice in the face of such destruction. As she would write, "Whenever someone urges international peace through international violence . . . I always wonder if the speaker has seen that kind of peace."

But just then, the realities of war took precedence. As she focused on the battle-ravaged city in her viewfinder, the room hushed behind her, then built to a loud hum. Iwo Jima ricocheted from table to table. Something had happened. Was happening.

Dickey rushed to the correspondents' center where wiremen crowded around a teletype spitting out reports from the assault fleet's communications ship, the USS *Eldorado*. A cloud of cigarette smoke circulated just above their heads. No one looked up as she came in.

The transmitter whirred to life and began to punch out the news in capital letters.

Offshore at Iwo Jima

THE MORNING OF D DAY PLUS THREE HAS COME HERE
FOR THE MEN ALIVE TO SEE IT. BUT INCOMPLETE
CASUALTY REPORTS INDICATE THAT FOR ONE OUT OF TEN
AMERICANS WHO CHARGED ASHORE HERE THERE HAS
BEEN NO SUNRISE. THEY DID NOT SURVIVE.

WITH THE ASSAULT FORCE AT IWO JIMA IT IS
UNDERSTOOD THAT UNITS OF THE THIRD FOURTH AND
FIFTH MARINE DIVISIONS HAVE BEEN COMMITTED.

The man beside her turned ashen gray. "God!" he whispered. "He's sentenced every man already there to death!"

The machine kept on.

ABOARD THE COMMAND SHIP OF THE ASSAULT FORCE
ANCHORED OFF IWO JIMA AN UNCONFIRMED RUMOR
IS SWEEPING THE SHIP . . . IT HAS BEEN OFFICIALLY
CONFIRMED THAT THE FLAG OF THE UNITED STATES NOW
FLIES FROM MOUNT SURIBACHI HIGHEST POINT OF THIS
VOLCANIC ISLAND.

Silence. Then a collective, spontaneous cheer that rang for minutes. The AP man to her left wiped his glasses in an attempt to hide a tear. Dickey scraped hers away with a knuckle. The fighting was not over, the island was not won. But the momentum had swung to the side of the Marines.

From the corner of her eye she saw Magee's flash of red hair. She ran after him.

"Did you hear?" she asked.

"I did," he replied, looking her up and down. She was wearing the same mud-splattered trousers as the night before. Magee pushed out his lips. "Where do you want to go now?" he asked.

In the blink of an eye she repeated her refrain: "As far forward as you'll let me."

4

As Far Forward

DICKEY SLEPT THE clock once around on the couch in the nurses' lounge. Magee had given her orders to report aboard the USS *Samaritan,* a hospital ship bound for Iwo Jima, at 0500 the next morning. Problem was, she lacked an alarm to wake her up at 0430 when her jeep to the port was set to arrive. So, she did the only thing she could do. She stayed awake, in the dark, all night, slapping and pinching herself while picturing on continuous loop the abject failure that awaited her if she closed her eyes even for one second. At last the jeep's headlights cut through the predawn. She managed to stay conscious just long enough to find a place to lie down.

By the time she woke up, they were halfway to Iwo.

She ran her hand along the steel walls as she searched for the press agent's office. The hull creaked as it slipped through the water. Taking a right where perhaps she should have turned left, Dickey found herself at the entry of the central medical ward. The sight stunned her where she stood. As she wrote in her autobiography, "A hospital ship is the only vessel that goes into combat empty. The one task of everybody aboard is to produce enough humor to suppress the significance of all those acres of empty beds."

Looking out over the field of white sheets that would soon turn red, Dickey could not fathom this task. But this was neither the *Samaritan's* nor its crew's first foray into war. On July 1, 1944, these beds had been filled within eight minutes of its first watch during the Battle of Saipan.

Unloading its bloody cargo in the bay of Kwajalein, the *Samaritan* returned on July 4, where its capacity was again met, then exceeded, this time fifteen minutes from taking watch. Subsequently shuttling ambulatory patients between Guam, Hawaii, and San Francisco, its crew had long since become adept at finding ways to cope with the gruesome promise of the *Samaritan*'s vast emptiness that Dickey now confronted.

"Ahem," said someone behind her. Dickey turned to see two hands holding a pile of linen stacked well above the carrier's head. "Little help?"

She took the top half, revealing the cherubic face of a corpsman barely out of his teens. "Sonny," he introduced himself. "Come help me count these," he said without asking her actual business. Dickey followed him to a mountain of sheets.

As they counted, Sonny reeled off the story of a recent ship-wide blood drive, though Dickey had trouble paying attention to his words or to the task at hand. The inevitability of the *Samaritan*'s purpose manifested in her imagination as teletype reports of Iwo Jima populated the room with specters of wounded soldiers. Their cries seemed almost audible.

Sonny kept talking. "Oh, we had a big time, all right!" he said.

She finished one stack and began another. The thought that at least she was being of help eased her mind for a split second until she realized her very presence displaced a doctor or nurse with the capacity to save lives.

"One of our boatswain's mates fainted right across the lap of the chief nurse when she pulled out the needle!" Sonny howled.

Suddenly realizing the implications of the need for a blood drive while on the way to the Pacific War's most gruesome battle yet, Dickey snapped out of her fog of self-pity. "What are all you giving blood for? Don't the folks back home give enough?"

Incredulity swept over Sonny's features. "There's never enough. You ever seen what happens in a battle when there isn't enough blood? Giving it don't bother us any, compared with those guys not having enough. Anyhow," he said, going back to his story, "it took three of us to lift him . . ."

In an instant, her purpose came into focus. She did not want to simply report the news: to coldly capture the story, record injuries and deaths, the kinds of bombs, the number of bullets. She wanted her journalism to affect the outcome, to change lives and maybe even save them. She would follow this trajectory for the rest of her career. But for now, she made up her mind to persuade Americans to give more blood, to help save the lives of those who fought for their freedom.

By that afternoon, she'd staged and photographed a blood donation drive with the ship's nurses, doctors, corpsmen, and sailors. At the end, she rolled up her own sleeve and watched the bottle fill. The photographs she took aboard the *Samaritan,* both of this donation drive and of the wounded soldiers desperately in need of blood, were used by the Red Cross for a decade in their publicity campaigns. The millions of pints of blood they helped raise saved tens of thousands of lives.

Her efforts endeared her to the crew, who in turn took it upon themselves to help her do her job. Sonny showed her how to reach the ship's searchlight, the highest point on the ship and the best from which to photograph an attacking Japanese fighter plane. Seeing her ascend its tower one-handed, a boatswain's mate made her a camera strap from a sling of rope. The chief nurse assigned her an actual bed rather than the sofa in the lounge. Finally, the deck officer taught her how to properly fasten her lifebelt and helmet.

Lights out was at dusk. Wanting to be ready for anything, she slept in her clothes with her boots positioned where her feet would land. She preloaded her camera with a flashbulb and positioned her helmet and lifebelt within arm's reach. It was a good thing too.

"The next thing I remember," wrote Dickey, "sound was vibrating the bulkheads and daylight pouring through the porthole. The noise was the alarm klaxon, and it lifted me clear up and into my shoes before I understood what I was listening to."

"All hands man your security stations," wailed the loudspeaker. "A Japanese bomber has just begun a run on this ship. I say again a Betty has just begun a run on this ship. We are the target. All hands take cover."

Dickey ran to the wide hatch that opened onto the main deck. There she hesitated. In another step lay the distinct possibility of being in the direct path of an enemy bomb. The *Samaritan* was completely unarmed, with only the First Geneva Convention's declaration against firing on hospitals as a shield. In the Pacific Ocean in 1945, these were just words, as effective against bombardment as the paper they were written on.

Unable to go either forward or back, she lingered at the cusp until a voice echoed down the steel hallway.

"Photographers are crazy!" exclaimed the voice of a passing sailor who saw the glint of her lens but not her hesitation.

Despite his low opinion of her profession, the mere fact that he believed she was a photographer gave Dickey the courage to step out onto the decks drenched in morning light, and utterly exposed to enemy fire. The single black dot of a Japanese plane grew larger by the second.

She froze. The rising sun on its tail became as clear as the bomb dropped from its belly that tumbled through the air until finally, miraculously, it splashed harmlessly in the water. The ship breathed a collective sigh of relief. Dickey composed herself and began to move.

"The bomber was circling and rising now," she wrote, "and I ran for the nearest ladder. I saw the whole war in that instant in clear terms. It was a race between him and me." She had to get to her lookout beneath the searchlight before he was able to discharge his second payload.

"I made it and threw myself flat on my stomach on the corrugated metal, bracing the camera into position with my elbows." The bomber began his second run. He had to change his release by only a few seconds for a direct hit. "Time spun out," recalled Dickey.

Somehow, she found calm behind her viewfinder. Enough, anyway, to keep her eye trained on the pilot's trajectory. Like him, she was waiting for the best possible moment to take her shot. But rather than a descending bomb, an orange lance arcing up from the water appeared in her lens. Dickey followed it down to its origin: a Navy destroyer opening up its antiaircraft weapons. The bomber turned tail and fled back into the blue.

The Samaritan's decks flooded with crew, waving to the destroyer and watching with relief as the enemy plane disappeared across the horizon. Dickey extracted herself from beneath the searchlight. A squadron of F6F Hellcats thundered above. She would have recognized their engines anywhere. They were the successors to Grumman's F3F fighter that she had reported on what seemed like an eon ago. Following their flight with her lens, their target came into focus: Iwo Jima. Japanese antiaircraft fire began exploding from its craggy landscape as they approached. The Hellcats flew straight for it.

"We could see first a single blossom of black smoke among the weaving dive bombers," wrote Dickey. "There was a flash of silver against the sky a hundred yards ahead of it, then the crippled plane spun down beyond the ridge and a thick spreading column of black smoke." The *Samaritan* steamed closer. Around the island's northern tip, the US Navy fleet became visible in all its enormity. Dickey watched as destroyers pounded the position of the Japanese gunner who had taken out the American plane. A cloud of volcanic ash followed and firing from that position ceased.

She was at last at war, and those for whom all the acres of empty beds were intended began to arrive.

In a speech for the Red Cross Dickey wrote, "When you read of a landing operation, you always think of the appalling D-Day morning when our men charge and stumble out of the landing craft onto the beach. After that, you rarely hear again about the boats and crews that put them there." But for the sailors operating these amphibious crafts, the initial landing was only the beginning of their mission. Every bullet, tin of food, and bandage that arrived on the shore of Iwo arrived in one of these boats. And every wounded soldier lucky enough to make it off the beach rode in one of them. Loaded to capacity and beyond, the small crafts had left shore as soon as they spotted the *Samaritan*'s bright white hull. The ship had not yet anchored when they began to arrive.

In a ballet of unfathomable proportions, the small boats circled the *Samaritan* still under steam while her crew lowered dozens of gangways into the churning sea. Dickey edged closer to the side, careful not to get in the way, and leaned over with her camera. The sound of the chop beating against the small boats' bows echoed up the *Samaritan*'s steel sides. Through her viewfinder she could see the agony of the wounded as they stared up at the readying gangways, waiting.

Dickey ran to the side of the first stretcher hoisted on deck. Like all of the wounded men she would see that day he was young and in pain. A nurse injected him with morphine. His writhing ceased. Dickey grabbed her pad and pen from her back pocket.

"Hey, who are you?" she asked, awkward with nerves.

Struggling for breath he answered, "Just call me Mac," then asked, "Who, who are you spyin' for?"

"The folks back home," she managed to reply, thinking the idea of Americans interested in his well-being might comfort him.

Blood and saliva foamed at the corners of his mouth. "Fuck the folks back home," he spat. He turned his bitter stare away from her back toward the island he had just been evacuated from, but would not escape. As Dickey learned, he died cursing those he died for. His words haunted her for years. She backed away.

Stretchers heaved over the side like waves in a storm. Nurses transfused the most critical patients on deck. Bags of blood swayed with the roll of the sea. Dickey kept focusing her lens, adjusting her light meter, and snapping her shutter. Behind her viewfinder, she could pretend she wasn't really there, wasn't really witnessing this carnage in person. She could make believe that like anyone looking at the newspapers back home, she was shielded behind the black-and-white veil of print.

"Some part of my mind," she wrote in her autobiography, "warned me that if I thought of them as people, just once, I'd be unable to take any more pictures and the story of their anguish would never be told since there was no one else here to tell it."

She didn't maintain this detachment for long. Pausing to reload her camera next to the stretcher of a man she presumed to already be expired, she saw his hand move and looked up. His eyes opened. The deep lines of volcanic ash on his face began to stretch. She realized he was trying to smile.

She stuttered, "Uh, soldier—how are you?"

His smile faded. The destroyer next to them fired off a deafening round. He waited for the reverberations to subside. Then, as Dickey wrote it, "he said carefully, syllable by syllable, 'Ma-rine. I'm a fucking Ma-rine.'"

Another salvo thundered. Dickey desperately wanted to return his half smile. Suddenly she knew how.

"Okay, you fucking Ma-rine," she said, imitating his intonation, "I asked you how you felt."

It worked. "I feel lucky," he said, smiling again.

Dickey quickly glanced down at his shrapnel-torn legs, then up to the large "M" written across his forehead, indicating he had been injected with morphine.

"Because," he answered her unasked question, "I'm here. Off the beach. I never knew the guys cared enough to get me the hell out of there. But they did. Three miles they carried me. Makes a guy feel lucky."

Two corpsmen came for his stretcher. Dickey quickly jotted his dog tag number in her notebook. "What's your name?"

"Johnny," he said as he was lifted.

Dickey watched as they set him down again in a corner of the deck reserved for those who had arrived too late, who had lost too much blood, who had little chance.

From then on she looked each man squarely in the eyes before she photographed him, acknowledging his anguish and fear, but also his hope. Rather than break her, it only strengthened her resolve to capture as many stories as she could. She wove between the endless streams of stretchers borne by corpsmen on the way to surgeries and wards. From the forecastle she took a panoramic photo of the deck as nurses triaged one patient after another. She climbed down the side of the ship into one of the small boats where a corpsmen unfalteringly held a bag of blood above a wounded Marine as the sea slammed them against the *Samaritan*'s hull again and again.

"There was hardly a wound that did not bleed on our welldeck that day," wrote Dickey, "and a pool of blood ceased to be a symbol; it was just something a man left behind him on the deck like his helmet or his gun." She understood now what Sonny had meant when he said giving blood before arriving was much easier than running out in the midst of their mission.

The *Samaritan* raised her anchor as the sun began to set. Her gleaming white hull and blazing lights would be a magnet for enemy planes in the dark of night if she stayed. Over seven hundred Marines had been loaded onto the ship, two hundred beyond its capacity. "Every corridor had become a ward," Dickey wrote. "Men couldn't be moved from the stretchers on which they had come aboard because there was no vacant bed to lift them into. Some who needed surgery were packed in ice so they would not die of infection before they could have their turn in the operating room."

But even away from the pitch of battle, the *Samaritan*'s odyssey was nowhere near over. It was eight days to Saipan, the nearest port with the capacity to absorb her load. That night Dickey returned to her quarters. The soles of her boots were soaked to the insoles with blood. She was exhausted in mind, heart, and body. And she was frightened for her own life in a way she had not been before.

On her portable typewriter, she pounded out the poem she had read so often that she memorized it by rote: "I Have a Rendezvous with Death," written by Alan Seeger, an American poet who fought and died in World War I while serving with the French Legion. She lit a cigarette as she typed the last stanza.

> But I've a rendezvous with Death
> At midnight in some flaming town,
> When Spring trips north again this year,
> And I to my pledged word am true,
> I shall not fail that rendezvous.

Leaning back in her chair, she pulled the paper from the bail, read it once more. She thought of her grandmother who had taught her to love poetry and who had wanted to be a bareback rider in the circus or a poet herself. For hours in the evenings they would trade reading Coleridge's ballads and Shakespeare's sonnets, and sometimes her grandmother's own compositions written in looping cursive on yellowing paper. She urged her youngest son's daughter to dream with ambition. And so she had.

As they steamed toward Saipan, Dickey captured as much as she could of the wounded Marines and the servicemen and women working around the clock to save lives and limbs. Like her hero, the esteemed combat reporter, Ernie Pyle, she spent hours listening, piecing together the whole from their individual stories.

Kit, the triggerman on a flamethrower, worked on a farm near Buckley, Washington. Jake Schiff, a rifleman from the Upper West Side of Manhattan, had been a student. Kit was a Protestant. Jake was a Jew. Their difference in faiths didn't get in the way of either of their prayers as 240mm mortars started raining down on them around midnight on D-Day. Almost half their company had been killed or injured, Kit told her, weeping. But they survived unscathed until D-Day plus nine when Kit took shrapnel in his right leg and the concussion of a falling mortar dislodged Jake's knee. By the happenstance of war, they ended up next to each other on the *Samaritan,* happy to see each other alive.

And she found hope. Johnny, the young man who thought himself lucky to be off the beach and whom Dickey thought would never see the States again, found her a few days into their trip to Saipan. She didn't recognize him at first, his skin no longer ashen gray but again full of life.

"Honest, Johnny," she said when he pointed to his name and number in her notebook, "I didn't know you. One shave can't make all the difference. What did they do to you?"

"Blood," said Johnny. "Ten pints of it. Cripes," he said, "I didn't know I was worth ten pints."

But this was war, and although displays of hope and camaraderie offered glimpses of humanity, horror reigned supreme. Nor did Dickey shy from its worst, found in the hospital's operating rooms.

"I remember those rooms," she wrote. "To photograph in it, the camera and I were both tied with rope by the bos'n to the pipes overhead, so if I fainted, I wouldn't fall into the incision." For three days and nights, an amputation of an arm or a leg was performed every thirty minutes without interruption. "The refuse bucket in here was a 50 gallon oil drum without a top. It filled up every three hours." Part of her never left that room, though she never did faint. Not once.

Finally, on the dock in Saipan, Dickey found something completely unexpected. Empathy.

It had been eight days and nights of steaming, of anguish that could not be quelled by morphine, of nightmares that would not let them rest even in their sleep, of canvas-wrapped bodies slipped into the sea. Finally, the *Samaritan*'s white bow warped into the pontoon docks of Tanapag Harbor. Ambulances had already formed a line. The wounded were loaded off in order of triage, the stretcher cases first and the walking wounded last.

But Dickey was one of the only people who knew that after the walking wounded Marines, there were five more patients to be unloaded: Japanese prisoners taken at Iwo. Because of an error in timing, their stretchers were brought above decks before the last walking wounded Marines had disembarked.

One of the Marines glanced back at the commotion behind him.

Then they all turned. Expecting violence, Dickey reluctantly lifted her camera that suddenly seemed heavier in her hands. "The nearest man was huge and square; his ragged jacket was in bloodstained ribbons and his left arm in a sling," wrote Dickey.

The Marine moved toward the Japanese soldier. The deck officer lifted his pistol. Leaning over the Japanese soldier, the Marine moved his hand toward the trench knife hung on his hip, then grazed past it and reached into his pocket. He took out a pack of cigarettes, removed one, placed it between the Japanese soldier's lips and lit it. The soldier struggled to free his hand from beneath the blanket. Realizing he could not, the Marine squatted on his heels, plucked the cigarette from his lips, and waited for him to exhale. He repeated the process until the Japanese soldier had smoked the entire cigarette.

"Okay, okay, move!" the deck officer shouted, uneasily.

The Marine crushed the butt beneath his heel, turned, and walked off the ship.

Nearly twenty years later Dickey reflected on her first view of war as well as this act of mercy. "I still don't understand why lookers on of battles try to use words to tell what they've seen. Or why I do. You don't remember the things of war with the part of your being that forms words.

"It's my stomach that remembers how the ship smelled. . . . And it's my ears that remember the ceaseless surge of small boat engines beside us as they delivered up their loads. . . . It's my feet that remember the blood that was slippery under your shoes and you had to be careful if you were standing in it not to fall down when the ship rolled. . . . I couldn't have guessed what my eyes would remember. It was how to fill with tears. It didn't happen there at all. But after the war, I was never able to see a helpless patient being moved in an ambulance or a boat or an airplane without feeling my eyelids sting.

"None of these impressions is as unfading as what the heart remembers. The eternal, incredible, appalling, macabre, irreverent joyous gestures of love for life, the fact of life, made by the wounded."

5

To the Front

THE PASTEL CLOUDS were tinged with red outside the freight plane's window. The cries of injured men echoed in her ears. Her memory replayed a Marine's last breath again and again. In between, doubt crept into her mind. Not of the worthiness of their sacrifice but rather doubt of her own intentions, her own justifications for reporting on the war. Her pride of being the first American woman to cover the Pacific Fleet came at the cost of thousands of dead and injured Marines. Her eagerness to get the story, get the scoop, follow the lead, seemed suddenly parasitical.

But another voice protested, insisted that were it not for her, the suffering of the wounded and the need for donated blood wouldn't be reported on at all. She argued with herself all the way to Guam. There, on the tarmac, she decided that she quite simply had a job to do. Though, hiking up the hill to her billet, it occurred to her she didn't quite know how. She'd already covered the hospital ship angle, and a story on a field hospital seemed like the next logical step. She just needed to figure out how to get to one. Luckily, the means and mode presented themselves as soon as she opened the flap to her Quonset hut.

Barbara Miller Finch had been assigned to the tent's second cot while Dickey was aboard the *Samaritan*. The British Reuters News's only female correspondent in the Pacific and the first woman to set foot on Iwo Jima, Barbara shared Dickey's passion and penchant for being the first on the scene. The two liked each other immediately.

As to how she had arrived on Iwo, Barbara explained she had flown under the auspices of a nurse's aide aboard *Peg O' My Heart,* a medical evacuation plane that brought wounded from Iwo directly to Guam.

"I'm going back tomorrow," said Finch. "Why don't you try to make the same run the following day?"

Dickey couldn't agree fast enough. It was the exact pretext she needed to photograph a field hospital and the delivery of donated blood. By midnight the next night, she persuaded Magee to grant her orders aboard *Peg O' My Heart.* He signed without protest and returned sleepily to his own reports.

"Good luck," he called after her as she gently closed his door.

At dawn, Dickey waited as the massive DC-3, specially outfitted to serve as a flying hospital, taxied down the runway. Though the Marines had recently captured Motoyama Airfield on Iwo, the still heavily en-trenched Japanese regularly bombarded the landing strip, making it impossible to store gasoline there. Any plane coming in had to carry enough fuel to get back. For *Peg O' My Heart,* this meant thirteen tons of fuel, over 80 percent of its total weight.

"We thundered into a takeoff run which seemed to go on for weeks," wrote Dickey. When their wheels finally lifted off the tarmac, they managed only to get a few inches of sky between them and the sea. "About ten miles out," Dickey recalled, "the pilot tried to climb. But the plane trembled and we made the whole run at about the same altitude as the tallest whitecaps."

Clouds of gray volcanic sand blossomed with the exploding shells of enemy mortar fire as they made their approach. The pilot circled, burning precious fuel that could not be replaced. Dickey glanced un-easily at the lifeboats. The possibility of having to use them ceased to be academic.

The shelling stopped, but the pilot kept circling. "He's making sure they're not luring us in," the flight nurse shouted over the propellers.

Finally earthbound, the pilot came back into the fuselage. He pointed out the field hospital that functioned in two wide tents. Rather than raised up from the sand, they'd been dug into the ground with only their pointed tops protruding. "Don't walk," he said as he let the stairs down. "Run."

As ever, Dickey did her best to follow orders but found her fastest sprint as rapid as a crawl through the sand that sank up to her ankles with every step. At last she reached the collection of rough-hewn boards laid on top of logs that passed for the base's road.

Emerging from a foxhole, a man with a shock of gray hair greeted them somewhat ominously. "Welcome to unmentionable island," he said. "You bring luck."

The man turned out to be Lieutenant Commander David Archambault, the surgeon in charge of the hospital.

"We haven't been so badly hit as to force us to stop operating for a whole day and night now, the first time that's happened," he said as Dickey followed him into the nearest tent. "Last night, we had to work for a time by starshells, but we were able to keep on."

Inside, the dug-in walls were lined with stretchers laid on the ground. In the center of the room, two more were suspended over crates marked WHOLE HUMAN BLOOD KEEP ICED, their contents long since having been expended. These were the operating tables.

"You call this a hospital?" Dickey guffawed.

"In the eyes of God and the US Army it is," Archambault replied and turned to his waiting patient.

Dickey backed up, sank to her heels, and lifted her camera as the doctor went to work. She tried not to notice as the man to her left watched her. His right leg lay askew, broken in more places than one. Even she could see it was doubtful he'd be able to keep it.

"Hey," he said. "You don't have a gun."

"Correspondents can't carry guns, Marine," said Dickey.

He fumbled with his belt. "Here," he said, holding out his trench knife. "Where I'm going I won't need one. And if you ever do, you'll need it bad."

She reached for it as if it were a talisman, as if he was bestowing on her the confirmation of the US Marines, which it was, which he was.

"Thank you," she managed to stutter as two corpsmen lifted his stretcher and placed it between the upended crates. She could not bring herself to watch as Archambault took a surgical knife from a roll of canvas. They had neither the time nor the resources for delicacy and Dickey could only guess at their morphine supply.

Outside, she shielded her eyes from the bright afternoon sun. Two

L-shaped berms meant to protect the hospital from mortars rose up to the left. Dickey realized they were tall enough for her to get a panoramic shot of the hospital area with Mount Suribachi in the background. She cocked her head to listen for the sound of incoming fire. Hearing none, she began to climb upward.

The sand fell away from her feet as she climbed, turning every step into three. Her legs began to shake halfway up but she reached the top, finally, stood, and focused her lens. The twin barrels of an antiaircraft gun rose in the foreground. Bombers and reconnaissance planes lined up on the runway. Beyond them was the mountain they were all trying to capture and the Allied fleet that had been shelling it for the better part of a month. Positioned between these landmarks of war, the hospital appeared as a lonely and brutal holdout of survival. Dickey's photographs were among the few to picture these humble structures where countless armed servicemen had bullets dug out of their abdomens and shrapnel dug out of their backs; got their legs set and their arms splinted; felt their hearts beat with transfused blood or breathed their last breath. There were no bloodless Hollywood heroics in a military field hospital and she didn't want that fiction in her photos either. She wanted only the simple and difficult truth.

Confident she got her shot, Dickey climbed back down, where she found Marines chuckling at her efforts.

"Now that's what I call doing it the hard way," one of them said. From his bars she could see he was a captain and his companion a lieutenant.

"What's the easy way?" replied Dickey, still struggling for breath.

"There isn't any. That's why it's funny. What are you doing here, anyway?"

"I'm photographing the Marines, sir," she said, unintentionally but effectively wiping the smiles from their faces.

"Where do you want to go?" asked the captain.

"As far forward as you'll let me," said Dickey.

The captain nodded at the lieutenant, who understood the implicit order.

"Come on then," he said to Dickey, pointing to a weapons carrier. "But I'll tell you right now girl, don't try and talk me any further than the front."

They drove in silence as the lieutenant struggled to keep the battle-worn carrier on the rudimentary road. It occurred to her then, too late to do anything about it, that asking a Navy man and asking a Marine to go forward were two entirely different requests. The Navy man would keep her in spitting distance of a hot cup of coffee. The Marine, however, would take her at her word. So here she was, on her way to the front, unsure if her courage would hold and terrified of what she might see.

Aboard the *Samaritan*, she had become used to the aftereffects of battle, as much as anyone could. But she knew nothing could prepare her to see a man shot, bombed, or mortared on the battlefield itself. She tried not to betray her apprehension as the lieutenant slid into a sandpit, cursing his luck and spinning the wheels. They broke free, then bounced down three terraces of shale. The lieutenant cut the engine.

"Here we are," he said.

There were no men, no guns, no exploding shells. Just the wind whipping over a lifeless island. Dickey looked around, thinking that perhaps she had missed something but didn't dare betray her ignorance. Instead she looked up at the ridges they had been driving between. Surely, she reasoned, there would be something to see from up there, just as there had been at the hospital.

Having done it once before, she scaled a ridge with more confidence this time, though not without imagining the Marines who had done so just days before under heavy fire, and laden with weapons and provisions. "Finally," she wrote, "I reached the top of the ridge. Now I understood why I hadn't seen anything below and heard so little. The whole area was honeycombed with sand ridges, their overall pattern like a waffle."

Standing up, she raised her camera to her eye. Three tanks rolled through the center of her photo. A moment later, their shells detonated over the ridge top to the north. She shifted the camera at right angles until finding three Marines digging a fresh foxhole into which they soon disappeared. Every hole, she realized, contained at least one man. Working from right to left, she methodically took eight photographs that composed a panorama of the front. But when she finished, she noticed the air seemed strangely alive with the sound of wasps. Her ignorance of its origin made the sound no less eerie. Though unaware of the full extent of the danger, she instinctively ran down the berm where the lieutenant was waiting, furiously smoking a cigarette. He threw it in the sand as she approached.

"That was the goddamnest thing I have ever saw anybody do in my life! Do you realize all the artillery and half the snipers on both sides of the war had ten full minutes to make up their minds about you!"

Her jaw dropped. The lieutenant continued.

"Didn't anyone anywhere ever pound into your pretty little head that you do not stand up, stand up, good God in heaven! On a skyline, let alone stand up for TEN minutes. And," he continued his rant, "do you realize that if you'd gone and gotten yourself shot I'd have to had spent the rest of the war and ten years after that filling out PAPERS?"

What sounded like the buzz of insects, as she later found out, were actually bullets flying in every direction.

He started the engine. Dickey silently crawled into her seat. They passed a Marine sitting on a rock, cleaning his rifle and chewing gum, marking the end of the front. The lieutenant slammed on the brakes.

"Are you trying to tell me that you honestly don't know any better? I mean, you're out here and you don't know what you should have done?"

It was her worst fear, realized. Being exposed as a dilettante, a pretender, in over her head. She had to say something.

"You mean," she began, "I should have made the pictures lying down?"

He punched the steering wheel. "That is correct," he said, his voice softening. "Do you think you could remember it?"

"I won't forget," she said. "It was too lonesome up there."

He looked her in the eyes and began to laugh. "Girl," he said, dropping her back at the airfield. "You made my day."

Dickey jumped from the running board. She felt at once foolish and grateful. In retrospect, standing on a skyline seemed unconscionably ignorant. But at least the lieutenant hadn't given her too hard of a time. If he wanted, he probably could have gotten her busted all the way back to Alameda. Or even home. Instead, his advice, though initially harsh, had taught her the single most important lesson when reporting on combat: keep your head down.

At the hospital, corpsmen were carrying the worst cases onto the medical plane. Dickey caught up with the flight nurse, who eyed her now filthy fatigues.

"You better get on board if you want to get off this rock," she said.

Dickey saw why the nurses at Alameda Hospital had trained so hard as *Peg O' My Heart's* engines thundered into takeoff. The temperature dropped like stone over the ocean. The blankets covering the wounded were crusted with blood and ash. Lifebelts hung behind the stretchers, parachutes cluttered the overheads, oxygen lines wound their way through the structural bracing. Nowhere was the quiet hush of a hospital, the order of a clean ward. Most difficult of all, no matter what happened, no matter how bad things got, there was no shortening the flight and no one else to call for help. The lives of the men rested entirely on the shoulders of the flight nurse on board. She alone was responsible for the lives of the wounded men on board. Yet even as she sutured their wounds, changed their dressings, and consoled those who would undoubtedly lose a limb once they landed, she maintained a cool confidence.

Dickey vowed to take a page from the nurse's book as the pilot began his landing approach. She shook off the sting of making a fool of herself on top of the skyline, replacing it with the singular desire to get back to the front, to report on the sacrifice war requires, to be a witness to that last full measure, and to try to tell the entire story.

When Iwo fell into Allied hands, only 216 of the 21,000 Japanese soldiers who had defended the island remained alive to surrender. Their terrible sacrifice took a heavy toll on the Americans, with 6,821 Marines dead and another 19,217 injured. But untold lives were saved by the nurses, doctors, corpsmen, sailors, and pilots who transported and treated these casualties, very much at the risk of their own safety. To Dickey, their efforts did more than just save lives, they helped win the fight. As she wrote in her article about flight nurses, every fighting man "can anchor his sanity to the thought that he is never more than hours from real security, the kind whose symbols are clean sheets, hot food, shaven faces, and concern for the value of human life." Knowing they might be saved if injured inarguably helped the Marines maintain their sanity and ability to fight.

But even with this comfort, Iwo marked a new low in the fiery pit of war. As Dickey later wrote, "The real odds were a little worse than even money on a man's being wounded, and flat one in seven that he would be killed outright. So nobody's faith in his own untouchability survived for many hours. Yet the fight went on for weeks."

But even now, with Iwo in Allied hands, the war was not over, not even close, and no one could have guessed how much further there was to go.

6

Floating City

"I'VE NEVER SEEN the plane before in my life," said Lieutenant John O'Hara as he climbed into the cockpit of a cub plane. A sheet of rain washed over the ocean while he took a moment to look over the controls.

"Well, what do you usually fly?" Dickey asked as the first drops began to fall.

"F-6. Want to ride in one of those?" he asked, closing the canopy as the rain began to pelt down on them. He didn't wait for a response before starting their takeoff run down the Falalop Island airstrip that looked no longer than a high school sprinter's track. The wheels left the ground as the breakers rolled beneath them.

Out of the rain emerged an enormous gray city of carriers and destroyers with radar towers and antiaircraft guns for a skyline. Between their hulls lay avenues of blue crowded with picket boats and tender ships. O'Hara took them in at a hundred feet, as Dickey wrote, "so low that the toy-like appearance of big ships that so many writers have commented on was missing entirely." Instead she saw them for what they were, utterly real and completely about the business of war.

In four minutes flat, they'd flown over this floating metropolis and begun their descent onto Asor, another of the isles that make up the Ulithi Atoll, where the Allies were amassing a larger naval fleet than even the coast of Iwo Jima had seen. As O'Hara pressed on the brakes all the way to the tide line, it occurred to Dickey that were it not for the war, this would have been the most romantic of island getaways.

Dickey jumped from the cockpit into the sand. O'Hara pointed her toward the press agent's office at the end of the runway. An attractive man in his midthirties who'd seen too many late nights and far too many journalists greeted her wearily. As Dickey noted, "He was properly devastated by the job."

She quickly told him her assignment. For her brevity, he gave her a chicken sandwich and forward-area lemonade, then assigned her to an acerbic ensign who seemed to purposefully slam the bow into the breakers as he piloted his dinghy out to the picket boat that would take her to the fleet. Gratefully aboard this somewhat more stable craft, she held on to the guardrail the entire way to watch the ships grow closer. But when they entered the blue lanes between the canyons of hulls, the picket boat began to rock violently. Still, Dickey stayed topside as spray smacked at her face and the sandwich she had vacuumed down cartwheeled in her stomach.

They pulled alongside the *Bountiful,* whose captain was, in her words, "the answer to a newspaper person's dream out here—red faced, beefy without being fat, and as much the disciplinarian as a puppy." He welcomed her with a pumping handshake and gleefully introduced her to his chief nurse, a "tiny and energetic and deliberately unglamorous woman."

But before she'd even gotten her sleeping assignment, word came that another picket boat was soon departing for a party back on Asor. Muddied, salt-sprayed, and unkempt, Dickey joined the perfectly coiffed nurses in their white silk shirts as they lined up to board. While they went below, Dickey doubled down on her harried look and stayed above deck to watch the sunset over the gray steel ships and white sand isles.

The Count Basie Orchestra wafted out of a double Quonset hut–turned–dance hall. The nurses made a run for it as the rain paused for a brief intermission. Dickey strode solemnly, trying to take it all in.

She got a drink from the bar where liquor was free and the bartender was pouring them strong. She drank the first one fast to take the edge off, and got another to sip. She had no interest in getting inebriated. "It was," Dickey immediately discovered, "very much a melodramatic eat-drink-and-be-merry-for-tomorrow-etc. party."

The whole scene seemed to embody the worst kind of loneliness that war can elicit. Marines and nurses wobbled around the dance floor and pressed against each other in not-so-dark corners while whispering "if only we had more time," before slinking back to the bar.

"Liquor drew a curtain over thoughts of the dawn," wrote Dickey in her notes, "and it seemed pretty worthwhile to remain hidden behind the thick folds for the last lingering minute."

It was March 25, 1945. Tomorrow, Iwo would officially end and preparation for Okinawa would begin. What further sacrifice peace would require, no one could say. But everyone knew there would be men who survived Iwo Jima only to be killed on Okinawa. It was enough to make anyone drown his thoughts of morning in whiskey.

Still, Dickey wanted nothing more than to follow the Marines on this next campaign, and she scanned the room for possible ins. She saw three generals sipping their drinks and watching their men break every prebattle regulation with benediction. A photographer she'd met on Guam soon gave her an introduction to these generals, if an odd one.

"Not drinking, huh?" said the photographer, eyeing her still almost full glass.

Dickey shook her head.

"How original," he intoned. "Me neither. Look," he said, "I need a favor. See those generals over there?"

"Yeah," she said.

"I want to get a photo of 'em with a woman, and you're the only one who's not drunk. Come on," he said, taking her by the elbow and practically pushing her onto the lap of one.

"I'm sorry, sir," said Dickey. The flashbulb exploded. The general looked her up and down and seemed to appreciate her ragged state of dress.

"Not a problem," he said in a Tennessee drawl. "General Shepherd. You just sit right on down, young lady."

"Dickey Chapelle," she introduced herself, sliding into the empty chair beside him.

"Well, what's a nice young woman doing in a place like this?"

Unknowingly, General Lemuel Shepherd had opened the floodgates.

The stories swelling in her chest came spilling out as the music played louder and the rain pounded heavier on the roof, as the dancers spun faster on the dance floor and drinkers drank faster. Somewhere in her storm of words of operating rooms and bombs and boys who died cursing the country they fought for were the reasons she had come here and what she wanted to accomplish.

Finally, she fell silent, suddenly aware she had been talking for ten minutes straight. General Shepherd looked at her patiently, took a draft from his drink and said, "I see. Are you going to see the Marines in the field on the next operation?"

"The Navy won't let a woman go that far forward," she replied.

"If you should be where my command is," he said, "please do not hesitate to visit us."

"I won't get that far," Dickey despaired, her second drink near empty now.

The general laughed. "I want you to be sure you understand that I have invited you to my command," he said and rose from the table.

The bartender emptied the last bottle. The lights began to flicker as the generator ran low on gas. The party spilled out onto the beach where picket boats waited to take them back to their ships. Back aboard the *Bountiful,* Dickey remembered she'd left before being assigned sleeping quarters and found a canvas tarp to sleep in beneath the stars on deck while the blinker from a carrier stabbed the darkness again and again.

She woke at dawn, found a cup of coffee, smoked cigarettes on the lookout deck until breakfast at 0800, then hopped a picket to Asor. She found O'Hara and his cub plane on the airstrip. A shipment of donated blood was due to arrive on Falalop any minute and she wanted to photograph it being unloaded. By the time she finished and hoisted herself back into O'Hara's jump seat, the squall bore down on them. O'Hara took off in its teeth, unfazed.

"How about some harbor aerials?" Dickey joked.

"Sure," said O'Hara, and he cut the engine at 120 feet to go in for a mock strafing run. They sank to the level of aircraft carrier landing strips. Crews waved at them as they glided by. Dickey stared back through her lens, snapping photos as fast as she could, sheer terror notwithstanding.

The squall they had left behind on Falalop caught up with them. O'Hara took another run.

"Hey, O'Hara," said Dickey, trying to keep the trill out of her voice, "I'm running a little late. Think we should land?"

"Sure thing," he said, snapping out of whatever trance of military training he had gone into.

The wind-whipped water lapped at their wheels by the time they came to a stop. Dickey shouted goodbye and ran to the picket boat readying to leave, hoping to make it back to the *Bountiful* in time for that evening's variety show meant to cheer up the troops.

But when they pulled alongside, the officer on deck shouted down that the show had been relocated to the USS *Franklin*, just down the way and to the left. The picket boat pilot sighed as they went in search of yet another ship. They found it where the officer said it would be, but not in the state they had expected. Drawing under its bow, they didn't find the usual gangway. Nor did they find one on the other side where half a dozen repair craft bobbed at her stern.

Dickey took the megaphone without asking permission. The pilot didn't object.

"Journalist for *Life Story*," she called. "Permission to come aboard."

"Permission granted," came the reply.

A steel cargo net dropped from the flight deck.

"Watch your feet," someone shouted down as they began to hoist her up. Dickey crossed her legs.

Somewhere between the cub rides and boat rides, filing stories and getting around protocol, she had missed what had happened to the *Franklin* a week earlier.

While on a secret strike force mission in the early morning hours of March 19, a Japanese bomber plane spotted the *Franklin*. Diving undetected out of low-lying clouds only a thousand feet away, the bomber managed to drop its payload before the *Franklin* was able to position its guns. Both bombs were direct hits.

The first penetrated the flight deck and ricocheted in the hangar. The second exploded only moments later, sending another fireball through the enclosed deck that ignited the fuel tanks of the hanger's planes. Blast flames shot up the elevator wells and out the sides of the ship. The planes on the flight deck were thrown into each other. Their propellers became steel swords. Dense black smoke enveloped the ship to the bridge. Communications were lost, blinding each section of the ship to what was happening ten feet away and what was about to happen to them.

Then, the *Franklin*'s own munitions began to explode.

As the surviving crew fought to extinguish the fires, ammunition stored in the planes, clipping rooms, ready service boxes, and the upper handling room sprayed them with unpredictable barrages of bullets. Sixty of its sixty-six 500-pound bombs detonated along with eight of its ten 250-pound bombs. All but one of its rockets went off.

But even as the *Franklin* burned out of control, the captain refused to abandon ship. There were too many men trapped below. On his lead, those aboard that could continued to endeavor to save them. As the *Franklin* floated dead in the water, its plume of smoke now 2,000 feet high, other ships from the fleet began to arrive. Several destroyers maneuvered bow to stern, allowing the walking wounded to jump to safety and able men from other ships to jump aboard the *Franklin*. In all, 807 of the ship's complement of 2,600 died. Another 487 were injured. The casualties would have been astronomically higher were it not for the actions of the crew that stayed and those that came aboard.

Pulling herself over the *Franklin*'s flight deck rail a week after it'd been hit, Dickey saw for herself how devastating the destruction had been. "From her hangar deck up was an almost solid mass of fire twisted wreckage. Not a yard of paint showed above the hangar deck, not a square girder, not a bulkhead or former gun that was not tortured steel."

The damage-control commander led her across the flight deck, burnt, buckled, and punctuated with holes the size of a plane's fuselage. The boards between the decks were rotting with the thousands of gallons of water it had taken to douse the fires. Dickey forgot about the variety show entirely until they walked by the crew's impromptu stage, constructed from the plane elevator lodged halfway between the flight and hangar decks.

Down one level, into the darkness of the hangar, he paused amidships. "This part was really the worst," he said. "We had 50 men killed here. It was bad picking them out of the overhead."

On some level, she had known this before he told her. The smell that permeated the air was one she had first come to recognize aboard the *Samaritan*. It was "the smell not of death, but of people who had died." The smell of death was the metallic scent of fresh blood, of cotton bandages and antiseptic. It was the pungency of cauterized flesh, burnt but closed. The smell of those who had died was older, mustier, stronger. It was the sulfuric smell of rotten eggs and rotting cabbage. The odor of mothballs and methane, of molded garlic and putrescine. It was the stench of an absence and grief and it could linger in the air for weeks.

Dickey suddenly felt on the edge of a sinkhole expanding outward. But still, true to the vow she had made to herself, she kept photographing the destruction and interviewing those who had survived it.

THE PERFORMANCE BEGAN just after sunset. Someone had run lights around the makeshift stage. Dickey found a seat on the bleachers of twisted steel girders and mutilated fuselages. The sailors, who had spent the last week digging their shipmates out of the wreckage, dead and alive, began to crack smiles as the vaudeville routine began. By the time it got to a Carmen Miranda number by an officer in drag, they were laughing outright. "But this was one show that the audience stole," Dickey reflected. "For a week little but fear and bitterness and horror had occupied their minds; now suddenly and a little surprisingly to themselves, they remembered how to laugh."

The picket boat had circled back for Dickey, who went down the way she came up, in a steel cargo net. It was dark now. The beacons of ships blinked along with the stars. Bits of bioluminescence washed against the *Franklin*'s hull. Dickey fingered the letter from Tony in her pocket that she hadn't yet read. It was the first she'd heard from him since she'd left Pearl Harbor, weeks ago now. She'd telegrammed him twice from Guam. Not having heard back, she assumed he was still sore that she left without him and felt a tinge of guilt about her departure. In any case, she'd resigned herself to not hearing from him for the duration of the war and was almost afraid to open his letter now. He had a way of getting to her.

Back in her berth aboard the *Bountiful*, she slit open the envelope with her trench knife. The letter didn't say much. There were no sweet nothings, no I love yous. Only that the army of Chiang Kai-shek was losing ground to Mao Zedong's communist forces and he wouldn't be going to Chongqing after all. But the Navy, he said, needed men like him in postwar Italy and he expected to be on his way in a month or so. He didn't know when he'd be back.

Despite his supposedly imminent departure, he signed off with a plea for her to return to New York. "If this reaches you in the trenches, dear doughgirl," he wrote, "just remember how good fresh cold milk tastes and come home right away where you can have all you can drink."

Soaked in seawater with the stench of dead bodies still clinging to her nostrils, the thought of creature comforts was, as Dickey put it, "calculated torture." Guilt and homesickness formed a single knot in her stomach. But after seeing the *Franklin* and with the Battle of Okinawa just days away, she knew she still had a job to do.

7

Okinawa

L-DAY ON OKINAWA and Easter Sunday both fell on April 1. A cruel joke if there ever was one. Word of a typhoon headed directly for them came over the loudspeaker just before sunrise service. No one knew what waited on the jungle island just ahead. As Easter Mass began, Dickey observed that "the line 'O Lord hear our prayer for those in peril on the sea' was a lot more sincere than melodic."

After the service, cigarette butts arced out from every deck of the *Relief* where Dickey had been reassigned. A general sense of live and let die ran through every rank. The crewmen pushed the limits of insubordination, talking back to officers and playing hijinks on one another. They hung by their knees from the overheads, wrestled in the wardroom, pretended to stab each other with carrots for Dickey's camera. All was forgiven as long as they continued to work as they did, never complaining of fatigue or refusing a chore, no matter how onerous.

Expecting another Iwo Jima, the Marines landed instead on ghostly quiet beaches. The *Relief* withdrew from the fleet at sunset without a single casualty coming aboard. Dickey retired to the nurse's wardroom, her sleeping quarters. Cigarette smoke escaped as she opened the door. The senior medical officer and five nurses howled as the queen of spades came out in a game of Hearts. Dickey took a seat on the pile of hospital cot mattresses that was also her bed. A sailor soon joined her.

"How is it," he griped, "that every goddamn officer on this ship has a liquor ration and a place to drink it?"

"I don't know," said Dickey.

"Well me neither," he replied and jumped off in search of a bottle.

The card game wound down and the men left. It was far too late for them to be there anyway. But the women stayed and got to talking about what they would do after the war. Be at home, they all decided, and picked out names for the kids they'd have as soon as this was all over. Though Dickey joined in, she couldn't quite convince herself of her own sincerity.

After the party crawled off to bed sometime around midnight, Dickey pulled out her typewriter. "I wish I knew what was expected of me," she wrote. "Am I to take the feminine psychology and do as I've been told? Or shall I adopt the admired virtues and grab the first shoreward vessel I can get to take me? I've got a fine case of split personality: the masculine lined up against the feminine," she reflected pensively, but concluded, "This is no place for the feminine, surely."

She fell asleep with this uneasy thought, though did not rest with it long.

The klaxon shattered the morning's silence at 0615. Dickey fell off her makeshift bed. As usual, she'd slept in her GI khaki shirt and survivor-gear trousers. By the time the speaker intoned "All hands to your security stations," she'd tied her boots and slung her camera around her neck.

Above decks she saw the Japanese Zeke long-range fighter heading straight for them. She started up the ladder to the flying deck when the first bomb began tumbling through the gray sky. By its arc, she could see it would miss.

She reached the top as the pilot unleashed his second. A deathly silence enfolded the ship as all eyes watched the bomb fall both impossibly slow and incalculably fast. This one looked as if it would hit. But under as much steam as the pilot could muster, the *Relief* outran the bomb that detonated a mere thirty yards astern.

The violent thunder of antiaircraft guns sounded off the port side. Dickey focused her lens on the destroyer sending a steady stream of bright orange into the sky. The Zeke took cover in the clouds.

For the next few days, Dickey hardly left the flying deck, the highest point on the ship. "I've seen dawn and sunset, storm and wind, smoke screen and ack ack and dog fights aloft and even the guns of a battlewagon," she wrote of her perch, where she was rarely alone. "We have a little society up there. Konicer, the Polish lookout, chunky and square; Evans slim and good looking, the radar operator who worries from one alert to the next, and I."

The three quickly fell into a pattern. Grim good mornings were exchanged followed by a long silence as each stared into the horizon. More often than not, a Japanese Zeke would appear, sending Evans to the controls and Konicer to the radio while Dickey adjusted her f-stop and aperture. Orange arrows of antiaircraft guns followed. Sometimes a couple of American F6s flew into the fray. Maybe the Zeke would get a bomb off. Most horrifying were the Japanese pilots that turned their planes toward the decks of ships.

But through all this, afternoon eventually rolled around, indicating their chances of surviving the day had increased merely from the passage of time. Silence thawed into quiet conversation and then an exchange of cigarettes, though regulations prohibited them from smoking up there. In a few days, Dickey started feeling at home on the *Relief*. "Funny how you can 'adopt' a ship like a town," she wrote.

Even so, she had not come all this way for the pleasure of some company. After less than a week, which seemed like an eon of inactivity, Dickey decided to act on her initial instinct and grab the first shoreward vessel that would take her. Within military protocol, of course.

She had requested permission to photograph Okinawa's field hospitals weeks ago, while still on Guam. The naval director of public information, Rear Admiral Harold Miller, promptly and crisply returned a resounding no. "Men, my girl," he began with chivalric chauvinism, "are very gallant. They will always risk their lives to save yours. Under the circumstances of an amphibious landing, I am sure you can appreciate the consequences yourself."

To a degree, she sympathized with his position. The amphibious landing on Iwo Jima had been one of the war's bloodiest battles. On the eve of Okinawa, the Marines braced themselves for history to repeat itself. Dickey had no intention of putting her own career ahead of the safety of fighting men. This was, however, the last time she would accept "because you're a woman" as an excuse to keep her from a story and would in the future often repeat her reason for rejecting such faulty logic. "As for the point that the front (any front) is no place for a woman, we heartily concur. We cannot too strongly agree. We say moreover that the front is no place for any human being. But if we are going to have wars if we are going to find ourselves as a nation in a position where our men must kill and be killed for months, even years—than no one except a woman can tell the story to other women."

In any case, the Marines had met hardly any resistance since landing and had marched across the island, established a field hospital, and appropriated the island's two airstrips. With the island seemingly all but secured, Dickey speculated that the reason for denying her permission to go ashore no longer held. Unable to consult with Rear Admiral Miller back on Guam, she hitched a ride to the USS *Eldorado*, the fleet's advance public relations headquarters where Rear Admiral Miller's own deputy, Commander Paul Smith, had his office. If she could get orders from him, no one could argue with the legitimacy of her landing on Okinawa.

Unlike many of the men who served as public relations officers, Smith had actually seen his fair share of combat. When World War II began, he resigned his post as an officer in the Navy and reenlisted as a private in the Marines. Only a battle wound convinced him to get back behind a desk, and Dickey dared to hope for his sympathy as she made her request in the best military voice she could muster.

"Sir, I'm photographing the use of whole human blood to save the lives of the wounded. Request permission to visit the Army's blood stockpile on Brown Beach. Sir."

Smith paused. Dickey braced herself for another denial. "You will eat in the wardroom now," he began. "There is an LCVP leaving the *Eldorado* after lunch. It will take you over and bring you back this evening."

She ate as much as she could as fast as she could.

The wind came up on the way over. The other two passengers in the amphibious boat were reporters as well. One hurled his lunch over the side. The other, a lanky Australian holding a portable typewriter, exchanged glances with Dickey as if to say, "What the hell is that guy doing here?"

"Surf's too high to land on Brown Beach," the pilot shouted over the engine as they neared shore. "This is Orange Beach." Releasing the gate, he added, "You know I won't be back for you today, don't you?"

The puking reporter declined to disembark. Dickey jumped into the knee-high breakers, followed by the Australian, who introduced himself as MacLean.

"I've been seven years in this business," said MacLean as they waded to shore, "and I must say, you Americans do it differently than anyone else."

Choosing to take this as a compliment, Dickey simply replied, "Which way is Brown Beach?"

"Where's it on your map?" he asked.

"I don't have a map. Can I see yours?" she deflected.

"I never use one. I just write my stories about the first fighting unit we come to."

Dickey paused to listen for gunfire. Above them the canopy of white birches spontaneously burst into flames. They ran. From what and to where they had no idea. It just seemed like the only thing they could do. But fortune smiled on Dickey again as two Marines pulled alongside them in a jeep.

"Give us a lift to Brown Beach?" Dickey implored.

"Brown Beach?" one said. "We got no Brown Beach. How'd you get here anyway?" they asked her.

"It's an Army beach," she clarified, ignoring his last question.

"We're Marines, ma'am," the other returned. "We don't know where any doggie beach is. We'll give you a lift to the First Division though," he said.

Dickey and MacLean hopped in the back and hoped for the best.

The divisional commander took one look at Dickey when they arrived. "Get her the hell over there," he said, referring to the next echelon of command up, the Third Amphibious Corps. He lent his own jeep and driver to the task.

She tried not to take it to heart. In any case, she'd been passed up, not down the food chain, and that had to be good for something.

Her luck held. She happened to know the Third Amphibious Corps's commanding officer, Johnnie Popham, who'd been a newspaperman for *The New York Times* before the war.

"But how did you get here?" he asked.

"Hadn't I descended from a jeep right in front of him?" Dickey thought, but didn't verbalize. Instead she said she was due back aboard the *Eldorado* before 1800.

"That's the least of your problems," he replied. "That's physically impossible. But what are we going to do with you? We've never had a woman here after sunset." It was already twilight then. "Here," he said, handing her a ration tin of scrambled eggs and bacon. "I'll think of something."

Her tent mates grumbled at the solution, seven male correspondents embedded with the unit.

"Put her in the middle. That's the safest place," one of them said.

"Safe from what?" Dickey asked.

"If the Japanese infiltrate the camp, they'll have to cut somebody else's throat before they get to you," explained one of the Marines posted to guard duty.

"We aren't going to have any infiltration," a columnist from Chicago piped in. "We're going to get strafed and we're right in line with the main runway, which will be the main target. So put her out on the edge. She won't have to run far to make it to the shell hole."

In the end the consensus—minus Dickey's own opinion, which hadn't been requested—was to give her the cot between the edge and the middle of the tent.

Lights out. Dickey covered her bases, placing her boots next to the cot and clutching her trench knife. She couldn't sleep. No woman had been on Okinawa after sunset. And she'd be here for at least another day. She thought she could see the stars through the canvas ceiling. When sleep finally overtook her, it didn't last long.

"MOVE!" shouted the Marine standing guard. "Uh, ma'am," he added.

"Everyone was charging out of the tent," Dickey later recalled. "Outside, a sector of the night sky was bright with lines of soaring silver . . . A Japanese plane had started to strafe near the main runway, just as the columnist from Chicago had predicted."

They made a forty-yard dash to the shell hole in the concrete, lay flat against the wall, and waited as the sound of machine-gun fire grew faint. Their collective breath steadied. An all clear sounded throughout the camp. Dickey refused a hand offered to help her out of the hole, managing just fine on her own.

Another near miss. It was becoming a pattern.

In the morning she warmed a ration can of beans on the fire and opened it with her trench knife. A jeep crept up.

"Anybody here heading for the Sixth Division command post?" called the driver.

Dickey looked up. "That's General Shepherd's outfit, isn't it?" she replied.

"Yes sir, I mean, yes ma'am. Say, how did you get here?" he asked, and Dickey wondered if there might be an echo on the island since she'd been asked this obvious question so many times.

But rather than ignore him, she replied simply, "I'm almost sure your general invited me," and ate another knife full of beans. As Dickey wrote later in her autobiography, "this stupefied the driver long enough so I could tell Captain Popham I'd be back after lunch."

"My dear," said General Shepherd as she got out of the jeep, "you are a brave girl. You're in time to lunch with us too." He ushered her over to a table of rough boards on ration cartons in a grove of pine trees.

The division's chief of staff, surgeon, and captain soon joined. A sergeant served them hot stew. The general held court, waxing poetic on his native Tennessee and how Okinawa's mountains reminded him of home. But when their plates were cleared, General Shepherd resumed his attitude of business, asking Dickey a pointed question: "What did you come to see?"

"I want pictures to show how you use whole blood to save the lives of Marines so more civilians will give it before the next operation," she said.

"And how long do you have?" the surgeon asked.

"I told the public relations officer at Captain Popham's unit I'd be back right after lunch," said Dickey, dejected.

The general smiled. "There will not be any transportation out of here till sundown," he said.

"Yes, sir," she said, trying to keep the corners of her lips from curling into a smile. She had until sundown.

But the day was not the success she had hoped even though the chief of staff arranged two outings. The Japanese army had not yet made its full presence known and she found little of note to report on. Back at camp, the sun slid beneath the tree line. For all her efforts, not to mention whatever hell she'd have to pay for not being back aboard the *Eldorado* last night, she didn't have a single shot worth the ink it would take to print. She was packing her bag when a lieutenant summoned her to the general's tent.

"You should be starting back," he said. "But there's been some sniper fire reported on the roads. So nobody's leaving tonight. Now," he said, "about your schedule tomorrow."

Tomorrow.

As she bunked down in General Shepherd's tent for the night, Dickey dreamed of morning. Though when she woke, little went to plan. Her ride to another field hospital was nowhere to be seen, nor were any who might help her find another. Unsure of her next move, she took her frustration out on a cold cup of coffee and her pack of cigarettes until she heard a familiar voice call her name.

"Hey Dickey," said Jay Eyerman, a war photographer she'd met in Guam. "Whatcha been doing?" he asked jovially.

"Nothing," replied Dickey, grinding her cigarette out in the dirt. "Do you know," she started, "I've been with this outfit all the time since yesterday noon? And either I can't find pictures or I can't get where they are or I don't understand about the arrangements."

Jay smiled. "Have you been going around asking these people permission to do things?" he almost laughed.

"Yes," Dickey replied.

"Come on," he said. "We've only got five minutes 'til the staff meeting."

"What's that?" asked Dickey.

"It's like a family clambake about this hour every day where almost everything that's happened usually gets mentioned. Shut up and listen," he advised, "and you don't have to ask questions, or ask permission."

"In half an hour," wrote Dickey, "I learned more about the Sixth Marine Division than I'd have found out by asking questions for a week."

Most importantly for her own purposes, she learned that medical battalion Commander John Cowan would shortly be setting out to search for a new field hospital site closer to the evolving front.

The meeting dispersed. Dickey followed Cowan to his jeep.

"You coming with us?" he asked.

Remembering Jay's advice not to ask permission, she replied, "Unless you throw me out of here I am."

"No," Cowan returned, "I don't think I will."

The jeep wound along the coast on an ill-defined dirt road. Cowan rode shotgun beside the driver, Lieutenant Brija, "who moved like a child and had the face of an old man." She sat in the back between their outfit's doctor and rifleman, whom Dickey supposed to be the Marine's smallest.

Conversation was sparse. The only words Cowan spoke for the whole ride were "keep your head down" when a mortar barrage thundered somewhere in the near distance. The road turned inland, inclined, then dove beneath a thick canopy of trees. What used to be a village appeared in a clearing.

"Pull over," Cowan ordered.

"Two hours earlier," wrote Dickey, "it must have been a characteristic Asian farm village. You could see how the community had grown in harmony with its own terrain. There had been no straight lines anywhere. The ditches and the rows of homes and the limits of the vegetable gardens all curved and crossed in deference to the rises and hollow of pink soil." But little remained beyond these broad strokes of the village's layout. "Our artillery had finished here. The village had had it."

The Marines had evacuated the hamlet before the strike. Its purpose had not been to kill, but to demolish any infrastructure that might be used by Japanese forces as ambush sites. Still, the absence of bodies did not mean that life had not been lost. As Dickey surveyed the completely razed village, the totality of its destruction washed over her in waves of rage and horror. Roofless houses meant exposure to the elements. Shattered hand-thrown clay cooking pots and shell-cratered gardens meant hunger and starvation. The leveled post office meant isolation. What it had taken an entire village generations to build had been wiped out in the course of an afternoon.

It was the first time Dickey had seen the immediate aftermath of an attack on a civilian target and she could not square its awful devastation with the US military's objective of liberating the Okinawans from Imperial Japan's brutal regime. The two realities were in her mind utterly at odds with each other. In the face of such a fatal contradiction the only emotion she could summon was one of pure, seething anger at those who had razed this once peaceful community. That they were US Marines mattered not at all to her at that moment.

In the end, they didn't find a single building still suitable to serve as a field hospital. Dickey bottled her anger into silence as they jeeped to another evacuated village that hadn't been shelled. Cowan halted their second sweep in the town's brewery. Its open floor plan made for a perfect medical ward and its office would do for a surgery. Cowan put in the call for supplies, donated blood included, and Dickey waited for them to arrive with her camera.

Before the gauze and surgical knives and blood could get there, a heavy weapons carrier pulled up. Dickey knew immediately they had laid waste to the last village. All of her ire rose up as she strode toward them. She wasn't thinking and she couldn't stop herself.

The captain jumped down. Dickey went straight for him.

"Remember that last little village before you got here?"

"Sure do," he said. "Hundred percent destroyed."

"Last I heard," she snapped, "we were liberating the Okinawans from the Japanese. They weren't our enemies. So do you mind telling me why you had to smear their mud huts all over the map?"

"Look, honey bunch," the captain barked back, "you civilians give me an unadulterated pain. We plastered the goddamn village because it was sitting on the goddamn front. Perfect for a sniper attack or whatever cute ambush the enemy might have had in mind," he spat. "I don't know how correspondents get around out here, but if you'd just get back to headquarters it would be all right with me. In spades."

Dickey glared. Within the logical matrix of war, his argument was unassailable. Within that of peace, hers was inarguable. But they were at war, total war, and there was nothing else to be said. Even so, she could not accept his explanation of the need for civilian casualties in war.

The captain whistled for the rest of his crew. "Roll out," he said. The driver winked as they went by.

The supplies arrived soon after, followed by casualties from a sniper attack. As ever, she buried her feelings in the mechanics of her camera.

Afraid they might draw sniper fire, the hospital went dark at nightfall. Only flashlights were allowed. By then the floor and walls of the surgery were splattered with blood. The surgeon, who hadn't slept in days, reached for his scalpel with shaking hands that somehow steadied by the time the blade reached the patient. He found the bullet, bandaged the wound. The corpsman leaned in to take the patient's pulse and Dickey offered to hold the flashlight.

"Give it to her," said the surgeon, "and go sack out. We've only got one more." Then he turned to Dickey. "Don't faint," he said.

"I won't," she said.

But the last patient wasn't a Marine. Two corpsmen laid a woman on the operating table. Her face was worn with a lifetime of harvest and childbearing, her clothes those of an Okinawan farm wife.

"When her wound was new," Dickey wrote in her journal, "it had been what American soldiers call a million dollar wound. Something heavy, sharp edged, and moving fast, like a piece of shell casing, had slashed her leg above the knee, inflicting one deep cut perhaps eight inches long. There had been enough force to break the thigh bone, cleanly."

But that had been hours ago and now, encrusted with dirt and pus, its outer edge had turned black and the flesh around it a lifeless gray. No one, it seemed, could survive this kind of injury or endure this level of pain.

"Think she'll make it?" asked Cowan.

"We can try," said the surgeon. "I'll take the leg off now."

Dickey held the flashlight without a single tremble. It was the most she could do. It was the least she could do. It was all she could do.

Afterward, she went outside for a cigarette with Cowan and Brija.

"How'd she get here?" Dickey wondered aloud.

"That big gun outfit that came through," replied Cowan, "the one you were talking to. They thought somebody might be left in the cellars of that village they bombed. So today they looked. And there she was."

The bright moon silhouetted the wings of bats and Atlas moths. The crackle of burning tobacco cleaved at the silence. Dickey exhaled a cloud of smoke and drew her legs toward her. Cruel mercy, it seemed, was the best war could offer to anyone.

8

The Limit of Human Endurance

THE FRONT MOVED overnight and with it, the Marines established a new field hospital in a former schoolhouse on a rocky plateau. Cowan's unit, Dickey included, set out to help.

Lieutenant Charles Ihle, a surgeon of slight build with bloodshot eyes, came out to greet them.

"How the hell did you get here?" he asked Dickey.

Cowan saved her from having to explain how a jeep works. "She wants to photograph how you use blood."

"Well, we don't have any transfusions right now, but the chief can show her how it's stored."

They ate first, hot stew, not from a K ration can. Fixated by the good-as-home-cooked meal, Dickey didn't notice as Cowan and Ihle stepped out for a smoke. They came back in as Dickey scraped the bottom of her bowl.

"Jeep's waiting," said Cowan.

Dickey rode shotgun beside Pat, a chief pharmacist's mate. Okinawa was his fifth landing with the Marines. "When he heard I was trying to make pictures that would raise blood donations for his wounded," Dickey recalled in her autobiography, "he began to smile as if his face didn't know any other expression." In the back rode another corpsman, Spaulding, who was no less pleased with her mission.

Pat turned onto a narrow road that hugged the mountainside before coming to a stop in front of a rock cave. Spaulding grabbed a lantern, and Dickey followed them through its entrance, without knowing why. Inside, the temperature dropped by twenty degrees. Spaulding set his lantern down on one of six plywood crates marked HUMAN BLOOD DO NOT DELAY KEEP ICED.

"This should last us a couple of days," he said. "It keeps here without any ice."

Shivering, Dickey had no trouble believing that it would, and turned to leave after popping off an appropriate number of flashbulbs. But Pat and Spaulding took a seat on the rock floor, leaning back against the walls.

"They tell me you were pretty impressed that we pick out sites for field hospitals as soon as the artillery lifts," said Pat laconically.

"Tell her about the company commander who came up to tell Ihle he couldn't put a defense line around the hospital," said Spaulding with a laugh.

For a quarter of an hour Pat recounted the story of how their hospital had been in no-man's-land for a half a day without cover. "We bandaged with one hand and fired with the other," he said, proudly.

This story unfurled a slew of yarns from the two corpsmen about the mortar shell that just missed and the Japanese soldier who came to on the operating table and tried to kill Ihle.

"He joined his ancestors," said Pat with the nonchalance of one who had seen a great deal of death.

Dickey listened as calmly as she could, but when her legs started to go numb and her ears felt like they might fall off from the cold, she stood.

"Not yet," said Pat. "It isn't safe out there for you."

Just then, they heard the sound of a jeep grind around the corner.

"Okay, we can go," said Spaulding.

Dickey looked at them, confused.

"Commander Cowan has left," said Pat. "And there won't be any more vehicles moving around out here tonight. Not going back anyhow."

"But that means you're stuck with me," protested Dickey.

"That was the general idea," replied Pat. "You didn't want to go back, did you?"

As Dickey wrote, "I felt like Wendy enjoying Peter Pan's approval for offering to do the pirate's housekeeping." It was a telling and accurate metaphor for the place she'd carved out for herself.

Since she first set out on the *Samaritan,* her coverage of the Pacific Theater had centered on the drama of wartime medicine, and specifically the need for donated blood. Every request to go forward included an assurance her coverage would be in service to the men who were fighting; that her photography and writing would help increase blood donations back on the home front. From the shiniest brass button to the dirtiest grunt boot, everyone knew how vital blood was in saving the lives of wounded soldiers. While the numerous contrivances enacted by several Marines of various ranks did in fact allow her to do her job, it is doubtful she would have been granted so many allowances if she had not positioned her journalism so deftly as beneficial to those she reported on. In this sense, Dickey's coverage performed the equivalent of domestic labor on the war front, the vital work that supports the work of others but to which women are often confined.

For the moment, she felt her presence only justifiable through this lens. This belief was pushed to its extreme back at the hospital, with the arrival of a Marine lieutenant named Jameson who was strapped to his stretcher and heavily sedated after suffering several bouts of what was diagnosed as homicidal mania. Dickey leaned over him in the ward. He looked like any other sleeping teenage boy with dirt on his face after an afternoon fishing or hiking or hunting.

"What's going to happen to him?" she asked Dr. Solomon, the unit's only psychologist, who had accompanied him.

"He can go either way," he replied. "If no gun-fire triggers his mind back to his original trauma, if what he sees and hears around him, and more important, what he says, all act to restore his confidence he may go back to duty at once as the most rock-steady Marine in his outfit. But," the doctor continued, "we can't do much for him really if he can't express what shook him in the first place. It would be too dangerous to leave it buried; it could trigger another mania too easily." At the front, he explained, the only treatment available to those like Jameson was talk therapy.

Then a Marine sergeant interjected, "What really set him off wasn't anything the Japs did. He got a dear-John letter last thing before we landed, and he never could make himself eat but twice the whole time he was on Okinawa."

Dr. Solomon looked up. "Sergeant," he said, "did you ever see a psychiatric casualty who had a good relationship with folks back home?"

"No, sir," the sergeant replied, "and I don't expect to. You can kill a man who knows his woman's waiting, but you can't crack him up." Then, the doctor and the sergeant looked at Dickey.

As she wrote, "The men were making me feel that being born a girl baby made one responsible for the crack-up of at least an entire platoon of fighting men." As she often did, Dickey simultaneously withdrew her heart and puffed out her chest. "Well, if I'm the big symbol of what's troubling Jameson, why don't you let him tell me about it?" she said.

"Oh, you aren't, Ma'am," returned the sergeant. "You don't look like a woman. You look like another damn Marine."

"I'll take that as a compliment," snapped Dickey.

"How long is your hair?" asked the doctor.

"Her hair's long," the sergeant answered for her.

Because thinking at the time reasoned that women, not industrialized warfare, were responsible for the mental distress of servicemen, the psychologist believed that by virtue of being a woman, Dickey would be the most effective at administering talk therapy. However unjust that placement of blame and responsibility, Dickey nevertheless accepted the task, agreeing to try to make Jameson talk about the trauma that had put him in this state.

The camp was running short on water, but Solomon authorized her an extra helmetful to wash her hair and lent her his personal bar of soap. She hardly recognized herself in the tiny shaving mirror. It had been a long time since she'd worn her hair down or had seen her face without a caking of dust.

In the medical ward, Dickey leaned over Jameson and asked him what was the matter. His lips were dry. His voice rasped as it whispered about the men he had killed and the ones he had watched die, about the sound a bayonet makes when thrust into a chest cavity and the grenade-shattered pieces of a man he had collected in a poncho and carried six miles back to camp to be buried.

Outside, in the distance she heard the sound of Japanese rifles. She said nothing, hoping they would remain at the perimeter.

The gunfire drew nearer. Dickey looked toward the shots, looked back.

"Jameson's face had been piteous a minute before," wrote Dickey. "But his face now was just that of a cool man identifying the noise." Dr. Solomon's words came back to her.

"Shambos," he said, using the Marine term for the champagne cork sound of Japanese rifles. He rose to his feet, found an M-1 Garand semi-automatic in the pile of guns in the corner, and gestured for Dickey to follow as he headed for the door. "I would have anyway," wrote Dickey.

On a flat high rock overlooking the road, he lay behind a screen of crabgrass. Dickey followed suit. Another corpsman joined them with a Colt .45.

Beyond the road lay a valley of rice fields flooded with mirrored water and beyond that another rocky hill.

"They're in one of those caves," he said. "Must be half a dozen."

Dickey followed the line of his barrel to a large cave on the left and two smaller ones directly below.

"The big one," said Jameson, and began to unload. The enemy returned fire, their bullets skimming across the rice paddy. The firing ceased. Three Japanese soldiers ran out and down the hill, under a hail of bullets from Jameson and the rest of the hospital that had come out to take aim. Tumbling and taking cover every few feet, the Japanese soldiers reached the opening to one of the smaller caves. Jameson waited. Another half hour passed. Several other corpsmen and walking wounded Marines, including the sergeant, joined them at their position. The sun grew low on the horizon. If they didn't clear the enemy from the caves soon, a night ambush was certain.

"Right now," said the sergeant, "we probably know where they are. Later, we won't. So we'll just make one small patrol up that hill and be sure the caves stay empty."

Dickey joined without asking permission. The sergeant and Pat broke off in a forward guard to make sure the caves were clear. Jameson, Spaulding, and Dickey brought up the rear.

"Listen for grenades," hissed Jameson as they began their ascent.

"This was the first infantry patrol I had ever tried to cover," Dickey recalled in her autobiography. "But I learned on it the one cardinal rule of patrol coverage: you can be sure there'll come one time and maybe more when everything happens at once. That moment was on us."

Two grenades detonated above them. The sound of three semiautomatics quickly followed from the forest on the far side of the road. Dickey pressed herself against the mountain, clutching her camera and struggling to control her breath. Lieutenant Jameson crouched beside her, his gun facing toward shots fired while Pat aimed his .45 up the road. She raised her viewfinder to her eye, adjusted the f-stop, and clicked. Then silence. Nothing. Jameson motioned for them to move back down the hill.

At the bottom, the sergeant emerged from the foliage. "The caves are empty all right, but we got one when we were all firing back there. There's blood on the grass." The hospital would be safe for the night.

On Iwo, she had seen men marching shoulder to shoulder. On Okinawa, she joined them. Years later, Tony would write he'd lost her there. He could not have been more right. She would never stop chasing this feeling the Marines call esprit de corps, an intangible and unshakable bond between comrades in arms. For the rest of her life, Dickey would often say, "When I die, I want to be on patrol with the Marines."

Cowan returned in the morning. The front had moved again, and another field hospital had been established farther forward, this time in the abandoned home of a wealthy Japanese landowner. For the first time in weeks, Dickey had an entire room to herself. She stayed there for two days. Fighting started to intensify and the wounded were more numerous. With ever more dedication and conviction, Dickey captured their sacrifice on film and in her writing.

On the third morning of her stay, a patrol invited her out to look for the wounded after a Japanese artillery barrage. Finding none, they turned back, but were stopped midway by a Marine MP.

"Mrs. Chapelle, you hadn't ought to ask us to do it anymore," he said.

"Marine," she replied, "I don't think I ever spoke to you in my life and I'm sure I never asked you to do anything at all."

"That's right," he said, "but they come on the radio two or three times every day to find out if I've seen you. There's an arrest-on-sight order out for you. Two or three times a day I have to say, 'seen a dame this far forward? What do you think, I'm nuts?' But today, you've driven by three times."

"Do you want me to come into custody right now?" she asked.

"No Ma'am. I won't arrest you. But if you could report back to division headquarters."

"What are the charges?" she asked.

"Don't know Ma'am. Just know there's an order out for your arrest."

Brija, Cowan's driver, took her to the public relations headquarters that afternoon. "Don't worry," he said as she was getting out, "they can't do nothing to you."

"Thanks," she said and closed the door, though not entirely sure she believed him.

Inside, Dickey was told to wait. On one of the room's several typewriters, a Marine correspondent for *Leatherneck* hammered at the keys while a fresh wound on his leg gushed blood onto the floor. He finished his copy, handed it to the sergeant, and fainted. Four men carried him to an ambulatory jeep on a stretcher.

The sergeant's face turned ashen as he read the report. Dropping it back on the desk, he rushed out of the room, leaving Dickey alone. She sidled up to the desk. Japanese shells had decimated a Marine command post with the precision of foreknowledge. Thirteen were killed. It was April 12, 1945, the day the Japanese revealed the full extent of their entrenchment in Okinawa's craggy mountains with a series of well-planned and expertly executed artillery barrages. It was also the day President Franklin Roosevelt died. The future that had for a moment seemed so bright dimmed once more in the shadow of these two tragedies.

What had appeared as an easy victory on Okinawa turned into a ninety-eight-day siege that took a higher toll than even Iwo Jima. As Dickey wrote, "The price of victory was more than 20,000 American dead [casualties]. There was no real count of enemy casualties, for thousands of their dead were sealed in the caves from which they had fought. But it is known that only a handful of the 100,000 defenders survived."

This onslaught was only just beginning as the press officer for Okinawa, Lieutenant Bern Price, called her into his office with more bad news, though of a personal nature.

"You're under arrest," he said, matter-of-factly.

"You can't arrest me," she replied. "I came in to surrender myself."

"Be that as it may," he replied. "The story we got, you embarrassed an admiral."

In finding other orders, she had evidently angered Rear Admiral Miller, who had initially refused her request to go ashore at Okinawa. This alone was her great crime. She had wounded his vanity, and, as a result, he issued a warrant for her arrest.

Still, for the moment, it seemed like no more than a misunderstanding. After all, hadn't she received orders from his deputy, Commander Smith, to go ashore? Hadn't she been stranded, through no fault of her own? Hadn't General Shepherd invited her to his camp? Hadn't he allowed her to stay and arranged for her to go farther forward still? And last but not least, hadn't she rendered the service she said she would by photographing the dire need for donated blood?

Surely, she reasoned, the consequences of her actions, many of which were beyond her control, would not prove overly serious.

"Anyhow," said Price, "I don't know what to do now that I've arrested you. There won't be any transportation to the rear anymore today."

"There never is from the Marines," muttered Dickey. Price chuckled at the roundabout compliment.

Rain pelted down the next morning. Dickey arrived at Price's office first thing. The only boats leaving were LCVPs evacuating the wounded. Dickey volunteered to get herself to the beach where they were disembarking and hitch a ride back to the fleet. He agreed to let her try.

By the happenstance of wartime, she boarded the same boat that had taken her ashore in the first place. Though, now, wounded Marines filled its hull. Crawling onto the motor housing, Dickey hung on for dear life as they bounced through rough seas and gale-force winds.

The skipper met them as they docked at his landing ship.

"How did you get here?" he asked.

Dickey was in no mood to answer and just gave him her name.

"I know who you are," he said and left to radio fleet command that she was no longer missing.

He received a top-priority reply in ten minutes. HOLD MRS CHAPELLE

UNDER ARREST IN QUARTERS SHE IS NOT REPEAT NOT TO LEAVE THE SHIP.

"What did you do?" he asked, showing her the dispatch, incredulous that a woman could have done anything to merit arrest.

But before she had time to answer, the klaxon wailed. All eyes turned skyward as a squad of Japanese suicide planes began to dive. It was Friday, April 13, 1945.

"For 58 of the next 72 hours," Dickey wrote, "the men of our ship and all the other ships in the assault fleet stayed at their battle stations. It was the heaviest kamikaze attack against the fleet of the entire war." Dickey went topside every time the klaxon sounded, which seemed to be every hour on the hour. "The routine was familiar to me by this time. Lifebelt, helmet, camera on a lanyard. Wait 30 seconds before starting topside to let the guys who really have something to do get clear."

Since she didn't get in their way, the crew didn't get in hers. As she had aboard the *Samaritan* and *Relief*, Dickey climbed to the highest point on the ship to photograph what lay above and below. Hundreds of enemy airplanes crowded the sky in terrible gusts of what the Imperial Japanese Army called a divine wind. The Allies answered with unending arcs of thunderous antiaircraft fire. Dickey focused her camera on the faces of the gunners, whose expressions moved between fear, hatred, and determination. She captured the last moments of pilots' lives as they were struck midair by Allied fire. And despite her instinct to look away, she snapped her shutter as a kamikaze plane struck its target, killing dozens, injuring hundreds, and inflicting crippling damage to the ship. It was a kind of warfare she had never seen or imagined, and hoped never to again.

The Allies shot down 270 Japanese planes over the four days Dickey remained with the fleet. Kamikaze planes struck ten ships, sank another destroyer, and crashed into the USS *Intrepid*'s flight deck. Dickey likened the suicidal aerial campaign to a "kind of ghastly roulette, with Fate the croupier and like all things in war, anguish and death as the stakes." By April 17, the Japanese had expended all the planes and pilots they could commit to this onslaught. It would be renewed once more on April 28 when two hundred Japanese planes would attack the fleet and damage several ships, including the USS *Comfort,* a hospital ship on which Dickey had been briefly billeted.

But for the moment, the storm had passed and the skies were calm and clear. The skipper received orders to take Dickey to Buckner Bay, a naval base on the southern coast of Okinawa with an airfield nearby. A Marine MP met her on the dock with four stripes on his arm and a .45 pistol in his hand.

"You will walk off this ship directly in front of me, Ma'am," he said.

"Sure sarge," she replied and waved goodbye to the crew, who wished her luck in return.

He didn't holster his gun as he drove her to the airfield. When they arrived she tried to assure him, "You know, you don't really need that thing."

"My commanding officer told me I did," he said, walking her at gunpoint to her flight out, a transport plane evacuating the wounded. One of the nurses Dickey had met at Alameda Hospital waited for her at the top of the stairs. Dickey clasped her hand, happy to see a familiar face.

"You got her?" asked the Marine.

"We got her," the nurse replied. "She's been delivered into the Navy's hands."

The Marine holstered his gun. "So long Dickey!" he shouted. "Whatever it is, you just tell them you didn't do it!"

The engines thundered to a start. The propellers began to churn. Her war was over. Her war had just begun.

Yet in the wider war, there remained one last unthinkable act of horror. On August 6, 1945, forty-eight hours after the Marines made their final sweeps of the island, America used an atomic bomb against the civilian population of Hiroshima. Its mushroom cloud, the very shape of apocalypse, overshadowed and obscured the sacrifice so many made on Okinawa.

"Nobody," wrote Dickey years later, "least of all this looker on, troubled then to assess Okinawa beyond its place in chronology, the last of the fighting. Yet over the years, its importance in shaping American foreign policy has grown plain. The terrifying casualty figure probably was the final factor in the persuasion of President Truman to order the atom bomb dropped. If an island 300 miles from Japan cost tens of thousands of lives, the invasion of the Japanese mainland could cost a hundred thousand."

But for as much as Dickey cherished the Marines, as much as she detested their deaths, and as much as she hated the extreme right-wing nationalism of the Imperial Japanese Government, she abhorred the atomic bomb and the decision to use it even more.

"I wonder how those Marines and sailors and soldiers would have voted if they'd been asked about the dropping of the atom bomb beforehand," wrote Dickey. "It was their lives that its use was saving. Could they have foreseen the decades of tension that would rest not alone on inexorable scientific advance, but also on the fact that the one use of an atomic weapon in war had been by their country? I think they might have, being so intimately familiar with violent death in all its forms. And I can't help but feel they might have balloted in favor of their own expendability."

9

The War at Home

In Guam, Navy censors confiscated Dickey's notes, camera, and film, then told her she would get them back eventually, probably. Still under arrest, she was confined to the Agaña Airport without a priority rating, an omission that sentenced her to the purgatory of perpetual standby.

Refusing to be defeated, she used the time to interview the wounded waiting for transport home. Through them she learned Jameson, the Marine suffering from PTSD at the field hospital, had been returned to his unit on Okinawa. It seemed cruel. His commanding officers must have known he could relapse at any moment, and Dickey, who couldn't unsee in her mind's eye the horrors he had described, couldn't help but imagine new ones that might set him off a second time.

After thirty-six hours of waiting, a passenger clerk called her name. He had been on duty the day before when she arrived. Somehow between then and now he'd learned who she was, why she was there.

"Now," he said at the counter, "you just mumble when anybody asks about your priority." He flashed her the clipboard of the next flight's passenger list. Her name was written in pencil, the rest in pen.

"Don't do it, Marine," she said. "Just erase my name. Thanks anyhow, but there's bound to be room for me on some flight later without anybody else getting in trouble."

"You're going out on this flight," he rasped. "You don't deserve to be pushed around. You didn't do anything but go too far forward and stay too long. And anyhow," he smiled, pointing to the single stripe on his arm, "where can they bust me to?"

In the morning, she arrived in Honolulu where she caught an Army Air Forces freight to San Francisco. Tired of flying and in no real rush to get back to New York City, where once and for all she would have to admit that it was over, she bought a ticket for the train.

California rolled by her window, redwoods giving way to cypress to oaks to grassland. She fell asleep until past Las Vegas and woke to the vast, empty desert. She pulled out her typewriter and cigarettes. Almost to a man the Marines at Agaña Airport had told her the same thing. They were glad to be going home but afraid no one would understand what they had gone through, how they were feeling, and why they didn't want to talk about any of it. Far from unfounded, their fears were based on three and a half years of letters from girlfriends and wives, mothers and fathers, sisters and brothers that avoided the subject of war wholesale. Homeward bound, they were afraid their loved ones would never want to talk about the war, never want to know what they had gone through, and never want to know the men they had become. They were afraid they would remain isolated, stranded with their recurring nightmares.

Dickey had written about the physical wounds that Marines endured. Like many, she had photographed them bleeding out on the decks of hospital ships and getting bullets dug out of their guts while lying on stretchers suspended between two K ration crates. But few were writing about the millions of men returning home without outward trauma, but who were tearing themselves open again and again as their minds made them relive the horrors they had witnessed. It seemed to Dickey that not enough people were trying to figure out what to do about these "combat fatigue" cases that numbered in the millions.

Though more widely accepted and discussed than during World War I, combat fatigue, now called post-traumatic stress disorder (PTSD), was considered a temporary and curable ailment at the time. One medical study in 1943 suggested "shower baths and ice cream" were an effective treatment while another in the same year held that unit cohesion and good leadership prevented the condition altogether. After the war, the popular media rarely mentioned combat fatigue outside the context of criminal proceedings when lawyers pleaded for leniency on account of a veteran's psychological condition. Otherwise, Americans did their best to turn a blind eye toward the plague of PTSD that affected millions of veterans. Dickey did her best to make them see.

"Somewhere behind every battle recollection in a man's mind," Dickey wrote, "lies an invisible line. He'll talk quite freely about what lies on one side; he will say nothing about all that lies beyond. But most of the misunderstandings, the heartaches, the irritations that sour his return could be cleared up if he could take his loved ones back there for a little while. Nevertheless, the words don't come." Since they couldn't talk about it to those they needed to tell the most, Dickey tried to give a voice to those whispered confessions of fear, apprehension, and anxiety.

In September 1945, *Cosmopolitan* magazine published her article, "It Still Hurts to Get Hurt," written in the first-person voice of a fictional Marine. "I don't want to talk about it, Mom," her character says. "I didn't want you to know how bad it was when it happened and I still don't. Besides, talking about it means thinking about it all over again. But sometimes I think I've got to, somebody's got to, anyway, and it might as well be me."

Her article went on to detail common symptoms of PTSD with almost uncanny accuracy given that the medical community had yet to form a comprehensive definition of the condition. She identified the phenomenon of flashbacks, when sufferers feel as if they are reliving events long past. She recognized the tendency to avoid memories, feel detached from loved ones, and experience survivor guilt. And she described the common belief among those who suffer from PTSD that a part of themselves died on the battlefield.

Dickey made her last notes on the war as her train pulled into Penn Station. She rushed to put her typewriter back in its case as the other passengers disembarked. Tony met her on the platform. He kissed her. Tired, dejected, and covered in the grime of travel, she let herself be enveloped in his arms. After everything she had endured, she desperately craved a safe port. She did not find it in his embrace.

"I was worried about you, goony bird," he said, then pulled an envelope from his pocket. It was addressed to him and had been opened.

She read it once, read it again, aloud.

"I regret to inform you that the credentials as a War Correspondent of your wife, Dickey Meyer Chapelle, were revoked because she failed to comply with specific orders and regulations regarding her movements in this area."

What she had assumed was a comedy of errors in an instant became a tragedy. Without her credentials, few editors would even look at her articles or photos.

In shock, she walked into Penn Station's concourse of high marble arches and grand Corinthian columns. It seemed so extravagant, so unreal, so far from where she had just been, where she had felt of use and part of something undeniably important, and where, this letter said, she would never be allowed again.

She didn't get out of bed for days after, exhausted by travel and betrayal and the feeling of failure. When she finally did get up, she found she couldn't speak, that words caught in her throat like fish bones. When they finally did come, they were halting, staccato. To her horror, she had a stutter. Tony laughed at her as she tried to talk. She began to cry, and for the moment, he choked back his own amusement at her difficulty. Years later she attributed her condition to the fear that her wartime experiences and the ways they had changed her would mark her as an odd "Riverside Drive housewife," as she phrased it.

Stuttering is often the result of deep-seated emotional stress, and Dickey's anxiety over failing to live up to societal norms may well have contributed to her condition. But her impediment could also easily be attributed to PTSD, which combat reporters often suffer from to the same degree as those they report on. Experiencing both forms of intense psychological stress, it is a wonder she ever recovered her normal speech, which she did, in only a few short months.

In the meantime, Dickey made her voice clear in a letter-writing campaign aimed at getting her credentials restored. Point by point, she recounted the order of events to Rear Admiral Miller, the Navy director of public information, which to her ran counter to the charges leveled against her. She wanted to explain how the cause of all fighting men, not to mention her career, were harmed by these fraudulent charges and his refusal to reinstate her credentials. Few if any publications were willing to print the stories of a journalist who lacked the proper paperwork.

He replied coolly, "I sincerely regret that your professional standing has suffered. An excellent time for you to have given this thought would have been at Okinawa prior to the disembarkation." He concluded with finality, "I see no reason to change my original position."

Just like that, he buried the majority of her historic work. A few of her pieces made it to print, notably her article on combat fatigue in *Cosmopolitan* and another about the first wave of Marines on Iwo in *This Week*. Then there were the photos she gave to the Red Cross that led to donations of blood that helped save thousands of lives.

But she felt there was so much more she could have done. Many of the drafts and notes she prepared about actual combat, not to mention photographs for which she risked her life, never saw the light of day. Worse, the book deal she'd landed about her experiences with the Pacific Fleet remained on hold until her credentials were reinstated, a date that now seemed would never come.

Meanwhile, Tony spent the little money they had buying up surplus war goods for a scheme he promised would make them rich, and fast. But for now they were broke and it was up to Dickey to find gainful employment. Luckily, it didn't take long.

She had recently submitted an article about the humanity of wounded Marines to a new magazine entitled *Seventeen*. Impressed by Dickey's gutsy photographs and passionate prose, the editor in chief, Helen Valentine, and the managing editor, Alice Thompson, invited her to their office for an interview. Besides, they had never heard of Rear Admiral Miller.

With no interest in working for a teen girl magazine but very much in need of rent money, Dickey accepted their invitation and on a late October afternoon, she rode the stainless-steel elevator up to *Seventeen*'s headquarters in the famed Flatiron Building. Dickey had done her best to clean up for the occasion, donning a clean silk shirt and the diamond bracelet Tony had bought her when they first married. But she felt like a slob across the desk from these two women whose precision in dress and coiffure reminded her of a Marine Corps general.

Their hair billowed beneath fashion's latest foray into millinery. Their tailored suits fit them perfectly. Their makeup elegantly accented their skin tones. They were both undeniably beautiful.

Turning to Dickey, Alice told her what she already knew. "We're not going with your story. But, we are impressed with your photography. I hope you make pictures on assignment? The fact is that we'd like to see some valid pictures of a particularly difficult subject right here in New York."

"More difficult than what I've been doing?" Dickey replied, envisioning a cushy assignment photographing a teen fan club or fashion show.

"I don't really know," Helen picked up, deliberately dismissing Dickey's tongue-in-cheek jab. "It's the rodeo in Madison Square Garden. There are teenage girl riders this year."

That night Dickey focused on a bucking bronco at close range. Unfortunately, the bronco did the same to her. Dickey's combat zone training abandoned her as the horse, after shedding its rider, began to charge right for her. Rather than run, she stayed stock still. The audience of eighteen thousand watched in elated alarm, half hoping she'd get out of the way, half wondering what would happen if she didn't. This was a rodeo after all.

Dickey came out of her trance in the nick of time, just making it over the fence. Predictably, she didn't get any printable pictures that night, nor could she blame the bronco entirely for her failure. Like jungle canopy in Panama, the audience's forest fire of cigarettes, coupled with the stampede-size dust clouds, filtered too much light for a decent exposure. Forced to admit hers was the only source of potential income they had going, Tony pitched in to find the solution. He built her a hoop of flashbulb holders that rose up from her shoulders and encircled her head to wear in the ring like a haloed guardian angel of rodeo. The next night, and every night after for a week, the audience accepted her luminescence as part of the entertainment.

The following Monday, she delivered her photos to Alice. They were fantastic. Looking them over, Alice said, "What we need is a staff editor to write and photograph articles which are not about fashion, food, or beauty. Would you like the job?" she asked.

"And," Dickey recalled in her autobiography, "she named a salary I'd never earned before." Dickey took the job in a snap.

For a moment, it seemed she had landed squarely on her feet, despite all her setbacks. But as was so often the case, whenever things were going well in her career, Tony cleaved at the edges from home. He hated that Dickey earned more than he did. He berated her endlessly for not acting the part of dedicated housewife, ignoring entirely his own lack of income, not to mention her complete disinterest in living a domestic life. For the rest of their marriage, as Dickey wrote to her mother, "I never looked for a job if I thought it was one Tony would have wanted, telling myself it wouldn't be considerate to get a bigger income than Tony."

For now, though, neither willing to give up her job nor subject herself to his ire, Dickey pitched her new bosses every assignment she could think of that would take her outside of New York City. It worked. During her tenure with *Seventeen*, she traveled to thirty states as a photographer. The magazine often teamed her up with Charlotte Straus, a writer who had a voice almost as loud as hers and with whom Dickey got along famously from the word go.

However well paid and far flung, her assignments lacked the sense of purpose she'd come to crave. Meanwhile, Tony's get-rich-quick plan of buying and selling military surplus paid off, and how. He put all cash down on 24 and 25 Riverside Drive, a pair of adjoined brownstone apartment buildings that had been drastically discounted on account of crumbling interiors combined with a massive cockroach infestation. Tony mounted a two-pronged attack, using one pound of DDT for every ten pounds of plaster. It was a war of attrition, but for the most part, the occupying force prevailed.

Then, the other shoe dropped.

In 1947, Carmel, Tony's first wife, arrived unannounced, with his son Conrad "Ron" Chapelle. Tony had never mentioned either to Dickey but now, forced to come clean about his previous marriage and his child, Tony admitted he had filed for their divorce in Mexico. Predictably, this turned out to be nonbinding in the United States, which meant Dickey and Tony were not legally married. Worse, Carmel suffered from acute depression and was no longer able to safely care for Ron. Out of need and desperation, she was suing Tony for abandonment.

As he always did, Tony tried to avoid responsibility, claiming Carmel had left him, that she was crazy, and that none of this was his fault. Dickey might have rejected his lies were it not for Ron, a skinny and melancholy teenager. Twenty-nine and without children of her own, Dickey was not a maternal woman. But she had an extraordinary capacity to love and an undying sense of responsibility to better the lives of those around her. Forgetting Tony's lies and betrayal, she took to Ron from the beginning, and he, in turn, took to her. Still, she could not responsibly take over Ron's care. Since Tony had no intention of playing father, it was decided that the best thing would be for Ron to be placed in part-time foster care and enrolled in boarding school.

Despite his own mendacity and the chaos it had sown, Tony continued to chastise Dickey for pursuing a career. Again, taking the burden of responsibility onto her shoulders, Dickey searched for another path forward. She found it through Alice Thompson, her editor at *Seventeen*. In addition to being one of New York's most fashionable women, Alice was a Quaker, and thus a member of a devoutly nonviolent Christian faith with a profound commitment to social justice and equality. The simple yet powerful theology of the Quakers appealed to Dickey in these darkest of times. When Alice mentioned they needed some PR photos of their summer camp outside of Louisville, Kentucky, Dickey volunteered her time immediately.

Like any summer camp, most of the day was spent splashing in the river, climbing trees, making crafts, and playing tag. But this was not why the teens had elected to go to this camp. Instead, they had chosen to spend their summer here to pick green beans in the morning and can them in the afternoon. The fruits of their labor were then sent to Europe where children were starving in the wake of World War II and where the Quakers had established a network of aid campaigns.

Even more inspiring, as Dickey wrote, the campers were of "assorted ages, creeds, colors, and hometowns." Dickey recalled the Black teenager from Philadelphia who taught her how to best pinch the pods from their stalks and the White farmer's son from Wyoming who showed her how the canning machine worked as he affixed one lid after another.

"Whether it had been their purpose or their character I didn't know," wrote Dickey. "But the youngsters had moved me with their joyous dedication to a hard job as if they wanted to make the same gesture of reverence to being alive that I hadn't seen since . . . I was covering the United States Marines in combat."

Dickey had personal reasons that attracted her to the Quakers' cause as well. Their work looked like an escape hatch. Rather than mailing her photographs, Dickey hand-delivered them to the Quakers' Friends Service Committee National Headquarters in Philadelphia. Standing outside their offices, housed in a redbrick Federal-style building, Dickey felt as she had aboard the USS *Samaritan*. As she wrote in her autobiography, "I felt at home at once."

The director of public relations, Jack Kavanaugh, "a serene man going gray with features that just missed being too even," welcomed her into his office. Dickey proudly handed him the portfolio. He smiled as soon as he opened it. In the past, counselors had done their best to photograph the campers' volunteerism for their newsletters and fundraisers. But as a professional photographer, Dickey had been better able to capture their spirit and drive.

After looking through her photos twice, Jack closed the portfolio. "I wish," he said almost wistfully, "we could get pictures like those from the other side of the Atlantic."

There it was again. That sliver of light that always seemed to appear in her darkest moments. First Panama, then Iwo, then Okinawa, now this. Her way out, another chance to report on history in the making. This time, rather than the waging of war, she would be covering the waging of peace. She was incandescent. But she was also not entirely free.

In the months that had passed since Carmel had arrived, Tony had rewoven the strands of his web keeping Dickey in their relationship. Ron explained it years later, calling his father "one of the world's greatest con men. He could con anybody into or out of anything."

In textbook style, Tony waged a campaign of gaslighting that never let Dickey find her footing. He belittled her and built her up. Guilted her and begged her. Told her she was nothing without him and he was nothing without her. He screamed at her and whispered sweet nothings in her ear. Dickey, despite all her sophistication, intelligence, and courage, became trapped again and could see no exit. But Tony had not broken her will entirely. Jack's need for a photographer in Europe meant she could fulfill her promise to Tony without breaking her promise to herself.

Dickey looked at Jack across the desk. "It wouldn't be hard to get more pictures like these," she said. "All you have to do is send Tony and me to Europe."

PART II

. . . .

10

The Crater of Recent Peace

THEIR TRIP BEGAN portentously. The entire success of their venture relied on their vehicle, a baby food delivery van refitted with beds, a kitchen, and a darkroom packed with every last item they might need on the road, from food to film to fuel. Yet when they arrived at the Hoboken Pier on a bright November morning, Dickey and Tony found their van still parked at the end of the dock.

Finding the nearest crew member, Dickey demanded it be put aboard immediately.

"It's too heavy," came back the laconic reply.

Tony quickly applied his trademark charm to the problem. The last lash around the wheel bed was tied as they passed the Statue of Liberty. The couple went below to find their quarters. Understandably, the Quakers had paid for the least expensive berth, furnished with two cots no nicer than those aboard the USS *Samaritan*. Dickey smiled at the spartan arrangement. Tony fumed.

"Don't unpack," he said and went off to find the chief steward. Dickey smoked and took out her book of Polish phrases.

"Miło cię poznać," she said and repeated, "Nice to meet you."

Tony returned with a grin and a set of keys to a stateroom. "No extra charge," he said. "It was empty."

"Wspaniale," said Dickey. "Wonderful." She did not ask how he had done it.

Ensconced in luxury, Tony played the part. Every morning of their two-week crossing, he rose late, then gorged himself on the liner's sump-tuous breakfast buffets of "fruits, juices, any hot or cold cereal, bacon, ham, sausages, steak, fish, chops, eggs or practically anything you can think of," as he described them in a letter to Jack Kavanaugh.

Meanwhile, Dickey brushed up on her German grammar, studied Polish, and tried to wrap her tongue around French as they made slow headway across the Atlantic. She'd managed some progress in each by the time they arrived in Gdynia, Poland, "on a morning so gray that you could hardly see the pier guards' guns." Wearing Soviet insignias and carrying Russian automatic rifles, they were as foreboding as they were prognostic. After the war, the Allies granted the Soviet Union con-trol over Poland. Though the Iron Curtain had not yet fallen over the last act of the Paris Peace Treaties, signs of its imminence were already manifest. For Dickey and Tony, chilled relations between the US and the USSR meant that the soldiers, without putting down their weapons, unloaded every single last item packed into their van as they searched for anything that could be deemed as evidence of subversive Western imperialism. Luckily, the Quakers had sent convoys into the Soviet Bloc before and had assembled their paperwork with expert precision. Every crate had its checklist, every item its stated purpose. Just before the win-ter sunset at 3 P.M. the customs agents reluctantly released them onto Polish soil.

Hours later, Dickey and Tony heaved a sigh of relief as they pulled into their lodgings at one of the country's only luxury hotels, meaning it had private rooms, hot water, and a dining room that actually served meat. They drank wine with dinner, commented on the boiled beets, and went to bed early.

The next morning, Tony edged their van through the streets cleared from the sea of rubble. Dickey had seen total destruction before on Guam and Okinawa. But it had not been on this industrial scale. The extent of the desolation only grew as they wound their way farther from the city's center. Bombed-out buildings teetered in the wind. Others that had completely collapsed spilled into the road. Children picked through the ruins for silverware, bits of clothing, anything they could sell. Tony turned up a hill, toward the once affluent suburbs that overlooked the city.

The translator met them in front of the house the Quakers had arranged for them to visit. Outside, Dickey wrote, there were "missing windows, machine gun pock marks, and a missing leaf on the front door." Inside, the ceiling creaked from the constant flow of footsteps on the floors above. Every room housed an entire family. There was no heat, no plumbing, no electricity. Children gawked as she and Tony climbed the stairs. Dickey noticed there were few between the ages of two and eight. "Few babies survived the war," the translator explained.

Dickey grew self-conscious about her camera, which likely cost enough to feed a family for a year. Still, she consoled herself that her photographs might do the same. As Tony set up his tripod to photograph one family's portrait, they explained how they had come to be here and where they hoped to go. They were poor beyond American measure but also understood that they were not the most destitute in Poland, Gdynia, or even in the house they occupied. The family who lived in the root cellar was far worse off than they.

Without having to ask, their translator led to the cellar's half door in the kitchen. The smell of earth and kerosene flooded their nostrils as they stepped inside. The last of the dimming afternoon light disappeared a few steps down. Then came the sound of children's voices, a baby's wail. The translator called out. A woman's voice responded.

The glow of a single kerosene lamp illuminated the faces of eight children and their mother, who introduced herself as Sofia Wisniewska. The translator explained why Dickey and Tony were there. Sofia nodded, said she was happy to have them and they were welcome to photograph her home.

Tony began setting up the lights. Dickey joined Sofia at her stove where she cooked five potatoes and one head of cabbage in a rusty pot over a barely perceptible flame. Offhandedly, she said it took five hours to cook their dinner. Dickey asked her where her husband was. He'd been killed by the Nazis during the first days of the resistance, explained Sofia. Despite herself, Dickey looked back at the eighteen-month-old lying between two of his sisters on the family's single cot.

Sofia answered her unasked question. In their retreat, the Nazis came through their enclave. One found them in their cellar, demanded food, and grabbed Sofia's oldest daughter, who was fourteen at the time. Sofia pleaded he rape her instead. In an act of cruel mercy he acquiesced. Eight and a half months later, she named her baby Jerzy. As she often did, Dickey marveled at the strength of women in the face of the seemingly unendurable. The original act of violence bore no consequence on the family's love for the child. As she wrote home, "The youngster is completely adored by his brothers and sisters and is quite adorable, high cheek bones and all."

Tony finished the lights. Sofia lined her children up and Dickey reflected that keeping all eight of them alive for the duration of the war was itself a formidable accomplishment. But when they smiled at Tony's antics behind the camera, Sofia's accomplishment seemed nothing short of miraculous. Through six years of war, hunger, and fear while living in a dank root cellar shared with innumerable rats, mice, and cockroaches, she had not allowed her children to forget what it was to be happy.

Leaving Tony to repack the van, Dickey ventured over to the cliff's edge. Dusk had fallen, though it was only three in the afternoon. Below, the city's few lights flickered on. Dickey tamped a cigarette against the space between her thumb and forefinger, wondered if she would have had the same strength as Sofia, and knew that she wouldn't. "In these folks' eventual survival," wrote Dickey in a letter home later that evening, "I have all kinds of faith—but I simply do not understand how come they do not simply walk off their loamy little cliff into the small sea of bright lights." Before meeting the Wisniewskas, Dickey had believed the limit of human endurance had been reached in the violence of combat. Now she knew that endurance had been tested further still by the suffering found in the crater pit of recent peace.

From Gdynia they drove to Nawiady, a small village where the Quakers operated a medical clinic and community center. Though only 180 miles east, it took them from sunup to sundown to traverse the distance. Built for America's paved suburban streets, their van shuddered and thumped over Poland's war-torn roads. They nearly rolled when Tony inadvertently hit a mortar shell pothole. Only a few miles later, a piece of sharp metal tore through the front tire. Tony cursed as he jacked up the chassis in subfreezing weather. Still, they arrived in Nawiady in one piece and before dark.

Like so many villages across Europe that had the misfortune of lying in Hitler's path, Nawiady had been burned to the ground. Cheap and quick concrete slab buildings had been built to replace the town's destroyed quaint two-story wooden homes. Driving through them felt like entering a strange canyon in the middle of an otherwise flat landscape.

Past the edge of town, the Quakers had purchased one of the few farmhouses left standing and converted it into a community center with a medical clinic. At the sound of their engine, a woman with the statuesque figure of an Olympian came out to the porch. Wiping the blood of a patient off her hand, she waved and welcomed them in.

"Welcome to our humble outpost," she said in Queen's English, an accent Dickey later learned was far from affectatious. The woman who introduced herself as Philippa was known in London as Lady Philippa Glynn, a baroness and physician who'd given up a life of luxury to care for those most in need. Dickey took to her immediately.

In the days that followed, Dickey accompanied her on house calls in neighboring villages and solitary farms. Dickey helped Philippa deliver a baby, set a leg, suture numerous wounds. Once, on their way to check on a family who had all come down with the flu, her jeep stalled in the snow. Unfazed, she walked the last mile in knee-high drifts, treated everyone, chopped some extra firewood, and walked back, whereupon she and Dickey had to dig the jeep out before disembarking once more.

After everyone had gone to bed, Dickey and Tony stayed up late stoking the fire in the kitchen's fireplace. Among other inadequacies, the van's heater couldn't beat back the cold enough to function as a darkroom as they had hoped. Instead, Tony improvised, using the great cauldron hanging over the fire to warm the well water for the chemical baths. Tony took pride in his mastery of the art of developing film, and there were few conditions under which he could not produce a crisp, clear exposure. A nineteenth-century kitchen proved no exception. Dickey watched in admiration as he clipped one perfect picture after another on the twine they'd strung between the wooden beams. Her gaze was not without pride. They were, after all, her photos, and they were good.

While they had been scheduled to spend only a few days in Nawiady, Dickey and Tony stayed for more than a month. Dickey took miles of film, wrote volumes about those she met. Many invited them into their homes, allowed them to document their lives, and shared what little food they had. The weeks slipped by to Christmas.

Christmas morning, Quaker volunteers working in the surrounding area began to arrive—on foot, by mule, and in jeeps. Philippa hung stockings above the great room's hearth. Someone stood a freshly chopped Christmas tree in the corner. At noon a local farmer brought them a gift of a rabbit that the cook simmered for hours with cabbage and potatoes. In the evening the village's fiddler and accordionist arrived, striking up their songs of love and harvest, war and victory, Christmas and miracles.

"They stayed," as Dickey wrote ebulliently to her family, "until the wee hours playing so we could have the one Quaker dance of the year." Tony took Dickey in his arms, held her close. She clung to him, wanting this moment to last. She had not felt this peace of purpose since she had been with the Pacific Fleet. But they could not remain in Nawiady for much longer. They had already overextended their stay and the Warsaw office had written more than once to ask when they were arriving.

In the first week of the New Year, a convoy of Save the Children delivery trucks on their way to Warsaw came through town. Since the roads of Poland were replete with highwaymen, the convoy was their last chance to get to Warsaw safely for what might have been another month. They said their goodbyes and left early the next morning.

Gray drizzle covered the city when they entered that night. The destruction here had been more complete and on a much larger scale than even Gdynia. As she wrote home to her family later that evening, "Warsaw was 64% completely destroyed, 30% rebuildable, and only 6% sound after the fighting ended here. I am giving you the figures because I cannot describe the horror of the reality. . . . There is not a place in Warsaw where you can walk or ride where naked buildings, splintered and burned and dynamited, are not close enough to touch. . . . The entire heart of the city is now a level place."

As a relatively small religious group, the Quakers weren't always able to establish independent projects and programs in larger urban areas, instead working in a supportive capacity with larger organizations. In Warsaw, they had partnered with a Franciscan children's shelter in a part of the city that Dickey described succinctly as "the worst rubble dump on earth, a district in which you think no one could live, until it snows and you can pick out, from fresh footprints, the cellars in which human beings still, unaccountably, survive."

Tony parked as close as he could to the L-shaped barracks the Franciscan monks had built by hand. Still, they had to clamor over snow-covered piles of broken concrete, brick, and stone to reach them. They were both drenched in sweat and freezing cold by the time they arrived. The prior welcomed them in, explained the plight of the shelter's orphaned residents. When their fathers and mothers, sisters and brothers mounted and maintained an entrenched resistance to German occupation, they were met with the mercilessness for which the Nazis are known. These children paid the price for surviving such horrors.

"The youngsters here were not diseased," wrote Dickey. "They were insane. Most of them were driven out of their minds by having to look on while first their neighbors and then their own parents fought and died."

Some had become mute, others catatonic, and still more acted out the nightmares playing through their heads at all hours of the day. Dickey recognized the kind of PTSD she had encountered among Marines. Even so, she did not realize what a flashbulb might signify to them as she loaded her film. The flash went off. "Then pandemonium broke loose," wrote Dickey. "For at least a half dozen of the 40 youngsters, a flashing light signified gunfire and the death of someone close to them."

Yet theirs were not even the most tragic of circumstances Dickey witnessed in Warsaw. These she found along the banks of the Vistula River.

Once the city's main artery of trade, the Vistula was now the heart of the black market where children went to work, beg, and steal. Aware that children congregated here to find means of survival, the newly established UNICEF located their primary food distribution efforts along the river's banks, and in doing so, were able to feed five hundred children at least one hot meal every day. Dickey had secured a contract to document their work and interview some of the children that waited in the line.

Many, as she discovered, lived in cellars and bunkers or in condemned buildings on the verge of collapse. Several she spoke to had watched their parents die or be dragged off to concentration camps. In many ways, these children not only represented but were in actuality the past, present, and future of their nation. But one teenage girl in particular seemed to perfectly articulate Poland's most pressing dilemma: independence or remain under Soviet rule.

Intelligent, with quick eyes and faster hands, she told Dickey how much she admired the anti-Nazi underground. "But she does not think her nation's real security lies in independence," wrote Dickey in her photo captions for the UN, "and she is as distrustful of laissez faire capitalism as she is fearful of the secret police."

Dickey was not philosophically opposed to an egalitarian vision of the future and, for a moment, reserved judgment as to whether Premier Joseph Stalin could deliver on his promises to bring such a society into being. But, as she traveled farther through the Eastern Bloc, it quickly became apparent that his overtures were only propaganda and that the Soviets were using widespread desperation as a lever to tighten the vise grip of their control. Eventually, her distrust of the Soviet Union grew to antipathy, then to hatred.

From Poland, they drove to Yugoslavia, where, as Dickey wrote, "the longest stretch of undamaged railway track measured only twenty-five miles." Retreating on trains, the Nazis had secured a hook the size of an anchor to the last caboose and tore up the track ties like toothpicks. They had equally mangled the country's roads with mines. Their well-planned and sadistic campaign of destruction cut tens of thousands of people off from vital supply lines.

With little other choice, the UN workers looked to the people of Yugoslavia to help deliver aid to their countrymen. With much of the adult male population wounded or dead, while women struggled to keep their families alive, children more often than not answered the call for volunteers. In one southern port city they visited, Dickey and Tony found a crew of twelve youngsters sailing the Adriatic Sea under a UN flag, unloading parcels of food, clothing, and medicine in coastal towns. In the mountains, children had learned treacherous terrain by heart while working as gunrunners and spies for the resistance during the war. Now they used that knowledge to guide UN workers to remote communities that were otherwise entirely isolated.

It was not the hardship of these children's lives that most struck

Dickey, but their bravery and willingness to help those among them in need. As she wrote in her report back to the UN, "The young Yugoslavs have probably done more for their country than any other young people of central Europe."

After they left Yugoslavia and changed half a dozen flat tires, Dickey and Tony arrived in Vienna on the first of February. To Dickey, the city looked like a collection of dollhouses sawed in half. "You just don't believe that such ruins are real until you've driven through them for hours," she wrote to her mother. "The yawning insides of the buildings go up and up, showing one floor after another of what must have been wonderful, spacious rooms."

Dickey and Tony's assignment for the Quakers was to document their school housed in a commandeered baroque mansion that had been spared the worst of war. The students it housed represented "most of the European nations that fought on both sides of World War II." Jewish girls loaned their pencils to Austrian boys who in turn shared their lunches with newly arrived students from Yugoslavia. The atmosphere reminded Dickey of the Quaker summer camp in Kentucky where she had first been introduced to their ethos of nonviolence and radical equality. In the classroom where the students practiced their spelling and arithmetic, the Quaker vision of a world without strife seemed like an achievable if not inevitable goal. The ruins they walked through on their way home told another story altogether.

In her reports back to the Quakers, Dickey detailed the tuberculosis epidemic and widespread malnutrition ravaging the city's less fortunate, many of whom included recent refugees fleeing starvation conditions in the Austrian countryside, Hungary, and Germany. Again, children were the most affected. She photographed them holding out their hands for spare change on street corners, overcrowding ad hoc orphanages, and practicing the art of pickpocketing in order to survive. Yet, for all these challenges, Vienna fared better than many European capitals. Numerous aid organizations coordinated their efforts. The country leveraged its prodigious banking industry to prop up the textile, construction, and rubber industries needed to clothe and shelter its people as well as transport its goods. International loans further buttressed the country's reconstruction.

As such, Vienna had an abundance of fresh food. "We dined on fresh milk, fresh oranges, and fresh eggs for breakfast this morning," she wrote to her family. "And boy did we make pigs of ourselves." And of all the cities and towns they had visited so far, Vienna was by far the most comfortable and it was the first place where Tony had access to an actual, bona fide, professional darkroom, courtesy of the American consulate.

Like everywhere on their trip, they stayed in Vienna longer than originally intended. Dickey picked up stringer work for other aid organizations in need of a photographer. Tony welcomed the extension of their stay. But when February turned to March, Dickey grew anxious to move on. Tony lobbied to tarry a little longer. Their next destination, Munich, Germany, promised to be bleak. But as the deep freeze of winter began to thaw, he ran out of reasons as to why they should remain.

Between them and Munich lay the Alps. Dickey thought of Hannibal as they began their ascent since their baby food delivery truck was as unsuited to the trek as his pachyderms. Their tires skidded on black ice toward the chasms just beyond the edge. Subfreezing temperatures meant they had to jump-start their battery almost daily. Mountainous grades forced them to beg tows from trucks better suited to the terrain.

Finally, on March 16, 1948, they reached the autobahn, the four-lane highway system threading across Germany that Hitler first used as an artery of trade and then as conveyor belt for his genocidal war.

Dickey had thought herself past the shock of destruction. Yet Munich's fresh hell proved her wrong. Not a single building they passed had escaped the war. Hollowed out, half-collapsed, or reduced to rubble, each was its own brutal monument to the war that came to a gruesome culmination in 1944 when the RAF and US Army Air Forces dropped millions of bombs on Munich. Four years later, the streets were not streets, but paths lined by berms of rubble.

But this was the city where the Nazi Party located their first headquarters; where they tried to overthrow the Weimar Republic during the Beer Hall Putsch; where Heinrich Himmler dreamed his terrible nightmare of industrialized genocide and made it come true in 1933 with the opening of the Dachau concentration camp. Dickey struggled to find her moral compass as they wound through Munich. Pulled between her fierce hatred of fascism and her want to empathize with those living in the ruins of war, she forgot to tell Tony to turn left past the destroyed post office. Furious, he unleashed another of his torrents of verbal abuse that were becoming increasingly frequent.

Dickey did her best to navigate them back to the right route, but an hour passed before they arrived at the American consulate. The night clerk handed them their clearance papers, directions to their hotel, and a stack of letters. Along with missives of familial love were notes of financial bad news. Though Tony had made a fortune selling war surplus goods, he'd spent almost all of it on clothes, cars, vacations, and lavish parties. The only investments he'd made with his quasi-legal gains were the adjoining apartment buildings of 24 and 25 Riverside Drive, the rents from which were supposed to be their primary source of income. In their absence, Dickey's aunt Lutie was looking after the buildings. But according to Lutie's letter, things were not going well. Two tenants had just vacated. Three more were demanding basic repairs.

More of a con man than a businessman, Tony replied to Lutie's letter saying that she should list the vacant apartments at a 15 percent increase from their past rents and not make any more repairs past those that had already been requested. In the end, these two strategies counteracted each other and the buildings continued to lose money. In the meantime, Dickey asked Lutie for a $500 loan to keep them afloat, which she deposited into Dickey's account, no questions asked, no strings attached.

Dickey couldn't care less about their modest means. The more time she spent traveling, the less attached to material things she became. Even if they lost everything, she reasoned, they'd still be better off than those on whom she reported. This conviction only deepened in Munich and its surrounding towns where the infrastructure of war had been half-transmogrified by the miracle of peace. Buildings that had housed the means to kill now sheltered refugees. But the bloodstains, real and metaphorical, remained.

In Munich, they spent time documenting concentration camp survivors now sheltered in former SS barracks. Like at the Franciscan children's shelter in Warsaw, the Quakers helped supply its residents with food and clothing. They had arranged for Dickey to follow and document the Hadsewycs, a family of five who in many ways typified those who found themselves in the shelter. Imprisoned in concentration camps at the outset of war and used as slave labor until its end, they survived on thin soup, straw bread, and the solace of each other. Barely. By the time American soldiers opened the gates of their hell, they had become skeletal. Even now their sunken cheeks and sallow skin betrayed the years of malnutrition they had endured.

Dickey spent days with the Hadsewycs, photographing their living conditions, their shifts volunteering in the shelter's kitchen, and most of all, the hours they waited in line at the American consulate. Like so many, they had been trying to obtain US visas for years. Finally, their applications were approved. Departing from Munich's train station, Dickey photographed them as they beamed with expectations of freedom and plenty. More than ever, Dickey understood the power of America's promise and the reciprocal cruelty of denying so many safe passage to its shores.

To Dickey, America's inadequate refugee policy represented the nadir of its apathy toward Europe's war victims. In a scathing essay entitled "Are We Committing Genocide in Europe?," she did not mince her words. "By the inactivity which we have forced upon them, by the hopelessness and frustration of belonging nowhere and to no one, we have not decayed their bodies, like the gas oven would have done in a flash. We have infected their minds, and it has taken us years. Now from among them, the wealthiest nation on earth has dared to vote to pick one out of five or six, like a slave master at an auction, and graciously consent—if his teeth are sound and his religion acceptable and his skill is one that we need anyway—to add him to our citizenry." Far from what a postwar America basking in its victory and drinking deeply from the river Lethe wanted to hear, her controversial article never found a publisher. More frustrating still, the Marshall Plan, which would eventually help rebuild Europe, remained deadlocked on the US House floor, stalled by a contingent of conservative Republicans.

Dickey, who read the news with rapacity whenever available, followed the bill's stymied progress. In late March 1948, she wrote to her family, "I think a great many of us are of the opinion that further delay on the Marshall Plan is simply insane and that the gulf of misunderstanding between the Continent and America is widening, not narrowing. Not that the Marshall Plan is in itself so sound, simply that any concerted and continuing action, anything to give people a hope alternative to another war, is of top priority."

As her exacting language suggests, the aim of her letter was not to elicit pathos, but action.

Her hometown of Shorewood was a bastion of conservative Republicans, and her father was one of the more active among their ranks. Moreover, Shorewood was almost completely German-American. Dickey learned German as a child because everyone spoke German. There were German-language newspapers in Shorewood. Most of its numerous mansions were built in the popular German-Flemish Renaissance style. Nearly every corner had a biergarten where Shorewood's residents went to talk about politics in English and German. By trying to convince her father of the need for hasty passage of the Marshall Plan, Dickey was lobbying the influential, affluent German-American Republicans of Wisconsin.

Amid her ire at America's inaction, Dickey could at least feel she was, in some small way, doing her part. In late March, Jack sent word that *Seventeen* was publishing several of her photographs from Poland. UNICEF would be using her photographs in their annual appeal. Even so, she knew her efforts were hardly a drop in the pail compared to the task at hand. As she wrote in her reply, she felt that "these few months have shown us that we haven't put an infinitesimal scratch even on the surface of the story."

Then, finally, spring. Winding up their coverage of Munich, Dickey and Tony headed north, this time to Berlin where the Quakers maintained a meeting house and the battle lines of the Cold War were being drawn in sharp relief.

After a long drive and a run-in with Soviet border guards, they entered Berlin about 11 P.M. and promptly got lost. Tony ranted, Dickey smoked. Like Gdynia, Warsaw, and Munich, Berlin lay in unfathomable ruins. A maze of nameless streets and alleys dead-ended in empty oil cans and barricades of trash. Streetlights were nonexistent. Their hope of finding a sense of direction let alone the Quaker house dwindled by the minute.

"There," said Dickey, pointing to a policeman in a little blue car. He took pity and pointed them right then left then right again down

Kirchweg Street, recognizable by its birch trees that had, against all odds, survived the war. There, at the end, stood Mittelhof, a Quaker Center housed in a redbrick Tudor mansion. Like most of Berlin's better buildings, it had once been occupied by Nazi bureaucrats pushing paper that killed millions. Now, wild wisteria arched over its entrance, framing a carved wooden sign that read, JEDER IST HERZLICH WILLKOMMEN, *Everyone is heartily welcome.*

"We entered at midnight," wrote Dickey, "with a deep and wonderful sense of coming home."

Dickey woke early to a cup of coffee and a table full of newspapers from both occupying forces. The top headline of each announced the passage of the Marshall Plan. National pride rushed over her. Yet the next headline down declared how much steeper the hill had become. A Soviet air force plane had collided midair with a British passenger plane while in clear violation of West Berlin's airspace. Known as the Gatow air disaster, the incident foreshadowed the Berlin Blockade that was eventually followed by the construction of the Berlin Wall.

But somehow, this turmoil remained trapped in newsprint as the residents of Mittelhof gathered for Sunday prayers. Rather than presided over by a priest, Quaker services were observed in complete silence, allowing each in the congregation to meditate on their own personal idea of divinity. In the roar of recent peace, Dickey had nearly forgotten the power of silence that contained the possibility to think, remember, forget, and to daydream about a future not defined by war, poverty, hunger, sickness, and death. From this silence grew the rest of the Quakers' work that Dickey documented for a month.

Within its sprawling seventy rooms, Mittelhof's staff and volunteers made space for everyone, just as the sign above the door promised. They hosted free daycare for the neighborhood's children. Teenagers crowded the recreation room and library. Job training for adults included classes in hairdressing and shoe cobbling, sewing and blacksmithing. In the evenings, local academics gave free lectures on topics from modern literature to macroeconomics. On the weekends, the great room hosted dances.

Most remarkably in Dickey's mind were the discussion groups that Mittelhof hosted every afternoon. Without fail, Dickey observed, a new participant would timidly announce, "'I was a fascist,' or 'a communist' or 'a criminal.'" With equal regularity the discussion leader said matter-of-factly, "You were?," and then change the subject. For the rest of the hour, participants talked about community initiatives, the role of education in rebuilding Germany, the importance of forgiveness, and other topics that faced toward the future and not the past. If bombing a city into oblivion was one way of eliminating fascism, Dickey concluded, certainly this was another.

11

Home Again

THEY ARRIVED IN Paris in late April. On a crooked side street near Gare du Montparnasse, the clerk at the Victoria Palace Hotel informed them the restaurant was closed and there were no croissants to be had in the morning. He handed them their key and forwarded mail. Up in their room, Dickey slit the envelopes open with her trench knife while Tony smoked in bed.

There were more bills and letters from home. Then one from Jack Kavanaugh. He told them their work had been a huge success and asked if they would consider signing up for another tour. Dickey beamed. Tony balked. What about their debts? The apartment building's vacancies? Her mother? His son? Wasn't seven months long enough to go gallivanting around pretending to save the world? Hadn't he endured enough of her delusions of grandeur?

Dickey bent beneath his barrage of excuses and insults, replying to Jack's offer by saying, "the only honest reply we can give is to ask you to wait until we have been home at least a short time."

They set sail on June 5, 1948, when Paris, even rebuilding from war, was at its most beautiful. Dickey hardly noticed. She had a mission but needed a plan, and spent the eleven days it took to cross the Atlantic drawing one up. Once they docked, she hit the ground running.

Rather than rely solely on the Quakers, she set up multiple contracts with nonprofit organizations including Save the Children, CARE, and UNICEF. She also landed a multi-article deal with *Scholastic Magazine* reporting on the plight of children in numerous European countries. Last but not least, after discovering the Massey-Harris Company had a Marshall Plan contract, she sold them on the idea for a documentary film tracing the trajectory of one of their tractors from the conveyor belt in their Wisconsin factory to a provincial French farm. She bought a film camera and taught herself how to use it.

All the while, she pitched articles on their last trip through Europe to every editor for whom she could find an address. *Seventeen* agreed to run a series on teenage refugees. The *New York Herald Tribune* published an extensive profile on their trip. The AP put out one of her stories for syndication.

She was on fire. Tony played the wet blanket.

As she became less dependent on him, he tried to exert more control over her: picking out her clothes, dictating whom she spent time with, even choosing the movies she saw. At the same time, he became pathologically needy, looking to her for constant reassurance about his career, his looks, his health, his vitality in bed. Her efforts to console him were never enough.

Making matters worse, Tony tore their already fraying finances to shreds. Having burned through his small war surplus fortune, he borrowed another to feed his addiction to a lavish lifestyle. In order to avoid bankruptcy, he sold 25 Riverside Drive, though he held on to 24 Riverside for the time being. The bleeding of one wound stanched, he opened another with a series of unfettered shopping sprees including one at Gimbels department store where he ran up a debt of $200, or nearly $2,500 in today's dollars.

In spite of all this, Dickey spent ten hours a day planning out her next trip to report on postwar Europe. In November, she performed her coup de grâce by registering the American Voluntary Information Services Overseas, AVISO, as a nonprofit foreign news organization with the IRS. Whatever excuses Tony might hurl at her about money were now moot since every last dime they spent on equipment, gas, repairs, film, food, and lodgings were 100 percent tax-free.

They flew to Wisconsin for Christmas. Doted on by Dickey's mother, idolized by her kid brother, and admired by her father, Tony seized his chance to play the hero and the star. He held court around the dinner table, recounting his savant-like photo-developing skills, the Alpine chasms avoided only by his expert driving, and the orphan children whom he made laugh with his colorful antics. From the way he told it, anyone would have thought he enjoyed his time in Europe.

Dickey did not step into his spotlight. Her focus remained singular. If Tony wanted to portray himself as the adventurous kind, so be it, better still that he believed his own story. But in truth, Tony was an alcoholic chain-smoker edging up on fifty, with few prospects of gainful employment. Meanwhile, Dickey was in the prime of her life with multiple client contracts starting in February 1949.

12

Incrementalism

THEY ARRIVED BACK in Paris on the last day of January. In the eight months they had been gone, the city had begun its ascent from the ashes. At the Victoria Palace Hotel, the same clerk that had checked them in the previous April welcomed them back with good news. There were croissants for breakfast now, and the restaurant would soon be open. Bread rationing ended last week and there was electricity all day, except for six hours on Fridays and Saturdays.

Delighted to find the water actually ran hot rather than just tepid, and feeling under the weather, Tony took a long shower. Dickey grabbed her cigarettes and went out for a stroll toward the Left Bank. Meandering on a side street, a flapping oilcloth outside a salon caught her eye. It'd been ages since she'd had her hair done and the sign said the price of a trim wasn't too expensive.

Frayed cables hung from the ceiling. A white spaniel gray with dirt licked the ankle of another customer. A box containing a four-day-old rabbit sat next to the till.

"Bonjour, Madame," said the stylist with flair.

"Bonjour," replied Dickey, removing her hat.

"Ah, Madame has an existentialist cut!" exclaimed the stylist. "Now what should we do with that?"

Paris was back.

Shops were once again full of the city's famous fashions, and fewer children begged for alms outside their doors. Traffic roared around the

Arc de Triomphe and rumor had it that cream for coffee could be found here and there.

Since Tony claimed to have come down with a cold, Dickey began their first assignment alone. Save the Children had hired her to document their clothing distribution warehouse in Paris's industrial district where a team of dozens had once processed half a million pounds of donations every year. Now the warehouse was mostly empty except for a long table of mismatched shoes running down its center. Having resumed a certain degree of normalcy, Parisians just didn't need as many donated clothes, and the warehouse's once enormous staff had dwindled to two: its indefatigable septuagenarian director, Madame Champenois, and her assistant. Proud of her obsolescence, Madame Champenois suggested Dickey photograph her and her assistant sorting the shoes into sizes.

She spent the rest of her time neck-deep in logistics. There were hotels to be booked and interviews to be confirmed, clients to be appeased and routes to be mapped. Though Tony had promised it'd be different this time, that they would share the workload, so far, nothing had changed. While he recuperated from a cold that stretched on for days, she hammered out letter after letter on her typewriter.

In mid-February, the hotel clerk handed them a telegram with the news that the ship carrying their truck and the Massey-Harris tractor would arrive the next day. They boarded the train at Gare du Montparnasse in the morning, pulled into Le Havre by early afternoon, and took a taxi down to the docks where Dickey struck up a conversation with a weathered stevedore. Dickey turned on her film camera and asked what the Marshall Plan meant to him. His eyes squinted out to sea where cargo ships lined up to the horizon.

"Cela signifie travailler," he said, *It means work.*

Last year, he explained, a wildcat strike in New York Harbor all but halted cargo into Le Havre. As a result, every single dockworker had been laid off for ninety days. Now that the Marshall Plan had come into effect, there weren't enough hours in the day for men in Le Havre to process all the ships that came in.

As if on cue, he pointed to theirs as it docked. Dickey filmed the boom as it swung toward a crate reading MASSEY-HARRIS / MARSHALL

PLAN. A few hours later, the whole ship had been unloaded, including their new van. Tony drove them to a nearby motel that had yet to receive its coal ration. They shivered under the covers until waking late to a cold gray morning.

But the roads had been repaved since last they had been in France, and they made it in time to film the Massey-Harris tractor being rolled off the flatbed in front of a stone farmhouse that looked like something out of a Grimm's fairy tale. Pigs nosed the mud. Chickens flapped their wings in the doorway. Two sheepdogs watched lazily as Tony and Dickey unloaded their film and sound equipment.

Dickey, Tony, their translator, the Massey-Harris Paris sales chief, the farmer, his wife, and their four children crowded around the audio equipment in the living room. Dickey pressed record. The reel-to-reel whirred to life. The farmer spoke at length about his farm, his fields, his horse-drawn plow, and how much more efficient he could be now that he had a tractor.

"So, the Marshall Plan will help you grow more food?" Dickey asked hopefully. She wanted this to be a crowning moment, definite proof that America's might was good for more than just war, that it could foster peace as well. But things were not that simple.

"The tractor will help me," replied the farmer, conspicuously omitting any mention of the Marshall Plan.

Seeing where she was trying to go, the sales chief rephrased, "But we would not have the tractor for you without the Marshall Plan."

The farmer chuckled. "I would not have the tractor if I did not pay three hundred thousand francs."

To Dickey's chagrin, the exchange illustrated the kind of detached, impersonal aid that fails to foster goodwill or understanding between the recipient and the donors. In a complex exchange, the Marshall Plan paid American companies, like Massey-Harris, to build tractors for Europe's farmers. The farmers who received them also paid for the tractors, albeit a discounted price. But rather than go to the company—which had already been paid—these funds went to the French government and were in turn used in rebuilding efforts. But neither the farmer, nor the factory workers whom Dickey had interviewed back in the States, understood how this exchange worked exactly. It was too abstract and the US government had done little to nothing to personalize or ground this academic if immense outpouring of aid.

Dickey observed this kind of alienated giving to varying degrees throughout Europe. As she wrote to her family, "If it comes without faith, without sympathy, without understanding (as so much of what we've sent and now offer seems to come) it won't quite do the trick." In a later article for *Reader's Digest,* she recalled an anecdote of an even more egregious breakdown of foreign aid efforts in rural Poland in 1947, when she and Tony found themselves in the living room of the town's mayor, along with a stack of United Nations crates. Their contents were listed on the sides in large white letters as winter clothes and shoes for men, women, and children. Still, the crates remained nailed shut in the dead of winter even though the entire town, mayor included, were in desperate need of warm clothes.

"Will you please load these boxes back on your truck and take them out of here?" implored the mayor. "You see, your colleagues drove through this street five months ago, and pushed them off the back of their truck into the street. When it started to rain, I took the boxes into my house so they would not get wet. But as you see, I have no room to store them any longer."

For a moment, she couldn't understand why he left the crates sealed, let alone wanted them removed. Then they realized the contents were written in English, a language no one in the town spoke. Dickey translated, the crates were opened, and that winter, everyone in town had a new coat. But were it not for that interpersonal interaction, the contents likely would have rotted inside the crates.

Dickey had hoped that the sheer scale of the Marshall Plan would overcome these shortfalls of impersonal aid. Yet in the months to come, she found US aid and anti-American sentiment were directly proportional to each other, a relationship she attributed in part to this kind of parachuted-in assistance that gave little thought to how the intended beneficiaries would be able to incorporate such charity into their lives. "Hasty, anonymous giveaways, however defensible," she wrote in the same *Reader's Digest* article, "yield no return of love—or hate—to the donor. The climate between nations may not warm a degree."

Worse yet, as she continued her tour of Europe, she found that even the Marshall Plan's unprecedented ambition fell short of the actual need. Nowhere was this immediately more true than at their destination of Dunkirk, where only 15 percent of buildings remained standing and a mere twenty thousand of its original one hundred thousand residents still called the city home. Systemic malnutrition and tuberculosis ran rampant.

The living conditions of many didn't make things any better. The prefabricated barracks that had been installed by the US Army in the aftermath of war were still the predominant housing in Dunkirk. Small and overcrowded, they were hot in the summer and cold in the winter. Rain poured through the ceilings all year round. There was no indoor plumbing. "Here are some of the children of the barrack city," Dickey wrote in her photo captions of children playing on the rubble heaps of what used to be their homes. "The war history of Dunkerque [*sic*] is written in their eyes, even though few of them are old enough to know what happened here."

They drove south along the coast to Saint-Nazaire, another of France's great port cities that had been occupied by the German Kriegsmarine. Like Dunkirk, much of Saint-Nazaire had been razed during the war, and its housing had likewise been replaced by prefabricated military barracks. But here, at least the hope of renewal existed in the forest of cranes building the city's future skyline. Tony parked their van in front of one of the few buildings that had survived the war and that now housed the Ministry of Reconstruction, where they had arranged to meet its chief architect, Jacques Laurent.

"You should have come in 1965," he said in his top-floor office. "We only have the map at the moment." He waved toward a ten-foot mural drawn on the office's newly plastered wall. "In clear pastels," wrote Dickey, "it showed a river-edge community with curving boulevards, a score of generous parks, a dozen neat square commercial districts." Ambitious, exquisite, and visibly cognizant of the inhabitants' needs, it looked like more than a map to her. It was a rebuke of postwar rubble and an almost unthinkably optimistic vision of the future. As Dickey photographed its details, Jacques tried to explain the idea behind his vision, but found himself coming up short between his broken English and her abominable French.

"It doesn't make sense on the wall," he concluded. "We'll have to go to the docks."

In the late morning, Saint-Nazaire came alive with the deafening ruckus of industry. In the absence of buildings the sound of cranes traveled unimpeded for miles. Five-ton trucks bounced over mangled streets. Dockworkers shouted their conversations over the din on their way to the yard.

"If you please," said Jacques when they arrived at the yards. He gestured toward a 180-ton crane and began climbing up the stairs.

At the catwalk's end, the ground beneath her feet started to move and the boom began to swing. Jacques looked unconcerned. Dickey tried to follow suit as they turned toward what used to be the heart of the city and was now a flattened wasteland.

"There," said Jacques, adjusting her gaze with his extended arm, "will be our central boulevard. And there will be our park by the river." He moved his arm ten degrees, and so on until he had drawn his map once more on the leveled city.

"Now do you see?" he asked.

"I think I do," Dickey replied, framing him in her viewfinder between two cranes.

In truth, Dickey's best vision never came from a bird's-eye view. She saw much better at ground level. After Jacques returned to his office, Dickey bought a brown paper packet of fried potatoes from a street vendor and waited for the yard's whistle to blow.

"The real story of St. Nazaire," wrote Dickey in an article for the Quaker newsletter, "streamed by us as the work day ended, the cranes ceased to turn, and the shipyard gates swung wide." Dickey followed the workers to the bus stops where they waited to return home and the few cafés that had managed to open. She asked them about their lives and what they thought the future held. Most were happy to talk. Several invited her to their barrack homes that were drafty, leaky, and far too small for the families that inhabited them. Nevertheless, the women managed to flood their buildings with the aroma of rich French stews and the laughter of children. But while the pots simmered, they told her this was the first year since before the war that they'd had enough to eat. Dickey never ceased to be amazed by the way women provided for their families with less than nothing, even within the ravages of war. She photographed their work accordingly, picturing them as heroes of their homes and, collectively, their countries.

For all the progress that had been made, the penumbra of war still hung over much of Saint-Nazaire. Nowhere was this eclipsing shadow more evident than in the reinforced concrete Nazi U-boat pens that measured three hundred yards long and rose five stories up from the sea. The whole of France wanted this monument to Nazi occupation that still marred the Saint-Nazaire seascape blown to smithereens. Yet until now, its fate remained unknown.

The city had arranged a press tour to address this structure's ulti-mate fate. Dickey and Tony queued up with a number of other report-ers who exchanged cigarettes and hellos in half a dozen languages. In true French fashion, their tour guide arrived late wearing a blue beret and wrinkled suit. Introducing himself as Yves Hameline, he flipped on his ten-thousand-candlepower flashlight and beckoned them into the monstrosity's innards.

"Each of us," wrote Dickey, "lived in a Stygian world bounded by cold concrete on one side and colder puddles of water underfoot."

Shining his flashlight to the right, he illuminated the mechanism used to open and shut the doors of the pens. Its massive lever looked like the rusted arm of a dormant giant. As if afraid to wake it, the re-porters crept silently past, then up a set of wide steps that went from concrete to sand to a marsh of decomposing life preservers abandoned by the Nazis after their final, unsuccessful stand.

At the top, daylight broke beneath an air shaft with a wooden lad-der to the roof. Yves moved a table beneath it so everyone could reach. Dickey volunteered to go first, slinging her camera over her shoulder and hoisting herself onto the ladder's first mossy rungs.

Imposing from below, this U-boat pen appeared even more fortress-like from above, presiding intact as it did over the ruined city. Flash-bulbs burst in quick succession as the reporters snapped photos of the panoramic view of destruction.

After a few minutes, one reporter asked what all France wanted to know: Would this structure be destroyed?

Yves cleared his throat. "No," he said firmly. "Our experts inform us this is impossible. But," he continued, "St. Nazaire has decided to lease the space within. Come," he said, ushering them to a second opening and another ladder leading into another part of the structure.

Overhead lights illuminated an open floor space with modern office furniture occupied by smartly dressed workers.

"Welcome," he said with bravado, "to the headquarters of Reno Hyposulphate." Below them, he explained, lay the company's factory, which processed and packaged phosphates into agricultural fertilizer. In addition to Reno Hyposulphate, almost all of the other former submarine pens had been leased to peacetime industries. But after the other reporters had asked their questions of how, what, where, and why, one more raised his hand with an entirely different type of inquiry.

"Monsieur," he said, "would this building protect one against an atomic bomb?"

The old war had ended, the new war had begun.

In her article for the Quaker newsletter, Dickey replied to his question with uncanny prescience. "The answer is probably no," she wrote. "But if not this building will some ill-guided leader try to put us all beneath another and heavier one?" Though the arms race between the US and USSR had only just begun, in many ways Dickey's inquiry foresaw its inevitable progression.

Shortly after the end of the tour, she and Tony drove back to Paris where their own personal apocalypse waited in a stack of mail at the Victoria Palace Hotel. Bill after bill, letter after letter revealed that Tony had sunk their finances to new lows. His shopping sprees put them back some. His overdue balance at Sofia's Storage on Amsterdam Avenue, where he stashed all the surplus goods he couldn't sell, cut into their savings yet more. He was behind on utility payments and let their health insurance lapse. There was a bill from the city housing office, which had recently discovered that he'd never paid the fee for converting 24 Riverside from a boardinghouse into an apartment building. Finally, and worst of all, he owed such a substantial amount of back taxes that the city Department of Finance subpoenaed him to appear in court.

Hoping to buy time, Tony replied to most that there had been some mistake, or that a check was soon to follow. Of course, there was no mistake and there were no checks coming. Tony didn't have a job other than working part-time for AVISO, Dickey's nonprofit. With an altruistic mission and expenses of its own, the organization groaned under the weight of this doubled financial burden. But, as ever, Dickey found a way to keep going, at least for now.

They drove east from France, back into Germany and on to Munich where Dickey observed "the grass through the ruins is thicker and greener," which she took as a good sign. Likewise, store windows displayed the city's incremental improvement. Where they were once empty, they were now full, though remained so because no one could afford to buy anything. Hunger had abated to the point where instead of having nothing and longing for potatoes, mothers now had potatoes and longed for noodles.

From Munich, they turned north, toward Westerwald, a mountain range where the United Nations had hired them to make a short documentary on the resurgence of the German mining industry. Rolling green hills of late April gave way to unscathed medieval towns. The Rhine ran low and fruit trees had begun to blossom with sweet, fragrant flowers along its banks. Even the sun seemed unhurried within this pastoral landscape, hovering high above the horizon before finally touching down as they pulled into the country hotel in the late evening.

A birdlike couple in their eighties checked them in, showed them to their room. Tony, ever gregarious, asked them how they came to run a hotel in the area. The husband answered they'd bought the building to retire in, but lost everything last year when the occupying Allied forces converted all German currency to the deutschmark. Now they had to work until they were dead just to live. Tony had nothing to say to this. To his silence the reluctant hotelier replied that the dining room was open until ten.

They ordered a bottle of wine. The waiter brought it with mismatched glasses. At the next table over, two mine officials were discussing the journalist arriving the following day. Dickey introduced herself and Tony as those they were expecting. The four pushed their tables together and spoke at length about the uncertain future of their quartzite mine, given the mineral's limited use.

Four turned to six when the hotel's two other guests joined, who happened to be the mine's chief foreman and his assistant. Dickey asked the foreman how he liked his job. To her surprise he talked only about his workers, the long hours they had to stand in freezing-cold, ankle-deep water, and wages that would buy them enough to eat only if they farmed on the side. They ordered more wine. Loosened tongues turned to talk of the war.

"I was a member of the Nazi Party," confessed the foreman, then added apologetically, "I had to be to run the mine."

"But, he said," wrote Dickey in a letter home, "he had believed in the party, remembering the unemployment, his own and his men's, before Hitler and the relatively better times which the Nazis made between 1933 and 1937. By 1938 our German friends agreed, it was too late to withdraw. His argument, apparently, was that the Germans so feared depression that they were led to war."

Though she had no interest in fighting the war again over tablecloths, Dickey found this widespread "German desire to explain everything in recent history as stemming from the Versailles Treaty" and the precipitating economic collapse too bitter a pill to swallow. Fear of deprivation was not a moral excuse for acquiescing to fascists. On the other hand, she knew all too well that demagogues brandished the threat of poverty and privation like a gun, relying on the fact that most would rather shoot than be shot. She saw parallels between these events and those unfolding back at home.

"I'm asking you now," she wrote to her family, "out of some of the headlines we read in US papers, could we take a lesson from his argument?" She referred to the increasingly hysterical Red Scare sweeping across America. Though Dickey abhorred communism, she did not consider its threat a reason to give up civil liberties as Senator McCarthy and his cadre would have Americans do. Instead, she viewed the expansion of communism as cause to work that much harder to preserve America's freedoms.

13

Naples

FROM GERMANY, THEY headed toward Italy, the last leg of their trip. Tony wanted to take his time on the scenic drive. Dickey knew they didn't have any, or money for that matter. They were already over budget on all their projects as well as late in starting a Save the Children documentary on Naples's most impoverished. In the end, he convinced her to stop over in Rome for a day to sleep, eat, and see the sights.

By impossible coincidence, somewhere between the Trevi Fountain and the Colosseum, Dickey ran into her old friend Charlotte Straus, with whom she had worked at *Seventeen*. Charlotte was on her way back to the States from reporting on the recently established nation of Israel and explained her circuitous route by the presence of her beau, Denis Plimmer, an English reporter stationed in Rome for an international wire service.

Cosmopolitan writers who were desperately in love, Charlotte and Denis would go on to have a flourishing collaborative literary career. Over the course of their marriage they cowrote a variety of books, from science fiction novels to travel guides to a critical history of slavery in America and England. They even wrote a seven-part series for *Dr. Who* that got cut just before going into production. They were the kind of couple Tony and Dickey wanted to be—and on the surface, were.

Over dinner, Tony announced that the four of them were going on an impromptu holiday. Without the energy or the will to argue, Dickey relented. In any case, after eight long months she needed a break from

Tony's cantankerous side, which had become more pronounced in recent weeks. His sinuses flared up everywhere except in the pure Alpine air of Geneva where they had stopped for a few days between France and Germany. Colds plagued him through the winter, spring, and now summer. The near constant mechanical problems of their truck left him in apoplectic fits of profanity. Money matters weighed on his mind yet his ill health provided a constant excuse not to work. Dickey was his nursemaid, psychologist, and emotional punching bag in addition to all the jobs she was doing for AVISO. But in the presence of others, Tony transformed into the boisterous and affable character she had fallen in love with. Besides, the company of an old friend was just the balm she needed.

"We've been eating a most luscious variety of lotus here," she wrote to her family in late August. For ten days, the two couples toured the ruins of Pompeii, hiked to the top of Vesuvius, and rode through the streets of Sorrento in a horse-drawn carriage. Tony's health and money problems seemed to disappear almost immediately. He paid for dinners that stretched past midnight, hired guides for their tours, and always insisted they see one more sight, get one more round, stay up just one more hour. By the trip's end, Dickey almost believed the facade Tony constructed of them as a happy-go-lucky couple, in love and lovable. Yet reality crashed down on them like a tidal surge as they waved Denis and Charlotte off at the port of Civitavecchia. They were deeper in the hole than ever before and completely unprepared for their last assignment in Europe.

The harbor lights flickered on as they arrived in Naples. Children sang the quintessential Neapolitan ballad, "Santa Lucia," along with Fats Waller's rendition of "Darktown Strutters' Ball" for tourists' pocket change. It was a surreal confluence of the old world and the new, of postwar Italy's abject poverty and the permeating influence of American wealth.

"Naples has to be seen to be believed," wrote Dickey in a letter to her family in late August when the afternoon heat rose off the white cobblestone streets in waves. "If Rome was a shell of a city, this one is a nice ripe and rotten hull."

Tiered hotels with panoramic views of Mount Vesuvius lined the coast for miles like an elegant row of colorful wedding cakes. But this was a city of "strange contrasts" as Dickey described it, where opulence and poverty abutted one another on every street corner. "All the natural beauty in the world," she wrote to a friend, "and a hundred thousand unemployed, the sick, the old, the crippled, the diseased, the homeless children sleeping in doorways on the street."

Save the Children had hired them to make a documentary about the poorest of Naples's impoverished inhabitants who had taken up residence in the coastal Mergellina caves. They had no electricity, no heat, no plumbing, no floor or roof except rock.

Before beginning their film, Dickey and Tony attempted to do their due diligence by visiting the Italian Service Mission, one of the few organizations that worked with the Mergellina community. The director's assistant welcomed them into their single-room office. Dickey offered to transport any pending donations they might have. Tony asked if the assistant had any tips on photographing the caves.

"I'm sorry," she said, "but the director prefers that the Mission not be associated with your work. You see, photographers come and writers come and they go there and the people are told it is all to bring help for them. But the help never comes. In 1947, we had food and clothing," she explained. "But now there is nothing." She pointed to a graph on the wall tracing the trajectory of donations since 1945 with its line dormant if not dead on the X axis. "Nothing," she repeated.

They started out for the caves the next day as ignorant of what they were to find as they were empty-handed of aid that might help those they met. Their only windfall had been their translator, Federico, a science student with a social conscience who studied at a local university. He met them at the hotel, rode in back, and cheerfully narrated what each pile of rubble used to be while navigating them to the sea.

Children flooded around the truck as they drove up to the cathedral-sized coastal caves. Stunned by the stark juxtaposition of objective beauty and abject poverty, Dickey wordlessly allowed them to lead her and Tony into their homes. Their parents welcomed them in, "admired every word we said, and murmured approvingly each time we were freshly shocked; they woke their babies with their little bare bottoms so we should see their sickly faces; they pulled aside their mattresses so we could see their tiny food stocks, and then they began to show us their news clippings."

The Italian Service Mission worker had not been exaggerating. Newspaper headlines in various languages declared them the poorest of the poor. Hundreds of black-and-white photos pictured their destitution. Nor were she and Tony the first film crew to arrive. As one inhabitant informed them, Warner Bros. had taken the whole top off a rock arch to get their generators in just last month.

"To the whole fraternity of news and cameramen, the caves are a kind of mecca," Dickey wrote to her family that evening. "For here, in arched stone holes, live several hundred of the poorest people in Western Europe. The writer loves them because they are as friendly as kittens. . . . The photographer loves them because their whole hideous poverty is plainly illuminated half the day in clear sunlight and the view of their misery is equally photogenic from the muddy roads below or the gravel cliffs above. . . . Like no other slum in the world the caves draw everyone who wants to record misery in any means for any purpose. Including, of course, us."

For all this coverage, their situation had not improved. Arguably, their lives were even more difficult for the attention they received since time and again they had been promised, and had waited in hope, for assistance that never arrived. In the end, the only ones to benefit from this reporting were the reporters themselves. Dickey had confronted the ethicality of this kind of journalism on Iwo Jima where she questioned if personal glory or collective action motivated her coverage. With the more concrete objective of helping to raise blood donations, which her photos in fact achieved, she felt her coverage of World War II was justified. She had been able to rationalize her work with the Quakers because it helped raise more funds for work already being done.

But Save the Children hadn't yet provided the Mergellina caves community with food, clothing, medicine, education, or aid of any kind. After seeing their scrapbooks, Dickey found it hard to believe her photographs would amount to anything other than further exploitation. Those that lived in the caves came to the same conclusion in the days that followed.

When she and Tony returned the next day and the next, the residents asked them for food and clothes. Without a different excuse, they tried the familiar line that the film they were making would bring those things later. To their relief, the residents let them continue for now. But on the fourth day the promise ceased to assuage.

A small crowd gathered around their truck as soon as they parked. Holding her suckling baby with one hand, a young mother banged on the passenger side window with the other. Reflexively, Dickey rolled it down. Federico relayed her demands in English.

"Since the whole community was pictured in the long shots," Federico interpreted, "each should be paid two thousand lira. Nothing," Federico continued the simultaneous translation, "compared to what you Americans will make out of holding us up to ridicule for the rest of the world to see."

"We're not ridiculing anyone!" protested Tony.

Dickey tried to explain they were not with a movie studio like Warner Bros. but with a small aid organization whose sole purpose was to help people like them.

In the meantime, more of Mergellina's denizens began gathering around the truck. Tony started to open the door.

"I recommend," said Federico, "that you turn the truck around before getting out."

"We don't have to be ready for a fast getaway," snarled Tony. "We're not robbing a bank." Regardless, he made a U-turn and parked the truck facing down the hill.

The small crowd that had gathered around them dispersed when they got out, drawn instead to the unmistakable cadence of speechifying coming from the upper cave entrance. With the craggy Mediterranean coast as a backdrop, a man in his midforties made a fiery appeal to those who had gathered to listen. Even in Italian, Dickey recognized the drumbeat of political platitudes meant to whip up a populist fervor.

"I thought there would be communist agitation here with such poverty," Federico commented laconically, recognizing the speaker. "That man's running for election to the city council on the red ticket."

"These can't be his constituents," said Dickey. "They can't vote without an address."

"Some day they will," replied Federico. "Now they'll follow him anyhow. They need a leader."

Dickey couldn't argue with this last point. As she had discovered in Poland and Germany, communism traveled in empty stomachs. While Federico ambled off to listen, Tony and Dickey began filming those whose hunger and thirst discouraged them from joining the crowd. Thinking she was doing them a favor, Dickey casually left her canteen next to one of the interviewees with the intention of offering a drink without offending his pride. Instead, a slow-motion fistfight broke out as two men struggled over a tepid quart of water. Powerless to do anything and without any more water, all she could do was look away, toward the communist organizer whose audience had grown since they arrived.

Suddenly, Federico emerged from their ranks, running.

"Get out!" he yelled.

Behind him, the crowd began to turn, then move toward them. She and Tony threw their film and sound equipment in the back. Federico jumped in after.

"Drive!" he shouted, slamming the doors.

Blessedly, the engine turned over on the first try. Tony hit the gas. Fists pounded on the back door as they sped away. Chants of "Yankees go home!" echoed in the caverns behind them.

Dickey could not help but sympathize with their ire. Describing the antipathy of those displaced by World War II toward insufficient American foreign aid, she wrote, "What our policy has really offered is not the dignity of human life—but the importance of its mere continuance on the rat level . . . I would have no love for those who continued to deprive me. And I would find bitterly empty declarations about the highly upheld dignity of human life."

Her empathy notwithstanding, the documentary was a complete and utter disaster. All the gas, film, flashbulbs, hotel bills, and the hundred other little expenses that go into a production had been wasted without hope of recuperation. They left Naples soon thereafter and under the slowly turning blade of their hotel room's ceiling fan in Rome, Dickey wrote letter after letter trying to explain delays and gaps in coverage to their various clients while Tony dozed in bed and drank at the bar. Their bank account had dwindled to almost nothing. Unless everything went according to plan, they wouldn't even have enough money to get home. Of course, nothing went according to plan.

From Rome they drove to Munich, a trip that should have taken them two days. Instead, it took the better part of two weeks. Their truck broke down six times along the way. When the engine failed near Milan they had to sell all their sound equipment piece by piece to finance the repair. Just outside of Munich, the carburetor got clogged and the fuel pump sprang a leak. Dead broke and miles from a garage, they pulled to the side of the road to make the repairs themselves. The storm clouds that had begun to gather somewhere around Windach let loose as she popped the hood. Tony cursed. Dickey cursed back, tired of always playing the punching bag. Sodden and sullen, they arrived at the city's Quaker Center after dark on the twentieth of September.

There, the full extent of their calamitous finances sank in. As an organization, AVISO was $3,800 ($45,000 in today's currency) in the hole and had to be folded, outright. Tony's overspending put them personally in debt to the tune of $11,500 ($137,000 in today's currency). Dickey sank into a fit of depression, only able to see her mounting failures and the increasing difficulty of the task at hand. "It's hard for me to feel what we've been doing is really useful," she wrote to her mother. "Tony and I are supposed to be over here getting a job done, and when the job is growing tougher and the chances of getting it done less, it's hard to assess how and whether we are really helping or just floating around the map over here for our own amazement." In Berlin, they had to sell their truck to pay for their tickets to New York. Perhaps worse than professionally futile, she felt her time in Europe had been a personal failure. She knew she had been a disappointment to her parents, who had hoped their daughter would settle down to a more traditional life.

"I haven't exactly been a satisfactory daughter," she wrote to her mother in the same letter. "You and probably Dad have kept asking yourselves the question, 'Why? Why do we have children and bring them up at considerable travail—and then they turn out to be more worry after all?" For all the sacrifice her parents had made, for all the worry she had caused then, she felt she had nothing to show.

But more than the guilt of being a disappointment to her family, Dickey felt a sense of obligation to those whose struggles she documented.

In the same letter to her mother, she wrote, "Lucky me to be among the comparatively few in the world who is lucky enough to have actually experienced security and love and orderliness and goodness and a kind of life where all these things come under the label 'normal.' They aren't normal, of course. Of the two billion some odd people on earth, an amazingly small handful would even know what I'm talking about."

She continued this train of thought in, "How the Other Half Lives," her article for *The Saturday Evening Post:* "We are the curiosities, the phenomenon, the forward tidal wave—they are the ocean that surrounds and bears us. This perspective is unsettling, even unreasonable at first. It involves the admission that we are not after all the vital element of the universe."

Dickey continued, "being human, we resist this truth wholeheartedly. And on the face of it, why shouldn't we resist? Almost every map we have ever studied placed America in the center; what wonder then that we think it is there by right? Almost every discussion of foreign peoples in which we participate involves comparisons of their way of life with ours which are flattering to us; what wonder that we think we have so much to teach and so little to learn?"

From these assumptions, she wrote, grew the original fallacy of US foreign policy, namely that experts had the answers, rather than those whom aid was purportedly trying to help. As she continued, "A flat perspective based on the untruth that we and we alone matter would be a solution which few of us want. But our actual point of view is far too often based on other untruths—our slanted childhood concept of geography, for instance, or school day recollections from history books concerned only with what happened west of Egypt." Such perspectives perpetuated a world in which a very small percentage enjoyed freedom while the rest endured oppression in its myriad forms.

Dickey did not propose any sweeping answers in her article. Rather she spent her column inches enumerating the living conditions of those she befriended and reported on. Safe transportation, new clothes, warm food, sound housing, and fair elections, she explained to her blissfully ignorant audience, were rare. Though the majority of the world lived without these things, they were in fact deserving of them. But she did invite Americans to shift their frame of reference when it came to administering foreign aid, writing, "Perhaps the first step would be to forbear every reasoning from smugness; most of us after all were born to our precious citizenship. And to remember the phrase the architects of America called 'self-evident': Men are created equal in the sight of God."

However insightful, her *Post* article did little to assuage the sting of their difficulty-plagued trip or the dearth of articles to come out of all their travels. Trying to make something out of past work, Dickey started sending out repackaged pitches about her World War II coverage now that any censorship objections had become irrelevant. No one bit.

But in the fall of 1950, *The American Mercury* editor made an ultimately pivotal comment in his rejection letter of her article on her time on Okinawa. He suggested she "try writing subjectively." In the era of "journalistic objectivity," which was objective only from a White male point of view, she had never felt justified in pursuing this style of reporting. In some small way, this letter gave her the permission she needed to write in a more authentic and narrative voice that would come to define her brand of journalism.

Almost another year would pass before she had the opportunity to put this new approach into practice. In the meantime, she settled for a job as the public relations director for the Red Cross. She was uniquely suited for the position, though it did not uniquely suit her. In June 1950, US Marines had landed in Korea, where tensions flared across the 38th parallel. Still deprived of military credentials, Dickey had no hope of covering the war. At least working at the Red Cross, she could carry on the work of raising donated blood that proved time and again instrumental in saving the lives of those in the armed forces.

All the while, Tony did what he did best: sell. Charming his way into publicity gigs and hustling some photo-finishing jobs on the side, he managed to cover their expenses. Rents from 24 Riverside Drive staved off their creditors. Profits from the remainder of his war surplus cache put a dent in their interest payments. But once this last revenue stream had run dry and the storage space on Amsterdam Avenue emptied, the remainder of their income proved insufficient to keep them afloat. Besides, Dickey was miserable behind a desk.

The only truly viable option was to go back on the road where they could keep their expenses low while renting out their own apartment.

While Tony found no joy in the prospect of devoting another year to travel, he could also read the writing on the wall. With little income and more debt payments just on the horizon, he too turned his attention to getting them a new gig. And, to his credit, he found one.

While in Eastern Europe, Tony and Dickey had befriended a member of Voice of America, an anticommunist radio station network broadcasting across the Iron Curtain. Through him, Tony arranged an introduction to the State Department, which had recently launched the Technical Cooperation Plan, soon to be known as the Point Four Program. With the purpose of improving infrastructure and technical knowledge in the Middle East and India, Point Four desperately needed documentation of their efforts. While ending in financial failure, on paper AVISO looked like the perfect corollary to the State Department's needs. Within a year, Dickey and Tony were again bound for overseas.

14

Iraq

IN MARCH 1952, the proverbial Cold War pork barrel buffet spared no expense in the quest to make the world safe for America's interests. The comfort of two photographers proved no exception as Dickey and Tony found when they boarded their Baghdad-bound flight at Idlewild Airport.

"Our plane was the double-deck Boeing Stratocruiser," Dickey wrote to her family. It carried a total of sixty-six passengers in plush-lined seats, "and the fine lower deck, if you please, is being used to provide a cocktail lounge for the passengers."

She and Tony adjourned to the bar soon after takeoff, where they fell into easy conversation with the other passengers, most of whom were also in the employ of Point Four. For their part, Dickey and Tony had been hired to document Point Four projects in Iraq, Iran, and India both to drum up positive PR and serve as a record of their programs for congressional review. Their first assignment would take them deep into the Iraqi desert where a team of Americans were spraying a newly developed insecticide on locust-infested fields from crop-dusting cub planes.

Sipping her whiskey at 360 miles per hour, Dickey looked over at Tony, eyes glistening on his second martini. He seemed happy. She hoped he stayed that way. Dark descended as they sped through the clouds. Dickey climbed back up to their seats and fell asleep in her fully reclining chair.

"Then came a blazing orange dawn," she wrote, "a bit of brown green

England, and London airport in clear sunshine." A double-decker Pan Am bus took them to a postwar hotel built on a bomb site less than a mile from Buckingham Palace. They ordered high tea to their room, courtesy of Uncle Sam, took a nap, and headed back to the airport for a midnight flight to Frankfurt, then on to Istanbul, Beirut, and finally Baghdad. The pilot pointed out the Euphrates on the intercom as they made their approach. Dickey marveled at how this thin blue line had once been a wide river supporting one of the world's greatest civilizations before the days of Genghis Khan.

In the taxi from the airport they drove by an Assyrian stone bas-relief beside which a sign advertised ice-cold Coca-Cola. Like everywhere they would travel in Iraq, ancient and modern commingled on a single temporal plane, joined by a film of yellow desert sand covering everything except the electric blue sky.

"There is no such place as Baghdad," wrote Dickey the morning after their arrival at Hotel Zia, one of the city's best. "It's a wicked legend, a sinister myth. It's the end of the camel caravan and the terminus of the Orient Express. It's the Old Testament and A Thousand and One Nights and Chapters III–V in A Child's History of the World. . . . But Baghdad is also a city about the size and substance of Milwaukee, Wisconsin." As such, she went about making herself right at home in this foreign land in the few days they had before departing for the desert.

She met this new environment with the eyes of a child, naive and sincere. Waiting in line at the grocery store, she couldn't stop staring at the woman in front of her, covered from head to toe in a black abaya that she had seen in photographs, but never in real life. Down crooked streets she glimpsed the bare hips of belly dancers gyrating amid clouds of hookah smoke. While having lunch at a sidewalk café she gawked as a sheik in flowing robes emerged from his two-tone Cadillac. He nodded subtly in her direction as he sat at the table next to hers. But by then, Dickey's attention had been drawn down the street to an approaching band of Bedouins with their caravan of camels.

The city seemed to her exactly as mysterious as it was said to be and yet she felt entirely comfortable chasing down its leads. Nor did anyone seem to mind her snooping. "Baghdad must be the most tolerant capital on earth," she wrote to her family. Men in ankle-length white robes stepped out of her way as she neared them on narrow paths. Shopkeepers enlisted the help of their children to translate English into Arabic and back again. When she met with the Iraqi directors of agriculture, propaganda, and social affairs, each plied her with tea and coffee, insisting she have what she liked, but that she must have something. And, as she started to notice, they treated her differently than American men did. They treated her like an equal, like a man.

Her letters home were ebullient, dense with detail, overflowing with praise for the city and its inhabitants. Better still, Tony's good mood had persisted past the luxurious air travel. Nothing kept him happy like opulence, or at least its facsimile, and that's exactly what they had in Baghdad.

In the mornings, from their king-sized bed in their palatial room at Hotel Zia, they gazed up at the ceiling's intricate mosaic. Never mind the fraying furniture from before the First World War and the bare lightbulbs that flickered now and then. Their floor had its own servant who brought them cigarettes and whiskey, laundered their clothes, and polished their shoes. At the hotel restaurant, Tony feasted on filet mignon and freshly made cheese, sugary dates, and home-brewed beer. For all of it, he paid pennies on the dollar. Yet this sojourn among the finer things in life was soon set to close.

The State Department had arranged for them to visit the Point Four anti-locust camp at Al Busaiya, a remote desert outpost on the border with Saudi Arabia that would take three days of hard jeeping to reach. Their guide, Albert Maymarian, an entomologist specializing in desert insects, picked them up in front of their hotel at 7 A.M. sharp on an unseasonable rainy day in March and introduced himself in a decidedly Nebraska accent. Tony poured himself into shotgun next to Hussein, an expert in desert jeeping, while Dickey sat beside Albert who presently launched into an academic disquisition on locusts.

"I don't take for granted anything with the locusts," shouted Albert over the traffic of Baghdad's central traffic circle, then paused to shake Hussein's arm and point at the speedometer. Hussein eased off the gas.

"The locust goes through several stages, you see, and he's very fussy,"

Albert picked up, "unless the humidity in the soil and temperature and the wind and the food are right, he does not survive, or he goes elsewhere. Locusts have traveled nine hundred miles in fourteen days when conditions were right."

Dickey scribbled his lecture as best she could in her notepad. The city gave way to fields of carrots, tomatoes, and broad green beans. She tried not to imagine a swarm of locusts descending on this season of work, this year of food, and failed.

"Tell me if I'm becoming too pedagogical," said Albert.

"Not at all," replied Dickey, and meant it.

"A single female locust," Albert went on, "can lay thirty-five to a hundred eggs at one time. This stage lasts about 40 days. Then, he is in puberty, he has three pairs of legs, a head, a thorax, and an abdomen. He can only hop. And this is the best time, the only time really, to kill them. We've got some of our arsenal there," he said, pointing to the buildings and minarets of the city of Hillah rising in the near distance.

The Euphrates ran through the center of this provincial capital, bringing with it food, crafts, people, and thousands of years of history. Hussein navigated the crowded streets, inching past camels who wouldn't budge and avoiding shoppers on their way home from the vegetable market. The midday sun shone almost white. Tony sweated profusely. Dickey lit a cigarette.

"Here we are," said Albert as they pulled up to the local department of agriculture.

In the courtyard, he gravitated to a pile of camel dung and sank his hands into it. "Not bad," he said to the supervisor, Abdul Jelil Rahim, who had come out to meet them. "Not too much foreign matter."

Dickey snapped a photo.

"The idea," said Albert, "is to use the dung as a carrier for the DDT-laced bran. It's just an idea. Haven't proved it'll work yet. But I think it might. In the meantime," he said, pointing to the cache of burlap bags that filled an entire room, "we give these to farmers to spread by hand the way they would broadcast seed. It's painstaking, but it's what we've got."

They made two more stops at municipal agricultural offices before arriving at dusk into the town of Samawah. The perfume of thousands of blooming roses washed over their senses as they entered. Their lodgings lay at the edge of town in the local agricultural office, an otherwise un-remarkable building except for its rose garden which Dickey estimated to be about the size of half a New York City block. Inside, Tony lashed two Navy cots together for their bed.

In the morning, Hussein woke them with Turkish coffee and a deep purple rose for Dickey which she kept until it wilted halfway to their destination of Nasiriyah, the capital of the province. Dhia Achmed, the director of plant protection for the Ministry of Agriculture, greeted them in his office with ice-cold bottles of Pepsi and a map of Iraq's locust-control camps. There were thirty in all and not a single road between them. Located deep in the desert where infestations might otherwise go undetected, the camps were the country's first defense against famine. Though officially staffed by four hundred civil servants, scientists, and students, it was the volunteer network of sheiks, farmers, villagers, and nomadic Bedouin that enabled these remote outposts to overcome the absence of roads, telephones, and reliable radios. So far, this coordi-nated egalitarian effort had prevented the devastating swarms like those the country had seen in 1945 when locusts had consumed the majority of Basra's crops in a single day.

Dhia had arranged for them to document one such anti-locust campaign with the local sheik of Al-Rifai, a village of twelve thousand, sixty miles to the north. As they neared, the desert road turned onto the banks of the Gharraf Canal, an ancient waterway connecting the Tigris to the Euphrates. Sand gave way to verdant fields of barley and wheat fed by mule-turned waterwheels that stretched into the horizon. Dickey would have sworn it to be a mirage had not everyone in the jeep seen the same thing. It took hours to drive the last few miles through this muddy island of green floating in a sea of white sand. Finally, Hus-sein unceremoniously parked at the edge of the infestation. Dickey got out of the jeep, kicked her legs awake, and stared at the hundred-acre mass of undulating insects.

"Hoppers," said Albert.

The locusts parted, then closed back around her feet as she walked out into the field for a closer look. Silhouetted by the sinking sun, twenty men marched shoulder to shoulder, hand-broadcasting the DDT-laced bran on the other side of the field. Dickey raised, then lowered her lens.

There wasn't enough light for a photograph. Instead, she gave the camera to Tony, squatted, and sank her hands into the locusts. They crawled up her forearms with alarming speed and she half worried they might mistake her for vegetation. Tony snapped her photo. The flashbulb didn't faze the insects at all. Dickey stood, brushed them off her arms, plucked one out of her sleeve halfway to her shoulder, and walked over to Dhia.

"Any chance we could photograph some eggs?" she asked.

Dhia looked across the field. "There are probably some fresh ones over there," he said, pointing toward an irrigation dike more than a mile away.

They had to drive around the entire field to reach it. By then, dusk had descended. Albert and Dhia dug into the earth with their pocket-knives like boys looking for treasure and pulled up enormous clods of earth from which they gingerly extracted fragile egg pods with matchsticks.

"Put them on the hood," suggested Tony. "It'll help with the light."

Fifteen minutes more and they had a frightening display of fecundity laid out on the jeep. Tony set up the Rolleiflex, a high-end camera with multiple lenses, along with its flash attachment. He used more film than they had the budget for, but it would be worth it.

"We'd better go," said Dhia. "The local sheik is expecting us for dinner."

"It was dark as we pulled into the sheik's outer courtyard," wrote Dickey in her notes. "There was heavy incense coming through the door, and oriental music drifted out with it." Inside, a blaze of candles lit the great room carpeted from corner to corner in ornate Persian rugs. Plush upholstered settees and easy chairs lined the walls. In the center, a small wooden table covered in lace was piled high with tins of English cigarettes. The sheik's retinue of servants began unwrapping them, then placed a tin by each table setting, which also included an opened but untouched fifth of Bisquit cognac. Tony's eyes lit up. Albert and Dhia were unfazed. This was not their first dinner among Iraqi desert royalty.

Sheik Shalaha Al Muz'az emerged from behind a curtained doorway. The gold trim of his floor-length cloak sparkled in the candlelight and Dickey couldn't help but notice that he bore a striking resemblance to Basil Rathbone, the English actor who famously portrayed Sherlock Holmes.

He sat at the center of the table and gestured for Dickey to sit at the head. In the corner, a servant kept the radio perfectly tuned to the fluctuating frequencies coming in over the desert from the station in Basra playing Arabic ballads. As everyone opened their cigarettes and began thanking the sheik for his hospitality, a newscaster broke into the music, inexplicably in English. "The Wisconsin primaries are expected to be hotly contested. Support for Senator McCarthy is . . . ," he said. Dickey and Tony burst out laughing. It seemed absurd that American politics, let alone the shrill xenophobia of the senator from Wisconsin, should somehow enter into the desert home of a wealthy sheik while, coincidence of coincidences, they were there.

Sheik Al Muz'az smiled curiously and Dhia tried to translate, but the joke was lost, perhaps for the best. Translations notwithstanding, the conversation remained lively. They talked mostly about the locusts' threat and the progress being made. As the owner of thousands of agricultural acres, Sheik Al Muz'az took a vested interest in the campaign, as he did in what Dickey had to say. He leaned forward when she spoke, listened intently to her thoughts and questions. The paradox of being the only woman in the room while also being treated as an equal once more struck her as strange and would continue to puzzle her as she traveled through the region. As she would later learn, Muslim culture lacked a general protocol for dealing with unveiled women and so, as a default, Dickey was treated as if she were a man. This both appealed to and troubled her. But for now, she said nothing, preferring to unquestioningly bask in the rare glow of equality for at least a little while.

Their dinner party ended well past midnight and they took turns singing to stay awake on the long drive back. Albert crooned the saccharine operettas of Romberg. Dhia sang traditional Iraqi songs. Tony and Dickey belted out show tunes from *Oklahoma!* and *South Pacific*. Desert wolves bayed them into the city.

The next day was their last before departing for the true desert and Al Busaiya. They spent the morning reviewing the remainder of their caravan, which had arrived while they were in Al-Rifai. They had to take everything they might need with them since supply lines in the desert were tenuous at best. They added two more jeeps to their complement along with trailers for each that were packed tight with bedrolls, film, suitcases, and water enough to get them to where they were going. Live chickens, cooking pots, kerosene lanterns, and tents were loaded onto a surplus World War II British transport truck. Two aides, three more drivers, and a cook joined their crew.

Organizing everything and everyone took until evening. Dhia suggested dinner at the agricultural club. Halfway there, Dickey realized women were not allowed inside. "But Dhia coped with that problem too," Dickey wrote in her notes, "he had tables and chairs carried into the garden, under a lamp post with four blue bulbs which reproduced exactly the effect of moonlight."

In the morning as they disembarked for Al Busaiya, Dickey soon realized how little she actually knew about the desert. An hour into their trek, she wrote, "we struck real desert and then the mirages began to come up around us. The most memorable featured the south view of the Pulaski skyway and its approaches, rising out of two of the greatest, whitest sand dunes I had ever seen."

They spotted Al Busaiya as the sun struck 45 degrees. It too seemed unreal. The site of an ancient Bedouin well, it had once been a popular smuggling stop until the Iraqi police built a fortress on the Saudi Arabian border. Its turrets reminded Dickey of the rooks of a chess set. Rolls of rusting barbed wire marked its outer perimeter within which lay the anti-locust camp with its half-dozen tents and two cub planes.

Iraqi police checked their papers at the gate and waved them through. A hot wind dancing with loose tent ropes traced lines in the sand. Laundry strung between two poles whipped as she passed beneath. Squatting beside a fire, a man pulled a dead diamondback snake out of a tomato can and put it directly on the coals. Nearby, a child stood watching the horizon with a gun slung across his shoulder and its shells holstered in the belt around his waist. Dickey found the two cub planes lashed in place at the edge of camp. Beneath their wings, she ran her hand over the nozzles that sprayed Aldrin, a new kind of insecticide that killed its target through paralysis. Unlike previous insecticides used in Iraq, it was nontoxic to humans.

Dickey recognized William "Bill" Mabee, Point Four's anti-locust director, from his photo and, in particular, his well-trimmed salt-and-pepper mustache. A rancher and entomologist, he'd cut his teeth flying crop dusters over locust infestations in the Rocky Mountain region during the Great Depression. For the last eight years, he'd been living in Middle Eastern deserts where he oversaw Point Four anti-locust operations from Beirut to Karachi. At the moment, he was squatting in a circle of Bedouins, one of whom had drawn a map in the sand. Bill spoke to him in unhesitating Arabic. Dickey could only guess they were talking about the location of recently spotted infestations. Bill didn't look up from his conversation as they passed, nor did any of his interlocutors.

"Howdy," came a Texas drawl behind her. She turned to see a portly Iraqi man in his midfifties wearing khaki pants and a polo shirt. "Darwish al-Haidary," he said. "We've been expecting you."

A PhD graduate of Texas A&M and an adopted son of the Lone Star State, Darwish had been Iraq's director general of agriculture for thirteen years. Knowledgeable and efficient, he was as famous for his success as he was for his short temper. Dhia later told them about the time Darwish threatened to poison a foot-dragging bureaucrat with DDT if he didn't get six hundred tons of it for his anti-locust army. Several truckloads of insecticide arrived promptly the next day.

Darwish poured out three cups of Turkish coffee in his tent and Dickey opened her notebook.

"How does your anti-locust campaign function when you have no roads and few lines of communication?" she asked.

He smiled, put his coffee cup down. "I decentralized it," he said. "Six years ago in my office in Baghdad, I got a report about a locust swarm. But by the time I got it and told my men what to do, it was too late. It would have still been too late if we had better communication, better roads. Now," he continued, "every agricultural supervisor in every province is his own locust control officer. He has stores of insecticide bran and the authority to hire men to spread it. I don't need to be consulted unless what is needed is far in excess of what we have planned."

Dickey looked over his shoulder at the enormous map of anti-locust camps and the infestations they were currently battling. Maybe it was all the World War II surplus equipment, but even his map looked similar to those hanging in the canvas tents of field generals she had seen in the Pacific. As she later wrote in her article for *National Geographic,* this fight, like the war against fascism, "cut across race, religion, tribe, wealth, creed, education, position and every other consideration except the need to kill insects."

Bill opened the tent flap and extended a hand to Dickey, then Tony.

"Sorry about the delay," he said and waved off a cup of coffee from Darwish. "Good news, bad news," he said. "My Bedouin friends told me about an infestation north of here on the Saudi border. It's going to be an early morning."

Albert, Dhia, and the crew had struck camp by the time Dickey and Tony got back. Dickey protested the four-man tent they had assigned to her and Tony. It was too much, she insisted. But Albert, Dhia, and Tony insisted otherwise. Outnumbered, she relented. They ate a dinner of C rations out of the can. Slicing them open with the trench knife given to her by a dying Marine on Iwo Jima, Dickey dared to hope that maybe she was living up to his memory after all.

It was still dark outside when Dhia called to them from outside their tent. "The planes are leaving soon," he said.

The cook handed her a cup of Turkish coffee. One sip and she felt awake as ever. The pilots checked their wings in the purple dawn. They introduced themselves as Will and Keith, neither of whom Dickey estimated to be a day older than twenty-five.

Meanwhile, standing on top of a teetering empty gasoline drum, Bill finished pouring the insecticide mixture into the planes' four-hundred-gallon tanks and jumped down. "Let's go. You can ride with me," he said to Dickey. Hussein, Albert, and Tony rode in the second jeep. Will and Keith gave them a fifteen-minute head start.

According to Bill's Bedouin contacts, the infestation could be triangulated between the wreckage of a British sedan, a couple camel skeletons, and a few discarded handfuls of orange peels.

"When they're spraying," said Bill, explaining these seemingly inconsequential signposts, "these'll be enough since dusting locusts is only effective if the plane works almost on the ground. Ten feet at most."

Keith and Will's planes appeared in the rearview sky. Ahead of them, the road diverged. In the half-light, it would be impossible for the pilots to see their sand-colored jeeps as they veered to the right, toward the infestation site. Bill pulled a white scarf from the back, held it above his head.

Spotting them at the last second, Will circled back and Keith soon followed. The two sank down in formation to fifteen feet directly behind them.

"You know," Bill said after a few minutes, "it sure does give one a turn to look in the rear vision mirror of an automobile, and see an airplane there, signaling madly to pass."

Dickey glanced back. Will gesticulated wildly through the cockpit windshield. For the planes to cut around them would be suicide at their present altitude. To fly any higher was to risk losing the path that led them directly to their target. Bill pulled to the side. Keith and Will zoomed by, barely above eye level.

It was not a large infestation as far as locust hatchings go. But the hoppers were packed so densely that from a distance, the patch of sand looked like a bubbling tarpit. If given the chance to mature and swarm, this hatching alone could consume up to twenty thousand acres of crops.

Dickey photographed the pilots as they dropped down for one run after another. Each pass stilled another swath of writhing insects. Keith wiggled his wings as he pulled up from his last run when the field had ceased to move altogether.

"Well, I guess that's it," said Bill. "Sorry there wasn't much more excitement for you."

It was true. This round of pictures wouldn't make much of an impression on any editor. "Would it be possible to photograph the planes from the middle of the field of hoppers?" asked Dickey on their way back.

"You'd get sprayed," Bill replied. "But Aldrin isn't toxic to humans, so I don't see why not."

It would be a few more days before Dickey got her chance for an Aldrin shower. In the meantime, she got to the deep desert where burgeoning Cold War politics were playing out far from view of the American public.

That night, their camp gravitated to her and Tony's tent. Ever eager to play the charming host, Tony made a table for ten out of their storage trunks and pulled the benches out of the jeeps for seating. The cook made chicken stew with beans and tomato gravy. Their Arab dinner companions taught the Americans how to eat the dish by curling their fingers around the rice and dipping it into the bowl. Tony made gin and tonics. Giddy laughter ensued long into the night. Dickey nestled up to Tony in one of the jeep seats. The stars seemed close enough to pluck. Even more amazing, it seemed Tony was at last enjoying the kind of aid work that fueled her own purpose and passion. In his smile and embrace of their colleagues, she thought she saw the faint outline of the marriage she had always wanted: a partnership of equals working together to achieve a common goal. Though here in Al Busaiya they were without Tony's much-loved creature comforts, he still had what he treasured even more: the spotlight. These late-night parties hung on his every word and these men, so used to silence and solitude, found welcome relief in Tony's skill as an entertainer. Tony shined and once more Dickey mistook this glow for change.

The next morning took them to a teahouse in a nearby town where the owner mentioned an "American camp," as he put it, ten minutes or so to the east. With nothing else on the docket for the afternoon, they figured they might as well take a look. But rather than a ragtag outpost like their own, they found an enormous oil field run by 150 Americans who had constructed a settlement of prefabricated, air-conditioned houses, stores, and restaurants almost overnight. The public relations officer met them in his office, introduced himself as J. C. Kelly in a Texan accent, then drove them in his enormous yellow truck to the settlement's diner where he ordered each of them a rare steak with fresh vegetables. After lunch, he treated them to a shopping spree at the commissary, gratis. They loaded up on cigarettes, pipe tobacco, tinned roast beef, canned fruit, baseball caps, and fresh baked bread. J.C. kept trying to get them to take more until they begged the excuse of not enough room in their jeep. Back in his office he told them a little bit about their operations, namely that they pumped out three hundred thousand barrels of oil every day, every last one of which was sent to the United States.

Dickey's articles from this time period made no mention of the implications of this or the other American-run oil fields like it in the region. In retrospect, randomly happening upon such an operation in the middle of the Iraqi desert seems all too obvious an indicator of what the future held. But at the time, very few had the prescience to understand what came next. However, the deeper she trudged into the Cold War's mire, the more expertly she read the writing on the wall.

The next few days were spent much as the last. Dhia arranged for them to meet another Iraqi sheik and another Saudi prince. Albert spent afternoons pontificating on how the Babylonians prayed to locusts like demigods, hoping to be spared their wrath. Keith took Dickey flying one afternoon. High above the desert, she realized she had not forgotten how much she loved the sound of an unpressurized cabin and the feeling of being caught in the slipstream. Evenings were always spent around the trunk-turned-table where Tony held court and Dickey felt almost like she had when they first met.

Then, on the evening of April 12, Bill received two reports. The first came from a frontier anti-locust camp an hour north of their location where scouts had spotted a 1,300-hectare infestation. The second came from a band of Bedouins stopping at the well who told them the season's largest sandstorm was gathering to the south. They had to get to the infestation before the sandstorm got to them. It was a race against time and they couldn't start running until the next morning.

Bill had already filled the insecticide tanks by the time Dickey opened her eyes at four fifteen. "We gotta go," he said. Since the size of the infestation exceeded the capacity of the planes' tanks, they had to take a water truck along for the pilots to refill their supply of insecticide. Likewise, the infestation was too large to rely on the inexact markers of desert flotsam. Instead, the local anti-locust camp staff would mark out the area with white muslin flags affixed to six-foot bamboo poles.

They were waiting beside the site when Bill and Dickey pulled up. Without bothering about good mornings, Bill began to give them instructions in Arabic. "Yellah," he said, *Let's go,* and they immediately fanned out.

Dickey looked out into the field of hoppers. "They made a shimmering, moving veil across the pink desert face. Always progressing in one direction, always growing, eating, spreading."

The cub planes became audible. Bill picked up a handful of sand and let it drain from his loosely cupped fingers to show which way the wind blew. Northeast, straight toward Baghdad and the nation's breadbasket. The ground crew who had staked out the infested area lined up at one side like an audience at an air circus. Dickey stood beside them as Keith made his first pass. Their heads whipped as he flew by just above eye level.

"See," said the driver of the water truck, "he doesn't miss at all. He starts this time on the row right next to the last he sprayed. I thought maybe he would forget a row, but no! he covers every one."

"Yes," agreed Dickey, "they are thorough."

The nozzles beneath the planes' wings ran dry. Keith and Will came in for a landing, already drenched with sweat. Keith took off his shirt. Will squatted in the shade of a wing. Bill started the arduous task of refilling two four-hundred-gallon tanks by hand. Dickey looked at Dhia.

"Can you take me over there?" she said, pointing to the western edge of the field. "It looks like they're moving that way."

Dhia shielded his face with his hand. "All right," he said. Tony climbed in the front seat before she had a chance. Keith and Will took off by the time they were halfway there. A hot gust of wind slapped her face as she looked back to watch them. From a normal altitude, this wouldn't mean much. But when flying a mere ten feet from the ground, a strong wind could tip a wing or change the pressure beneath the fuselage and pull a pilot straight to the ground. It wasn't far to fall, but it was an abrupt stop at a high speed, and often a fatal one.

On the other side of the infestation, the hoppers had already started to spill beyond the flags. Dhia sighed, and began to move them to the new edge of the sea of insects.

"This means we're all going to get soaked," he said, waving a flag at Will to signal the edge moved. Tony began to help.

Dickey ran into the field as Will readied for his next pass. She lay on her stomach, put Will in her sight, and snapped as he dove, his wings tilting against the wind that swept across the sand. At ten feet the nozzles began misting, then raining Aldrin on the insects below. His engine roared over her head, the insecticide soaked through her clothes, fogged her glasses, greased her hair. Dickey set up for his second run.

The hoppers around and on her stopped moving, and though not dead yet, as good as.

Three more passes and she felt she got her photograph. Wiping off the crust of dead locusts from her pants, she rejoined Dhia and Tony in the jeep. They had gotten their fair share of dousing as well.

"Missed one," said Tony, scraping off a handful from her shoulder.

The gusts of wind grew more frequent as they drove back. Bill looked worried. "I don't like this," he said. "It's not good to try to spray in this wind. It's like waiting, waiting for something," he trailed off, not wanting to finish the sentence.

Keith and Will came in for another payload, took off as a dust devil swirled down the length of the landing strip.

"Last one," said Bill.

"The burden of waiting for each of the planes to return grew heavier," wrote Dickey. "Even the crew were silent now as time and again a plane would seem to touch the ground on one of its spraying runs. The wind would rise, the plane steady itself on a run at ten feet. Then the wind would drop, and the sound of the engine being gunned as the plane lost a little precious altitude would reach us. The roar always seemed to come across the intervening desert too late."

Then the gusts became unrelentingly steady. Bill looked to the southern horizon. Everyone followed his eyes. A dark gray wall formed where there should have been nothing. As the pilots circled back, he signaled for them to head home. The center of the field still undulated beneath the sun, now at its noon apex. But it was all they could do for the day. Hopefully it had been enough.

"Within ten seconds," Dickey wrote in her Point Four report, "our entire panoramic view ahead disappeared in a whirling curtain of sand." They had time, Bill assured her. This wasn't the worst of it, not even close. But they had to go, now.

Tony crawled in the back of Bill's jeep, his face looking ashen. "I'm fine," he replied to Dickey's concern.

Bill wrapped a scarf around his mouth. Dickey and Tony followed suit and the three of them drove in silence as curved curtains of sand several hundred feet high thundered over them at regular intervals. Their visibility shrank to almost nothing. Dickey and Bill kept their eyes peeled on the road, looking for camels, oil cans, cars, and humans. At the last second, Bill spotted the outline of three camels, swerved, and by luck didn't hit a sand trap.

Between the sheets of sand and threat of collision, Dickey hadn't checked on Tony, had almost forgotten about his ashen pallor. Finally, safely back at camp, she found him slumped over in his seat, unconscious. Dickey tried to slap him awake. He didn't stir. Bill came back with the cook and three camp aides. The five of them carried him into their tent, laid him on the cot. His forehead felt like fire beneath her palm. He murmured something incoherent.

Bill took off his hat. "We can't leave," he said. "And the radio's out."

Dickey nodded, pulled out a bottle of whiskey, and lit a cigarette. She sat with him for sixteen hours a day, moistening his lips with water, wiping the sweat from his forehead, monitoring his pulse that varied between racing and barely alive. The raging sandstorm cut them off from the outside world, from any hope of an ambulance or even a diagnosis. Her watch turned around six times and she realized it must be Easter. She had not felt the need to pray for intercession since she was on the USS *Relief* when a typhoon bore down on the fleet and the Marines readied to land on Okinawa. For all of his faults, Tony had been by her side since twenty. Now, at thirty-four, she didn't know who she would be without him. Especially now when it seemed they were on the cusp of finding the kind of partnership she had always envisioned. She found herself desperately wanting him to live.

Childhood memories of church before dawn and the scent of lilies stirred the prayer she thought she had forgotten. "For the angel of the Lord descended from heaven," she whispered, "and came and rolled back the stone from the door and sat upon it." She put her hand on Tony's wrist, feeling his racing pulse. "His countenance was like lightning and his raiment white as snow," she continued but could not remember the next words. She squeezed her eyes shut tight, trying to find them in the recess of her mind.

"And for fear of him," said a voice behind her, "the keepers did shake and became as dead men." Dickey looked at the hand on her shoulder, looked up at Dhia's face, caked in grit.

"And the angel answered and said unto the women," he continued.

"Fear not yet, for I know that ye seek Jesus, who was crucified," they said in unison.

Dhia squeezed her arm. "Don't forget," he said, "I went to Ohio State for four Easters. But I've been praying to Allah as well," he whispered and slipped out of the tent to let her be alone.

Dickey let out a sob. Tony stirred.

"Water," he said.

15

Iran

THE SANDSTORM CLEARED. Tony recovered enough to be driven to Basra where he slept for days in their hotel room overlooking an enormous rose garden. Dickey wore out her typewriter with two hundred pages about her time in the desert.

They returned to Baghdad and waited for their plane tickets to Iran, which were delayed in coming. Tony recovered his strength, went shopping, threw a dinner party in the hotel restaurant. As he wrote to Dickey's family, "She does all the work and I do the rest."

Nothing had changed.

Their tickets to Tehran arrived in early July. Whatever shred of optimism she had left about Tony changing his ways vanished the moment their wheels touched down in the sumptuous city. Snow-capped mountains rose in the distance above the bustling streets where princes rode in Bentleys and common folk in jewel-tone buses. Tony drank it in.

Their lodgings in Tehran's famous Park Hotel were even grander than those in Baghdad. A concierge attended to their every wish. A chambermaid tidied their room and changed the linen every morning. A ten-piece orchestra serenaded diners in a perpetually blooming garden restaurant. "Caviar," wrote Dickey to her parents, "comes in quarter pound portions and fine wine is all of eighty five cents a bottle." Still, she wished the State Department would make up their minds as to what they wanted them to do in Iran.

Long days turned into weeks without word from Washington, which at the time displayed little interest in Iran beyond its shared border with the Soviet Union. To a large degree, America's apathy hinged on its access to Iran's oil, or more accurately, its lack of access. Unlike Iraq with its undiscovered and underexploited oil fields, those of Iran were already being plumbed to their depths by Anglo-Iranian Oil Company (AIOC), a British-owned corporation. For a time, AIOC maintained unfettered access to the country's wells through its cozy ties to the ruler of Iran, Shah Mohammad Reza Pahlavi. But, in April 1951, under pressure from popular opinion, the shah appointed the leftward-leaning political figure Mohammad Mosaddeq as prime minister. Immediately after being sworn into office, Prime Minister Mosaddeq nationalized Iran's oil.

Predictably, England did not take kindly to having a valuable energy pipeline shut off overnight. In response, MI6, England's version of the CIA, stepped up its campaign to sow dissent in the streets as well as the halls of power. Their campaigns were beginning to bear fruit when Tony and Dickey checked into the Park Hotel, where a growing cohort of the international press corps was covering the story as it evolved.

They wasted no time endearing themselves to this clique over drinks at the bar. In one letter home, Dickey listed a few of the more idiosyncratic members of their crew: "One lanky Associated Press correspondent in a corduroy jacket, soft voiced, complaining into his Scotch-and-water that his office did not understand him; one equally skinny National Broadcasting Company correspondent in a tweed jacket squinting at a set of news pictures showing his interviewing the prime minister and complaining that said prime minister had caused him to be scooped on the interview; and a chunky correspondent from a British sensation newspaper seeking sympathy for a Sunday feature he was drunkenly assembling on how insects were about to take over the earth." To her they seemed like a cast of characters from a B-movie. Not that she meant it disparagingly, well aware that she was also an actor in this particular film.

Then, there was Albion Ross of *The New York Times*. Unkempt and perpetually underwhelmed, Albion embodied the archetypal foreign correspondent. Over dinner one night he told Dickey that he suffered from "neurasthenic boredom" and viewed the Middle East as "a cat's playground with an oil can in it." When he mulled over the menu, she suggested he try the pork chops.

"Bah! Trichinosis! Hookworm!" he scoffed.

"The watermelon is superb," she tried again.

"Watermelon! Doubtless solid with typhoid," he replied.

"What happened at the foreign minister's press conference?" Dickey asked, hoping both to get a glimpse of the action and soften his mood.

"Conference!" he guffawed. "Just filed my dispatch—don't even want to think about it," he said, waved the waiter over, ordered the pork chops and watermelon, then proceeded to launch into a dramatic disquisition on the conference, its historical background, as well as its future significance.

Scotches all around.

Jocularity aside, Dickey couldn't help but feel a twinge of jealousy that they, and not she, were covering the hard news. The all-male cadre rubbed salt in her wound by talking down to her with "an avuncular disposition," as she wrote to her mother. With more experience than the lot of them put together, this was a bitter pill to swallow. But beyond this aside to her mother, she said nothing, indulging their hubris as she had with so many other male correspondents before.

In late July, the State Department finally sent her and Tony on assignment to cover a few Point Four projects along Iran's border with Azerbaijan. Their first stop took them to a small town just over the border where three successive failed harvests had forced its inhabitants to eat their draft animals and seed to stave off starvation. As an ameliorative effort, a Point Four agricultural consultant had introduced a drought-resistant strain of wheat and their visit had been planned to coincide with the harvest of this initial crop. Adequate rainfall had ensured its success. Dickey photographed their host family standing at the edge of the field. Their faces, gaunt with hunger, seemed antipodal to the golden stalks swaying behind them. Dickey tried not to let hope get the better of her. But it was hard not to daydream in a wheat field.

From there they traveled to a nearby village where a Point Four nurse had established a medical clinic. Her fluent Farsi engendered trust within the community, an important asset when trying to save lives. She introduced Dickey to one of the families she'd been able to help. The winter before, their infant daughter contracted pneumonia. Having built a relationship with the mother, she'd been trusted to administer a shot of penicillin before it was too late. Now, Dickey squatted on her heels while the mother placed her healthy one-year-old daughter on the floor beside her.

Their last stop took them to a community on Iran's border with the USSR where Point Four technicians were building a well. As in Europe, Dickey discovered that here too aid efforts directed at a distance often fell afoul of the actual needs of the community. While water was important, what the community really wanted was a school. As it so happened, the Iranian Ministry of Education had given the town's mayor the money to build one and further funds to pay the salary of a teacher. But dispensation of the teacher's salary came with the contingency that the building had to include a window. Since windows were antithetical to the architecture of desert borderlands, no one in the town knew how to frame one.

In response, the Point Four technicians on the ground agreed to frame the window on the condition that they be able to build the well nearby and attach an indoor bathroom to the school. The community's mayor happily agreed. Yet without this personal connection and willingness to listen to aid recipients, the town would not have gotten a well or a teacher. What's more, in the absurdist play of government bureaucracy, the six dollars it cost to frame the window qualified as a capital improvement, therefore subject to congressional approval. As a result, the Point Four technicians ended up paying out of pocket for the materials, though happily so. Dickey delighted in the illustration of her theory that the best kind of aid is determined in concert with the community it seeks to benefit.

Still, for as much as she enjoyed reporting on these successes, the trip was less than comprehensive. Their stay in each community didn't last more than three days, far less time than Dickey would have preferred. Throughout her career, she strived to spend weeks if not months with those on whom she reported, convinced that the whole story could neither be understood nor captured in a mere matter of hours. But in Iran, she had to stay and go on the State Department's schedule and tried to make up for their haste by shooting over forty rolls of film.

Tony, on the other hand, couldn't wait to get back to the cushy environs of Tehran, even with the mountain of exposures he had waiting for him on their return. But unbeknownst to both of them, the political terrain of Iran had shifted while they were touring the countryside. Just a few days after their departure, British attempts to rig the upcoming elections in favor of candidates with pro-British sentiments came to a head. Aware of England's meddling as well as the shah's complicity, Prime Minister Mosaddeq resigned from office in a bold move of brinkmanship. The shah responded rashly, appointing an openly pro-British prime minister. This in turn spurred the broad leftist coalition of the National Front to organize massive demonstrations calling for the return of Mosaddeq.

The tactic worked. On July 21, 1952, Mosaddeq was swept back into office, but only after 69 were killed and another 750 injured when the demonstrations became violent. By the time Tony and Dickey arrived back in Tehran in mid-August, the demonstrations had been quelled, but evidence of the disturbance lingered in the streets where martial law had been imposed. "Every street corner and public building and shopping center," Dickey wrote to her family, "was decorated by a fine upstanding pair of soldiers." The gates of their hotel remained locked when rumors of riots grew too numerous to be ignored, and Dickey noticed for the first time how high the walls had been built around these luxury accommodations. What's more, the staff had been armed. The headwaiter prominently displayed his Colt .45 as he took orders for lamb, sour milk soup, and vodka martinis.

But the orchestra played on and the caviar supply didn't flag. When the gates were open, she and Tony went down to Avenue Lolazar, "Tehran's Fifth Avenue" as Dickey described it, where even she purchased a skirt or two. When the National Front headquarters were set ablaze by counterprotesters down the street from the hotel during dinner, the kitchen didn't miss a beat. Though Albion, not usually one for rapid movement, was seen running through the courtyard and out the gates to get the story.

In March 1953, the newly elected President Eisenhower's administration upped the ante by accusing Prime Minister Mosaddeq of collaborating with the Soviets, then tasked the CIA to orchestrate a coup that would install the pro-American General Fazlollah Zahedi.

In reality, Mosaddeq had made numerous overtures to the United States, which he viewed as a counterweight to the meddling British. His cardinal sin was his demand that Iran control its natural resources. In hindsight, numerous US government officials involved with the coup acknowledged that Mosaddeq was no friend of the Soviets and, under different circumstances, would have made for a stable ally. The full repercussions of this antidemocratic coup staged by the United States came to pass years later in the spring of 1979 when the ongoing Islamic Revolution, largely galvanized by Western interference in Iran, deposed the shah and swept Grand Ayatollah Ruhollah Khomeini into power, ushering in a new stage of conflict between the United States and Iran. In addition, the tactical shift in Iran signaled a universal repositioning of strategy within the CIA that increasingly sought to play God on the geopolitical stage.

As Dickey trudged deeper into the Cold War's mire, she would find herself crossing paths with the CIA again and again. To Dickey, their presence would become not only unwelcome but antithetical to American freedoms, and in particular, freedom of the press.

But for now, the State Department directed Dickey and Tony to close up shop in Tehran and sent them their official itinerary for central India.

16

India

THE MAIDENS HOTEL in New Delhi made opulent an understatement. Built for the coronation of King Edward VII as emperor of India, it embodied all the pomp and pretension that British colonialism came to signify. Its edifice of white marble shimmered beneath the hot blue sky while its expansive classical architecture floated on a sea of manicured grass. Tony was taken. Even Dickey couldn't help but be impressed, particularly by the snake charmer whose cobra eyed them suspiciously as they passed into the hotel's foyer.

But there was little time to enjoy the local sights. There were photographs that needed captions, reports that had to be written, and letters that had to be sent to their handlers in Washington. Most importantly and for the first time since leaving the United States, she had enough time, coffee, and cigarettes to start writing pitch letters to editors for articles about her experiences covering Point Four.

With few bylines under her name, she took a birdshot approach, sending queries to both local papers like the *Milwaukee Sentinel* and international outlets like *National Geographic*. At thirty-four, she very much felt that time was running out for her to become a successful journalist and burned the midnight oil like her career depended on it, which in many ways, it did.

Occasionally she came up for air between reams of paper, mostly to appease Tony, who was always being invited to one cocktail party or another. While she didn't always welcome these interruptions in her work, she did appreciate the excursion Tony organized to see the Taj Mahal for their wedding anniversary.

"The night of October 4th was the brightest moonlight of the year," wrote Dickey to her family, "and along with your daughter, the people of India came to discover the Taj." She took Tony's hand as they walked toward the famed tomb's red sandstone gate beyond which ten thousand people spread out over the expansive lawn to watch the moonlight glint off its polished marble dome.

"I think everyone in that vast crowd exclaimed again and again, but not a voice was high, not a child cried, not a soul shouted. It was the warmest sound in the moonlight that you can imagine—all those hundreds marveling at once." Brief moments of pure magic had long sustained Dickey and Tony's ailing relationship. But as they drove back to Delhi and she tried to nestle against his chest, she did not find that same sense of solace she once had.

The following day they left for their first assignment in Patiala, a capital city in the southeastern Punjab region where the State Department was waging war against communism. America viewed the People's Republic of China, rather than the Soviet Union, as enemy number one in India. As such its foreign aid policies were informed by Mao Zedong's galvanization of the peasantry during the communist revolution. Accordingly, instead of guns, the United States deployed seeds, plows, and the knowledge of how to use them as its primary weapons in India. This endeavor, which came to be known as a "rice roots" movement, enlisted thousands of American technicians to engage and educate India's villagers in modern farming methods.

Yet for all the pretense of social advancement under American leadership, the specter of British colonialism hung heavily over nearly every aspect of their trip, beginning when they pulled up to their lodgings. They had been told they would be staying in the former summer home of a local maharaja. Such principality rulers often worked hand in glove with the British as they plundered local resources, resulting in massive concentrations of wealth that made for the resplendent palaces, such as the one in which Tony and Dickey found themselves. Predictably, Tony felt right at home.

"The staff detailed to care just for us numbers about a dozen," he wrote to Dickey's family, then added in parenthetically, "(I should know—I just tipped 'em)." He went on to describe the palace's double-height ceilings, marble floors, and sterling silver flatware with which they ate "three sumptuous meals a day." Equally unsurprising was Dickey's disinterest in these materialist trappings.

The day after arriving, their State Department–assigned driver, Sumner, took them into the Punjabi countryside, where the local Point Four employee, Perry Jameson, was demonstrating the efficacy of American farm equipment. As they pulled around a sharp corner, a crowd of over a thousand farmers came into view. Clad in white turbans and loincloths, some held babies on their hips, others sat cross-legged on the ground. Most stood craning their necks as Perry stepped onto a wooden crate. Dickey grabbed her camera, clambered on the hood of their car, and snapped a photo as Perry began to speak through a Hindi translator.

"I came over here to be a friend," he said. "And I think it would be right and friendly of me to tell you about some new ideas I brought with me." He gestured toward the oxen yoked to two plows. One was wooden, belonging to the local farmer who stood in front of his oxen. The other was made in America with American steel. Perry invited the farmer to plow a row while he did the same. The difference became immediately obvious in the heaps of broken earth turned over by the American plow as opposed to the thin scratch made by the traditional plow. Nods of approval made waves in the sea of white turbans. Perry smiled proudly.

Good intentions have rarely paved such a direct route to hell.

The introduction of American farming equipment in the Punjab precipitated the rapid erosion of fertile topsoil, ultimately decreasing agricultural yields rather than increasing them. Farmers were then forced to supplement naturally occurring fertilizers with chemical ones. This in turn flooded the groundwater with poisonous nitrates that led to a massive health crisis since groundwater is the central source of drinking water in the Punjab region. The more time Dickey spent with non-Eurocentric cultures, the more she came to see the danger in trying to transpose American values onto others. But for now, all Dickey could see was the rich earth turned over in a straight row and the earnest man trying to bring about a better harvest.

The farmers dispersed slowly in the afternoon heat. Dickey waited for the last to leave before introducing herself to Perry, shaking his hand vigorously and congratulating him on a successful demonstration. He smiled with a puckish grin, and invited them to dinner that evening.

For the next few weeks, Dickey shadowed Perry on his rounds to Punjabi farmers whom he never belittled or spoke down to. Instead, he seemed genuine in his desire to help them improve crop yields. To Dickey as well as many more, Point Four seemed like a successful program. Only years later would its agricultural methods bear its poison crop.

Their last day in Patiala fell on Diwali, a celebration of the triumph of good over evil. The Jamesons offered to drive Dickey and Tony around Patiala to see the festival's fireworks and elaborate lantern displays. It was their first year in India, too. None of them were really prepared for the radiance they were about to encounter.

"Every porch and window and rooftop from palace to hovel was illuminated not by one flame, but by long rows of them, flickering in the soft wind," wrote Dickey, nearly knocked breathless by the spectacle. As they drove farther into the city, its residents wound down curving earth-paved streets holding sparklers, igniting spinning chakkars, and setting off rockets that exploded above rooftops in brilliant showers of gold.

Tomorrow they were leaving for the Bastar District in the state of Madhya Pradesh where they would be reporting on efforts to modernize the farms of the Madia Gond, indigenous peoples of central India. Part of Dickey could hardly wait. Few Western reporters had or were willing to visit this remote region, and she would be the first to get the story on how American-funded programs were improving their lives. Besides, she wanted to see it for herself and to meet those whose experience of life was so different from her own.

But another part dreaded their departure. There would be no maharaja's palace, no team of servants, no dinners with the Jamesons, no cocktails on the veranda. Tony had only so far grumbled under his breath about this change in environs. She fully expected him to erupt in the morning when the imagined became the actual.

Sumner packed their bags in the morning. Dickey offered to help but he refused. Tony sulked on the veranda until it was time to go. It took eleven days of hard driving to reach the Bastar District in the state of Madhya Pradesh. They slept on bedrolls in thatched-roof government shelters, ate out of C ration cans, drank boiled water. Predictably, Tony flew into rages over every inconvenience. Dickey pulled a thin blanket over her head to sleep.

He tore into her anew every morning. Her exposures were all wrong. Her captions were too long-winded. Her stories stank of sentimentality. She did her best to ignore him, paying attention instead to the camels, cattle, elephants, and four species of monkeys that streamed past her window. "The trip, " she wrote to her parents, "was like being locked in a movie where the projectionist had all the travelogs in history loaded on an endless loop."

On their last day of travel he started again. Unable to suppress herself any longer, Dickey fired back, flush with cold rage.

Tony recoiled.

Sumner pulled the car over, parked in front of a thatched-roof rest stop. "Lunch," he said, and began unloading the food and pots from their trunk.

Dickey got out of her side, slammed the door. Tony left his open, leaning against the side.

"Mum," said Sumner, burdened with his load, "don't talk mad with Master. Master, don't talk mad with Mum."

Tony held out his hand. Dickey looked at his swollen face and crumpled posture. Sweat soaked through his clothes. He could no longer keep up with her. There was nothing to be done about it just then. Dickey, as she always did, felt pity for him, tinged with compassion. She laughed, took his hand.

"We won't, Sumner," she said. "And I'm sorry."

With nothing else to say they rode in silence to their last stop, a government outpost on the edge of an enormous teak forest where monkeys howled and hyenas cackled in the falling dusk. Tony looked desperately at the building, little more than a shack, and said nothing. Dickey helped Sumner with the bedrolls and boiled water. They were all tired and even Tony, for all his grumblings of discomfort, started to snore soon after his head hit the pillow.

The sound of a motorcycle engine woke Dickey. She splashed water on her face. They had been told to expect a local administrator sometime that day and she was a little embarrassed not to be more prepared. Outside, the bike's owner leaned against its seat, rolling a cigarette and gazing absentmindedly into the forest. He looked up as she approached.

"Good morning," he said in an Oxford accent, "Ronald Noronha," and held out his hand.

An incredibly competent man who looked the part in a tweed jacket and round tortoiseshell glasses, Ronald was the deputy commissioner, district manager, and development director of the Bastar District. Born locally and educated at Oxford, he was perhaps an archetypical administrator of the Community Development Program (CDP), a government project designed, funded, and implemented largely by Indians in over one hundred thousand villages. Since the US Congress had recently allocated $45 million in support of the billion-dollar program, they expected a report, which Dickey had been sent to provide.

Sumner drove the three of them toward the village of Bhirlinga where the CDP had arranged for them to tour local farms. The road wove in and out of the forest that ebbed and flowed like a tideline on the seashore. Where it receded, rice fields shimmered in the hot morning sun. A little more than an hour into the landscape and Sumner slowed to a stop at the edge of a mud slick stretching a hundred yards ahead. Anyone could see they wouldn't make it through. But Bhirlinga's residents had already anticipated their trouble and sent a dozen men and boys to carry their camera equipment the remainder of the way. Dickey objected that she had nothing to carry. The villagers only smiled at the notion that a visitor should carry anything.

They followed in single file across a maze of earthen walls that edged acre after acre of rice paddies. Finally, they arrived at a burnt-out teak log bridge stretching across a stream and into Bhirlinga where a receiving line waited for them with garlands of Indian aster and flame of the forest. The villagers piled flowers up to their chins, then presented the visitors with woven leaf bowls of cucumber and cane sugar. Dickey felt guilty for taking so much from a community of subsistence farmers in which hunger remained chronic and persistent. But it was their custom, she was told.

After the ceremony, Ronald introduced her and Tony to Chano, one of the village's more successful farmers.

"How is your harvest this year?" she asked through an interpreter who spoke Bhirlinga's local language.

"You just walked through it," he said, gesturing toward the way they had come. "It's the most we've ever grown," he said.

Rather than fertilizers and plows recommended by the American Point Four Program, Ronald and his CDP team suggested techniques that neither fundamentally changed the Madia Gond's way of life nor the ecosystem in which they lived. Where farmers in Bhirlinga had once allowed monsoon rains to wash away the remnants of the last crop, Ronald suggested they plow the rice stalks back into the soil after a harvest. This simple technique helped enrich the soil with nitrogen for the next planting. He also helped them build the earthen walls they had just walked along to retain the water throughout the growing season. This in turn aided nutrient retention and diminished soil erosion. As a result, several of the farmers, Chano included, had not only enough to eat but a surplus of rice to sell. But one good harvest does not erase generations of hardship.

Their visit had been arranged to coincide with the harvest, and every day for the next week Dickey walked through the maze of rice paddies to Bhirlinga at dawn. As in Poland, Germany, France, Italy, Iran, and Iraq, as she would all over the world, Dickey saw that women here bore the brunt of poverty. In the captions for a series of photographs, Dickey wrote, "Women's work in the fields is vital to the family's survival in most of the world. The fact that labor like this in blazing summer sun takes years from their lives deters these women harvesting rice, no more than the danger of tigers, snakes, and wild boars, animals that claim more than a thousand victims in this area annually."

While their mothers worked in the field, young daughters filled earthen jugs at the village's watering hole, then hoisted them onto their heads for the long walk home. Early in her trip to Bhirlinga, Dickey tried to photograph them at their work. But shy and embarrassed, they turned away from her camera. Remembering the Marines who had found her overwrought attempt to scale a berm on Iwo Jima comically endearing, Dickey asked if they might let her try their balancing act.

One hesitantly handed her a jug. Dickey waded into the water, pushed it beneath the surface, and with farcical but not feigned difficulty, she hoisted the overflowing jug onto her head. Water sloshed on her shoulders. She walked with uncertain steps back toward the water's edge, where she plunked the jug into the mud and wiped her brow in hammed exhaustion. The crowd that had gathered laughed hysterically. The young woman who had lent her the jug scooped it up in one graceful motion and posed with a proud smile for Dickey to snap her photograph.

Even beyond these responsibilities, all of the domestic labor fell to women, as Dickey discovered when Chano's wife, Punie, invited her into her home of mud walls and an earthen floor. Punie had made all of their furniture by hand out of water buffalo dung, a material Dickey compared to plaster in her State Department report. In addition, Punie cooked and cleaned, fed her children, and tended their religious shrine.

"Women's work in homes outside the western world is incessant," she wrote in her photo captions, "while the rice cooks, tiny fish smoke over the raised wood stove. . . . Yet the stove is hard to light and must be constantly tended, the floors and walls must be constantly renewed as the mud dusts off, utensils must be hand polished with clay, and the fish baskets woven and re-woven. A woman finds it hard to feed ten people from these facilities, as Mother Punie does. She is now in her late twenties; her life expectancy is perhaps five years more."

After Bhirlinga, their assignments took them to a few more stops, a training camp for Indian civil servants working for the CDP; a village where a well was being dug to supply the community with clean water; and the construction site of the massive Hirakud Dam across the Mahanadi River. Dickey documented each with due diligence and enthusiasm. But for Dickey, those she met in Bhirlinga fundamentally changed her, profoundly influencing her appreciation of cultures other than her own, and set her down a path from which she could not turn back. Nor was it one that Tony could accompany her on.

Finally, on November 19, 1952, they arrived back at the Maidens

Hotel. Tony took a long shower and retired to the bar. Dickey checked the mail. There, along with the letters from her family, bosses, friends, and creditors, was an envelope from *National Geographic*. They wanted her story on fighting locusts in the deserts of Iraq. Here, finally, was the break she had been chasing for a decade.

17

Leaving

THE DECEMBER WIND hit hard at Idlewild Airport. Still, as the New York City skyline appeared over the Triborough Bridge, it felt good to be home even if for a short while.

The following week, they were due in Washington, DC, to give a congressional briefing on the programs and projects they'd documented. The US Foreign Service, State Department, Department of Agriculture, as well as the National Museum and the League of Women Voters had also booked them to lecture on their time with Point Four. Dickey had yet to finish the text for their talks, let alone organize a slide presentation from the more than ten thousand negatives she'd taken over the course of their tour. Daunted but undeterred, she made up her mind to go to work as soon as they got home, jet lag or no. Her urgency only increased when she checked the mail.

During their last two weeks in New Delhi, Dickey had written a draft of her article "Report from the Locust Wars" and sent it to George Long, her editor at *National Geographic*. His revisions were waiting at 24 Riverside Drive when they arrived. They were thoughtful, kind, and, better yet, not too overwhelming. Still, they were another item on an already long list and couldn't be put off since he'd invited Dickey and Tony to discuss her article in person while they were in DC.

While Dickey set to work, Tony took to bed, complaining of a stomachache. She would have chalked it up to his usual malingering if she too weren't feeling under the weather. But on the brink of the success

she had been working toward for so long, she didn't allow a little un-
ease to get in her way. By the time their train departed for DC, she'd
perfected their presentation and gotten through most of George's edits.

Accompanied by her vivid photographs, Dickey's lectures were an
unequivocal success, lauded by both government officials and the directors of multiple nonprofits. Point Four director Colonel Stanley
Andrews gushed, "Mrs. Chapelle, a distinguished photographer and
former war correspondent, has done remarkable work, under hardship
conditions." Various departments used her photographs in internal
publications and press releases while also printing large-scale versions
to be displayed for the public. Dickey had every reason to believe their
Point Four contract would be renewed and that she could go on in the
same manner with hard-to-find pride and purpose. Yet unbeknownst
to her, the tectonic plates of Washington politics were shifting in the
convection currents of Eisenhower's new administration.

In the meantime, their whirlwind tour of Washington's halls of
power had been a bit of a slog. Whatever stomach bug they had landed
with wasn't going away. Fortified with antacids, they managed to get
through their meeting with George at *National Geographic* at the end of
the week, albeit a little green around the gills. Dickey walked away with
a better grip on what George was looking for and sent back a fully re-
vised version a few days later. George replied on Christmas Eve with her
payment enclosed and the encouraging words that "we are all pleased
with the manuscript you sent us."

Then, just as her career began to gain steam, another roadblock appeared. Tony grew sicker by the day. She could see by his weight loss
and ashen pallor that he wasn't faking. The task of taking care of him fell
once again to her. She spent the majority of her days cooking, cleaning,
and catering to his every complaint, of which there were many.

Though unable to write full-time, she worked smart. Capitalizing on
her new relationship with *National Geographic,* she successfully pitched
them another article on the Community Development Program work
with the Madia Gond. By late February, she had sent in a draft and se-
lected photographs for her editor. Then Tony took a turn for the worse,
and Dickey took him to the hospital.

Based on their travel history and symptoms, the doctor diagnosed both of them with amoebic dysentery, a common ailment in communities without clean drinking water. They could have picked it up anywhere on their travels. Treatment required they remain hospitalized for a three-day course of antibiotics, after which they were as good as new. But by then, Dickey's momentum had slowed to a crawl. Even more damaging, the changes set in motion by the inauguration of Eisenhower had begun to solidify.

In the sweltering summer of 1953, McCarthyism lumbered to its apogee and cast its long shadow over every aspect of government. Dickey's attempt to document foreign aid proved no exception. In this climate of politically motivated paranoia, the State Department began requiring that all employees and contractors pass an FBI background clearance as well as a Loyalty Review Board test. Dickey's chances were stymied anew.

"It seems like McLeod," she wrote to a friend in reference to the administrator of the State Department's Bureau of Security, R. W. Scott McLeod, "has such jitters that no one has been cleared since the investigative blues settled over Washington. Basis of the whole thing of course is that everyone either on contract or otherwise is to have an FBI and State loyalty clearance. For fear of errors, they seem to have decided to clear no one."

While Dickey told her friends and colleagues that paranoia and bureaucracy were to blame for the delayed renewal of her contract, her quietest thoughts suspected Tony. Though Dickey and Tony lived together, shared a name, and stated they were married, in legal terms, they were not since Tony's first marriage had not been dissolved at the time of their ceremony. By now, Tony had finally divorced his first wife legally but never formalized his and Dickey's union. Dickey believed their living arrangement was to blame for the FBI's refusal to sign off on their accreditation as Point Four documentarians. No evidence exists one way or the other, but the culture at the FBI dictated by then director J. Edgar Hoover would not have been sympathetic to Dickey and Tony's nonconformist relationship.

Still, for the rest of the summer Dickey held out hope that their clearances might still come through. But by early fall, she had to accept that the last nail in the coffin had been hammered and did what she always did. She made a hard pivot and kept going. She pitched two more articles to *National Geographic;* hawked her and Tony's services as documentarians to as many organizations as she could think of; queried the United Nations Technical Assistance Board and International Children's Emergency Fund; contacted the embassies of Iran and Iraq; and even wrote to the Canadian Department of Agriculture in an effort to find an avenue back to reporting on international development efforts. Her zeal notwithstanding, these efforts came to naught. Money for the softer side of Cold War diplomacy all but dried up with Eisenhower's election.

Covering her bases, she kept pitching articles about those she had met documenting Point Four's international development projects. For months her avalanche of query letters fell on deaf ears. Then, in October, a positive reply. As she wrote breathlessly to Alice Thompson, "Just got a dream of an assignment from *The Saturday Evening Post*—sold them a story, and am working on picking pictures from five countries to illustrate it. Deadline's next week."

Published on December 26, 1953, under the title "There'll Be No Christmas for Them," her article described the difficult conditions faced by those in urban postwar Europe, rural Iraq and Iran, as well as by the Madia Gond in India. She lauded their collective grit as well as their ingenuity and capacity for joy regardless of their lack of material possessions.

She soon received several more positive replies. The first came from the managing editor of *Mademoiselle* magazine, who commissioned her article on newly dug wells supplying clean water to Iraq's frontier farming communities. *World Magazine* accepted her piece on the death of a young Iraqi girl whose family refused to let her travel to the Basra Hospital for blood poisoning treatment. Finally, *Reader's Digest* agreed to publish her story on Tony's near fatal fever in the middle of an Iraqi sandstorm over Easter.

All of these were national magazines with enormous readerships. But *Reader's Digest* could conservatively be described as a juggernaut. When her article was published in April 1954, no less than one in four households in the United States received *Reader's Digest,* which also boasted forty-nine international editions in nineteen languages with an additional circulation of twenty-eight million. Not even her triumph of two *National Geographic* articles could compare. And it paid better. As Dickey put it to an old friend, "This gives us a chance to catch our breath money-wise and makes us feel a little less unemployed."

Her career, it seemed, had finally begun in earnest, again. Tony was furious.

He took it out on her in endless streams of verbal abuse. He told her she couldn't be a real woman, a real wife, and a journalist at the same time. By Tony's estimation, every part of her belonged to him. As he wrote in a letter to mutual friends, "If Dickey has any fault on the 'interest' problem it is the one that goes way back to 17 [magazine], when my only complaint was that I was jealous of her job. It took too much of her away from me that I felt was mine."

At the same time, Tony matriculated his alcoholism to a graduate level. No hour was too early nor too late. He spent his nights gambling at the American Legion on West 132nd Street and came home in the predawn hours stinking of cigarettes and other women.

In the past, Dickey might not have allowed herself to react. But now at thirty-six, she had grown incredulous of Tony's version of their relationship. Where he told her she was weak and vapid, their friends and colleagues affirmed the opposite. While he insisted she was a bad writer and a middling photographer, the national and international magazines now publishing her work extolled her as a multifaceted storyteller. In his version of their life together, he was the hero. Yet she constantly took care of him physically, financially, and emotionally. And while he insisted she would be nothing outside of their relationship, it became increasingly apparent that the only place she didn't matter was within it. She could not yet fully disconnect these dualistic versions of her life. But she did start to glimpse the irreducible contradictions that existed within them.

Like so many victims of emotional abuse, Dickey could not fully accept that her abuser could alone be responsible for his actions. In a long letter to her mother, Dickey expressed feeling partially at fault for his behavior even after the relationship ended. "I tried to set the example of confidence myself," she wrote. "I advised confidence; I said 'sure you can do it' as often as I could. I cooperated in everything he said he wanted to do up to a degree of which I was proud whether I should have been or not." She exhausted herself appeasing Tony's ego in the hopes it would assuage his temper. Of course it did not, and this too she blamed on herself. "But the assumption that all Tony needed was a world in which he could have confidence and peace of mind, was a lot of nonsense. Maybe nobody on earth would flourish in such a world. I wouldn't; why did I think it would do him any good?" If only she had been more, done more, maybe things would have been different.

Dickey even blamed Tony's prolific philandering on her indulgent attitude. "Sure he was that kind of guy in the first place," she wrote to her mother. "But he might not have stayed that kind of a guy if I hadn't been so tolerant and kind and so forth." It would be years before she came to realize the fault for the abuse she endured rested with Tony alone. But at least she knew then with lucid clarity that she had to leave.

In the winter of 1954, she went about formulating an escape plan. Building on her recent slew of published articles, she secured Marie Rodell as her agent, a literary powerhouse who would later represent pioneering environmentalist Rachel Carson as well as Dr. Martin Luther King, Jr., for his first book, *Stride Toward Freedom: The Montgomery Story*. Next, she wrote to General Lemuel Shepherd, who had invited her to his command on Okinawa, to see if he might once again welcome her presence as a journalist. Finally, she took a job as Jack Kavanaugh's assistant, with whom she had worked during her stint with the Quakers and who had since become the director of public relations at CARE, a nonprofit international aid organization. The job was decidedly beneath her, but it was a steady paycheck when she needed one.

More important than all of this from a psychological perspective, she took up jujitsu. The competitive martial art's central philosophy of using the strength of one's attacker against them spoke to her current need. For long hours, she practiced harnessing the momentum of her sparring partners into throws and traps, pins and strikes. Jujitsu's tactic of redirecting an enemy's energy allowed her, at five-four and 125 pounds, to punch well above her weight. Taking control of her body enabled her to imagine the next steps in taking back her life.

The weather turned warm in early May. She had a job, an agent, and could throw a man twice her size across the room. She took to running along the Hudson River in the mornings. Magnolia and cherry trees smelled sweet in the soft spring air. Nothing could stop her now. Jogging home one morning, she took little note of the ambulance parked outside their building. Then, four men walked out, carrying Tony on a stretcher.

He'd had a heart attack. Suddenly, all Dickey's progress disappeared once more into the never-ending void of his need. Again the sole bread-winner, she put in extra hours at CARE and took over Tony's flagging army surplus business. When not earning money, she worked for free as Tony's cook, maid, and psychologist. She comforted him when he woke screaming from his habitual night terrors. She placated him as his insecurities over diminishing masculine prowess blossomed into neurosis. His care usurped all of her time to pitch, plan, write, and take photos. Even for all this attention, time, and energy, he resented her for working outside the home at all, necessity or not, taking out his jealousy on her in fits of rage that edged ever closer to physical violence.

In the midst of all this, Dickey's father passed away suddenly at sixty-eight. Even for all his misgivings about his daughter's nonconformist tendencies, her father had proved to be one of Dickey's most ardent fans. Sensing she would not find support from her husband, Dickey chose not to express her grief outwardly. Tragically, her intuition proved all too accurate.

They had met Helga and Ernst Riemschneider at Mittelhof, the Quaker house in East Berlin. She was young and blond with pouty lips. He was the wiry type, an intellectual with telltale round-rimmed glasses. In 1954, the Quakers helped them immigrate to New York and sent Dickey and Tony a note about their impending arrival. Tony offered to play the tour guide. Dickey joined when she could and the four of them became friends.

The more he got to know her, the more Tony thought Helga looked like Dickey once had—unsuspecting, unquestioning, vulnerable. To Helga, a German refugee who had seen the worst of war, Tony seemed like a safe harbor. Though broke and less than hale, Tony still portrayed himself as the embodiment of American bravado—wealthy, content, comfortable in his own skin. One Friday, only weeks after her father had died, Dickey came home early from work and found them in bed.

She walked out without a word.

For a few days she stayed with her friend Selma Blick, who went by Stevie. She and Dickey had become friends, somewhat ironically, because

Stevie worked as the secretary for Tony's cardiologist. Stevie never could figure out why Dickey would stay with Tony and fully supported her leaving. Indeed, Stevie would become not only one of Dickey's closest companions but also an invaluable partner in her career as she often filled the role of confidante, executive assistant, and sometimes PR manager. For now, she helped Dickey find a new place. Without references or much money, Dickey rented a studio in New York's only nondescript neighborhood of Murray Hill. Hers and hers alone, the inexpensive and anonymous efficiency overlooking Bellevue Hospital suited Dickey just fine.

Dickey wrote very little about her relationship with Tony in her subsequent autobiography, mentioning her divorce only in terms of her career. "Can a woman be both a foreign correspondent and a wife?" she asked her readers.

> My answer is never at the same time.
> I can't make the reason sound sentimental, although I'm sure it has to do with the heart and not the head. But good correspondents are created out of the simple compulsion to go see for themselves what is happening. There's competition for their assignments, and the odds are heavily in favor of the man or woman who yields to the fewest distractions in obeying the compulsion. It's a twenty-four-hour a day task till a story's done and you cannot know as you start covering an event where it may lead you. Till it's done, people you love always receive less evidence of love than the correspondent wants to give them . . . some marriages survive this deprivation indefinitely but mine (and most of them) did not.

Dickey never remarried, never had another serious relationship, instead curtailing her romantic life to occasional trysts. She had a Cuban lover while reporting on anti-Castro militias in Miami. She slept with a Marine while covering a war-game exercise at Fort Bragg in North Carolina. She exchanged veiled love letters with a Turkish diplomat. Later in life she maintained a yearslong affair with the pulp fiction novelist Shepard Rifkin, who had once served aboard the SS *Ben Hecht* that tried to evacuate Holocaust survivors. She formed the closest she came to a steady relationship with him, exchanging love letters while she was on the road and spending long days in bed during her short stays at home. But even he knew better than to try to tether her since to do so would be to lose her entirely.

For now, settled into her studio with her orange-crate bookcases and secondhand furniture, Dickey's initial reaction to her split with Tony oscillated between relief and confusion. As she wrote to Charlotte and Denis Plimmer, "The truth is that I must have been rather psychologically ready for a place and routine of my own for a long time, since adjusting to that has seemed not-so-hard. Or maybe," she conceded, "I'm still shock cushioned."

To her mother, she confessed much more. Presbyterian, midwestern, Republican, and under the spell of Tony's charm, Edna did not understand or agree with her daughter's decision. In response, Dickey wrote her a long and painstakingly detailed letter trying to explain her reasons for leaving Tony. In it, the rare admissions of vulnerability slipped out of her fingers and onto her typewriter keys. "It leaves me, personally, in a largely paralytic state. I'm quite frightened of my own bad judgments and quite unwilling to go on making them."

Aware she had to find firmer ground, she continued: "I think there is just one wise course for me to go to work in some field in which I do think I know something—a professional one—and let the personal relationships business alone for a while. God is good," she assured her religious mother. "I'll get my confidence back step by step and one of these days I will again trust my judgment of love and people again."

Tony, on the other hand, went out of his mind.

Panicked that the one who had shored him up for so long had left for good, Tony began an all-out assault to get her back. He opened with the obvious protestations of undying love. "I am writing this an hour after you have gone and already there is an emptiness in the house and in me." Sobbing on, he continued, "I am a fool and I know it and still I feel that I am on a merry-go-round that never slows down and I can't get off. I can't explain it and my heart knows that all of whatever life that I have left will always regret it."

Dickey didn't bite. Tony kicked his campaign up to stalking mode. He called at all hours of the day, frightening her with his fevered and at times angry exhortations for her to come back. His letters arrived in twos and threes, sometimes as many as five in one day. He buzzed her buzzer, got someone else in her building to let him in, knocked on her door, then pounded. Never knowing when to expect him, she started expecting him always. She couldn't sleep, couldn't eat, couldn't write.

After months of this onslaught, Dickey agreed to refer to their break as a trial separation and meet for dinner dates on Thursdays. In return she asked him to cease contacting her outside of their prearranged meeting times. Though he agreed, it didn't take long for Tony to break his word. "I don't know why I keep talking to you in this letter," he admitted in a letter on a Tuesday, "except that I guess I just want to talk to you and I know that you don't want me to call you up. I suppose that I could wait until Thursday and tell it all to you, but when I see you I always forget the things I wanted to tell you." Without fail, these things he so vehemently wanted to tell her fit into one of two categories: either the mundane details of life or efforts to manipulate her into returning.

Meanwhile, Tony kept sleeping with Helga and, according to some of their friends, other women as well. As he wrote to Dickey in August 1955, he started a photography school out of his apartment. The majority of his students were "photographic minded damsels" as he described them in a letter to Dickey while alluding to their apparent attraction to him.

His next ploy proved even more insidious. Earlier that year, CARE had to lay Dickey off for lack of funds. Seizing his opportunity, Tony took great pains to spotlight Dickey's financial instability. First, he cajoled her into allowing him to develop any freelance photo work she had, thus ensuring that he controlled at least part of her livelihood. Next he reminded her of her money woes, writing, "You'll never make both ends meet anywhere in the middle if you don't take on some extra work or get a temporary bachelor to take you to dinner more often." He of course being the "temporary bachelor." It's also worth noting that he entitled this letter "& Now it's the 7th of June—in 1955 Ten minutes to time for a drink or in other words it's 5.20 P.M." Heart condition or no, he hadn't eased up on drinking.

Then came offers of cash, an air conditioner, maid service for her apartment, and a hundred other attempts to hold something over her veiled in gestures of magnanimity. She refused them all. Finally, he secured a public relations contract with the United Nations and all but insisted she join him on the job. "The payment per day for us as a team would be one hundred dollars per day and expenses with a maximum for the job of between three and four thousand dollars," he wrote as if she had already accepted his proposal. When she turned him down, he replied scornfully, "You are a very foolish girl. Of course in turning it down you are also doing me out of my half."

While Tony waged a campaign to recapture her attention, Dickey fought her own war of liberation, enlisting no less than the US Marines to her side. In early July, General Shepherd answered her letter from earlier that year by inviting her to his headquarters in Washington, DC. Since she last saw him on Okinawa, he had been appointed the Marines' highest-ranking officer, Commandant of the Marine Corps, and served on the Joint Chiefs of Staff. For him to invite Dickey to his office was about as big of a coup as it was for him to invite her to his camp during the Pacific Campaign. Her comportment there influenced his decision to make room for her in his overtaxed schedule. So did his need for good PR on behalf of the Marine Corps.

When it came to the Corps's success in adapting to the rapidly evolving combat conditions of the Cold War, the buck stopped with General Shepherd. But without a traditional conflict with emergent dangers that could easily be depicted, it was difficult to demonstrate the necessity for increased funding. Indeed, the Department of Defense's budget had been cut by nearly 15 percent from its 1953 height. General Shepherd needed positive PR to convince Congress of the necessity for armament upgrades, especially when it came to what he considered to be the most important military technological advance: the helicopter.

In command of the Fleet Marine Force during the Korean War, General Shepherd witnessed the first major deployment of helicopters by the US Armed Forces in combat. Though the end of the Korean War proved ambiguous at best, the tactical advantages of helicopters were unmistakable. Among the first to recognize the effectiveness of this relatively new technology within an evolving theater of war, General Shepherd strongly advocated the expansion of their use, famously saying, "No effort should be spared to get helicopters . . . to the theater at once—and on a priority higher than any other weapon."

His words would reverberate in the rotors of every Chinook, Huey, and Cobra flying over Vietnam, where Dickey would be the first journalist to photograph Marines in combat while aboard a helicopter.

But now, before all that, General Shepherd needed to prove the advantage of helicopters to the public and to their elected officials. For that, he needed a sympathetic reporter, and he saw one in Dickey. In turn, she saw in him the opportunity to break free from the box that Tony was once again trying to build around her life. In September, Dickey boarded a plane to Camp Pendleton in San Diego, California, the premier training ground for Marines.

18

Starting Again

THE MARINES BILLETED her in a women's barracks. Dickey quickly filled her room with camera gear. General John C. McQueen welcomed her in the hostess house after she settled in. They recognized each other immediately from Okinawa where he had served under General Shepherd as a colonel. Enveloped in cigarette smoke and coffee steam, they talked about the war and the way things used to be. She told him about the time she flew between the fleet's destroyers in a cub plane at deck level. He recalled the last days on the island that no one seemed to remember anymore.

"I do," she said.

He was happy to see her again, he said, lightly punching her on the shoulder.

The Santa Ana winds swept down the San Diego foothills at nightfall. She felt desperately lonely. The closest person she knew was a long-distance phone call away that she could not afford. Further still seemed the days of her and General McQueen's reminiscences when she had thought herself a part of history's slow stride toward a better world. Recapturing that rare moment of clarity and purpose seemed impossible, here, a decade later, a decade older. She feared she had missed her chance and the years she had compromised suddenly came back to her in one deafening rush of failure. Between consciousness and sleep, she let slip the thought that maybe Tony had been right when he told her she wasn't good enough for her dreams.

The sound of a bugle playing reveille woke her in the morning. Dickey put on fatigues for the first time since the war. The cotton twill felt like armor, just as she remembered.

Her primary purpose in being there was to report on the Marines' Test Unit One. As Dickey put it, the mission of this elite group was to "evolve a new fighting man and the tactics for him that will be effective in atomic holocaust or limited police action." In time, it would seem the Vietnam War had been conjured by the military industrial complex as proof of concept. But then, in the fall of 1955, Test Unit One remained in its incipient stage with its logical conclusion too far off to anticipate. Very much the brainchild of General Shepherd, the idea of Test Unit One arose from his experience with amphibious landings on Iwo Jima and Inchon, South Korea. Though best practice at the time, he knew this concentrated and inefficient method of troop deployment would be no match against tactical nuclear weapons. The challenge then became how to break battalions into small, highly mobile units that were able to evade targeted weapons systems.

Half of that answer lay in mobility through the air. Instead of clunky transport planes and cumbersome amphibious boats, versatile helicopter fleets would ferry troops in small units. But the other half of the solution couldn't come until boots hit the ground. Since the nuclear battlefield required greater agility on the part of those engaged in combat than ever before, the Marine Corps designed their most rigorous training to date.

As with the Bushmasters in Panama, Dickey planned on marching with the troops as they went on practice maneuvers. Though now instead of twenty-three she was thirty-six. Looking out onto the Santa Margarita foothills encompassed by Camp Pendleton's perimeter, she wondered if she hadn't made a mistake. Still, she planned to try and ate another forkful of powdered eggs, hoping it might be enough to get her through the day with fifteen pounds of camera gear on her back.

After breakfast she joined the Second Platoon of Company C that General McQueen had arranged for her to follow. Before she arrived, he had given written orders that Dickey be "treated with the utmost courtesy by all Marines with whom she comes in contact and to be rendered the fullest cooperation in her effort." But Dickey knew the Marines didn't base their respect on orders alone. It had to be earned, and standing on the side of their formation, she didn't know if she still had the mettle.

The drill sergeant barked his orders. The troops turned in unison and started toward the hills. They were training for a war game that would test their experimental ground and air tactics on a mock nuclear battlefield. Dickey ran ahead, dropped to one knee, focused, and snapped. Looking at the squadron of young men marching as one she asked herself the same question she had on the volcanic sands of Iwo Jima: "How do you get human beings, with all their fears and frailties, to team up in a single concerted effort, so simple and so limitlessly hazardous, until finally they are one moving inexorable force?"

She remembered the answer in a few steps more. It was that feeling she had had on Okinawa when she followed Lieutenant Jameson on patrol. She felt it again here too—esprit de corps—that outlying French phrase in an otherwise gruffly American military parlance that literally translates to "spirit of the body." In many ways, this concept is the closest thing to religion in the Marine Corps. Describing this spirituality, General McQueen wrote to Dickey, "This esprit has been put to every test under every condition and has never faltered. To a civilian this great pride might be comprised of patriotism or loyalty or self-sacrifice, or possibly a combination of all these things. We Marines feel it even more."

For the next two weeks, Dickey witnessed this intangible camaraderie take hold among these new recruits. In turn, as she kept pace and kept up, this next generation of Marines warmed to Dickey until finally, near the end of one march, the platoon opened their ranks around her, encircled and enfolded her, then closed again. She entered the base as one of them.

It is not the best practice of journalism to so thoroughly identify with a subject. But in hindsight, the lasting importance of Dickey's stay with the Marines had little to do with writing about their new training regimen. The articles she wrote about Camp Pendleton would never be published, and she herself would admit that she had grown too close to the story for her writing to be of editorial interest. But she gained something much more valuable. For her, Camp Pendleton proved the ideal training ground for reporting on the Cold War's interlocking theaters of war.

Marching with the Marines day in and day out, she learned how they spoke, slept, ate, mouthed off, and followed orders. She learned how to dig a foxhole, fall on her stomach in the face of live ammunition, and roll away from an attacker. In a general sense, she learned how to soldier, and because the Marines' training did not fundamentally differ from that of other militaries the world over, Dickey was able to seamlessly integrate herself into the ranks of armies from Algeria to Cuba to Vietnam. As it specifically related to the US Armed Forces, Dickey developed an early and comprehensive understanding of their shifting strategies, updated weaponry, and evolving objectives, enabling her to stay one step ahead of her peers in nearly every major armed conflict of the Cold War.

Fully aware of the opportunity she had been given, Dickey worked for twelve hours a day. She also fundamentally changed her health regimen, permanently swearing off alcohol other than dark beer, committing to getting at least eight hours of sleep a night when not on assignment, and eating a protein-rich diet. She kept up her rigorous exercise routine of running, weight lifting, and jujitsu. If she wanted to report on fighting men, she reasoned, then she'd better train like one. Her logic served her well. Though, she never did give up cigarettes.

On a personal, if not more fundamental level, the Marines taught her, as ideally they teach all of their recruits, her own worth and value. General Shepherd had seen it ten years before at a party on Falalop Island in the eye of the war's end. His men had recognized it in the way she unflinchingly photographed their wounded and dying. Now, this new generation of Marines recognized her as one of their own.

By November, a month after arriving, Dickey did what she had not been able to do in New York. She wrote to break it off with Tony once and for all.

Tony responded all too predictably. Refusing to accept her decision, he tried to invalidate her experience at Camp Pendleton. "What you forget," he replied, "is that you are among many new people and in a way you have become a center of attraction and respect. People are looking up to you and that's not a part of normal, everyday living. It's fascinating but do you think it would wear off in time? And thrills and pleasures constantly repeated tend to dull their ecstasy in time. And as exciting as it is—you can't spend the rest of your life as a gal reporter at one Marine Base after another. After that what?"

When Dickey did not reply to his insulting letter, Tony intensified his entitled intrusions, calling the hostess house multiple times a day, writing ad nauseam, and employing every form of emotional blackmail he could muster. He even resorted to begging, writing at one point, "How about calling me—please—collect."

But Dickey didn't phone. Didn't write. Didn't even get his calls and letters. The war games had commenced and she had been given permission to stay in the field.

In order to best mimic an actual scenario, the Marines devised an elaborate backstory for the exercise in which the fictitious Malagania, "a Western European country very similar in size, shape, topography, and climate conditions to the state of California," had been invaded by a Soviet-style aggressor that had started installing a thermonuclear guided weapons system in the surrounding mountain range. "When completed," the brief continued, "missiles launched from this site will be capable of accurately striking friendly forces within a 360-degree radius of two hundred miles." By land, sea, and air, Test Unit One was tasked with overtaking this target at any cost. The reason they had climbed so many hills became clear.

As they left camp on their mission, Dickey noted, "Test Unit No. 1 has changed the very face of infantry assault so that the nostalgic ex-soldier would hardly recognize it. Gone is the 60-pound pack, the tent, the eight man squad, the landing craft, the jeep. The new pack weighs less than 20 pounds. The new shelter is called a geodesic dome and comes into battle, set up, by air. The new squad is now a five-man heliteam, with every man as able and better trained than many of the non-coms of Saipan and Korea."

She had spent the days and nights leading up to their departure planning her shots, mapping her compositions, predetermining her exposures. With all of her reflexes primed and firing, her hands kept steady as the dust devils swirled in the wind of rising helicopters. She snapped her lens just in time to capture the profile of the Marine being illuminated by an exploding napalm bomb. She photographed them charging onto the beach out of a whale mouth transport plane and leaping from helicopters hovering above a mountainside. Though her photographs from Camp Pendleton would never go to press, they are an accurate and artful depiction of warfare at the moment it shifted to address the new realities of the Cold War battlefields.

After extending her stay twice, Dickey finally left Camp Pendleton for a Thanksgiving visit to Shorewood. Sunburned, sore, and exhausted, she welcomed the softness of her childhood home and the warmth of her family, who since her initial split with Tony had rallied around her in support. But nor could she ignore him now. His increasingly desperate and angry letters filled their mailbox. His incessant calls rang out from the kitchen phone, permeating the house with the promise of insults, profanities, pleas, and drunken apologies.

Finally, on Thanksgiving Day when the phone rang as her uncle carved the turkey, as her aunt served the string beans, as her mother scooped ice cream for the apple pie, Dickey reached her limit. She picked up and told him simply that it was over.

"This is just a few hours after I talked to you," wrote Tony in his first letter of the day. "You made things pretty clear. I will be as clear," he promised, then immediately contradicted himself. "The association I continue with you is too untenable to endure very long. So, until the Marine Corps story is out of the way—provided it is done by the end of the year—I will go along and back you up—do your processing and do the best I can to help on your photographic problems. After that I feel that I cannot continue a relationship that seems to hurt the both of us." Ending his letter on a spiteful note, he wrote, "Again much love and I promise—that this will be the last time I mention the word to you." Of course, it was not.

His second letter of the day insulted her photographs of Camp Pendleton, criticizing her use of the light meter, pointing out under- and overexposures, claiming she could have completed her task with a tenth of the film she used. In short, desperately trying to revert to their early student-teacher relationship that Dickey had long since left behind.

He saved his worst for last. "I am just a little drunk, or otherwise

I suppose that I wouldn't be thinking this way but I wondered how it would be to have someone else in your bed." He continued on in licentious detail, imagining a fictional other woman, who had already been many other women, in the silk sheets they bought in France, putting her things on the bedside table Dickey had carried home in a cab, and wearing the clothes she left behind in her rush to leave. Yet his cruelest attack was on her professional abilities. "I'll do your finishing for you and do it better than I ever did it for anyone else," he wrote. "After all, I did get you into this and in a way it's my fault that you can't use an exposure meter—or you think that you know more than I do about exposures. Send your stuff along . . . and if you can't pay for it—what the Hell—it will still be cheaper than AVISO." What little you are, he tried to say, you are because of me.

He redoubled this campaign of verbal abuse once Dickey got back to New York. He called her a cocktease, a gold digger, and a whore. When he demanded she repay him for the jewelry he bought her, she obliged, delivering every last piece he'd ever purchased back into his possession. His bluff called, Tony folded and refused to take them back, since to do so would be to surrender one of the last things he held over her. He phoned her endlessly, rang her buzzer at all hours, and pounded on her door regardless of her neighbors' vociferous complaints. Soon after the New Year she broke down and picked up the phone.

"What do you want from me?" Tony sobbed into the receiver.

"All I want from you is a divorce!" she hurled back and hung up.

Later, he forced his way into her building, screamed at her from the hallway. Through the peephole she could see he had a gun.

Dickey contacted a divorce lawyer. Though Tony and she were never formally married, she wanted the legality of their separation written and recorded beyond the shadow of doubt. Her considerations were not only financial should Tony one day decide to claim part or all of her income as his own, as he had recently threatened to do, but also for her own protection. Getting a restraining order against an ex-husband was far easier than obtaining one against an ill-defined cohabitant since courts frequently saw things from the male point of view.

A friend recommended her to Sol H. Cohn, whose office in a Tribeca Romanesque Revival skyscraper couldn't help but inspire confidence.

"I'm asking you on the record to represent me in my—shall we call it quasi-marital?—problem," she wrote him after their meeting in late January 1956. "My immediate problem is Mr. Chapelle's unwelcome efforts to maintain a relationship with me," she continued, adding as an explanation, "The last time he became what I considered abusive (this was on the phone), I said I didn't believe we had anything about which we needed to communicate. But," she went on, "if such existed I thought he should get in touch with me only through you." Talk to my lawyer, in other words.

But therein lay the rub. "Now of course, I don't know whether I could have afforded the luxury of this remark or not," she wrote, since in truth she didn't have any money to pay his retainer if Tony did call. She even had to ask him to delay the court filings. "I will not have the funds to start on February 1st," she explained, "I'll have them when I find the job I'm looking for now."

Undoubtedly having dealt with similar situations in the past, Sol assured her he would fold any such charges into his final bill. Luckily, Tony never called. But none of this changed the fact that Dickey was dead broke.

Since getting back from Wisconsin, she'd been calling in favors from old friends and cold-calling strangers for work. She even went to the employment bureau. January came and went. February took the last month of rent she had in her account. Tony pressed on, now pressuring her for money. "It seems that I was wrong about my life expectancy," he wrote regarding a better than anticipated physical, "and I am told that I may even be around for months or years. In this case it behooves me to scratch about for living expenses and your bill is the only overdue one on the books." Incredibly, he signed off as "Affectionately."

But Dickey remained resolute, writing to her mother at the nadir of her bank account, "Did you think I'd go running back to Tony? Did you think I'd borrow money from strangers? Did you think I'd take something unsuitable, whatever that is?" By then, she had some reason to hope the tide would turn. She had a few solid leads on a job. Smith & Street Publications seemed to show some interest in her resume and her agent had recently put her up for a job as public information director at the International Rescue Committee. Something had to break her way eventually—though she didn't for a second expect it would be the IRC job.

Founded by Albert Einstein in 1933, the IRC first became renowned for evacuating two thousand of the Nazis' most wanted from Vichy France, including artists Marc Chagall and Max Ernst as well as the philosopher Hannah Arendt. Now, headed by intelligence community wunderkind Leo Chern, the IRC turned its attention to those escaping persecution behind the Iron Curtain. Just to be considered for the position was an honor and Dickey couldn't believe her good luck when they called her for an interview. "But I gave up hope myself," she wrote to her family, "because I understood the [IRC] wanted a man for the job."

With the passage of Valentine's Day and the calendar hurtling toward her thirty-eighth birthday, unavoidable self-doubt added its pall to the already dark days. Her mom sent her fifty dollars, supposedly to buy something nice for herself, but she knew it was meant to keep her afloat for a few weeks more. Then the phone rang just before the March rent came due. Dickey picked up, though she feared Tony's voice would be on the other end. But it was Jack Kavanaugh from CARE. Their budget looked good this year. Would she like her job back? Could she start next week?

She bought calfskin black gloves and a new dress, and opened a savings account with her mother's fifty-dollar check. She wrote to her family about the good news, her tone carefree for the first time in a long time. The job started the next day at 8:45 A.M., she told them. It wasn't her wildest dream, but it offered financial security and in that, freedom. This, she decided, was as good a place as any to start again.

Early the next morning she ironed her white silk blouse, polished her black high heels, and brushed off her pencil skirt. In the mirror she looked older. Her once soft features had hardened, made more severe still by the way she tied her hair back in a tight bun. Time and the sun had carved thin lines around her eyes. But she could say with confidence that she liked who she had become.

She put on her horn-rimmed glasses, checked she had everything in her purse, and steadied herself. Things could only get better from here. She had climbed steeper hills.

Then the phone rang. "Please hold for Leo Chern," said the woman on the other end.

PART III

....

19

The Iron Curtain Is a Cornfield

FLURRIES STARTED FALLING on March 16, 1956, the Friday of her first week of work. By Monday, the plowed snow piled up to her shoulders in front of her apartment on Twenty-Ninth Street and First Avenue. With trains delayed and buses out of service, Dickey walked the twenty blocks to the International Rescue Committee office on Fifth Avenue. Unlike most Manhattanites in their chic footwear meant for cocktail hour, Dickey had no trouble traversing the icy sidewalks in her boots made for Wisconsin winters, a recent birthday gift from her mother.

But before she even stepped onto the elevator, Dickey slid out of her salt-clad clompers and into a pair of black stilettos. She took pride in her appearance at work. Dark suits and white silk shirts were an every-day canvas onto which she painted her personality. As she wrote to her family, "I'm the only gal in the office right now who <u>always</u> has a clean lace handkerchief, polished shoes and handbag, ironed hair ribbons, one-of-a-kind jewelry and a smooth hair-do." As the only female department head and one of the few women in management, she wanted to at least appear the part and she did more than that. By the time the late snow thawed into early spring, Dickey's competence and charm had endeared her to the IRC team, putting her on even firmer footing professionally than she had dared to hope.

Dickey spent her evenings and weekends as she had told her mother she wanted to: alone. Wrapped in silk pajamas and cozied in her easy chair, she read racks of dime-store whodunits with a pack of cigarettes and a quart of buttermilk. As she wrote her family in late March, "I know I should have some other news for you, but my weekend was a heavenly quiet one." With her career on the upswing and her personal life blissfully banal, it seemed like the storm of the moment had passed. Then, her mother fell ill. What began as an undiagnosed discomfort in the early summer emerged as late-stage cancer by August. The family flew Edna to the city for treatment at the New York Presbyterian Hospital, one of the best at the time. But her cancer had advanced too far and on September 24, 1956, Edna Meyer passed away.

The suddenness of her death sent Dickey into a shocked silence. Her letters about her mother's passing concern only the logistical details of insurance premiums and estate appraisals, funeral arrangements and inheritance tax. Yet her actions after Edna's death said much more.

In many ways Edna had been a grounding force for Dickey, who often wrote about the sense of safety she derived from their home in Shorewood. But nested within this security lay a degree of constraint. For Dickey this manifested as guilt that she never settled down to a more conventional life in their affluent suburb as her mother would have preferred. Were it not for Edna's deeply felt anxiety over her well-being, Dickey may well have never even tried to walk the well-trodden path of expectations. In her grief, Dickey found herself at once liberated and unmoored, the last rope tying her to safe harbor severed. Had her mother been alive, she may have never embarked on her next endeavor.

It began on October 23, 1956, when news broke of a student movement in Budapest, Hungary, protesting repressive Soviet-imposed policies. When a group of demonstrators breached a government-controlled radio station in order to broadcast their demands, the state police, known as the Államvédelmi Hatóság or ÁVH, opened fire on them. Rather than back down, the students stripped the ÁVH troopers of their guns and returned fire. So began the Hungarian Revolution.

Spurred by the students, citizens organized into ad hoc militias that battled ÁVH and Soviet troops in the streets. In a matter of days the Soviet-backed Hungarian regime collapsed. By the end of October, the guns fell silent, the dust settled, and business, for the most part, returned to normal. It seemed for a moment that a group of teenagers had done what the entire West could not: put a chink in the Iron Curtain. Dickey, who had witnessed the USSR's incipient reign of terror spreading its tentacles across Europe, knew firsthand the audacity required to throw off this yoke of tyranny. Awed and inspired, she quickly helped organize a fundraising drive through the IRC to support widows and orphans of the uprising. In one day, the IRC raised $100,000, or just over a million dollars in today's currency.

In early November, terror had replaced hope when the USSR sent ten divisions of tanks into Budapest. Armed with stolen guns and soda bottles filled with pilfered gasoline, the city's youth again raised a valiant resistance. But the Soviets had come prepared this time and by November 10 the resistance had been silenced, the revolutionary government ousted, and an unimaginably brutal regime installed. Meanwhile, to Dickey's horror, America refused to lift a finger in support of Hungary's freedom fighters. Believing she could convince the American public to support the resistance by documenting their bravery, Dickey devised the mode and means to get herself to Hungary even before the revolutionary government had fallen.

In order to gain the goodwill of those she sought to cover, Dickey secured ten pounds of penicillin to help treat the epidemic of pneumonia that at the time was killing even more Hungarians than Soviet guns. Next, she sold her pitch to cover the Hungarian freedom fighters and refugees to *Life* magazine, the pages of which she had been trying to get a photo in since before the war.

Finally, she convinced Leo to allow the IRC to sponsor her mission with $3,000 in funding along with the loan of a subminiature Minox camera, a favorite among spies. By the evening of November 15, 1956, Dickey was halfway over the Atlantic eating caviar in first class on Pan Am flight 72 to Vienna.

Arriving at the Bristol Hotel where she had stayed the last time she had visited Vienna, she could hardly believe how well the city had been restored. Its dissected confection cake buildings were returned to their prewar glory. Its ground-up streets had been repaved. The clink of champagne glasses and erudite murmurs once again filled high society's most fashionable salons. Yet at the same time, the refugee crisis was far worse than she had even dared to imagine. Over a thousand Hungarians a day flooded across the border. Wearing the muddied clothes they arrived in, these asylum seekers snaked around the city's consulates, hoping to find sanctuary somewhere, anywhere west of the Eastern Bloc.

Dickey interviewed them as they waited in line, in her hotel lobby, and in Vienna's cafés over warm cups of tea. She met a teenage freedom fighter who had escaped a Soviet labor camp by crawling through a sewer pipe and stealing a military jeep. She interviewed a dancer in the Hungarian National Ballet who had been one of the best machine gunners in Parliament Square during the uprising. But what struck her most were the scores of those she met who survived being held in Fö Street Prison. Almost all of them bore the outward signs of torture in deep scar tissue, twisted limbs, and empty nail beds. Even the bravest blanched at the mention of the prison's name, and Dickey began calling it the "headquarters for horror."

But the stories she gathered on the Austrian side of the border were only half of what she had come to cover. For the rest she would have to cross into Hungary, though she had little idea of how. "What I'd overlooked," she later wrote in her autobiography, "was that the Austro-Hungarian border reached south from Nickelsdorf for several hundred miles." Then, a rumor started to spread beneath the crystal chandeliers of the Bristol Hotel's dining room that refugees had begun to cross near the village of Andau, a tiny farming community to the south of Vienna. That evening, Dickey splurged on warm socks and bandages to give to those crossing the border along with extra rolls of film. She hired a driver who agreed to meet her at 7 P.M. in front of her hotel.

"I will love the Viennese forever for what happened after that," she wrote. "The roads were jammed with cars of people from Vienna. Trucks and buses and limousines and jalopies and sedans and ambulances and finally farmer's tractors. Over the ice at night in cold seven degrees below zero, all going one way." They were headed for the border with the intent of driving Hungarian refugees back to the city where food, shelter, and medical care were more readily available. Not to mention the opportunity to apply for sanctuary.

Machine-gun fire erupted regularly. Starshells replaced starlight, illuminating the contorted faces of those running for freedom long after they exceeded their known limit of endurance. Tracer bullets followed, fired above their heads for now, but for how much longer no one could say.

Before she even arrived, Dickey could see exactly where Hungary ended and Austria began. Farmers had built enormous bonfires in their fields as beacons for those crossing the frozen tundra between the two countries. Housewives waited beside them with tea and soup. Volunteers from Vienna joined them, handing out blankets and bread, rubbing the feet of those in danger of frostbite and cradling the babies of exhausted mothers.

"This is really Austria, isn't it?" one recent arrival after another echoed incredulously.

Then a woman ran past Dickey, toward Hungary, away from Austria. She wore chic heels and a fur-lined coat.

"Lisa! Come back!" yelled a young man behind her.

"But Hans, there are people lost out there!" she replied and began to run again, fading into the darkness beyond the firelight.

The young man followed and Dickey felt her legs begin to run, too.

The ice-covered stubble of cornstalks caught at her boots. Frozen puddles of water broke beneath her soles. Hans started to disappear from view and, for a moment, Dickey worried she would be left alone in the dark on the wrong side of the Iron Curtain. But Lisa had paused to catch her breath. Hans steadied her with his hand. Neither seemed to notice Dickey. Then the three of them froze, suddenly aware of the sound of other footsteps.

A man in round-rimmed glasses and a raglan overcoat emerged from the darkness. Improbably, he looked familiar.

"Dickey Chapelle. *Life* magazine," she introduced herself in true foreign correspondent style.

"Michener," he replied.

They shook hands and a sporadic wall of tracer fire erupted in front of them. Lisa began to run. They followed her, again. Midstride Dickey realized who he was, the Pulitzer Prize–winning author of *Tales of the South Pacific,* a collection of interrelated short stories about World War II, which she had devoured in a single sitting. But before she could apologize for her momentary ignorance, the four of them found themselves standing absolutely still. They had all heard it: the sound of a woman crying. They found her with a dozen others, crouched within the banks of a canal, lost only a few hundred yards from freedom. The tracer fire had subsided and the ad hoc band of scouts led them to safety.

Dickey crossed the border fifteen times during her stay in Austria. Her boldness made for stirring photographs of families traversing the frozen cornfield, edging over logs and ladders in place of the bridges that had been burned, and arriving, at last, to safety. *Life* cabled to say they were pleased with her negatives, which eventually ran in the December 3 issue. One full-page photo pictured a family of four trudging through the ice-glazed stubble of last year's harvest. Behind them, the backdrop of complete darkness that both enabled and endangered their escape seems to swallow the world of their past. Illuminated by Dickey's flashbulb, a volunteer reaches out his hand, welcoming them into Austria.

Though she had dedicated years to humanitarian work in Europe just after the war, she never felt as if she had done all that she could. Taking photographs and writing reports for fundraising campaigns was vital work, to be sure. But here, on the Hungarian border where the Iron Curtain fell across a cornfield, she could see the results of her efforts in the faces of those she ushered to safety. As she wrote later in her autobiography, "There I felt deeply and for the first time since I'd flown off Okinawa, that I was serving something bigger than I was."

After a night's work, she exchanged adventures over beers at the Bristol's bar with Michener and the few other journalists brave enough to put their lives on the line for the story. Michener offered Dickey a standing invitation to dinner with his wife, Mari, which she accepted on more than one occasion. The three of them became fast friends and later Michener would include Dickey in his famous chronicle of the Hungarian Revolution, *The Bridge at Andau*, under a fictional name.

But all this was a precursor for the next phase of her coverage. After a week, she started looking actively for a guide to take her into Hungary among the volunteers who carried supplies and information to those still fighting the occupation. It was among these that she found someone to show her the way.

Short, slight of frame, and quick on his feet, Zoltan Dienes had been an engineering student in Budapest when revolution broke out. Soon after, he fled to Austria with his family. Dickey met him in Andau where he had gone to cross back. Since she had ten pounds of penicillin and money to pay him, he was happy to have Dickey accompany him. Besides, by then Dickey's reputation was well known among volunteers and refugees. Zoltan had no trouble believing she'd be able to keep up on the ten-mile march to the nearest village where freedom fighters were organizing. They agreed to depart the following night, All Saints' Eve.

In the meantime, Dickey visited the border once more, though decided to stay on the Austrian side so as not to test her luck. That night she witnessed what she recorded as "the last tragic note of the whole Hungarian revolt—the sealing of the western border of Hungary by Soviet Russia."

For the entirety of her time in Andau, Hungarian guards had been posted at the border. Out of deference to their fellow countrymen and perhaps a sense of humanity, they often, but not always, looked the other way as families collapsed over their finish line. That paradigm had now changed.

"Mein Gott!" cried the man beside her. Dickey looked up. He pointed toward the guard station where the next shift was relieving the last. "Look at the insignia on the caps of the new people!" he said. She saw the flash of a tin Soviet five-pointed star on one of their hats. Their presence meant there would be no more looking the other way, no more omissions of mercy. Dickey lifted her camera. The Soviet guards smiled, proud to have their picture taken as the first Soviets to patrol the Hungarian border.

Dickey went back to bed early that night, shaken but undeterred. The next morning she woke late, ate as much as she could, and meticulously packed her bag. She did not look at the news, did not see that the changing of the guard coincided with fraying relations between the United States and the Soviet Union with the Austro-Hungarian border serving as a rusty blade. As the USSR's state newspaper, *Pravda*, contended, "Some people from the United States Embassy in Budapest spoke to the Counter-revolutionary bands time and time again, urging them to continue the struggle." The state mouthpiece further alleged "that American vehicles with Red Cross signs on them had distributed weapons on the streets of Budapest." Finally, and most dangerously, the USSR had begun to assume that American journalists "who went to Budapest during the trouble, had no relation at all to the press and were just agents of the [American] intelligence services."

Unaware of all of this, Dickey made her way to the border on the night of December 5, 1956, where she met Zoltan along with Ferenc Welsch, another compatriot of his, and crossed once more into Hungary.

20

Imprisonment

DICKEY'S BOOTS SLOSHED through the same canal for a third time. The icy wind cut through her overcoat. In the clear night sky to their left, Ursa Major told them they were still traveling east. But north or south of where, Zoltan no longer knew. Somehow he had missed a major landmark that should have directed them onto the railroad tracks. They were undeniably lost.

Rocket bursts searched at random for wayward refugees. The flaring magnesium falling slowly to earth illuminated a tiny hamlet of thatched-roof homes ahead. They'd have to find a haystack to hide out in during the day, edging ever closer to the horizon. But there might be danger in this too.

"If I were a Red patrol sent out to comb these fields for people trying to escape," Zoltan whispered, "I'd stay behind that haystack to keep out of the wind. I'll scout the far side of the stack, you two wait here for a minute."

Dickey and Ferenc watched him run into the darkness until the ragged pink stars of a tracer rocket exploded directly above them. Her feet involuntarily left the ground. Midair, she remembered her Marines training and fell flat onto her stomach. From twenty yards away an automatic rifle screamed its bullets toward them. Ferenc, who had not fallen, stepped forward toward the Soviet guns.

"Stoi!" shouted the submachine gunner. Russian for *Stop*.

Ferenc put his hands on his head. Dickey stood, now caked in mud, and followed suit. The guards walked them for another five miles, prodding their backs with gun barrels when their steps faltered. Dawn broke in slashes across the horizon. She had been walking for nine hours. At last they reached a farm that had been converted into an infantry command post. Dickey and Ferenc were thrown into an empty barn surrounded by barbed wire. One of the soldiers tossed two thin blankets on the ground before bolting the door. She and Ferenc shivered together, eating the chocolate bars and oranges they had brought with them.

Eventually, Dickey's adrenaline crested and pulled back, dragging her into an uneasy sleep. The light seemed the same when she opened her eyes again. Cold and gray. Another guard brought them enamel plates of mashed potatoes, sausage, and sauerkraut. Dickey made herself eat as much as she could, well aware this might be her last meal for a long time.

Different guards entered. Unlike the skittish border patrolmen fresh out of basic training, these men carried themselves with disconcerting ease. The insignia on their uniform was one Dickey hadn't seen.

"They are like your military police," Ferenc whispered.

Again at gunpoint, Ferenc and Dickey were marched across an isolated field. The setting sun cast their shadows ten feet in front of them. It occurred to her that this would be the ideal location for an "administrative execution," a term used for the extralegal murder of refugees by border guards. On the other hand, Dickey continued to speculate, they might be headed for the Soviet slave labor camps. Though this seemed unlikely given her American passport and the long distance to the nearest gulag. In her most optimistic estimation, she imagined they would be passed into the hands of the Hungarian infantry, who would likely release them since they were unarmed.

But there was one more unlikely and almost unthinkable scenario that Dickey labored to put out of her mind as soon as it entered: that they would be handed over to the ÁVH. However, Hungary's secret police rarely ventured this far out into the borderlands. Even so, the two unmarked black sedans that came into view on the road ahead suggested they might have.

It was then that Dickey remembered the Minox subminiature camera taped to her bra that would immediately brand her as a spy if found.

Panic rushed through her veins as they forced Ferenc in the back of one car and her into the other.

Her mind spun in a search of a solution. None came. Beside the driver sat another guard whose sole task was to watch her while keeping his gun pointed in her direction. They drove for half an hour like this, Dickey trying to keep the terror off her face, the guard trying to stay awake as dusk slipped into darkness. Then the driver pulled over, got out of the car, and returned some minutes later dragging a sobbing woman in her thirties with a baby in her arms.

Dickey offered to hold the baby. The woman recoiled, unwilling to part with her child. But perhaps steadied by the kindness of the offer, she composed herself somewhat, retrieved a tin of cigarettes from her coat pocket, and offered one to Dickey. As the two women began to smoke, silently sitting in their private hells next to each other, the guard motioned for them to flick their ashes out the window. In a flash Dickey realized she might have a chance at purgation.

As the guard's gaze wandered toward the front windshield, Dickey slid her left hand beneath her sweater and tore the tape from her skin while forcing herself not to flinch. Slipping the camera into her glove so as to dampen the sound were it to hit the side of the car, she let the most certain piece of evidence against her slide out into the night. It was only later she realized her mistake. She'd kept the other glove. Consumed by the paranoia specific to those in the custody of secret police, she worried the glove containing the camera might be discovered and matched to the one remaining in her possession. No such epic game of lost and found ever transpired, but it didn't stop her from agonizing over the possibility.

Around midnight they left the highway for the streets of a city grid. The bright moonlight lit its quaint cobblestone streets and elegant Renaissance-style buildings. Reaching for hope, Dickey imagined an entity as insidious as the ÁVH could not exist in a place as beautiful as this. The black sedans, the military police, the long silent drive ceased to be signs of foreboding, and for a brief moment became only the happenstance of a great misunderstanding that would soon be resolved.

Then, they took a right through a pair of wide gates flanked by gun towers and washed in yellow floodlights. German shepherds strained against their chains. An imposing gray prison complex came into view. Yet this is not what convinced Dickey that the worst had come to pass. Instead, it was the small brass plaque set into the concrete wall beside the door they were prodded through. ÁVH, it read in embossed letters.

Ferenc, Dickey, and the mother with her baby were herded into a small room with a single table and several straight-back chairs. The baby began to cry. Her mother opened her dress to feed her. Ferenc mouthed the word "Győr," which Dickey knew to be a city in northwest Hungary that had been the site of some of the most intense fighting in the revolution outside of Budapest. Soon after, Ferenc was ordered into an adjoining office. Dickey had another of the mother's cigarettes. Ferenc came back, pale and perspiring. He said nothing. The same guard ordered Dickey into the same office.

"Why did you escape to Hungary?" demanded her interrogator in German. It was the first time she'd been addressed in a language she understood in twenty hours. Yet the question itself confused her.

"I did not escape to Hungary," she replied, nonplussed.

"You were arrested in Hungary," he volleyed.

Dickey returned, "I don't know where I was captured. But I wasn't arrested. Your men opened fire on me without warning. I had nothing in my hands, I wanted to help deliver the medicine you took from my knapsack as a token from my people to your people."

The interrogator laughed. "I have never heard such a fairy story since I was too old to read the brothers Grimm."

Dickey protested, grabbed her passport from her pocket. The interrogator took it, smiled. "You will see your counsel in the morning," he said and motioned for the guards to remove her. He did not return her passport.

They walked her down a hallway of curved steel doors and opened one with a creaking groan. The door closed and locked with an echo. Dickey climbed onto the wooden sleeping platform, wrapped herself in its rough blanket, and despite herself, fell asleep.

The door opened again at 4 A.M. Four men, including last night's interrogator, entered the cell.

"Good morning, gentlemen," she said with all the composure she could summon.

The interrogator took a beat to recover from his surprise, then launched into a reenactment of his previous line of questioning. Dickey repeated her answers verbatim.

"We do not believe you," he concluded.

"I want to see the American Consul," she said.

The four men left her cell, slamming the door behind them.

Breakfast was bread and ersatz coffee of acorn brew. Dickey ate slowly to pass the time. Midmorning, the cell door swung open again.

"Now we will take you to see your counsel," the interrogator said. She believed him.

They put her back in the sedan with the same guard, same driver. She glimpsed Ferenc being loaded into the other car but saw no sign of the mother and her baby. Outside of the city she spotted a sign painted with two white arrows. One pointed right toward Vienna, the other left toward Budapest. Dickey oscillated between hopeful anticipation and dread as they approached the fork. They turned left. Her heart felt as if it had been drained of blood. Hours later, they arrived at their destination.

"Our cars turned off the street, passed through huge sheet steel gates set in high stone walls, and parked in a cobblestone court entirely surrounded by buildings of five and six stories, every one of whose windows were barred with steel," wrote Dickey. The driver went inside. The guard kept his gun trained on her. Dickey tried to distract herself watching sparrows bathe in a nearby puddle. The driver returned, took her inside. She knew she would not be going to the American consulate, not then anyway. But in all her fear and disquietude she still held hope that the cloak of her citizenship would save her from the worst.

This too was ripped from her.

The driver led her down a long corridor lined, as Dickey wrote, with "a row of six pineboard cubicles, looking just like vertical coffins." He pushed her into one, locked the door behind her. All the light disappeared. There was no heat. Dickey sat on the bare board meant to be a bed. "I tried not to be noisy about it," she wrote, "but the tears running down my cheeks were warm and welcome."

Five hours. A new guard, this one with a square face and a limp. He led her through the corridor of coffin-shaped cells and into a long room. One half looked like a modern office. The other was filled with empty burlap bags. On the office side, the guard collapsed into a chair behind a typewriter and slid a form into its guide. Someone told her in German to print her name on a scrap of paper lying on the desk.

"American Consulate," said Dickey, pointing to the phone.

"Nem," said the guard, *No*, and pointed at the paper scrap.

Georgette Meyer Chapelle, she wrote with as steady a hand as she could.

A woman barely out of her teens led Dickey to the burlap-bag side and took her behind a privacy curtain hanging in the corner. She pointed to her bootlaces. "American Consulate," Dickey repeated.

The young woman looked confused, then made the pantomime of being hung. Dickey unlaced her boots, though misunderstood the gesture. She thought her cellmates would hang her with them. But as she would later understand, the woman meant that Dickey might hang herself were she allowed to keep the laces. The woman went on with her search for potential means of suicide, indicating Dickey should take off her coat, sweater, pants, shirt, and socks.

The guard made a pile of the things Dickey would not be allowed to keep. In it were the pearl earrings she had bought in Tehran, a compact that had been her mother's, and a flint lighter she'd had since covering the Pacific Fleet. The woman gestured for Dickey to get dressed again and carried her personal effects over to the guard still sitting at the typewriter. They discussed her possessions. The woman snapped open Dickey's compact to check her makeup. Galled, Dickey reached for it but the woman quickly drew it away, pointing at the mirror and then mimicking the motion of slitting her wrists.

All of these things, along with her hairpins, watch, notepad, and pencil were slipped into a burlap bag. The woman then took her arm and along with two other guards crammed into a tiny elevator. She pressed five. The elevator rose. The doors opened.

"My last doubts about the building were painfully removed," wrote Dickey. "We passed through two walls of steel bars into what could be nothing but the cell block of a huge and high-security prison. I looked again and felt every nerve of my body tingle with shock. I had heard of this cell block; the refugees had described its architecture to me. I was not just in jail. I was in the Fö Street Prison, the most dreaded of them all."

The guards halted her in front of Cell 504. Dickey stepped in. The walls were made of unevenly whitewashed brick and the floor of cold gray stone. There was a window covered by a grid of steel and muted by a thick pane of opaque glass through which she could see only the iron bars beyond it. Planks belted by wrought iron made the sleeping shelf. The bedding consisted of a thin mat and a blanket in the faded colors of the Hungarian flag. On its center white stripe she could see the blood stains of those it belonged to before her.

The door closed and locked. Dickey turned to look, half believing that at this last second the error would be corrected, the odyssey ended, that it would open again. But the door remained unmoved. Its red rusted iron interlaced with oak recalled Torquemada's Inquisition. Its peephole told her she would always be watched. Its Judas window said that even to eat she would remain alone inside. Dickey pressed herself against the far wall as if to test its firmness. It had no give.

Shouts to go to sleep echoed down the corridor. Dickey crawled beneath the blanket, pulled it around her. The door opened. Paralyzed, she didn't move. The guard grabbed her hands and put them outside the blanket where he could see them at all times.

"Nem," he said, making the sign of a slit wrist, then left, slamming the door behind him.

Dickey squeezed her eyes closed against pale yellow light from the bulb that remained lit twenty-four hours a day. She willed herself to sleep but woke with the sounds of a man being beaten in the next cell over. She recognized his pleas to stop even in a language she didn't speak.

His screams echoed in her ears for hours, ringing with the terrible clarity that she would not see the outside of this prison for a long time, if ever. Terror overtook her like a squall, enveloping her in torrential visions of possible futures, each more painful than the last. Of being raped, beaten, hung, shot. Of being forgotten by the ones she loved. Of war between America and the USSR about which she might know nothing before that last flash of a nuclear bomb. But within this deluge of waking nightmares, she glimpsed the certainty that were she to get out of here with any amount of her mind intact, she would need to keep track of the days. That if nothing else, she had to be able to anchor herself to time.

Without turning toward the wall, she made a hatch mark in the white-wash with her nail. The guards might erase it if they saw her. But what day was it now? And how would she remember where to count from? Adding up the hours since crossing the border she realized that it must have been December 7, Pearl Harbor Day, a date she would never forget.

Her eyes hadn't yet closed again when the guards shouted for the inmates to wake, well before the sun had risen. Soon after, the Judas window opened and an empty bowl was thrust through. In gestures and broken German she understood she was to draw three inches of water from the metal sink in the corner of her cell, wash herself, her laundry, her floor. Next came breakfast of cold ersatz coffee and a hunk of bread.

Then nothing. Nothing came, nothing happened. She had nothing to read or to occupy her hands and nothing with which to break the time nor any way to tell what time it was. Hunger started to gnaw at her stomach. No food came. Hours stretched out. Or were they minutes? She silently recited all the poetry she had memorized by the fireside with her grand-mother as a child. Finishing this, she began to sing the songs she knew, but the brick walls deadened the resonance of her voice in a way that reminded her all too clearly that she could not be heard outside of this prison. She thought living in her memories might bring her solace for a while. Yet reminiscing about the past produced the opposite effect. "My mind jumped back from it like a finger from a hot stove," she wrote in an essay about her experience, "I found that I always came back to, Will I see the people I love again?"

Still, no food.

She stared at the Judas window, willing it to open. She began to pace, seven steps from front to back, four from side to side. Her stomach churned. The cell did not have a toilet. She pounded on the door. No one came. She paced, then pounded. The door creaked. The guard took her arm, pushed her toward the toilet that was a hole in the ground.

Back in the cell. Nothing.

She would come to call this period of the day between the first and second meals the "Long Wait" that was made longer by the fact that it never had a set rhythm. Nor did anything in Fö Street Prison.

"It was erratic for a purpose," Dickey wrote later in life when enough time had passed to look back with a degree of disinterest. "You must never know how long it would be before the next food or rest. And you would know, almost from the first, that you were being systematically cut loose from time as a pillar of sanity."

Sunrise and nightfall had no meaning. As Dickey would find in the weeks that followed, she and her fellow prisoners were never shouted awake at the same time. Nor was there a set period between waking and breakfast, the second meal and the third, and the shouts to lie down.

"Time," wrote Dickey, "is the only real enemy. What I tried to do with time was splinter it. I stopped trying to foresee a whole day. But another hour? Even the time until the next food? How to make this <u>now</u> into that <u>later</u> was the only problem."

She grew more adept at fracturing her days. But she didn't know then on this first day, during this first Long Wait, how vast time could become.

The Judas window opened. Two bowls. One of clear broth. The other potato stew. She ate quickly but the guard came before she had finished. She scooped the remaining stew into her hand as he grabbed for her bowls.

The door closed. Then two guards came in and took her to the interrogation room. The routine repeated itself the first two times. The guards sat her at a desk facing the light in an otherwise bare room. A man with a hawk nose and a plump young woman with rimless glasses and immaculate makeup sat on the other side. The man slid a confession across the desk. The woman told her to sign. Dickey balled her fists in her pockets and said, "I will not sign."

Next came the kind of questions that made a prisoner miss home, made her more susceptible to confessing to whatever they said would shorten her sentence. "Do you remember how good food is—outside of our prison?" asked her interrogator. "Do you realize that your employer has already betrayed you? Is there not a man you love? What is he doing while you are here? Do you know your country has abandoned you?"

Sufficiently primed, a flurry of accusations followed.

"You are not who you say you are. You are not telling the truth. You have escaped into Hungary. You are not telling us what happened. We can wait until you are ready to tell the truth."

During the first two interrogations, she kept her answers concise and polite, believing the truth would set her free. By her third interrogation, having endured more than ten days of imprisonment, hunger, and privation, she had learned "the only two sound rules for being interrogated in a horror prison." The first: "Facts do not matter. To observe this rule is, I admit, appallingly hard. But any time the facts get in the way of the structure the interrogator is trying to build, they will be discarded." The second rule was "the interrogator does not have the power to free you. . . . So any civility he practices does not need to be returned in kind."

As such, she did her best to keep her answers clipped, at times managing to verge on sardonic, even as their questioning stretched on for hours.

"You tell us that you are not an agent of the imperialist conspiracy?" the interrogator fired.

"I am not."

"You tell us you brought medicine. We know you are lying. We know you are a photographer. Have you put away your camera?"

"I have no cameras."

"You tell us that this passport belongs to you?"

"It does. If you will examine the picture—Look," she broke, "surely you cannot shoot as a spy a woman walking toward your guns unarmed who speaks not a word of your language."

"We will not shoot you," he replied. "Under Hungarian law, spies are hanged." The threat of being hanged resonated in the sparse room, its echo conjuring the image of standing on the gallows, a noose around her neck.

Her veneer of placid effrontery crumbled. And it was not just his threat. The feeling of wanting food had grown into something she had never known: hunger. Real hunger. Not the discomfort of missing a meal or even two. But the state of the body consuming itself. She estimated her caloric intake to be at about 1,200 per day, enough to live but not to think, plan, hope, or dream. After only ten days hunger became not an idea but a tangible object, as if an organ of absence. As she wrote, "It was a local pain as big as my hand, dull or sharp but never still. More important, I watched myself become another person."

Every morning her clothes hung looser and heavier around her shoulders. Her hair came out in fistfuls. The hearing in her left ear started to dull and would eventually disappear entirely. She felt she would not recognize herself if she ever had the chance to look in the mirror. But most disturbing still, she could no longer think the way she wanted to about the things she wanted to for the amount of time she wanted to. Hunger broke her consciousness into shards with a dull, aching blade. "There was only one mood I knew how to show," she recalled, "a sullen and terrible ugliness."

As this interrogation dragged on, and she missed the already meager first and second meals of the day, she discovered something new about hunger. "Fear, too, seemed to originate in the part of my body where hunger hurt."

"Do you have any questions?" the interrogator asked after a long pause.

Dickey shuffled her feet. "How much longer will I be held here, like this?"

"Under Hungarian law, one cannot know," he answered.

"Days?" she asked.

"Perhaps," he replied.

"Weeks?"

"Possibly."

"Months?"

"Maybe."

"A year?"

He called for the guard and did not answer.

Her dinner was in a bowl on the floor when they thrust her back in her cell. She almost cried for joy. A two-inch piece of clear bacon fat. This was the best of what she had come to call the "Good Food," food that contained fat, food she would have thought nothing of back in America. A two-inch cut of pork sausage. A half-inch slice of salami. A wedge of chalk-like cheese. A slice of firm apple jam. But here, a piece of fat that she would have asked her butcher to throw away meant the hole the size of her fist in her stomach might shrink enough to let her sleep.

The guards shouted for the prisoners to close their eyes. As she always did, Dickey welcomed the night.

The next day, she began taking stock of the things she had as a way of grounding herself in this new reality, ever shifting as it was. She had her health and though it was failing, she put her money on getting out before she became too sick to survive. She found a way to roll an extra cigarette from the butts of her daily ration of five, and made half a set of checkers from bread crust and cheese wrapping. The prison lacked heat, but at least her cell stayed dry. The clothes she had been captured in were ideal for winter in jail: her trench coat stretched to the floor, her sweater and socks were made of wool, her pants were thick, and her ski underwear provided her with more warmth than most prisoners ever dared hope for. Most importantly, perhaps, Dickey gave herself a job on which she could focus all of her attention: staying sane.

For inspiration Dickey looked to those whose struggles and triumphs far outweighed her own. She recalled the immigrants she had photographed on "I Am an American Day" in 1945 when a million and a half new citizens gathered in Central Park to celebrate their naturalization. Almost all had fled persecution under fascism and the ravages of war. Most were from Europe, but others were from Africa, Asia, and South America, anywhere war had touched with violence. More than their faces, she remembered their panoply of accents that rose together in a stunning harmony as Mayor Fiorello La Guardia led the crowd in the Pledge of Allegiance. Sometimes in rare moments of silence, she thought she could hear it still, the song of America she loved best— global, diverse, and composed of voices who knew the true meaning of freedom.

She thought of Mahatma Gandhi, whose international funeral procession she had witnessed, here, in Budapest in 1948, after his assassination. In truth, she had not known the whole of his heroism at the time. But the Quakers she was working with explained the extent of his patience and fortitude in pursuit of his goal of a united and free India in the face of unimaginable persecution at the hands of the British. Dickey did not suppose she could summon his equanimity or courage. But knowing that he had gave her something to strive toward, something to hope for.

And she thought of Anna Kéthly, whom she had met in New York before flying to Vienna. A prominent Hungarian politician since 1919, Kéthly had always opposed the Communist Party. Shortly after coming to power, they arrested her and held her in solitary confinement for long stretches of time. Freed by the revolution, she had been appointed as a delegate to the United Nations General Assembly and by chance was in New York when Russian tanks rolled into Budapest. Dickey asked her how she had survived such a long ordeal. Kéthly replied calmly that one could make a life in prison, too.

Even so, fear inevitably crept in. Dickey found herself worrying far more about being raped or tortured than she did about being hanged or committing suicide. At least in death there would be an escape from what she feared most: that she would be left here indefinitely, condemned to go slowly insane.

She could not think her way back from the edge of this abyss. Only movement would do. Exercise was not officially allowed but she discovered the guards did not protest when she did sit-ups and push-ups on her sleeping shelf. She began to do as many as she could on the days they gave her fat or meat, about three times a week. Improbably, she began to feel stronger.

One day after the Long Wait, after the second meal, she felt what she had not for a long time, defiant. She spread her bloodstained blanket on the floor. Immediately, her guard opened the Judas window and pointed toward the floor.

"Nem!" he yelled, and motioned for her to put it back.

"Fine," she said, sweeping it back onto the sleeping shelf. "I don't need a blanket." While he watched, Dickey practiced the combat rolls the Marines had taught her at Camp Pendleton. Back and forth across the stone floor. She bruised her shoulders, her back, her hands. But the movement was exhilarating and the guard did not try to stop her, perhaps having learned the same technique in his own military training.

The next morning, through the Judas window, along with her bowl for water, the same guard furtively handed her a slim volume of German poetry. It was the first thing she had to read in weeks.

Then another week passed without anyone speaking to her. Since she had spoken to anyone. She marked another hatch mark in the whitewash. Last night was New Year's Eve. The guards celebrated with a short burst of automatic fire in the courtyard. Today was 1957, and she tried not to speculate on how many days of this new year she would spend inside this cell.

She began to lean against the walls as she paced the floor. Her shoulders wore a trail in the whitewash. Her coat began to tear at the seams but she could not stop. Something about the movement, the pressure, the friction helped her hold on to her sanity.

Everything seemed so loud now, even in the ear going deaf. Her teeth grated every time the steel gates scraped open and slammed shut. She heard the prison vans sputtering in the courtyard and the shuffling feet of new prisoners freshly damned to this hell. She heard the screams of those being tortured echoing through all five floors of the cell block. Fingernails being torn off. Women being raped. Bones being broken. Faces being beaten beyond recognition. Death being made to walk in the living.

"At one time or another," she wrote, "I heard too, every human sound but those of joy. There was talking, whispering, whistling, shouting, retching, sobbing and screaming. Sometimes singing, the saddest of all music."

Another night. Another round of shouts to wake up. Through the steel and oak she silently implored her interrogator to request her. Her sanity slipped down a rung. "Whatever I was," she thought, "has already been thrown away. Why is my body so slow to understand this? And my brain—why does it continue to reason and scheme and weigh? Why should the whole organism that was me try so hard to go on? What's left is like the leg nerve on some dissecting table. I've had it: why don't I die?" Shouts to go to bed. She had never come so close to confessing to anything they asked as long as they would talk to her.

Think think think. Her mind was the prison. The key was inside. She dreamed of Okinawa. Eighteen Marines lay in stretchers around the room, wounded by a Japanese sniper attack. The air was still, hot, humid. She held the flashlight as the doctor operated on the first. She could hear his breath moving through torn tissue and shattered bones. The doctor hung another blood bottle, then another. Dickey glanced at her watch. Two hours went by before they closed his wound.

She said to anyone, "How can he stand it?"

The corpsman, holding the blood bottle in his hand, paused beside the stretcher. One of the flashlight beams moved across his face and the deep lines of weariness made black slashes on either side of his mouth.

"She's Ready to Defend America," a portrait of Georgette Louise Meyer (aka Dickey Chapelle) as a member of the Women Flyers of America, an organization formed in 1940 to teach women to fly and then to ferry American bombers to Great Britain.

A soldier from
the Fourteenth
Infantry trains
his submachine
gun at the camera
while preparing
for World War
II combat in the
Darién Gap jungle,
Panama.

Soldiers in the
Fourteenth
Infantry fording
a stream in
Panama's Darién
Gap jungle.

A soldier from
the Fourteenth
Infantry rests after
training exercises
in the Darién Gap
jungle.

Medical facilities, Iwo Jima. Dickey landed here on the *Peg O' My Heart* medevac plane as one of the first and only female correspondents to visit Iwo Jima during World War II.

Dickey spent several days on Okinawa during the initial push to overtake the island. Here, she captures a military truck driving by three Okinawan women and a small child who are picnicking in the grass.

Marines wounded during the Battle of Iwo Jima wait to be evacuated to the hospital ships stationed offshore.

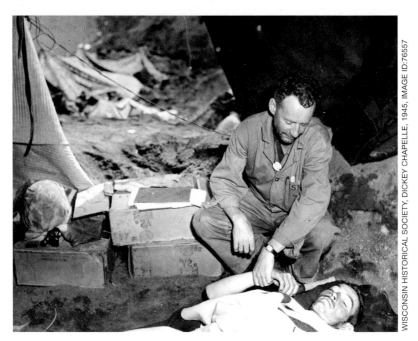

Lieutenant Commander Leonard (Leo) Thelen, commanding officer of the field hospital Dickey visited on Iwo Jima, takes the vitals of a Marine whose legs have been injured by shrapnel.

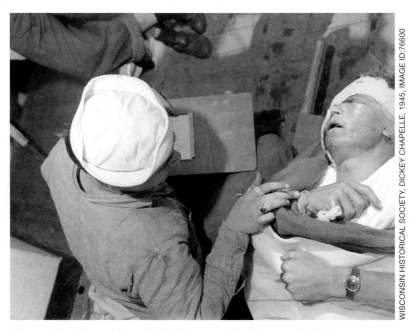

Wounded with an abdominal injury on Iwo Jima, this Marine was one of thousands to be treated on the hospital ships stationed offshore to aid the campaign.

Strategically located between Pearl Harbor and Japan's outer archipelago islands, Guam served as a vital staging location for airfields as well as a field hospital. Here, a C-47 transport plane returns to North Airfield, Guam, after completing its mission.

Returning from Iwo Jima aboard the *Peg O' My Heart* medevac plane, flight nurse Gwen Jensen treats Private First-Class George Berier, who suffered a head injury.

Dickey documented the immediate aftermath of World War II in Europe for two years from the vantage point of retrofitted trucks like this one that served as a darkroom, kitchen, and sometimes bedroom.

The early Cold War years marked a period of enormous American investment in foreign aid as a method of countering Soviet influence in strategic regions. Dickey spent several years documenting these extraordinary efforts. Here, Dickey photographs an Iraqi farmer driving a Wisconsin-made McCormick tractor, delivered as part of a larger aid package.

For weeks in the winter of 1956, Dickey documented the refugees risking their lives to escape the brutal Soviet-installed dictatorship that toppled Hungary's democratically elected government.

Hundreds of Hungarian refugees line up outside the US embassy hoping to gain entry.

For nearly a month in 1957, Dickey was embedded with the Algerian National Liberation Front (FLN), the first reporter of any gender to be granted the honor. Her photos, like this one, uniquely highlighted both the humanity and bravery of those fighting for their independence from French colonial rule.

As she often did, Dickey focused her lens on the efforts of doctors, nurses, and medics risking their own lives to treat casualties of war. Here, an Algerian Red Crescent worker treats a Bedouin herdsman injured in an illegal bombing of civilians by the French colonial forces.

Stationed in the foothills of the Atlas Mountains, Dickey regularly accompanied and documented the FLN while on patrol.

Dickey's familiarity with military training made her comfortable with soldiers the world over, and likewise, they with her. Here, she shares a cup of Turkish coffee with members of the FLN Scorpion Battalion.

FLN lookouts keeping watch for French planes and foot patrols.

Major Antonio Lusson, battalion commander for the 26th of July Army, fires on a Batista government B-26 as it strafes the town of La Maya, Cuba.

In the foreground, leader of the 26th of July Movement and later Cuban president Fidel Castro takes a rare respite from his usual frenetic movements for a cup of coffee.

Though women's war efforts were often overlooked, Dickey regularly focused on their contributions. Here, she photographs a Cuban female guerrilla fighter outside of a university in Havana after the 26th of July Army seized the capital city.

On the same Milwaukee beach where she learned to swim as a young girl, Dickey photographed "Operation Inland Seas" to celebrate the opening of the St. Lawrence Seaway. This was her favorite photograph of herself at work.

In Camp Pendleton, San Diego, California, Dickey photographs two Marines from Test Unit One, an experimental regiment designed and trained for the nuclear-age battlefield.

WISCONSIN HISTORICAL SOCIETY, DICKEY CHAPELLE, 1963, IMAGE ID:85529

This shot was taken by Dickey while embedded with the Commandos L, an anti-Castro militia made up of Cuban exiles, in Miami, Florida.

WISCONSIN HISTORICAL SOCIETY, DICKEY CHAPELLE, 1960, IMAGE ID:11731

Much of Dickey's expertise in war came from covering military training exercises such as those at Fort Benning, Georgia, where she documented the development of Cold War helicopter strategies that would later be put to ubiquitous use during the Vietnam War.

WISCONSIN HISTORICAL SOCIETY, DICKEY CHAPELLE, 1962, IMAGE ID:11736

Aboard a helicopter Dickey photographed the first US Marines engaged in actual combat in South Vietnam as they fired on Vietnamese National Liberation Front (NLF) regulars in the process of laying siege to the village of Vinh Quoi. The Kennedy administration later tried, and failed, to censor her photos of this event that foretold a paradigm shift in American involvement in the Vietnam War from an advisory role to one of direct engagement.

WISCONSIN HISTORICAL SOCIETY, DICKEY CHAPELLE, 1965, IMAGE ID:115824

Abuse of Vietnamese combatants and noncombatants at the hands of American and South Vietnamese forces became increasingly and horrifyingly common-place as the war went on. Here, Dickey photographed a suspected Viet Cong soldier who had been executed. Though she rarely commented on such acts of egregious violence directly, she let her photographs speak for themselves.

Having been a prisoner of war herself, Dickey was often outraged by the treatment of suspected Viet Cong combatants. In her mind, the abuse of an individual's human rights and civil liberties, such as those she documented here, could and would not win the war.

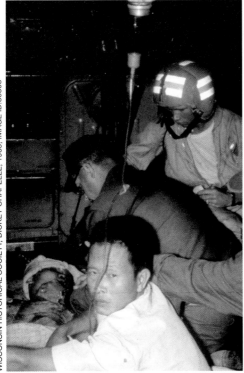

From World War II to the Vietnam War, Dickey highlighted the importance of medics on morale and the overall war effort. Here, she captures the cool stare of a Vietnamese medic treating an injured South Vietnamese soldier.

WISCONSIN HISTORICAL SOCIETY, DICKEY CHAPELLE, 1962, IMAGE ID:86864

In this photograph for her *National Geographic* article "Helicopter War in South Viet Nam," Dickey was one of the first to capture the ubiquitous use of this relatively new technology in warfare.

WISCONSIN HISTORICAL SOCIETY, DICKEY CHAPELLE, 1965, IMAGE ID:86862

Dickey insisted on accompanying fighting forces on patrol during all of the conflicts she reported on. Her coverage of the conflict in Vietnam was no different as she accompanied multiple branches of the South Vietnamese military as well as anticommunist guerilla forces, such as those pictured here, as they searched for enemy combatants.

Taken during Dickey's coverage of the helicopter war erupting in South Vietnam for *National Geographic,* this photo shows a suspected NLF operative involved in the siege of Vinh Quoi.

Though adamantly against the abuse of prisoners of war, Dickey had no sympathy for the NLF and their North Vietnamese allies, the Viet Cong, having seen all too often the aftermath of their attacks. Here, Dickey captures the fear and uncertainty of the inhabitants of Vinh Quoi whose homes were completely destroyed by an NLF raid.

Though the Geneva Conventions prohibited journalists from carrying firearms, the realities of the Vietnam War required that they be able to defend themselves—as well as help the battalions they were embedded with—if the need arose. Here, Dickey is pictured carrying a semi-automatic rifle while embedded on the Vietnam-Cambodia border with the South Vietnamese marines.

"The limit of human endurance has never been reached," he said and tossed the empty blood bottle into the great pile of red waste.

The door opened in the morning. Dickey felt as if she just now breathed for the first time in eight days.

"Consul!" they shouted, smiling, gesturing for her to come with them.

Elation swept over her as the nightmare, it seemed, would soon be over. They led her to the marble stairs, worn with the footsteps of unknown numbers of prisoners. One guard remained at the top of the stairwell, watching her and the other descend, though Dickey didn't notice in the moment, fixated on counting the flights to freedom. She counted three before the guard grabbed her by the shoulders. The one who had remained at the top burst out laughing.

"April fool!" he yelled.

Another five days without human contact. "The awareness of being starkly alone can swell like a true sound, a dissonance so vast that no other hurt is real," she wrote of this period of solitary confinement. "You can know of other dangers close by—being hanged the next time you wake up. Or being tortured, not sometime but today. Or growing sick here where there is no chance to heal. But to be afraid of these would be an anti-climax. They are drained of drama. Only the pain of the present is real," she wrote, and then with all the knowledge she had gained of war's cruel mercies, "but it won't always hurt this much."

The door opened again. The guard who grabbed her seemed like a savior. Hawk Nose and Pudding Face, as she had come to call them in her mind, resumed their campaign of interrogation. At first Dickey found she had forgotten how to speak. Silence had built a dam in her throat. But when it broke, words came flooding out, not always in order, not always correctly pronounced, not always making sense. Words spilled out, all at once, despite herself.

She eventually regained control and never lost so much as to confess to their false accusations. Meanwhile, she had resigned herself to the possibility that the United States had broken off all diplomatic ties with the Soviet Union and that she would have to make a life for herself, here, in prison.

Now as the guards sat her at the desk once more, she noticed Hawk

Nose seemed tense. Even Pudding Face's makeup lacked its usual precision, a smear of lipstick trickling onto her chin.

Hawk Nose fired his questions in staccato as soon as she sat down.

"Tell us in detail how you escaped to Hungary. Tell us how many people you were. Tell it again."

"I refuse to answer any further questions," replied Dickey.

Hawk Nose raised his eyebrows, almost as if he was hurt.

"I will ask you several more," he said, "but it is not necessary that you answer to me. We know what is the answer to these questions. First, are you alone in your cell? Next, are your guards men? Now," he said, "tell us in detail what you did on the evening of December 5th."

"I refuse to answer any further questions," she repeated.

Hawk Nose motioned for her to be returned to her cell.

Dinnertime. The guard opened the Judas window holding a tray full of bacon. He slid it halfway in before pulling it back, laughing, and gave her a cup of water without anything else.

The shouts to sleep were late that night. A guard she had not seen before with a pointed jaw noisily opened the door holding a pair of pliers a foot long.

"Beteg?" he asked. *Sick?*

"Nem," said Dickey.

Opening his mouth wide, he pretended to pull at his front tooth, then pointed at her.

"Nem," she said.

Though solitary confinement is an acute form of psychological torture, this was the first time she had been threatened with physical torture. Nor, she knew, would it be the last. Something about this confrontation with its possibility of unbearable pain changed her, hardened her, made her want to push back even if it meant endangering her body further. At least, she reasoned, they would not take the only thing she had left: her dignity.

Shouts to shut and open her eyes. Her guard slid breakfast through the Judas window, but not before taking a piece of jam off her plate, just for spite.

Long Wait. Short Wait. The guard with the pointed jaw and the pliers came back in.

"Beteg?" he asked, again.

"Nem," repeated Dickey.

Putting his cigarette between his lips, he tucked the pliers under his arm and spread out his fingers. "Ön," he said, *You.*

She knew what this meant. "The last photograph I'd made before I was captured," she wrote, "was the spread hands of a woman escapee. The [ÁVH] had torn off every one of her fingernails and ground out two cigarettes in the back of her right hand."

Dickey smiled, reached toward him. Two other guards entered the cell. "Slowly I took the pliers. Very carefully I closed them over my own index fingernail. I rotated them until it hurt, stopped, smiled and looked up at the now attentive faces of the guards, saying in English, 'You do it like that, huh?'"

21

Scar Tissue

IN THE PURPLE dawn of January 14, 1957, two guards pushed her out the doors of Fö Street Prison and into the back of a windowless van. She tried to keep from imagining the worst, which was not the scaffold of a hangman, but an unnamed prison known only to those held within and their torturers.

She exhaled in relief as they unloaded her in front of a minimum-security jail on a street she recognized. In the few steps between the van and the door Dickey drank in the sun that even on a winter morning seemed incandescent. Inside, two female guards with diamond earrings and submachine guns led her up two flights of stairs and opened the door to Cell 21.

She wept with joy when the lock bolted. There were seven other women in the cell. After five weeks of solitary confinement, she was no longer alone. Her cellmates immediately crowded around her.

"A sírás itt nem megengedett," they cooed. *Crying isn't permitted here.*

But after the block had been shouted to bed and Dickey had crawled into her bunk, she could not stop from shaking uncontrollably in release and relief, from the weightlessness of euphoria. That feeling of communion she had searched for from Iwo Jima to East Berlin to Camp Pendleton flooded over her once more. As Dickey wrote, "Surely this experience—to be with other human beings—is the ultimate proof of the presence of the Deity."

The depth of her feeling only increased in the days that followed. Through broken phrases and learned words, she discovered each of her cellmates was a revolutionary in her own right. One had assassinated an ÁVH officer. Two had been gunrunners. One had been a union striker. The youngest among them had been a student demonstrator. Sisters in arms, they formed a fast community. "That they welcomed me among them, that they were human beings to love and be loved by when I could imagine no greater gift—this I will not forget," wrote Dickey. "I cannot feel that an ocean or a way of life separates us now."

Yet even all the sentiments of solidarity could not dispel one fundamental difference between them: the lottery of birth had conferred Dickey with immeasurable privilege. After her release, Dickey never ceased to acknowledge the advantages of her race and nationality. But for one brief moment in Cell 21, even this gulf seemed erased as Dickey had lost all faith that she would ever again be the beneficiary of her status as an American. When the guard said she'd be able to see the consul, Dickey merely shrugged. She'd been tricked by the cruel games of her jailers before and maintained her incredulity even when sat across from Richard Selby, who claimed to be her lawyer.

"Can I see your credentials?" she spat and studied them carefully after he slid them across the table. Minutes passed before she could convince herself of his legitimacy. In reality, since her disappearance her family and friends had been working to get her home. It had actually been Mari Michener who first reported her absence to the State Department after Dickey uncharacteristically missed a lunch date. As soon as her abduction had been confirmed by Zoltan, who had managed to escape, Dickey's aunts, uncles, and even Tony did what they could to pressure the US government into lobbying for her release. In the end, Leo Chern leveraged his contacts within the intelligence community and State Department to pressure the Hungarian government into admitting they held Dickey in custody. Having done so, they had no choice but to allow her to see the consul.

"Are we at war anywhere?" Dickey asked, handing him back his badge.

"Not actively," he said.

"Do I sound sane to you?"

"You are still putting verbs in your sentences," he replied.

"When do you think I might be free?" her voice cracked.

"I don't know," said Richard, "but you will be."

Eleven days went by. Dickey and her cellmates settled into a routine. They shared rations of food and water. The assassin, "a graceful woman in her thirties," as Dickey described her, became their de facto leader. She quelled hot tempers and allayed fears of the future by telling their fortunes with handmade tarot cards. The results were not always good, but at least they knew what was coming. Prepared to go on like this indefinitely, Dickey's most pressing concern became her quickly disintegrating socks. The heel had worn through and the toe would soon follow. Come summer, her leather boots would give her terrible blisters.

Without fanfare or warning, on the twelfth day of her imprisonment in Cell 21, one of the guards announced Dickey would be tried later that afternoon. The assassin removed her tarot cards from their hiding place behind the water container and dealt three cards: the King of Swords, the Grim Reaper, the Star. From her gestures and a few words of German, Dickey gleaned they represented a lawyer, a change, and a woman. When she asked if this meant a good or bad omen, the assassin pantomimed the leveling of a scale. It could go either way.

Two guards opened the door, motioned for Dickey to grab her coat. They wound her through the jail's labyrinthian halls until finally reaching a snowy alleyway. Dickey paused. The guards adjusted their machine guns in case she tried to run. Dickey took out her last cigarettes and offered them each one. She needed to pause, to think. The next set of doors led to the courtroom. She knew the Hungarian justice system to be more akin to a house of mirrors than a bastion of law and order. A verdict of not guilty could mean indefinite imprisonment. A sentence of a few days might end in a noose. On the precipice of hope, she had to step back to the safe ground of doubt.

The guards ground their cigarettes beneath their boot heels. Dickey took one last deep drag.

In the courtroom, they deposited her in the accused's box. Richard tapped on her shoulder from the lawyer's box behind her. "We'll have you out of here before you can smoke them," he whispered, handing her a pack of Pall Malls, her favorite. At least, she figured, she'd replaced the cigarettes the guards had smoked. But as she turned, she glimpsed an improbable familiar face. Carl Hartman of the Associated Press, whom she had known for years. Hope crashed against her wall of disbelief and for a moment she allowed herself to think his presence signaled the court's intention to let her go. But her doubt held steady, countering that it more likely meant they planned on making a spectacle of her trial in order to demonstrate the power they had even over an American citizen.

The beginning of the trial did not assuage her misgivings. In a classic indication of a kangaroo court, the judge, rather than the prosecution, cross-examined her. More troubling still, his line of inquiry went on for the better part of an hour and mirrored that of her interrogators.

Finally, the judge finished. Dickey lit a cigarette with trembling hands. The prosecutor stood to make his closing argument. He urged a lenient sentence, "out of humanitarianism of the glorious Hungarian people's democracy." Dickey wondered at what the word "lenient" meant in the context of a communist court.

During the judge's oration Dickey's mind slid into reciting Thomas Gray's "Elegy Written in a Country Churchyard." Around verse eighteen she thought she heard the judge say the Hungarian word for year, or was it years? Both made equal sense to her, and she went back to her poem, her mind far from the madding crowd. The courtroom rose and she with it.

"His Honor says you have been judged guilty," said the interpreter. Her heart stopped as she waited for the sentence. "His Honor says that you are sentenced to the fifty days you have served already. His Honor says that you are hereby expelled from Hungary forever. Is there anything you wish to say?"

"No, your Honor."

"Do you understand your sentence?"

"Yes, your Honor," she said and sank down to her chair in shock.

She watched as her lawyer spoke to one of her guards. Nothing seemed real. Carl made notes a few rows back. Richard walked toward her.

"You're to go back to your cell to get your things together," said Richard. In a flash, she saw her darkest suspicions coming to pass.

"Carl!" she waved for his attention.

Carl cocked his head, cupped his hand over his ear to signal her to speak up.

"Don't file that story!" she yelled. "They say they're taking me back to my cell for a few minutes! Please, wait across the street for me, for twenty minutes, by your watch! If you see me come out with earrings in my ears, write the story. But don't file before—please!"

Through the court building, the halls of the jail, back to Cell 21. The guard handed her a cardboard box, motioned for her to get her things.

"I thought I was simply being transferred to another cell," Dickey later remembered. Even so, she gave her cellmates the cigarettes and food Richard had handed her before the trial began. After unloading them from her pockets, she began to cry. Wherever she was going, she would miss them. The assassin threw her arms around her, kissed her cheek.

"My release is real enough to her, I thought, returning the hug," wrote Dickey. Her other cellmates embraced her one by one. "Then a wave of the last feeling I'd expected overwhelmed me—deep guilt. Guilt that, under whatever circumstances, I was leaving these women to whom I owed so much. The only Magyar phrase I knew that expressed affection was *szeretlek*—I love you. I said it and it sounded right."

They echoed it back, *szeretlek, szeretlek,* gently walking her toward the door. "Their joy was so sincere, and my own feeling that I was deserting them so strong."

The guard pulled her out the rest of the way, turned her shoulders forward as she tried to look back. On the first floor they handed her the burlap sack she had been ordered to put her things in when she first arrived. Her mother's compact was missing. But her pearl earrings were inexplicably there. Dickey's hands shook as she pushed the studs through her lobes, still believing this might be a trick. But there was Richard waiting on the sidewalk with a taxi. And Carl across the street. Dickey waved, frantically pointing to her ears.

Dickey later wore those same pearl earrings into the combat zones of Algeria, Cuba, the Dominican Republic, Laos, and Vietnam. They were a reminder of those heroines of Budapest, the preciousness of a freedom they might never know, and of the great debt she owed them.

"Nobody is ever prepared to become a prisoner of terrorism," wrote Dickey, years later, "but when I returned to New York, the first thing I learned was that there's another side to the coin. Nobody's ever really ready to come back either. Not to a free world. You can't accept that both are real."

Like a diver surfacing too quickly, Dickey struggled to adjust to the rarified air of her aunt Lutie's luxury apartment on Sutton Place overlooking the East River. Sometimes she thought her imprisonment might have been a long nightmare. Or worse, that this current life was a dream from which she would wake to the walls of her prison. Mostly, she found herself somewhere in between.

Accustomed to talking to herself in solitary confinement, she muttered under her breath without noticing her aunts Lutie and George were in the room. Lutie diligently cooked all the dishes that had once been Dickey's favorites. But now the smell of steak and pork roast made her stomach churn. Her jaw ached trying to chew them. More than once she vomited from the fat she could no longer digest. Forgetting she had others, she often went to sleep and woke up in the same clothes, wearing them until George helped her pick out a new outfit. But these were only ripples of the tempest swelling beneath.

Her mind ran rampant with memories of burning fear and cold loneliness. Her body relived the visceral pain of prison, the straining tension in her shoulders, spasms in her back, and soreness of her feet from pacing the stone floor of her cell for hours. She woke up nights with visions of what might have happened. Of rape and torture and the slow descent into madness that ended with her hanging by her neck. These onslaughts clawed at her consciousness until she relented, balling herself up on the bed and sobbing in desperation.

As it had in her cell, movement proved the only way to stave off these thoughts. She wore a path in the living room carpet walking back and forth, a cigarette always between her middle and index fingers. She traversed Manhattan, river to river, and took the sky tram to Roosevelt Island, circling it twice around. But eventually her legs would tire and these thoughts, only one step behind, would catch up as soon as she stood still.

George and Lutie did their best to comfort and console her. But at the time, little was known about the lasting effects of solitary confinement or how to treat the deep psychological wounds it causes. Dickey eventually sought psychiatric care, and luckily so. Even with the limited knowledge that existed, her psychologist recognized her pattern of behavior as associated with solitary confinement. As she wrote to friends, "I'm not physically marked, says the doctor, but I do have all the psychological problems of having been in solitary confinement, incommunicado, and without identity for almost six weeks."

She turned to her typewriter for solace. First, she dedicated herself to writing 138 thank-you letters to the friends, family members, strangers, journalists, politicians, and diplomats that had played a part in her release. These letters were a kind of sweet revenge on her jailers who insisted her loved ones had given her up for dead. Every postage mark proved how very wrong they had been. They also allowed Dickey to replace bitterness and fear with gratitude, a process that in turn went a long way to covering her wound with scar tissue.

Still, this was not enough to get her back on her feet or to quell her stormy mind. The intrusive thoughts, the paranoia, the unquenchable restlessness were symptoms of deeper, more permanent change. The mean alchemy of prison had turned what was gold in her to iron. She had to recast herself into a new mold capable of containing and controlling this harder metal. She began to write this new self in hundreds of pages about her ordeal in which she always appeared as the hero and never the victim, showing weakness only to overcome it in the next paragraph. For her own survival, both psychologically and physically, she would make this fictive coping mechanism real, never again allowing herself a moment of fragility. At least not outwardly. At the same time, it was this perception and projection of self that would land her in ever more dangerous situations.

Above all else, her new sense of self required that she find her way back to combat journalism, to reporting those fighting for democracy. When Leo Chern welcomed her back to her job at the IRC, she had to refuse. As she wrote to her former boss and longtime friend, Jack Kavanaugh, "Now that I'm truly back and able to see my experience in a little clearer perspective, I find I've brought something very good back with me. I have a real compulsion to both write about and study the kind of government that held me—government-by-terror, of course, but also a kind of government that just now is ruling more people than any other one form."

Dickey took her first step back to reporting by pitching the story of her imprisonment. Despite its drama and timeliness, she received no favorable responses. Through whispers and backhanded compliments at the Overseas Press Club, where she had been a member since World War II, she found out why. Most of her male colleagues believed one of two things about her capture. At best they surmised she knew the risks of crossing the border and had gotten what she deserved. At worst they conjectured she had allowed herself to be arrested on purpose. Were she a man, her feat of daring and subsequent endurance of psychological torture would have been viewed as heroic and extraordinary. But because she was a woman, print journalism's establishment settled on the general consensus that she shouldn't be rewarded for risky behavior.

Luckily, TV producers had no such compunction.

Both NBC and CBS requested on-air interviews for their evening news programs after she returned. Contradictory desires howled inside her, one side urging her to tell the world her story while the other begged her to hide. The former won. She appeared as she wanted to, unfazed and unchanged, resolute in the face of improbable odds. These televised interviews cemented her reputation as America's first Cold War heroine.

But in a few months' time, telling her own story no longer satisfied her increasingly urgent need to help beat back the tide of communism that she equated with totalitarianism. The best way for her to do this, she knew, was to go back to telling the stories of others fighting for their freedom. She soon got her chance.

22

The Algerian National
Liberation Front

IN MID-JULY 1957, Dickey received a curious invitation to visit the New York office of the Algerian National Liberation Front (FLN), which claimed to be fighting a war of independence against French colonial rule. Intrigued, if incredulous, Dickey climbed the stairs to a cramped one-bedroom apartment that doubled as their headquarters on the Upper East Side of Manhattan the following afternoon.

The FLN's special envoy to the United Nations, Abdel Kadar Chanderli, opened the door and led her back to his desk in what would have been the living room. With a furrowed brow, thick glasses, and a slightly rumpled suit, he looked every part the rebel army diplomat. Dickey smiled and took a seat across from him at his desk.

"I'm sure you're wondering why you're here," said Chanderli.

"Sure, I'm curious," she replied, tamping a cigarette. Blue smoke hung heavy in the humid July air.

"My country is fighting for its life," he said, "and no one knows about it. The French control everything. Our borders are lined with razor wire. They own the airfields, the radio, and the telephones. There is no way to get information out from the front."

"That's not entirely true. There's a headline every other day about your Battle of Algiers," she replied, referring to the coverage of the capital city's violent civil unrest.

Chanderli sat back in his chair with an air of disdain. "This is not a matter of bombing and mobs," he said, waving his hand. "This is a true war. Here," he said, retrieving a file from his desk. "Read for yourself."

Dickey reluctantly accepted his dossier. It was hard to believe the American press corps could have simply missed an entire war anywhere in the world, even Algeria. At the same time, all the coverage she had seen so far had shared in common one glaring omission: it never included the Algerian perspective. Were there a fresh lead, it would be in this potential if improbable blind spot. Besides, she consoled herself as she walked the twenty blocks back to her apartment, Chanderli seemed sincere enough to warrant a glance.

Back in her own studio apartment, her doubts faded as she read the first page that detailed a campaign of international subterfuge. At the United Nations General Assembly, the French government falsely accused the FLN of having ties to the Soviet Union, then deployed half a million troops to Algeria, twice the total it had committed in the Indochina War, their last attempt at subduing a colony. The sheer number of soldiers, she wrote in her autobiography, "could not be explained by the café and department store bombings or by the mob demonstrations alone."

Against these five hundred thousand French stood the FLN, a guerrilla army of intellectuals and Bedouins, shopkeepers and farmers that waged an all-out war of independence with World War I rifles, homemade explosives, and the determination of revolutionaries.

Immediately Dickey knew this was her best chance to get back in the game, to report on a story that mattered. But she worried Chanderli wanted her to write a sympathetic article or two from afar. What she really needed was accreditation with the FLN and permission to march with them on maneuvers. No American had been granted such access and as a White, middle-aged woman, she worried she hardly appeared as the ideal candidate. Faced once again with a familiar hurdle, Dickey's mind began to churn, looking for ways to clear it.

The next morning, Chanderli opened the door with an air of satisfaction. "Back so soon?" he asked.

"If a reporter were to get to the front," she began her opening salvo, "how would you get him there?"

"It's never been done before," said Chanderli. "But, I have a plan. We'd have to smuggle them in."

Dickey's eyebrows arched as she listened to his proposition. It was illegal for journalists to enter Algeria without the permission of Algeria's French government. As Chanderli explained, "The last journalist we tried to get through was imprisoned and sentenced to death. We broke him out, of course. But we might not have such an opportunity next time."

Plausible deniability for the reporter was therefore imperative. Chanderli proposed the reporter be kidnapped by FLN sympathizers in Madrid, transported to Morocco, then passed through the Algerian underground until arriving at the foothills of the Atlas Mountains on the border of the Sahara Desert. where the main forces of the FLN made their stand.

"I see," said Dickey, leaning back in her chair. "So what you really need is a guinea pig with no dependents, no commitments, little backing and a positive taste for being a kidnapee."

"Indeed," said Chanderli, looking amused.

Dickey rolled a cigarette between her thumb and forefinger and took a deep breath. "I know a member of the US press who might meet the description."

Chanderli leaned forward with a broad smile. He had heard about her refusal to give her communist jailers any information about the resistance even while under intense interrogation. "Did you really think I meant to turn you down?" he said.

THE FLIGHT FROM New York City to Madrid seemed both interminably long and altogether too short. On one hand, part of Dickey still dreaded the thought of embarking on another exceptionally dangerous assignment. She'd been imprisoned in Budapest not seven months ago and here she was, entrusting her life to soldiers she didn't know fighting for a cause she was not yet certain of. But it was too late to turn back now.

Soon after landing in Madrid, a group of Algerian rebels "surprised" Dickey, blindfolding and bundling her into the back of a truck. She played the part, putting up enough of a struggle to make it look like a real kidnapping. She recorded only the vaguest details of her bumpy trip to the Mediterranean in order to protect the identity of her escorts, but it's likely they drove to Gibraltar, where she was then disguised as a German tourist and loaded onto a World War II–era DC-3 propeller plane to Tétouan, Morocco.

Above the roar of the engines, Dickey listened to her supposed kidnappers talk about their struggle. They spoke "pure revolution," she recalled in her journal. "The French have become too rich," said one. "They eat while we starve and play while we die," said another. "Surely justice is on our side. Their jails are full—50,000 of us. Five hundred thousand are dead, and who can count those held in the camps?" Their words ricocheted around the cabin as Dickey scribbled furiously. Neither she nor the rest of the world had heard these opinions, these stories, these voices that all pointed directly to a well-hidden but full-blown war of independence.

That night, a man who introduced himself only as Ali met her in the hotel lobby and loaded her bags in the trunk of his car. She got in without comment, having learned that when dealing with an underground militia, it's best not to ask too many questions. But it was a long drive, and as the desert passed by hour after hour, Ali began confiding in Dickey about times before the war. Educated in France and a scientist by profession, Ali's background was "no less Western than my own," as Dickey wrote. The French government's perpetually broken promises of reform coupled with its systematic practices of violent repression catalyzed his change in profession, as it had for many Algerians. Ali was an arms smuggler now, and apparently, it suited him. He cheerfully boasted to Dickey that he'd become so effective that the French placed a $20,000 bounty on his head.

The sun came up as they entered a Moroccan village that seemed to arise from nowhere. It had rained recently. Their tires slipped and spun on the muddy roads. Even so, Ali drove like he had been there a hundred times before, effortlessly navigating the unmarked streets to a building with an improbable sign simply reading, HÔTEL.

The clerk showed them to Dickey's room by the light of an oil lamp that made Ali's face look even more ashen with fatigue than her own. He stopped short of the door's threshold and turned back to Dickey. She was to expect him at eight in the morning. "Be ready to leave at once," he said, then disappeared into the dark hallway.

At 10 A.M. Ali had yet to return. Dickey's mind raced with thoughts of his arrest or even execution. Nor did it escape her that without him, she was stranded without contacts or even a working knowledge of the language. She took a dog-eared deck of playing cards out of her suitcase, shuffled, and compulsively dealt game after game of solitaire. She cursed when she won her fifth game in a row. So many coincidences had to be a bad omen. She kept playing nervously until she heard voices coming from the sidewalk outside. But rather than Arabic, she heard French.

Sidling up to the window, she risked a long glance through the shutters. White soldiers with submachine guns casually slung over their shoulders crowded the sidewalk below. Trucks and jeeps bearing the French flag came and went from the building adjacent to the hotel. Dickey knew Morocco allowed the French to maintain military bases within its borders. But she had no idea that Ali would be so brazen as to have her sleep next to the enemy. She didn't know whether to be annoyed, angry, or impressed.

Retreating, she went back to her cards (and kept winning) until a soft knock at noon startled her. She watched with relief as Ali slipped in the door, slightly out of breath.

"I am sorry I am so late," he said. "But we have to change the route for you. We think the French expected you in the place we were going." He unholstered his Colt .45 and checked the clip. It was full. "How was your breakfast?" he asked.

"I haven't eaten."

"You deserve a good lunch. Come on." He took her to a nearby café with white tablecloths, fresh-cut flowers, and a dining room crowded with French soldiers. Dickey shot furtive glances around the room, certain one of these soldiers, all of whom wanted Ali dead, would recognize him. When she said as much in a low whisper, Ali shrugged and coolly replied, "It is the best place to eat in town."

Afterward, they drove to where a French convoy was departing for Algeria. The officer who had sat at the table adjoining theirs at lunch rode shotgun in the lead jeep. Again to Dickey's amazement, Ali seemed unfazed. After the last of the French departed, another sedan pulled alongside them. Ali exchanged a few words with the driver, then transferred Dickey's bags.

"You will go with him now. Good luck and bon courage."

Far more stoic than Ali, her new guide drove in total silence to a sympathizer's house in a town just shy of the Morocco-Algeria border.

That evening, her host led her through the courtyard, one wall of which was stacked from top to bottom with enormous crates stenciled with the words GUNPOWDER SECOND GRADE 50 KILO. Dickey quickly counted seven across and five high. Almost two tons, more than enough to blow up the entire compound and the city block surrounding it.

"If the French come," said her host, noticing her gaze, "we'd sooner blow it up than be captured." He ushered her through an arched doorway. Six men sat cross-legged on the carpet, each with a gun on their belt or resting on the floor beside them. All looked to be in their twenties.

"It is very dangerous for you to be here, with the French around," said their translator. Dickey counted the loaded weapons in the room and silently agreed, though for different reasons. But it would be fine. She had been around armed young men before.

She let out a deep breath, then took out her notebook and calmly asked each of the men why they had joined the FLN.

Before the war, three of them had been studying in France and the other three working in Algeria. At the time, the French government promised true reform and full citizenship for Algerians, including the right to vote. But when the Europeans living in Algeria staged violent protests to demand the pledge be repealed, the government acquiesced. An organized movement of Algerians revolted and angry mobs followed close behind. The French military reprisal was equally swift and even more brutal.

Each man in the circle was the last surviving member of his family. The rest had been killed by French soldiers in their campaign of repression and revenge. Of course they signed up to fight.

By now Dickey and the soldiers had exchanged cigarettes, a diplomatic gesture that seemed universal among fighting men. Tea was poured and the air started to assume the chill of night. Their stories were undeniable and tragic. But Dickey knew what Americans would think, what they always thought regardless of the atrocities visited upon the downtrodden by the powerful.

She looked around the circle and asked them outright: "Are you a terrorist?"

"Yes," said one.

"Against terror one uses terror," said the next.

"I am a counter-terrorist," replied a third.

The next morning before dawn, another guide arrived to take her the rest of the way on horseback. The soldiers' answers rang in her ears as the sun rose. She had not yet considered that the French might be using terror against the Algerians. Surely, she had assumed, they would abide by the Geneva Conventions they had been so instrumental in bringing about after World War II.

It took three days of traveling on foot, horse, and mule to reach the foothills of the Atlas Mountains where the FLN's Scorpion Battalion waited for her. She'd read about these men in Chanderli's file. Famed for blowing up more French train tracks than any other unit, they were the closest thing the FLN had to an elite force. With their leather-tanned skin and wild beards, they looked the part.

Their commander greeted Dickey warmly, chuckling about the lengths she had taken to get here. "I've never known anyone who worked so hard to do their job," he said. "But we must hurry. There's a full moon tonight. The French will be able to see us if we don't set out."

The setting sun painted the mountainsides with the deep shadows of desert twilight. "One was so long," wrote Dickey, "that I climbed for minutes in its blackness." With the light playing tricks, it was hard to tell how long their ascent would take, and Dickey didn't want to betray her fear by asking. But the nights spent half sleeping in the back of cars, desert-town hotels, and Bedouin tents were catching up with her. She tried to distract herself with visions of the cataclysmic upheavals that gave rise to the jagged and sublime landscape of the Atlas Mountains. Night soon enveloped even the tallest peaks.

Dickey could feel her legs giving out beneath her. She stepped out of line and didn't get far, collapsing behind a flat rock jutting from the side of the trail. Her chest heaved and her mind spun with the fear that she couldn't make it. The same terror that had gripped her in the frozen Hungarian tundra came over her in this Algerian desert. The threat was as real. As one of her Algerian guides told her, if the French found her, "They'll cut your throat. But first they'll face you toward Mecca and then say we did it."

Trying to conjure the will to get back in line, she didn't notice the soldier standing above her. She recognized his face and broad mustache as Felga, the first Algerian infantryman she'd met at the bottom of the hill.

"Missy?" he said, holding out his hand.

She accepted gratefully, giving him half of her weight as they made the rest of the climb. It was another hour before they reached the Scorpion Battalion's base. Felga disappeared into the darkness as she whispered her thanks. Laying her horsehair blanket over the rock floor of a cave, she fell into a dreamless sleep. The aroma of Turkish coffee woke her at dawn.

With her legs slung over a cliff, coffee in one hand and camera in the other, she surveyed how far they had come. She couldn't help feeling a little proud she had climbed yet another hill, albeit with a little help. Then, anxious voices sounded through the camp.

"L'avion! L'avion!" *Airplane,* they yelled, their cries punctuated with the unmistakable hum of an approaching twin engine. Just a week earlier the French spent ten hours flattening a nearby peak with bombs, rockets, and napalm.

Just as she had aboard the *Samaritan* and *Relief,* Dickey looked for a spot that would give her both cover and a decent angle for photos. She found one beneath a thick rock jutting out over the cliff. Peeking her lens out, she spotted the plane veering directly for their position. Its silhouette came into focus. She recognized it immediately as a B-26, the Martin Marauder, built in Baltimore, Maryland, and used to great effect against Nazi-occupied France during World War II. She snapped her lens and wound the film forward as fast as she could, not quite believing that the French would bomb those demanding the same freedom that this plane had once defended. It seemed incomprehensible. Yet there it was, captured on film in black-and-white.

Twice it passed over their position. Dickey expected to see one of its bombs tumbling through the clear blue sky at any second. But the camp had concealed itself well. The pilot swung right. When the sound of his engines disappeared in the distance, the soldiers emerged from their hiding places and popped their guns off like celebratory champagne corks. They had lived to fight another day.

But then came the sound of a deep and distant roar. The camp's cook, a gray-bearded veteran of both world wars, squinted up from his rack of lamb roasting over brushfire. "Four rockets and a 100-pound bomb," he announced.

"Later in the day," wrote Dickey, "a runner confirms the report. The victims were a group of shepherds tenting in the valley beyond us here. They are eighteen dead. One of these was the tribal elder's baby son."

The commander arranged for horses to take her to the scene there the next morning. Having tented with Bedouins on her way to the Atlas Mountains, she had an idea of what to expect. A nomadic people, the Bedouins had few possessions and could move to new grazing lands at a moment's notice. Developed over thousands of years, this strategy made them adept at surviving the harsh conditions of the region, but it could not protect them from modern warfare. She imagined the situation would be bleak.

But the worst she could picture paled in comparison to reality. A full third of this tribe had been killed, and a good many more injured. Their tents were burned to ash in the conflagration of rockets, leaving them vulnerable to the desert's scorching days and freezing nights. All but eighty of their fifteen hundred sheep had been wiped out, ensuring many of the survivors would go hungry if not starve. Dickey carefully noted the losses in her journal, knowing full well her report would be the only place in the Western world where their losses would be recorded.

DEAD
> 6 old men
> 3 boys
> 9 women

WOUNDED
> 3 old women
> 2 men
> 7 children

She had come to expect such atrocities from communists. They were the enemy who sought to rob the world of its birthright of freedom and self-determination. Now, here, she had found that the French, one of America's staunchest allies, had murdered defenseless civilians. Yet more horrifying, America, her America, had supplied the murder weapons.

"What justification," she scrawled furiously in her spiral-bound notebook that night, "can there be for using rockets fired from a fighter plane on shepherds in the desert?"

Dickey's articles and photographs on Algeria were unlike any that had or would come out of the country by a Western reporter. She compared the Algerian desire for independence to that of American revolutionaries. While other reporters dismissed the FLN as either foolish ideologues or dangerous extremists, Dickey sympathetically outlined the conditions that gave rise to the rebellion.

"The anguish of Algeria is real," she wrote in one article. "The Algerians are not criminals or communists or primitives; there are ten million of them and they are a people being united by civil war, and after a month underground with them, to me, they are a nation."

She unflinchingly described the brutal slaughter of civilians, including children who had been bayoneted in the back by French soldiers. She exposed French tactics of forcing Algerians to inform on their own countrymen and using civilians to test the terrain for land mines. She dredged up France's history of torturing and mistreating those over whom they ruled. And her photographs served as unimpeachable evidence for anyone who doubted her words.

She even criticized her own government for its complicity. In her article "A Hill Is to Climb" for *Pageant* magazine, she quoted an FLN lieutenant as saying, "You know, your country is really my country's chief enemy. Not France, for we can bleed France white. But always America revives her with arms and money when she would faint without them." The article was accompanied by a photo of an unexploded bomb discovered near the decimated Bedouin village. The markings on its fins unmistakably identified it as made in America. That Dickey published this piece of political analysis running counter to her government's position was nothing short of subversive. That she wrote it about a faction accused of Soviet ties during the quickly escalating Cold War was a radical act.

But most of all in Algeria, she saw the American ideals, her ideals, vanishing beneath the brutal grays of the burgeoning Cold War. And she saw that even for all her patriotism—precisely because of her patriotism—she could not subscribe to this aspect of American foreign policy. Though Dickey held fast to the belief that her nation's better angels would one day prevail, she knew for now she had to find a new home for her loyalties. One that did not exist within proscribed borders but that resided with those, regardless of nationality or religion, who fought for the freedom that she cherished now, more than ever. In that moment, the cause of freedom fighters around the world became her cause. As their wars for independence continued to erupt around the world, Dickey made it her life's mission to be the first to the front, time and again.

23

Becoming a Perpetual
Motion Machine

RUNNING IN LOCAL newspapers around the country, Dickey's coverage of the Algerian War fomented her reputation as a "bayonet border correspondent," as one editor called her. Meanwhile, she continued to send out her personal story of resisting communism while in Fö Street Prison until finally, in November 1957, *Reader's Digest* accepted her essay "Nobody Owes Me a Christmas."

The article painted a moralistic veneer over her experience with its climax on Christmas Day when she received double her usual dinner portion. "Somewhere hidden in this monstrous world," she wrote in summation, "in the heart of one cook or one warder or one guard—the spirit of Christmas still lived. . . . Christmas, even here, was bigger than communism." But even this sanitized version conveyed, at least in part, the truth, heroism, and horror of her story to millions of readers. More, it expressed Dickey's unyielding belief in the power of empathy, the possibility for human connection even in the frozen hell of Fö Street Prison.

Reader's Digest received a slew of laudatory notes about Dickey's article. Undeniably, she had an audience. In the years to come, the *Digest* would become her most consistent publisher. They needed a reporter who would risk anything and go anywhere to report on the Cold War's numerous fronts. She needed a publication willing to send her where she was hankering to go. They cemented this pact of mutual benefit soon enough. Even so, one stumbling block remained in her path: her Department of Defense credentials to cover American troops overseas were still re-voked from her time on Okinawa. But this too soon fell by the wayside when her growing fame as a fierce patriot, combined with their own des-perate need for positive coverage, finally convinced the DOD to reissue Dickey's credentials. In October 1957, with contracts from *Reader's Di-gest* as well as the Spadea News Syndicate, Dickey took off from Idlewild Airport on her way to cover the Navy's Sixth Fleet in the Mediterranean.

It took twenty hours to get there, first by commercial jet to Rabat, Morocco, then by military transport to Naples, and finally a propeller ferry plane that blew a tire upon touching down on the USS *Franklin D. Roosevelt* aircraft carrier. Dickey held her breath and reinvested her faith in the pilot who managed to keep them out of the turquoise sea.

Composed of sixty warships spread over an area the size of New York State, the Sixth Fleet was far from a peaceful Aegean cruise. Much had been made of its numerous deployments to Egypt, Lebanon, and Libya as a deterrent to Soviet activities in the region. Less well known was the Sixth Fleet's function as a mobile nuclear launch base. Lacking a fixed position, it would be that much more difficult to destroy in the advent of nuclear war, thereby giving the United States the upper hand, if only by remnants. The full capabilities of this fleet had only just been declassified, and upon landing, Dickey became the first woman, and only the second reporter, to be granted permission to cover its opera-tions. What's more, she had been given permission to fly aboard one of its nuclear bomber jets for a test run—again, the first woman to do so.

During her nine days with the fleet, Dickey visited as many of the ships as she could, traveling between them by ferry plane, helicopter, and with old-fashioned flair on a boatswain's chair tied to a high-line. She explained this last means for transport to her aunts with characteristic mirth: "A high-line, kids, is a piece of rope from the upper deck of one warship across 100 feet of roiling water to the upper deck of another warship when both of them are moving about 15 miles an hour. From the piece of rope they had a chair in which sits the person wanting to get from one ship to the other and then the chair is moved, by sailors hand-hauling on one ship, over to the other across the water. I've now done eight such crossings between carriers, 2 destroyers, and a missile cruiser." In a nod to her grandmother, she added, "Remember Grammy always wanted to be a ballet dancer or a tight-rope artist?" Certainly Dickey thought of the woman who had first dared her to dream as she swung her legs above the blue sea.

Much as she had on the USS *Santa Marta* on her way down to Panama, she crafted her story by talking to as many of the crew as she could, regardless of their rank or station. On flight decks she interviewed the men who caught planes as they came in to land. "For sheer drama, no task I've ever covered can equal this man's," she jotted down in her notes. "Once every 40 seconds, a fire spewing monster roaring like the dragons of nightmares and weighing anything up to 35 tons comes directly at you, moving 125 miles an hour. It grows bigger, roars louder, spews lethal red exhaust, can't possibly miss you—it passes 15 feet away, catching its tail hook on an arresting wire and with a bone-crunching, spark-showering impact, becomes just another plane landed on the carrier deck."

Taking off proved even more complex, as Dickey learned from the sailors responsible for launching jets off the deck and into the blue. Since the airstrip on a carrier is far too short for a jet to gain enough speed on its own, they had to be catapulted, quite literally, in order to get airborne. This process began in an engineering room where a technician poised his hands on the handle of two enormous steam pistons that were attached to two metal lugs that protruded through the flight deck. These were in turn connected to a small shuttle, itself connected to a towbar that was then fastened on the underside of the plane's fuselage. For all the high-tech mechanization involved, two men performed this last step by crawling on their stomachs beneath a plane after it was in position and while its engines spewed burning jet fuel inches above their heads. Finally, on a catwalk at the edge of the flight deck, an invariably young lieutenant triple-checked the equipment before signaling the technician below to pull the handle and launch the plane.

Having interviewed each and every member of several catapult teams, Dickey felt she had a pretty good grasp of what was in store for her as she climbed the ladder of a largely nondescript jet differentiated from all the others only by the numbers 303 painted on its nose. She was wrong.

The pilot taxied into catapult position. The men below affixed the towbar.

"All clear," said the young lieutenant on the catwalk.

"Ready for takeoff," said the pilot.

"Impact sound and color instantly were gone inside the plane," wrote Dickey. "One thousand one," she counted. Her seat, the cockpit, the plane ceased to be tangible and only the invisible air had weight as she felt her organs being pushed toward her spine. "One thousand two." Shades of gray replaced color as the blood rushed away from her eyes. "One thousand three."

The moments stretched out into an eternity. Her teenage flight in a Grumman F3F at 9 Gs seemed like an amusement park ride.

Then a tiny clang as the catapult released the plane. The sky was blue again. Dickey dug into her flight suit to find her notepad and pencil and began to write.

More than just a test flight, this was a practice run for a nuclear attack. Traveling at 657 miles per hour, about half the engine's capacity by Dickey's estimation, they made it to the test site somewhere around Athens in just a few minutes. Rather than a missile, the plane dropped radar pings picked up by equipment below that measured for accuracy. The strange ease of it all unnerved her. The men appeared to be doing hardly anything at all and yet they were staging a dress rehearsal for the apocalypse. The era of the push-button war had arrived, and suddenly Dickey realized how very much the world had changed since the war. "For a minute, I felt I'd outlived Methuselah and I guess I should have felt that way. None of the men in the plane were old enough to have lived for years out of a truck in destroyed cities," she wrote, recalling her time in Europe's bombed-out capitals.

As they passed back over Athens, Dickey could not help but imagine a mushroom cloud enveloping the ancient city. The thought made her sick. But her aversion was no longer without qualification. She had started to think of nuclear weapons as a necessary deterrent in the struggle for power between the United States and the Soviet Union. Though she never condoned, supported, or advocated for their use, she no longer considered them wholly unnecessary and immoral. This shift in her thinking marked the first of many moments when Dickey bent her once rigid code of ethics.

After finishing her coverage, she received a letter from the fleet's admiral at her hotel. "It was a real shot in the arm having you around," he wrote, then invited her to join him again, anytime. She had come a long way from being marched off Okinawa at gunpoint.

Now, her editor at the *Digest* had telegrammed her to say that they were sending her on another assignment, this time to Turkey. No stranger to conflict with Russia, the Turks had brought their centuries-old conflict into the twentieth century with a recent purchase of bomber jets, tanks, and heavy artillery from the United States. *Reader's Digest* wanted Dickey to visit a few of their bases to get the latest.

Christmas Eve found her holed up in Ankara finishing her Sixth Fleet copy until 4 A.M. in front of her hotel room's fireplace. Dropping it with the front desk to be mailed, she caught the 8 A.M. train to an air base in Eskişehir on Christmas Day, where its officers impressed her both with their hospitality and soldiering. They were equally taken with her as not only the first female reporter, but the first journalist in modern times to visit their base.

Nostalgia washed over her when she saw her ride to her next assignment in Bandirma—a World War II–era DC-3 transport plane. Shortly after they thundered into takeoff, two enlisted men got out their accordion and clarinet. Dickey and her fellow passengers jitterbugged amid the cargo crates for the entire flight. "I was in tears—from laughter—when we landed," she wrote home. "Who needs language?"

Practically in the shadow of Mount Ararat, the base was Turkey's closest to its border with the Soviet Bloc. As such, the air force concentrated the majority of its fighter jets here. They let her fly in a few, just for fun. By then her reputation had begun circulating among the ranks. When an officer found out she had been in a communist prison last New Year's Eve, he arranged for her to patrol Turkey's border with Bulgaria, supplying her with three brigades, a pack of dogs, and an armory's worth of semiautomatic rifle ammo.

Just before dawn, they marched back to the command post. "The Turkish soldiers held a concert for me by the light of two kerosene lamps," she wrote, "singing without accompaniment, one by one, of death and glory . . . No music has moved me like that, before or since."

Back in her New York City shoebox apartment, Dickey pounded on her typewriter until her fingers ached. Hobe Lewis, her editor at *Reader's Digest*, had sent back both her articles at the same time. *Pageant*, a large-format monthly magazine, had made last-minute changes to her piece "Now I Know Why the Algerians Fight." She was enormously content and, by the end of February, so were her editors.

Coming out from the haze of cigarettes, long days, and late nights, Dickey found she had nothing set up for the spring. No writing assignments, anyway. Rent was due, not to mention taxes were coming up, always the bane of her existence. She never seemed to put enough aside without some serious belt-tightening come April. But she had an offer from the University of Minnesota to go on a lecture tour through America's heartland. At a hundred dollars a stop, she could hardly refuse.

She rented a puke-pink Cadillac for a discount and left the city in mid-March. The road suited her just fine at first. She didn't mind being solo. Besides, she enjoyed talking to high schoolers, church congregants, service organizations, and social clubs about her time with Algerian rebels and Turkish infantrymen, her experiences surviving a communist jail, and flying in the Sixth Fleet's bomber jets. "As far as I can figure," she wrote to Stevie, who was working as her assistant, "I am now a traveling salesman for Freedom of the Press." It was a job for which she was well suited and well received.

She turned forty on the road and didn't mark the occasion. After winter's thaw came the early spring deluges of April over the Plains states. Dickey headed back to New York where she had television and radio appearances scheduled. Stevie hired a maid to clean her apartment before she arrived. Dickey ordered lamb chops to be delivered from the butcher shop as a belated birthday dinner for herself. The woman on the other end of the line recognized Dickey's voice as soon as she said hello. She had been patronizing the same butcher for years, long enough to watch the oldest son replace the father behind the counter, long enough to know they were Cuban, and long enough for them to know she was a reporter of revolutions. The buzzer rang, a knock on the door. Rather than the delivery boy, the butcher stood at the threshold, holding her order, wearing his bloody smock.

"Why haven't you been to cover Fidel Castro?" he asked without preamble.

"Because I don't know any of Castro's people," she replied.

"I thought it might be that," he replied. "Go to Bab's Luncheonette on MacDougal at ten o'clock on Friday morning. Sit on the third stool from the end. You'll meet them."

He left. She fried the chops, rare.

That Friday at Bab's third stool from the left at precisely 10 A.M. a blond man in his thirties paid her 45-cent check and handed her a thick manila envelope. Dickey accepted it without expression, then ran to get the subway back to her apartment. Inside the envelope were dozens of translated articles from *Bohemia*, a Cuban magazine and one of the only publications covering Cuba's ongoing civil war. As she had after reading Chanderli's dossier on the Algerian rebels, Dickey immediately wanted to cover the Cubans' fight against tyranny.

PART IV

. . . .

24

Cuba

MORE THAN ANYTHING, Dickey searched for hope as she looked toward Cuba. The revolutions she had covered were in disarray, with Algeria still embroiled in a fierce civil war and Hungary squarely beneath the thumb of a communist dictator. But ninety miles off the coast of Florida, she thought she saw an authentic folk hero in Fidel Castro and believed he might be a George Washington for his people.

While her contacts finished her travel arrangements, Dickey spent a few days in Miami gathering information about the state of the war at the Cuban underground's office, located, ironically, in the same downtown skyscraper where she had worked as a teenager for the Miami Airshow.

Back in 1939 Fulgencio Batista had not been in office when she visited Cuba as a tyro reporter. But he was the man behind the throne, initially engineering a military coup in 1933, then orchestrating a string of puppet presidents before occupying the position himself in 1940, when his despotism kicked into high gear. While Cubans starved, he amassed a personal fortune of approximately $300 million, or about $6 billion in today's currency. When newspapers began to expose his corruption, he shut down their printing presses. When the people began to object, he built a secret police force to abduct, torture, and kill suspected dissidents. By the time Dickey planned her trip, almost every police station in Cuba's major cities had its own torture chamber. In 1957 alone an estimated twenty thousand citizens were murdered by their government.

In Miami, Dickey interviewed those who had managed to escape this campaign of terror. Their scars and open wounds, stilted words, and frightening silences recalled those of the Hungarian refugees she had interviewed in Austria. Her experience in Fö Street Prison dispelled the myth that her citizenship would spare her the worst if she were captured.

She knew America bore its own culpability in the horrific pain inflicted by the Batista regime. The United States had backed him for decades, selling him guns, planes, and tanks while turning a blind eye as he waged a war against his fellow Cubans. All the while, Batista made sure there was nothing to see should America ever turn its good eye his way. Like the French in Algeria, Batista cloaked himself behind a press blackout. He killed domestic journalists who dared lift a pen against him and dropped a dragnet across the island's airports that had so far kept out all but nine foreign reporters. Without information, without the truth, there was little hope of shedding light on these atrocities or of convincing the American people that their government should cut off any and all military aid to the Batista regime. In every sense, Dickey felt it was her duty as an American journalist to report on the Cuban revolutionaries.

That, and she hated dictators. The thought of playing a part in Batista's demise made her heart race with giddy anticipation. Afraid but undeterred, she boarded her plane to Havana.

Getting this far was easy enough since the war had not yet reached Cuba's resort city of casinos and white-sand beaches. To explain her camera equipment, she simply claimed to be a portrait photographer. But now came the hard part. She had to get to Santiago de Cuba on the opposite end of the island in the Oriente Province where the two armies had centered the bulk of their forces.

Since the underground could not secure her overland route, Dickey had to fly into Santiago's airport and right into the police's blockade where her bags would undoubtedly be searched. The camera and Marine trench knife in her luggage would be viewed as irrefutable proof of her profession as a reporter and earn her a one-way ticket back to Miami enforced at gunpoint. Her contacts insisted she turn them over for safekeeping and promised to return them before she crossed into Castro's territory.

Though unburdened of damning evidence, she still needed a cover for her presence in Santiago. Unlike Havana, the city lacked the tourist attractions that would otherwise give her a reason to visit. It did however have one location that might provide a believable excuse: the Guantanamo Bay Naval Base where the United States stationed thousands of Marines and sailors. Dickey turned to her imagination for the rest.

Slipping a photo of a young Marine into her wallet, she boarded the plane in a shirtwaist dress with spike heels and hoop earrings to finish the look. The flight lasted barely an hour. Dickey tried to breathe deeply as they deplaned and act calm as a police officer began to search her bags.

"You say you are a tourist?" he snapped, angrily closing her luggage, having found nothing out of the ordinary.

Dickey nodded.

"How can that be?" he said. "There is nothing for visitors here. The city is encircled by the bandits. We do not even have enough to eat. You cannot be a tourist here."

Dickey batted her eyes. She had practiced for this in the mirror of her hotel bathroom. "You see officer," she half whispered, "I'm trying to evade the authorities."

"Evade the authorities?" he repeated, incredulous.

"American authorities don't want Marine wives in the vicinity of the Guantanamo Naval Base," she replied, surreptitiously opening her sequined wallet to the picture of the Marine.

The police officer grabbed her left hand. "But you don't have a ring," he said.

"Well," said Dickey coquettishly, "we're *going* to be married."

The officer let go of her hand. "Incredibly," Dickey recalled, "he was smiling."

"Okay, go ahead," he winked and waved her into Santiago. Part of her could not believe her ploy had succeeded. Most of her was not surprised.

While she waited for the final go-ahead, the underground arranged for her to stay in Santiago's only hotel that could boast luxury amenities like hot water and electricity. She passed the time making notes on what she had seen so far while waiting impatiently for her camera and trench knife to show up. But on the day she was scheduled to cross over to Castro's side, it became clear her belongings had been appropriated in the service of the revolution. In the grand scheme of things, she could care less about the camera. But her trench knife could not be replaced.

Unable to fault a guerrilla soldier for taking a weapon, the significance of which he could not have surmised, she blamed herself for relinquishing it in the first place. Still, she had to go on now. In the few hours she had left in Santiago, Dickey scraped up enough parts to Frankenstein together a workable camera and found a few rolls of film gathering dust in the back of a drugstore.

That afternoon, a young woman of no more than twenty met her in front of her hotel, walked her across the golf course and onto the front lines of the Cuban Revolution. It was not long before she heard the sound of bullets.

Around the bend of a mountain road, the courier deposited her with Captain José Valla, a traffic clerk turned rebel. But as Dickey would find, Castro's army was made of men and women from all walks of life. When she arrived, Valla's troops were busy making the last touches on what Dickey described as "a textbook ambush site" for her article "How Castro Won" in the *Marine Corps Gazette*. Steep ridges lined a nearly mile-long horseshoe of asphalt. Some soldiers hacked machine-gun blinds out of the jungle on either end. Others laid the last of several 200-pound homemade land mines packed with explosives salvaged from undetonated aerial bombs. Valla told Dickey they had been working for thirteen days. Their intelligence had it that the government, or Batistiano army, would be passing through later that day, and their intelligence never failed. She soon found out why.

Made up of villagers and farmers, teachers and grocers, parents and children, the revolution's ad hoc spy network reported every move made by the Batistianos. As Dickey described it in the same article using the military's sometimes coarse parlance, "The Batista commanders could not go to the 'head' without a perspiring runner arriving a few minutes later to tell Castro about it." Their collective ire and motivation stemmed from the regime's terror campaign. Dickey saw evidence of this herself in two communities that had been completely destroyed by napalm. Since Batista claimed to bomb only rebel camps with these incendiary bombs, Dickey dug through the charred remains of barns and houses to find and photograph proof otherwise: the telltale aluminum containers in which napalm is air-dropped. The Batista regime reaped what it had sown and Castro's army knew where and when the government planned to strike before they had even left camp.

Just before noon, the enemy column rolled into view with a lead jeep, four armored cars, two tanks, and three buses loaded with soldiers. Dickey crawled into a blind with Valla as two B-26s began flying figure eights along the road. Spooked or eager, the rebel's advance guard opened fire before Valla gave the order.

Still, they had the element of surprise on their side and managed to halt the entire convoy in a few bursts. But the counterattack came soon enough while the B-26s laid into the mountainside from above. Some rebels turned their guns skyward while others continued to concentrate on the armored vehicles. Then, to Dickey's amazement, the battle turned on a dime. The government troops began to flee en masse. The tanks, the armored cars, and the two buses that had not been destroyed sped back down the mountain. Even the B-26s retreated toward the horizon. Valla was furious.

"My orders were that you should fire and withdraw, *fire and withdraw!*" he shouted at his lieutenant, whose face grew red with embarrassment.

"We would have, Captain, but we had no cover from the B-26 and—" the lieutenant began before being cut off.

"If you had done what I told you to do, we would have captured the whole convoy. Now all we have is two wrecks and some blood on the Central Highway! And that is all there is to show for thirteen days waiting!"

At first, Dickey could not understand Valla's ire. After all, they had decisively won the battle without losing a single soldier. But she soon understood that to win the war, the rebel army engaged the enemy not only for territory but also for weapons. With limited funds and an arms embargo, necessity required that the vast majority of the rebel's arms be requisitioned from government forces either in battle or night raids. "The weapons which I saw," she wrote in her analysis for the *Marine Corps Gazette,* "were not new, and the great majority were of the type which we furnished to Batista—Springfields, M-1s, BARs, and Tommy Guns. And Colt .45 automatics, many of the latter demonstrably captured weapons with buttplates still carrying the insignia of the Cuban Army." She estimated that only 15 percent of the rebels' armory had been purchased new. Had Valla's ambush succeeded in the way he had planned, they would have added multiple combat vehicles and at least a hundred semiautomatic rifles to their armory. Not to mention any other light artillery they were carrying. In this light, the battle had been a complete and utter catastrophe.

But more than the dictator's army, rebel soldiers and villagers alike blamed the United States for the asymmetrical war they were forced to fight. "It was repeatedly emphasized to me," wrote Dickey in *Reader's Digest,* "that everyone, including myself, was being fired at by American weapons, and that US strictness toward arms smuggling prevented Castro from shooting back more effectively." This was particularly true in regard to the American-made B-26s that regularly strafed noncombatants. "The planes," she wrote for the *Marine Corps Gazette,* "no matter how badly flown, utterly terrorized the province and moral judgements entirely aside, the fact is that we are heartily hated because they caused such fear." As in Algeria, she could not ignore the evidence that her own country was propping up a repressive regime with weapons.

NIGHT FELL EARLY beneath the thick jungle canopy. Dickey thought back to her time in Panama's Darién Gap, though few parallels could be drawn other than the humidity. Whereas Darién Gap crawled with animals and insects that could kill a person where they stood, "Cuba," wrote Dickey, "has the kindest jungle in the world. Guerrillas or Boy Scouts or reporters can sleep where they grow tired anywhere along the trails. There is no dangerous snake or insect life, and the only wild game is a pygmy boar with an incurious disposition." After a hard morning's hike and an

afternoon of gunplay, she fell asleep easily in these cozy environs to a chorus of tree frogs and the sound of snoring guerrillas armed to the teeth.

It was time to move in the morning. Orders for more men came
from La Maya, a town three days' march away where the 26th of July
Army were in the middle of besieging one of Batista's last strongholds.
The soldiers carried no food with them, both to keep their packs light
and because there was little to be had. Instead, they lived off the land
and from those that would feed them. This meant they sometimes ate
well, and sometimes ate nothing. Most times, their food supply fell
somewhere in between. Dickey's experience at Fö Street Prison and
subsequent assignment with the FLN prepared her well. Over the
course of their march to La Maya, she ate one meal a day provided by
farmers.

They arrived in La Maya on a steely gray morning just as the streets
came alive with the sound of gunfire. Dickey leveled her viewfinder at
the men as they rubbed the sleep from their eyes and punched another
magazine into their assault rifles. It occurred to her that before the war
the town must have been "quiet and quaint," as she wrote in her notes.
A church lay at the end of the cobblestone main street lined with a few
cantinas, a pharmacy, and a general store. "Around this heart, a dozen
crooked streets bordered with houses that needed paint but did not
want for love or laughter. Now, La Maya had lost its national character.
I could have been anywhere in any war. It was just an infantry front, a
place where people had been trying to kill each other for so long that
they did not remember there was another way of life."

The soldiers eyed her with a combination of suspicion and bemuse-
ment as her escort led her to their daytime command post located in
a second-floor apartment with a veranda overlooking their primary
target: a garrison of fortified barracks at the edge of town where over
325 government soldiers along with 150 family members had retreated
after the rebels had taken the town. Major Antonio Lusson, whose long
black beard signaled he had been fighting with the rebels for years, welcomed her with a grunt. She recognized him immediately from the articles in *Bohemia* given to her by the underground in New York. He had
been childhood friends with Castro and an early adherent to his cause.
Since then, his exploits had made Lusson one of the most celebrated

commanders in the revolution. Neither he nor his men had once balked at running at tanks armed with only their Browning automatics and so far, they had taken the tanks every time. Dickey addressed him with respect and thanked him for welcoming her into his camp.

"Americana," he half scoffed. "Our people tell us there will be planes at nine o'clock."

Dickey lit a cigarette and looked at her watch. They had about an hour. The smell of food wafted up from the apartment below, reminding her how hungry she had become.

"Abuela Fernandez has something for us," said Lusson.

Dickey followed him down the stairs to what must have been a typical home before the war. A woman in her seventies with white hair and deeply tanned skin stood at the edge of the oilcloth-covered table, watching contentedly as soldiers served themselves the beef and rice she had set out for breakfast. Dickey noticed she had left her flowerpots out on her veranda. The paradoxical nature of guerrilla warfare never ceased to amaze her.

She ate, traded cigarettes with one of the soldiers, and had to admit his was far superior. Then, the sound of twin engines approaching from the west. The men put down their plates, picked up their guns, and rushed into position.

Two B-26s appeared in the sky. Dickey crouched beside Lusson against the second-floor veranda wall.

"They might hit a cow that way," he grumbled, "if the cow is careless."

But, spotting the concentration of men on the command post balcony, "they committed and thundered in, their wings showing continuous handsome winking pink flashes," as they unloaded their .50-caliber guns. Dickey focused her lens on their barrels pointed skyward.

"Five times the planes strafe in and over," wrote Dickey. "Five times the weapons, air and ground, seem to spit directly into each other's faces for long seconds. But the range is always too long and the speed too great and when we look around, no one has been hit." Even so, it did not escape the soldiers' attention that Dickey had neither hid nor cowered nor ran away but only held her hands steady as she photographed them. Finally, the B-26s disappeared.

"When they come back, Americana," said Lusson, "we'll get one for you."

But almost immediately his attention was taken away by a teenage runner with torn sandals and a shotgun. "Lanzamiento aéreo al cuartel," he panted. "Probablemente lo intentarán en media hora." *Airdrop to the barracks in half an hour.*

Wanting to photograph the drop, Dickey headed for what they referred to as "The House" where the majority of the rebel force was garrisoned. Machine guns talked to each other as she ducked from doorway to doorway. Two men seemed not to notice as they debated in the open about where to fire from during the next B-26 attack. One argued for the front porch of a burnt-out house. The other for a nearby foundation pit. But both their points were rendered moot as a bomber roared toward them not twenty feet off the ground with its machine-gun fire marching toward them double-time.

They dove through the House's doorway where a squad of six were firing through venetian blinds. The windows had long since been blown out. The sound of the twin engine grew louder as it circled back for another pass. Dickey found cover behind a large cabinet. Only later did she realize it contained the previous occupants' collection of crystal.

"The B-26 does not miss this time," wrote Dickey. "His shells tear out the supports of the veranda room at the front of the house and almost with a sigh, the porch roof folds down over the main door . . . bringing darkness and dust into the living room." They were blinded by darkness. The engines grew faint, but not for long. "Coughing, we move along a corridor toward the back rooms."

There were already more riflemen there, firing at the barracks through the seven slatted blinds. Then six, then five. For all the bullets going out no one noticed the incoming ones until a soldier sounded the alarm. The Batistianos had been using the window as a target. Everyone hit the floor and hustled on elbows into the next room, including Dickey.

Looking out onto no-man's-land, they saw the reason for the B-26's risky attack. It served as cover as the other plane unloaded its airdrop halfway between the two camps, but to no avail. Men in the blue-green fatigues of the rebel army were already dragging it back toward their command post. The men cheered and opened fire to give their comrades cover. Dickey hustled back down the main street to see what was inside.

She found Lusson supervising while his soldiers carefully unpacked its contents. He handed her one of the hundred or so packs of cigarettes. "The best I ever smoked," she jotted in her field notes. In addition, there were thousands of rounds of ammo, several boxes of medical supplies, and most importantly, a sack of the enemy's personal mail. He read through them until he found what he was looking for: a letter from the Batistiano captain's wife with a photo of their ten-year-old son. She is sick with worry, the letter said, and she begged him to leave the military.

Lusson refolded the letter and placed it back in the envelope with the photograph, then added a note of his own.

My dear captain: I have three sons I hope to see again some day myself. For the sake of our children, will you not reconsider my demands for your surrender?

Then he turned to Dickey. "You, Americana," he said, "didn't you say you might go to Batista's people so your readers would hear the story of their—ah, their resistance?"

"Yes, comandante," replied Dickey, "I did."

"Then you have my permission to go," he said and handed her the letter with his note.

He arranged for a cease-fire with the town's priest, who accompanied her across a no-man's-land pocked with shell holes and littered with bullets. They each held the corner of a white tablecloth for a flag of truce. The gates of the barracks swung open as they approached. A government soldier waved the priest into a room where Dickey glimpsed a portly man with a gold shield on his visor, whom she assumed to be the captain. The doors closed. She took a seat on a hand-carved wooden chair that looked like it was from the Spanish days. Minutes passed. Dickey smoked. Then the doors opened. The priest shook his head, which Dickey understood to mean she would not be granted an interview. With their tablecloth flag, they began to walk back.

But this time, the soldiers standing guard by the gate stopped the priest and began speaking too quickly for Dickey to catch a single word.

"No, no," said the priest, and removed two cigarettes from his lapel pocket.

The soldiers took them, smiled, and waved them on.

They were stopped twice more on their way back to no-man's-land. Each time the priest produced two more cigarettes before the soldiers waved them on. At the command post, Dickey asked Lusson to translate for the priest, who spoke no English.

"They were deciding whether to shoot you," he said. "I guess you are just lucky that they would rather have a cigarette than a reporter. Now," he said, "tell me, are they going to surrender today?"

"I don't think so," she replied. "Not today."

"I wouldn't either," he said.

LIKE CLOCKWORK, THE B-26s returned the next morning at nine. But this time they stayed too high to do any real damage or risk being shot down. The rebels emptied a couple clips into the blue just for show. After they flew off, Dickey went into the streets, trying to find the day's action. Scanning the soldiers in ragged uniforms carrying dusty weapons, she saw a mop of light-brown hair. No matter. She'd learned Cubans were some of the world's most ethnically diverse people. The man who'd handed her the dossier at Bab's had been blond and one of the rebels here had dark red hair. But his uniform gave her pause. USMC, it read across the arm. Could have been that a rebel soldier got hold of the uniform. Except for one thing: the wearer had hardly ten days' stubble in an army where the length of one's beard marked the length of one's service.

"Hey, Marine!" she yelled.

He turned to her and she saw a deep weariness in his eyes. "You must be from the press," he said casually. "I don't mean to be impolite, ma'am, but, drop dead."

Dickey paused. "I'll never write a word about you if you ask me not to," she said, "but I am dying to speak English to someone."

The Marine sighed. "So would I, ma'am. But not right now. I got to find some ammo," he said and kicked his boot toward a 20mm baby cannon.

"I think I know where some are," said Dickey, remembering a few rounds in the major's jeep.

"Jerry Holthaus," he introduced himself.

After retrieving three shells, he took her to the rebels' central defensive position, colloquially referred to as the Hole.

Centered in the foundation pit of a burnt-out house, the Hole looked directly onto the Batistiano army's strong point, a concrete blockhouse set back 150 yards from the compound's serrated walls. Serendipitously, the Hole jutted into the narrowest part of no-man's-land, which Dickey estimated to be no more than a hundred yards across. The rebels then dug a trench another dozen feet out with a sandbag embankment at the end of which stood another monument to guerrilla warfare's impossible juxtapositions: a full-length vanity mirror angled at 45 degrees toward the blockhouse that allowed them to aim without sticking their necks out, literally.

In terms of guerrilla warfare, the Hole provided as ideal a defensive position as one could ask for. The Batistianos treated it as such. "The Hole was incessantly under blockhouse fire," wrote Dickey, "and always it fired back. All my life I had heard how Latin Americans knock off their wars for daily siesta. But I knew now that the soldiers in the blockhouse and the rebels manning the Hole had never heard about it."

Even so, the Batistiano blockhouse was too far and too well fortified for the rebels' bullets to do anything other than wash the dirt off its walls. Thus Holthaus's haste to set up the baby cannon, which itself proved to be a complicated affair.

This piece of light artillery "originally came to Cuba in one of Batista's planes, or rather," she added, "US made planes delivered to the Cuban Air Force" on which it had been wing-mounted and fired electronically by pressing a button. Now, the cannon was mounted on a machine-gun tripod and fed homemade ammunition by hand. Horror and awe occupied Dickey equally as she watched Holthaus, along with a two-man volunteer crew, load and eyeball-aim this artless contraption that might prove more deadly to those who fired it than those who were fired upon.

In the end the baby cannon proved benign to all parties. A dozen rounds were dispatched, only to flame out nowhere near the target. Having expended most of their ammo, Holthaus and his crew gave up in favor of a more familiar weapon: rifle grenades. Each man in the Hole knew how to fire these. Yet again, Dickey couldn't believe the courage, or insanity, that it took to use them.

Packed with appropriated mining explosives, these handmade sheet metal cones with painted red tips were affixed onto a rifle barrel and then fired by lighting the fuse with a match. Dickey could hardly watch as grenade after grenade malingered on the rifle barrels after the fuse had expired only to rocket off at the last second and explode, impotently, halfway across no-man's-land.

When they had nearly expended their store, Lusson slid into the Hole, grabbed a rifle, loaded a grenade, and lit the fuse with his cigar. Like all the others, his exploded fifty yards out.

"Let's make a patrol," he said and ran, without cover, into no-man's-land. A dozen soldiers followed with their guns and Dickey with her camera. Midway across they dove into another foundation pit where Lusson opened up his machine gun on the blockhouse. The others soon followed suit. Only nominally closer, their rifles had no more effect on the structure than they had in the Hole. Dickey surmised that Lusson must have known this before setting out. But to be that much closer to the whites of their enemies' eyes boosted morale after the repeated failures of homemade ammunition. Dickey watched in wonder as the rebels pushed their heads and shoulders above ground to unload clip after clip.

After a sufficient number of bullets had been fired, Lusson signaled for them to fall back. While they had been out, another runner had dropped off a new piece of artillery wrapped in a flowered tablecloth. Lusson looked like a boy on Christmas morning when he unwrapped the World War II–era 57mm recoilless rifle with original, made-in-the-USA rounds—but only two. The task of firing it fell to Holthaus as the only one with any proper artillery training.

Unlike the rest of the weapons so far fired out of the Hole, the recoilless's size required that Holthaus stand with his head and torso above the embankment of sandbags long enough to fire, about a minute, more than enough time for the Batistianos to take aim. Dickey held her breath. Holthaus stood, eye to the site. "The flame, the noise, the smoke is shocking, tremendous," she wrote, "and the round fell short." Immediately the entire blockhouse started firing back at him, who looked unspeakably depressed. But, there was another round.

Summoning the remainder of his resolve, he loaded the last shell, checked his aim in the mirror, stood up, and adjusted the counterweight. The mirror burst into a thousand shards. He fired. Wide.

Dejected, Holthaus climbed out of the Hole. Twilight gathered. With all the pyrotechnics expended, Dickey followed him to a stone wall off the main street where they could sit and have a few smokes. By then, everyone had started to trust her, Holthaus included, and when Dickey asked, he told her the strange story of how he arrived to the rebel side. It started with a kidnapping.

In late summer of that year, Holthaus had been on guard duty at Guantanamo when Raúl Castro, Fidel Castro's younger brother, abducted him along with forty other Americans. As prisoners of a guerrilla army, they often had to live off the land, sleep in barns, and march for miles a day. But as a Marine, Holthaus was used to all this. Basic training had been far worse. Instead, he noticed that the hostages ate before their guards, that they were never mistreated, and they always had a roof over their heads while the soldiers often slept in the rain. This was not a typical POW experience.

After a few days, Holthaus started to ask questions about why they were fighting. "They told Jerry of 250 suspected rebels whose bodies were bulldozed into a mass grave near Cienfuegos," Dickey wrote, "about the 21 bodies of suspects (never tried) left in the streets of Holguin nearby in one 24-hour period; about the teen-ager who died in Santiago with long nails driven through his forehead. Finally they made sure he knew about the boy who had been castrated when caught while serving as a runner for them."

Three weeks later, Raúl returned all the hostages unharmed. His point had been to show America that Batista could not protect even its citizens against the 26th of July Army, not to harm anyone. Back at Guantanamo, Holthaus returned to his duties and said little about the event. He gave no indication that he had been swayed toward the rebels' side. But then, on the day before Thanksgiving, just after midnight, he hopped Guantanamo base's forty-foot chain-link fence and disappeared into the night to join Castro's forces.

"I'm no kid," he told Dickey, "I mean I'm over 21 and I took a couple months to think about it. I still think I did right. But I sure don't like being called a deserter for it," he confessed.

"I don't care what you're called," Dickey replied, "you'll always be a Marine to me."

The guns fell silent for a while around midnight. Dickey went back to the House to sleep. In the morning, she woke late in the absence of automatic weapon fire. At the command post she found out why: the Batistiano force had surrendered. Lusson allowed her to attend the negotiations where she gained a valuable, if not unique insight into the reason for the rebels' continued success in the face of a much better-equipped army.

After Lusson promised that his men would not be killed, that their wives would not be raped, and that their children would not be harmed, the Batistiano captain relaxed into his seat and the two veterans began talking about the battle.

"What was that big thing you fired?" the captain asked. "The one that, praise be to God, came at us only twice?"

"That was the time I got disinterested in the whole war!" chimed a Batistiano noncom.

The captain shrugged in acquiescent agreement.

They were referring to the 57mm recoilless rifle that Holthaus had fired at them, albeit unsuccessfully. And therein lay the moral.

"My own conclusion," wrote Dickey for her *Marine Corps Gazette* article, "was that they [the rebels] earned all the real estate by making every mistake in the book—*but one*. They consistently delivered a high volume of fire. After they started shooting, they rarely let anything—the enemy's reaction or their own commander's orders—stop them from continuing to fire until there was nothing left to fire on." This incessant barrage of bullets, Dickey argued, manifestly communicated the rebels' superior will to win. "This virtue fully exploited the major weakness of the well-equipped government forces, which was a near-paralysis of the will to fire at all. If there is any military lesson from the Cuban revolution for all Americans, in and out of uniform, I think this is it: Machinery does not win wars. Men do." Despite her crystal-clear analysis in one of its premier magazines, the US military would fail to recognize the analogy as it applied to their own engagements with guerrilla armies, particularly in Vietnam.

Though the Cuban rebels' strategy of an unabated barrage of bullets won the war, it did not always win the day. After all, the Batistiano army did in fact have superior firepower. Dickey soon found out the true danger of being overmatched.

After the terms of surrender were exchanged at La Maya, Dickey moved on to the next front, the small mountainous village of Maffo, a few hours' jeep ride away.

The tinny acoustics of music broadcast through a horn loudspeaker grew more distinct amid the orchestra of nocturnal insects as they reached the edge of town. Turning onto its main street, she recognized the tune as the battle hymn of the rebels. "Gente de Cuba, Destruye tu tirano," sang the singer above brass and drums. *People of Cuba, Destroy your tyrant*. The driver parked in front of its origin, a pharmacy that had been converted into a command post where the village's only light flared from a gasoline pressure lantern on the counter.

The song finished as she entered. A stocky man with the triple V of a captain's insignia on his shoulders lifted a silver microphone from the counter. "Soldados de Cuba en la fortaleza, ¡ustedes son nuestros hermanos!" he said, "No deseamos matarte."

Her translator rushed to catch up: *Soldiers of Cuba in the fortress, you are our brothers! We do not wish to kill you. Ask yourself why you should die for the tyrant Batista. Does he risk his life as you risk yours? No! He counts his millions of dollars in Havana while he uses you! As he has always used the people of Cuba. I tell you, cross to us here in free Cuba. We are waiting for you and you will not come to any harm with us, your brothers.*

Dickey recognized him as Luis Orlando Rodriguez, the revolution's great propagandist. When Rodriguez had finished his impassioned oration, an aide touched the needle back to the record and the battle hymn crashed back out into the night.

As if he had been expecting her, he gestured toward her camera. "You must have thought they were going to shoot me," he shouted in

English over the music. "It is tragic. I will try to talk with them again. But, the cease-fire will end in a few minutes. You should get back in the jeep and out of the light. My mortar crew has no ammunition. Here," he said, waving toward four soldiers standing to the side, "they'll take you."

The four walked double-time to the jeep where Jorge, the driver, waited for the song's crescendo to start the engine so as to camouflage the engine as it turned over. He drove in first gear out of town and pulled over beside a tree-covered rise.

Another guerrilla named Luis gestured for the four to follow him into a deep ditch. "We'll be safe in here from anything but mortars," he said.

"But you know they're going to use mortars," replied Jorge, who was proved correct when a shell exploded too close for comfort on their left. The sound of the phonograph needle scratched over the loudspeaker. The buzz of bullets and the crash of mortars replaced the music.

"Let's go," hissed Luis. They ran back to the jeep.

Half a dozen other men jumped on as they sped off. Dickey knew they were too heavy, and that there was nothing to be done. Luis said something about the mortars targeting the road. Jorge grunted in assent and pushed the pedal against the floor.

"Suddenly," wrote Dickey, "the jeep was speeding faster than I had ever ridden in a jeep before. Then, we crested a hill."

Jorge tried the clutch. She heard it grind into nothing. The jeep's brakes had given out long ago. They had no headlights. Dickey looked at the jungle rushing by in a solid mass of green, then back at the driver's seat. Jorge was gone. The road turned, the jeep did not. She felt herself flying then falling and saw nothing in the black night until she came to, facedown on the warm asphalt. Guttural screams pierced the resounding stillness. Jorge appeared by her side.

"Horses," he mumbled. Then she saw Luis pushing himself to his knees before collapsing. "But you'll have to wait to go to the hospital," Jorge went on as if in a trance. "The one villager who is screaming is dying. I think. Gasoline drum fell on him. Cut him apart. Luis," he said, "I know I should not have jumped," then disappeared into the thickness of trees.

Luis rolled over. "Él sabe," he whispered. "Sabe que era su deber quedarse con el jeep." *He knows it was his duty to stay with the jeep.*

Improbably, Jorge reappeared with two draft horses from a nearby farm. Dickey tried to stand for the first time and feared her left ankle was broken. For two hours she thanked the Algerian soldiers who had insisted she learn how to ride a horse as the three of them plodded through barely cut trails, finally arriving at a coffee plantation warehouse the rebels had converted into a field hospital.

Inside, the surgeon pushed a morphine syrette into the arm of a soldier. "With a sad spare gesture," wrote Dickey, "she threw it onto a cardboard carton of used bandages. 'Final,' she said to no one in particular. The last anesthetic."

The surgeon eyed Dickey suspiciously until Luis explained what had happened.

"No está roto," she said, examining Dickey's ankle. *It's not broken.*

"Then," wrote Dickey, "all the casualties from the mortar barrage arrived at almost the same minute. Before the next hour passed, there were a dozen newly wounded in the hospital. Four bodies, candles burning at their feet, lay in a row at the dark end of the shed. The floor was wet with blood."

Among the last was Captain Rodriguez, the propagandist. Dickey limped over to him. "Are you wounded?" she asked.

"No," he said, "but he is." He pointed to a soldier lying on the floor with his hands pressed against his stomach. "Shrapnel. We put the loudspeaker on the truck and drove it into the field in the dark under their fire. We never stopped talking to them. Then their mortars hit our truck. Three times." He grabbed her lens. "Look, Americana," he said, staring directly at her now, "you must tell this man's story even if you do not tell other stories. He is not even Cuban. He is Dominican. He fights with us against Batista now so we will fight with him against Trujillo later. If," he added fatalistically, "he is able to fight again."

"I will," said Dickey. It would be seven years before she was able to keep her promise when she tracked the man down in the midst of the Dominican Republic's civil war. She didn't know it then, looking at him as he almost bled to death in this coffee warehouse turned field hospital. But Ramón Mejía Pichirilo was known as Castro's Boatman for his uncanny ability to smuggle arms, goods, and people through Batista's near impenetrable blockade. As in the Cuban Revolution, he would become a hero of the Dominican civil war.

For now though, Rodriguez had no choice but to leave Pichirilo in the hands of the surgeon who promised to do her best to keep him alive.

Turning to Dickey, he said, "I have a truck outside and am going back to Castro now. If you can make it to the jeep, you can ride with me." He handed her his carbine for a crutch.

"Through a pelting downpour at dawn," wrote Dickey, "I was led a mile on foot, limp and all, out to a cave on a hillside, the command post of the 26th of July forces." There, she found radio equipment enough for a pirate station, towers of half-empty food crates, and enough ammunition to fend off a battalion or two. But not Castro. To see him, she had to hitch a ride to his forward base located in a farmhouse a thousand yards from the front at Jiguaní, a small village sixty-five miles west of Santiago and where the rebels began their last push of the revolution.

By now, she had been with the 26th of July Army for two weeks and her reputation had already come to Castro's attention. He welcomed her into his command post with an indifferent grunt. Still, she was granted more access than most of the journalists who had reported on him in the past.

Like her, Castro never stopped moving. "The normal state of ease for Castro is a purposeful 40-inch stride, forward then back," she wrote. She had to set her camera shutter at a speed usually reserved for Olympic events to capture his swift gait. His speech came at an equally quick clip. A relay team of runners were required to send his orders to the front. He screamed his dissatisfaction and embraced those that pleased him with bear hugs. He filled every room he entered with his outsized ego and charisma.

By coincidence, Dickey arrived in Castro's camp the same day Raúl returned from a successful campaign to the north of the Central Highway. Dickey photographed their reunion with Castro clapping his brother on the back. Celia Sánchez, the revolution's first female guerrilla fighter and Castro's longtime partner, smiled at the edge of the frame, her five gold crosses flashing around her neck. Off to the side, Vilma Espín, Raúl's girlfriend, played with the new Belgian submachine gun

Raúl gave her as a token of his victories. Later, Dickey would spot them making out in a rock cave like teenagers.

Dickey tried in vain to publish a piece about these two women warriors and those like them who fought with equal ferocity and valor as their male counterparts. But no matter how heroically she wrote them in her pitches, Dickey's editors didn't think their stories were worth printing. As was often the case, Dickey's journalistic instincts and her sense of the historic outpaced the imaginations of her peers. For the time being, Dickey focused on Castro, who after all was inarguably the man of the hour.

Yet Dickey was not as taken with Castro as she had been with his commanders and soldiers. Even then, she saw the characteristics that would later bend him toward dictatorship. Like many despots, Castro had the gift of oration, able to hold the attention of the masses as if by hypnosis. Almost every night, he practiced his art for hours through his increasingly famous radio addresses broadcasted from a rock cave command post.

Most of all, as she wrote in her article for *Reader's Digest,* Castro's greatest weakness lay in the fact that he was "at his best when he is against something." Later, in her autobiography, she fleshed out this initial thought, writing, "The overwhelming fault in his character was plain for all to see even then. This was his inability to tolerate the absence of an enemy; he had to stand—or better, rant and shout—against some challenge every waking moment."

But even for his faults, as far as she could see in late December 1958, neither Castro nor his forces were aligned with the USSR. As she wrote, "Application of the Red label to the Castro movement caused great indignation among the rebels. 'You won't call us Communists, will you?' I was asked dozens of times. The fact is that I found no evidence of Communism in the rebels' talk—none of the typical jargon. And neither the Batista Regime nor the US embassy in Cuba was ever able to present proof that Castro personally had been at any time a Communist."

Her vehement affirmation that the movement held no ties to communist Russia was aimed at American politicians and opinion makers who claimed the Cuban Revolution had turned Red. As evidence, they pointed to Raúl's criticism of America's support of the Batista regime. As a critic of any country, her own included, that would arm a dictatorship, Dickey saw no fault in Raúl's analysis. Nor did she oppose America's other central concern, Castro's plan to nationalize some of Cuba's sugar and mining industries. She well understood Batista's grift had long since drained Cuba of its wealth. To Dickey, this stance made Castro an egalitarian or perhaps even a socialist. But if socialism that shared nothing in common with Soviet communism was what the people of Cuba wanted, they were surely entitled to it since in Dickey's estimation, self-determination was the birthright of all people.

On January 1, 1959, Dickey was one of the only reporters in Havana to witness the victorious 26th of July Army streaming into the city. It was not lost on her that she found herself in the crest and fall of revolution on yet another New Year's Day. But rather than the frozen hell of Fö Street Prison, she found herself on the verge of a tropical utopian dream. Crowds converged in spontaneous celebrations. Boy Scouts who had trained in secret directed Havana's traffic. Soldiers self-organized into patrols to prevent the looting of small businesses. "There is hope of democracy in the air," Dickey wrote with exuberance in her article for *Reader's Digest*.

Two days later, the man of the hour walked through the city's gates.

"Castro's arrival," Dickey wrote, "was a day of delirium." Thousands poured into the streets to welcome him as he walked the entire length of the parade route, without bodyguards. That night, he opened the gates of Camp Columbia that just days ago had been the geographic center of the Batista regime. Thirty thousand crowded its parade ground for a final victory celebration.

"The revolution was over," wrote Dickey. "The real challenge of Cuba is now symbolized to me by two women I knew before the fighting ended." The first she had met when Havana still lay under Batista control. "She was a wealthy matron serving as a rebel courier. She flicked her beringed finger to the switch of her Cadillac's air conditioning so the grenades she was running across the city in the back seat would not become overheated as she told me, thoughtfully, 'The trouble with Cuba is that we always have had too many heroes and not enough citizens.'"

The second woman, Thelma, served as her guide back to Santiago from the front lines. Hiding in a drainage pipe while a B-26 strafed a nearby field, Dickey asked her how she came to join the revolution. For Thelma, the last straw had been the government murder of her friend, a fellow dancer at a Havana casino. After that, she signed up as a courier, smuggling guns beneath her full skirt and coded messages in her purse.

Her career nearly came to an abrupt end when the police raided the café where she was having breakfast while in possession of rebel military orders. Luckily, she managed to get rid of the evidence before the police searched her. Still, they arrested her on suspicion and held her in prison for five days. "Each day they told me they would shoot me," she recalled.

"What did you say?" asked Dickey.

"Nothing at first. But finally I told the captain everybody has to die some time, and if he wanted to kill me, well, maybe this was my day. Then," she shrugged, "they released me."

"This," wrote Dickey, "is the answer to how Cuba's rebellion produced something new—a genuine folk revolution surging toward a government with every kind of person, even pretty dancers, playing a proud part. That's a brand of democracy it would be fine to foster an hour by air from Miami."

But neither Castro nor the United States would foster this kind of democracy, and instead cultivated its opposite. Worse, in the coming years, this became a pattern among all the revolutions she covered. In Algeria, the United States continued to both withhold funding from those who fought for freedom while supporting their oppressors. As a result, the FLN were forced to turn again and again toward its more radical flank until the revolutionaries she marched with became unrecognizable in their war-pitched fervor. In other cases, American inaction allowed revolutions to be crushed, as in Hungary where the Soviet-backed regime imprisoned more than twenty thousand suspected freedom fighters. Dickey knew their fate only all too well.

Still, she would take up the search for this increasingly elusive ideal of American freedom once more in the jungles of Southeast Asia. And she would find it, though rarely with her own countrymen. Instead it was while on patrol with Chinese, Lao, and Vietnamese soldiers and civilians fighting for their own survival against communism that she discovered what she was looking for. Yet here too, she heard the echoes of history repeating itself all too clearly.

25

With Her Eyes Wide Open

By 1959, DICKEY had become a celebrity in her own right. She appeared on the game show *To Tell the Truth,* on which contestants try to guess the unique occupation of the guest. William Morrow and Company asked if she might be interested in publishing her autobiography with them. Oregon senator Richard Neuberger read her *Reader's Digest* article "Remember the 26th of July" into the *Congressional Record.*

When things started to get bloody in Cuba, her hometown paper, the *Milwaukee Journal,* called her for comment. "No," she said on the record, "I can't get very excited about the four hundred terrorists Castro has shot. Not when my own country refused to get excited about the ten thousand victims of Batista . . . US correspondents failed to keep the country informed about conditions in Cuba. Instead of taking a stand against Batista, we supported him. We have our own errors in judgment and interpretation to blame." Her answer surprised the paper's readers, but no one who knew her. She always took personal responsibility first.

Meanwhile, General Lemuel Shepherd, who invited her to his camp on Okinawa, came back into the picture. Though he had retired from military service, the Inter-American Defense Board had appointed him as chair. Best described as a think tank made of high-ranking military personnel, the IADB advised the US government on security matters pertaining to the Western Hemisphere and particularly those relating to South and Central America. Once again, her and General Shepherd's paths dovetailed.

He wrote to say he enjoyed an article she penned on the Marines' intervention in Lebanon. She replied to ask if he would like to see photographs of US-made planes terrorizing Cuban villagers. In turn, he invited her to lunch in Washington, DC, in late February. They spent several hours discussing the tactics and motivations of guerrilla soldiers in the numerous conflicts she had covered in recent years.

"After I came back from Washington yesterday," she wrote in a thank-you note, "it occurred to me (with characteristic immodesty, I'm afraid) that I'd printed a good deal of material on the subjects we've discussed during the luncheon, and drafted even more which have not seen print." She enclosed so much that she apologized for the bulk. It would seem the general did not mind.

Soon thereafter, she received an invitation to brief the naval deputy director of plans for special warfare and his staff. Later, this branch would be referred to as the Navy SEALS. Dickey then secured an assignment for *Leatherneck,* a Marine Corps magazine, to cover their upcoming vertical envelopment maneuvers, aka, paratrooping on the USS *Boxer* off the coast of Puerto Rico. In late May 1959, the secretary of the Army invited her to Fort Campbell, Kentucky, where Major General William Westmoreland had cofounded RECONDO, a school specializing in Army Ranger tactics for the 101st Airborne Division.

For two weeks, Dickey accompanied the 101st Airborne on their RECONDO training missions, including their paratrooping runs. Somewhere above the rolling bluegrass of western Kentucky, she heard several students talking about the likely location of their next deployment in Southeast Asia, where the only way to reach their target was by jumping out of a plane. Dickey realized immediately that if she wanted to follow this next war, she'd better learn how to do the same.

Earthbound, Dickey looked to the 101st Airborne's tower that recruits had to jump out of before being given permission to parachute from a plane. She asked if she might try. As she wrote in her autobiography, "They told me that I was welcome to jump out of their tower any time." But first, she needed civilian training.

In the middle of her coverage, Dickey left for Orange, Massachusetts, where the East Coast's first ever civilian parachuting school had just opened. Fittingly, to get there, she had to fly through Worcester, the destination of her first flight while covering the airdrop of supplies in 1934 after the city had been cut off by a historic flood. From there she took a bus to Orange where she jumped out of planes for six days. On July 1, 1959, she stood on top of the 101st Airborne's training jump tower.

"If I could learn to do it right twice in succession," she wrote in her autobiography, "the US Army would permit me to jump with troops on a maneuver that same night, the first time a woman had ever done so." Harnessed into her chute and staring down at the ground from the jump tower, Dickey heard the instructor shout advice she would never forget. "There is absolutely no reason to close your eyes." Though intended as literal, she couldn't help but hear its allegory. All her life she'd been trying to see the world around her with open eyes. As she prepared to jump into the next phase of her career and a new era of history, she heard these words as a directive to work that much harder, be that much more rigorous, and uncover the truth no matter how deeply buried. The further she journeyed into the Cold War's morass, the more difficult this became, especially as the light shining on her beloved Marines faded in the crepuscular jungles of Vietnam. But even then, as in this moment, she kept her eyes wide open.

Harold C. Lyon, Jr., a member of the 101st Airborne, best described Dickey's time at RECONDO in a letter to her *Reader's Digest* editor, writing, "While with us at RECONDO School, Dickey walked miles and miles through rough terrain as a member of several of our patrols. . . . Through her own determination and perseverance in obtaining clearance from Washington, she managed to make a night tactical parachute jump onto an unknown drop zone from an L-20 aircraft thereby becoming the first woman to accomplish this feat. To have been associated with Dickey Chapelle while on her visit has been for me an enlightening experience and a personal pleasure."

The feelings were mutual. "I doubt if any letter can constitute a proper thank you," she wrote to Major General Westmoreland, "for the privileged adventure of covering the 101st, but I want to make this on-the-record try." She continued, "I hope that I can now do my job as well as I saw them do theirs, and I don't know of a higher standard. Or of a more challenging reminder of it than the RECONDO certificate bearing your signature which now hangs on the wall in front of my typewriter." Much more than a memento, this certificate cleared Dickey to jump with the 101st in peacetime operations, which is exactly what she did—and in the process, secured an almost unbelievable tip.

While flying over the rolling Kentucky hills during a war games exercise, Dickey struck up a conversation with Rufe Philips, a former member of the 101st Airborne turned military instructor. Right before they got to their drop zone, he happened to mention his last teaching assignment not in America, but Laos. Dickey pitched *Argosy* magazine a story about what he had told her. In a letter dated October 11, 1959, Dickey wrote, "I believe the Laos thing is much hotter than public prints indicate. The big story is the effort of Laotians to counter Red infiltration with 'village development teams' trained in part by us. Because there are no roads, these six- and eight-man teams parachute jump into their assigned areas and walk out. According to ex-paratrooper, Rufe Philips (as American as apple pie), who just came back from training these people, there is a very good chance that I'd be able to jump in with the Lao army teams close to the Reds pretty damnquick."

She couldn't have known the full extent of the story.

For years, the US and USSR had been waging a proxy war in Laos, with the Soviet-backed Pathet Lao on one side and the US-supported royal government on the other. That both superpowers were arming and aiding their respective proxies had been widely reported in the press. But what the US government kept secret, and what Dickey had glimpsed, was that the military and CIA were laying the groundwork for a much larger conflict.

Under the code name Erawan, America started sending CIA and military special forces to train Hmong soldiers in unconventional warfare techniques, an action that remained classified until 2006. It can be safely assumed that Philips served in this initial detachment. Because Special Forces stints in Laos tended to last six months, it might be inferred that Philips and his fellow Green Berets had been deployed even before the declassified report's earliest timeline of July. If he told Dickey he had just returned from Laos in October, six months would put him there in May 1959.

Despite this once-in-a-career scoop, *Argosy* passed.

Whether Dickey's story was nixed by editorial myopia or government censorship is unknown. Regardless of why she didn't immediately pursue this story, she had an on-the-record first-person source stating that the US government was conducting covert operations in Laos as early as the spring of 1959, forty-seven years before Erawan became public knowledge. Still, she would get there soon enough.

In the meantime, she had to content herself with parachuting into Korea's demilitarized zone with the Army's First Special Forces Group, aka the Green Berets, as the first woman to paratroop with the US Armed Forces.

Through her seasoned connection with General Shepherd and her new relationship with Major General Westmoreland, Dickey secured an assignment with the First Special Forces Group. Stationed in Okinawa, they were tasked with supporting anticommunist guerrillas in South Korea. Touching down on the island she had been escorted off by gunpoint brought back memories, good and bad. Making it all the more nostalgic and perhaps poetic, she would be paratrooping onto the longitudinal line that defined the Korean War from which she had been barred from covering because she had dared, as a woman, to set foot on this very island during the last days of World War II.

Though pulled between what this place meant to her past and what it meant for her future, Dickey showed no sign of stress. She felt indelibly at ease, even at home, when in the company of military men, all the more so when they were as well trained as this group. "You have no doubt of what kind of men they are," she wrote in her article for *Reader's Digest*. "That casual absence of expression on the lean faces, not all young or unscarred, comes from looking hard for a long time at hazard. These are the men who have survived, and they swagger a little even sitting down." The very same could be said about her.

Not long before takeoff, Colonel James B. Mills, who had blown up Nazi train tracks with the French Resistance during World War II and then landed on Omaha Beach on D-Day, found her to deliver the good news. "You have been cleared to jump with us tonight," he said, then looked at the rest of his troops. "You people know what to do," he told them and left.

She suited up and walked out onto the airfield in the cool dim of an island winter twilight. Before boarding the C-130 Hercules, an officer asked her to write a release in her notebook: "I hereby release the government of the United States from any liability for my person or possession in connection with the parachute jump I am about to make." She signed it, tore it out, handed it over.

"If we lose her in the water hazard," he called to the staff sergeant, "make sure to recover the body. I'm signed for that jacket she's wearing." Dickey was the first to laugh.

The propellers thundered into motion. Some men dozed with their weapons. Others played a mean game of pinochle. Dickey ate a sandwich and apple, both of which tasted like they were made from the box they came in. Outside the portholes the sky grew dark. She made notes in her notebook, rehearsed the jump in her head. Night jumps were notoriously difficult. She wouldn't be able to see her landing site until just above it, too late to change course. Broken bones, concussions, and even fatalities were not uncommon occurrences. But as ever, she placed her trust in the men she reported on. She hadn't been let down yet.

Time came to chute up. The plane lights were turned down to a faint orange glow, allowing the jumpers' eyes to adjust before jumping into the darkness. The airmen slid the door open to the night air howling like a hurricane. Dickey reached her mind beyond the slipstream. "It will be so quiet out there," she told herself.

Her turn. Choice disappeared. The light turned green and she pushed her palms against the cold metal door, gasped, then felt herself pulled into the sky. Fast suddenly became slow as a plume of silk opened above her. The lights of Seoul gleamed to the south. The moon faintly illuminated the silver forks of the Han River beneath her feet. "I am a rag doll," she whispered to herself and relaxed every muscle in her body. Her chute tore away. In the sky, a dozen men floated toward earth beneath the stars.

A band of South Korean guerrillas met them at the river's edge. "Merry Christmas," said the colonel in charge of the jump.

"Happy New Year," returned their leader, Kim.

The Americans and Koreans took turns poling two flat-bottom boats toward their destination, a steep cliff on the right bank overlooking the demilitarized zone.

"I used to play here when I was a boy," Dickey quoted Kim in her *Reader's Digest* article, intentionally highlighting the tactical importance of local knowledge. "There is a path—too steep for boys, but men can use it.

"My heart sinks," wrote Dickey. "The way is craggy, steep down and steeper up. But the intuitive magic which turns many individuals into a single entity on any night patrol begins to spin its web around us."

As if they had all been training together for years, they marched in perfect formation to the end of their patrol in a flat valley. An American radioman turned to Kim. "We're almost to a safe area," he said, "I don't need to keep a lookout anymore. Let me take your pack." He paused. "I gave you the heavy one, you know," he said, clapping him on the back.

The two began laughing. "I find now what I remember is not the jumping or walking. It is the sound of the laughter of those two wet, cold and weary men, one American and one Asian. The real joke is on the people who believe their wills and muscles can never be pooled, that one must distrust the other even at the price of alliance in the struggle against tyranny."

The future would prove her optimism tragically misguided.

26

Laos

JUST BEFORE CHRISTMAS, Tony called to say he'd been arrested for waving a gun around at O'Hare Airport after Helga left him for a younger man. Dickey told him never to call her again. In true Tony fashion, he responded by writing a long letter.

Too busy redecorating her apartment, she didn't bother to reply. "I mean the yellow bookcase is OUT," she wrote to her aunts George and Lutie. "I destroyed it happily one midnight with the purple-handled hammer, and erected in its place a nobbish oak-and-steel job which braces between floor and ceiling and has no truck with the wall plaster at all." Despite being loaded with "tons of books, the globe, my stereo speaker, and a few favorite prints," it still looked airy in her studio apartment. Even better, she could finally afford "a real writers' chair which has slightly more adjustments than I have."

These humble yet invaluable improvements came with her growing financial success and the little bit of time it afforded her from the otherwise grueling schedule of living paycheck to paycheck. Rather than having to query endlessly for new assignments, she had six magazine stories to write about her jump from a Special Forces airplane over South Korea. This, along with the advance from her publisher at William Morrow and Company for her autobiography, meant she didn't have to spend the winter and spring crisscrossing the heartland while giving three lectures a day in order to make ends meet.

For the first time in almost a decade she stopped moving. She didn't drive hundreds of miles a day or fly across multiple oceans or march for hours along the Cold War's embattled borders. Instead, every day she sat in front of her typewriter with a pack of cigarettes and a bottle of buttermilk, looking not ahead, but only backward on the life she had lived so far. From the way she told it, she had few regrets. Not even about Tony, whom, despite their soured relationship, she only ever described as hardy, hale, and good-natured. Not that she mentioned him often. In the final version, his name appeared sparingly and mostly in the section between their wedding ceremony in 1939 and her coverage of Iwo Jima and Okinawa in 1945—a period when they spent more time apart than together. Otherwise, she portrayed him as a side note, a sidekick, an also-ran, even when she wrote about the end of their pseudo-marriage. She did not want to be defined even in the slightest by their relationship.

Instead, she focused on the adventure of her career. Turning back to notes, letters, drafts, and articles, she created an accurately frenetic portrait of a life filled with grit, bravery, and perseverance, doused with self-deprecating humor. True, at times her anecdotes ran longer than merited and several sections were disorganized in their logical progression, as is the case with all first drafts. But overall, she wrote a compelling narrative of a unique life and a career spanning one of the most decisive epochs in American history.

Yet stillness did not suit her. No longer on the run, her loneliness caught up with her. "My social life is not in the league of yours," she wrote to her aunts in February, "well it's in no league at all, being largely confined to discussing the weather with the landlord if I meet him when I go down for the mail." Knee surgery in April kept her grounded even longer. By August, her enforced torpor had become almost intolerable. "What I am doing," she wrote to a friend, "is leading a sad and solitary life writing the inevitable books," referring to her autobiography as well as a history of military training which never came to fruition.

Once in a while though, she allowed herself a date with Shepard Rifkin, a man she had met when he was a struggling novelist working at a bookstore. He had since become a successful author of whodunits, Dickey's favorite genre. More than any other lover he understood she would never stay too long in one place. Paradoxically, this acceptance of her need for freedom drew her closer to him and she let him in more than anyone since Tony. Even so, she had no intention of settling down, not by a long shot.

In July 1960, she received a tip from a contact in the 101st Airborne. "Major Millett," he wrote, referring to Lewis Millett, a cofounder of the RECONDO school, "is on his way to Viet Nam where he is to set up a Viet Namese Ranger School—no less." At the time, few in the American press corps were paying attention to South Vietnam, where an insurgent communist guerrilla force known as the Viet Cong were beginning to make inroads against the US-backed government of President Ngô Đình Diệm.

But, Dickey knew when she heard boots on the march. "In Vietnam," she wrote to her photography agent, Nancy Palmer, "whatever happens, I have been told I may accompany paradrops in frontier villages with their anti-Red troops. There is a great untold story of American participation here." She could not have known just how right she would turn out to be.

It would be a while still before she found her way to Southeast Asia. For the time being, she kept her head down, focused on finishing her autobiography and rehabbing her knee according to the latest Armed Forces physical therapy techniques sent to her personally by the Army chief of physical standards. With Nancy's help, Dickey also sold a teaser article for her autobiography to *Coronet,* a large-format monthly magazine. Published under the title "I Roam the Edge of Freedom," the article spanned the enormous scope of the latter part of her career, from Hungary to Algeria to Cuba. But more than this, it served as a record of the paradigmatic shifts she bore witness to and the lives of citizens and soldiers caught up in this great swell of change. Dickey's writing and photography captured these surges of revolution crashing onto every shore with more speed and force than history could account for. They would only gain momentum in the years to come. Intuitively, Dickey knew this would be the case and raced to keep up.

By fall of 1960, she had worked her knee into good enough shape to run two miles a day along the East River. On Christmas Eve, when the thermometer registered an icy negative four degrees, she sent a complete draft of her autobiography to her editor. After the holidays, she went on the road again, zigzagging the Midwest in her rented Chevrolet, talking to three and sometimes four audiences a day. Service clubs and church groups applauded her dedication to democracy while seventh-graders asked her why she hadn't been tortured in Hungarian jail. She cut down on cigarettes to preserve her voice and spent her rare off-hours making the changes her editor sent rather than writing letters home. Highways and motels and auditoriums bled into a moving panorama across the American Midwest.

Within this blur, she took little note of the inauguration of John Fitzgerald Kennedy. Though his liberal attitudes toward social issues and hard line against communists won her vote, she never was one to pin her hopes on a politician. Her reserve proved percipient in early April when back in New York City, her friends in the Marines began to murmur about something big about to go down in Cuba.

Dickey called her contacts, got a commission from *Reader's Digest*, and secured credentials from José Miró Cardona, the Cuban prime minister in 1959 and now chief of the Cuban Revolutionary Council (CRC), a CIA-funded exile group working with the Kennedy administration to overthrow Castro.

On April 17, a 1,400-strong brigade of Cuban exiles landed on Playa Girón in the Bay of Pigs. Immediately after hearing the news, Dickey flew down to Miami to at least get closer to the action since the US government had effectively banned reporters from being on-site. There, she visited the office of Richard Osborne, a public relations professional the CRC had supposedly hired to handle press for this combat unit, which called itself Brigade 2506. Yet Richard's operation hardly seemed like the stuff of a ragtag bunch of grizzled counterrevolutionaries. Dickey immediately suspected the CIA as behind this incursion.

"He had offices in a high-rent building which were newly decorated with wall-to-wall carpeting, indirect lighting, and a modern-architecture desk presided over by a pretty blonde girl," Dickey wrote to her editor at *Reader's Digest*. "More ambiguous yet for a mission for destitute and desperate invaders was the sight of the mimeograph operator turning the crank of a brand new machine. In a publicity office, this character is low man on the totem pole, barely considered skilled labor"—as she well knew, having spent a great deal of time working in press relations. "But this one was very well-groomed, very athletic and very alert. After he'd squinted at me long enough—I stared back to make sure I'd never seen him before in my life—he came out with 'Dickey Chapelle! I can't tell you how much I enjoyed that last article of yours! About Cuba, wasn't it? My, you certainly called that turn!"

Dickey raised an eyebrow and flicked her cigarette ash. The secretary ushered her into Richard's office where she said without intonation, "Tell that mimeograph operator to cut that stuff out; he's breaking your cover."

Richard of course pretended not to have the foggiest idea of what she meant and proceeded to give her the runaround, which she approached with due incredulity. Instead of heeding his advice to stay away from the naval station at Key West, she flew there posthaste, chartered a light plane and—hanging out the side, as she was prone to do—snapped more than a few recon photos of five US Navy destroyers in operational formation. On the ground, she went back to the naval base to submit her photos for censorship, a common practice among the old guard of World War II photographers. She fully expected them to redline national security concerns while leaving the rest. But when she approached the master-at-arms he informed her there were "no mechanics by which the pictures could be admitted to exist." In other words, she had not seen what she had seen. And she'd better forget it. Ultimately, she had witnessed the buildup for the CIA-implemented and completely disastrous Bay of Pigs invasion.

This was not the first time Dickey had run into the CIA during an attempt to cover a story. That had occurred in Cuba when, betting on both sides, the CIA supplied Castro's army with $50,000 for arms and ammunition. But it was the first instance she recognized their glove covering the hand that acted. It would not be the last. Frustrated and unsettled over this burgeoning era of government censorship and CIA meddling, Dickey called Hobe Lewis at *Reader's Digest* and asked for a transfer to Southeast Asia where she had wanted to go in the first place. He said yes and she bought a ticket to Vientiane, Laos. Little did she know that the Bay of Pigs served only as a preamble to what she would find in Southeast Asia.

DICKEY CHECKED IN to the Constellation Hotel in Vientiane at the beginning of the monsoon season when downpours marked every afternoon like clockwork. The porter carried her bags to her room where she fell asleep almost immediately beneath the whirring ceiling fan. In her wildest dreams she could not have imagined the tangled labyrinth she would be stepping into come morning.

Unlike the slapdash Bay of Pigs operation, the CIA had been laying the groundwork for mass government, military, and civilian manipulation in Southeast Asia since 1950 when it purchased Civil Air Transport, a private airline that it used to fly thousands of covert missions. During the Korean War, CAT air-dropped agents and arms over mainland China. It provided air support to the French during the Indochina War. Afterward, CAT continued to air-drop supplies into the Lao jungles where the CIA waged a secret war with Hmong soldiers against the Soviet-armed Pathet Lao. By the late 1950s, this burgeoning proxy war had spilled down from the mountains and into Laos's capital, complicating an already mired political landscape.

In 1959 Eisenhower responded by authorizing Operation Hotfoot. In conjunction with the CIA covert program Erawan, Operation Hotfoot sent Special Forces, including the one who'd given Dickey her initial tip, into Hmong militia units, supposedly as unarmed advisors in civilian clothes. As early as the spring of 1959, Special Forces were being transported into the brushfire battle arenas of Laos via the CIA's private airline, which by then it had rebranded as Air America.

At the same time, North Vietnam began work on the Ho Chi Minh Trail, a logistical network of roads that ran from North Vietnam down the Lao and Cambodian borders, then into the Mekong River Delta, a vast maze of rivers, islands, streams, and swamps. The Ho Chi Minh Trail soon became a massive thoroughfare of weapons, supplies, information, and soldiers supplying the communist Viet Cong insurgents in South Vietnam and feeding the war that would rage for over a decade. The stage had been set for the Vietnam War.

President Kennedy provided the players. Since assuming office, he had expanded the scale and scope of the CIA and Special Forces activities in Laos. In April 1961, one month before Dickey arrived, he replaced Operation Hotfoot with Operation White Star that deployed thousands more Green Berets and authorized them to engage directly in conflict. Tasked with logistics, the CIA's Air America received new aircraft as well as the military personnel to service them. Simultaneously, the Kennedy administration granted the CIA authorization and funding to recruit and equip thousands more Hmong for guerrilla operations. By the summer of 1961, their army grew from three hundred to nine thousand soldiers.

The Soviets and North Vietnamese government responded in kind, increasing the number of arms supplied to the Pathet Lao as well as upgrading the types of weapons they sent. Rather than surplus weapons from previous wars, Pathet Lao soldiers now carried brand-new AK-47s, recoilless rifles, light and medium mortars, and 14.5mm mounted machine guns. Since North Vietnam had every interest in creating a buffer between the US forces in Laos and its own precious Ho Chi Minh Trail, they also sent an increased number of advisors to train the Pathet Lao.

The killing fields of war grew larger by the day, threatening to upset the delicate detente between the US and the USSR. Fearing further escalation, the two superpowers sought to bring their respective proxies to the negotiation table. Yet these conversations of cease-fire that were taking place when Dickey arrived did little to diminish the hailstorms of bullets ripping through Laos's jungle foliage and into the lives of those who inhabited its mountains.

Despite the clandestine nature of the CIA's and military's operations in Laos, Dickey had no trouble finding her way to the center of this deadly game of geopolitical chess. Because war remained undeclared, the military had no real authority over who was and wasn't accredited. The only litmus test she had to pass before heading into the jungle was presented by a crusty colonel who asked her, "Will you eat bats?" since the Special Forces she wanted to cover were expected to live off the land if supply lines failed.

"Yessir," she answered unflinchingly.

Three days later on May 5, 1961, an Air America helicopter dropped her in a mountainous village where two battalions of the Royal Lao Army (RLA) and seven Special Forces advisors were stationed with the local Hmong guerrilla militia. None of the Green Berets were surprised by her presence. They were the same men she had paratrooped with in South Korea.

Over the next five weeks, Dickey would witness and document every aspect of the Kennedy administration's Operation White Star. Because she was one of the few journalists intrepid enough to go behind enemy lines, her reporting proved to be rare. As the only journalist willing— and welcome—to spend such a long period of time with the Special Forces in Laos, she had a unique perspective. As such, her notes and drafts reveal nothing less than the CIA's early efforts to shape the very landscape of the Lao countryside in order to build the foundation for an expanded war.

The first indication of what lay ahead arrived with the appearance of an unarmed Curtiss C-46 plane. With his first four passes over their jungle base, the pilot air-dropped half a dozen 200-pound burlap sacks of rice that fell to the earth like deadly missiles. But the cargo starting on the fifth pass was different. Crates clearly stenciled with the words .81 MORTAR AMMUNITION, 4.2 MORTAR AMMUNITION, and M1A1. M/45, BROWNING came floating gently to earth beneath silk parachutes.

The pilot signaled his last pass by buzzing the helicopter landing pad at an altitude of no more than thirty feet.

"That old Shower Shoes," said one of the American advisors. "He comes so close, man, close!" Central casting could not have found a more suitable character for an Air America pilot.

"Shower Shoes," Dickey explained in an unpublished article, "is the nickname for flier Art Wilson, who has been a professional transport pilot in Asia ever since he left Seattle, Washington, his hometown, in 1941. As for his nickname, Dickey explained that in addition to his aerial antics, "he is just as famous for the costume he wears in the cockpit. It is a flowered shirt, slacks and a pair of green rubber shower shoes. Most of Art's colleagues, anticipating an impromptu jungle landing someday, fly with infantrymen's boots on their feet. But Art, whose planes have been holed by fire from the ground more times than he can count and who has been forced down twice, expects to do again what he did then— walk home in shower shoes."

Soon after Shower Shoes's engine had disappeared into the distance, Hmong unit commanding officer Major Kob Gao ran out to the drop zone. He had just been on the radio with his CIA handlers. Through the translator he explained they wanted to enlarge the drop zone that Shower Shoes had just buzzed to be large enough for four helicopters to land. In her own analysis, Dickey noted, "He doesn't have to describe the circumstances under which four helicopters could be needed at once, and badly, to bring in ammo or take out wounded." Captain Frederick Gordon, the senior American officer, nodded and turned to his demolitions specialist, Sigward.

"Blast out that clump of trees at the end," said Gordon. "With the trees out, we'll have a four chopper pad."

Very carefully, Sigward packed and then placed four sticks of dynamite into a knothole in the largest tree.

"The whole jungle down to the earth shudders," wrote Dickey of the explosion.

Once the reverberations subsided, fifty people from the nearby village trod out to help clear the drop zone. "Two carry new shiny axes," wrote Dickey, "and several have big army machetes and entrenching tools." Again, Dickey witnessed and documented direct CIA involvement in and incitement of the civil war in Laos. Not until years later was it revealed that the CIA actively employed Hmong villagers to clear drop zones, helicopter pads, and landing strips. Along with the brand-new tools, Dickey noted that each of the villagers were paid one dollar each for their labor, no small sum in the highlands of Laos at the time. Both clearly indicated CIA funds were behind the operation.

Driving the point home with all the subtlety of a B-movie, the first helicopter to land in this enlarged pad the following day was an ex-Marine Air America pilot by the name of Johnnie Cople whose cargo included beer, cigarettes, small arms ammunition, and of course, more dynamite.

As Johnnie unloaded his cargo, Major Gao again approached with intel from the radio, this time about a company of Hmong guerrillas that had gone quiet for too long not to arouse worry.

"The innards of the helicopter are stripped down to one stretcher, one Tommy gun and one gallon of water," wrote Dickey. "Then in go six sacks of rice, eight cases of ammo and the human cargo," which included the captain, a gunner by the name of Turken who wore a gunbelt but no shirt, and Dickey.

Ten minutes west, Johnnie started circling around a steep ridge of two thousand feet. Turken peered out the open chopper door through field glasses for a white flare that would indicate the company was still alive.

Johnnie widened his circles but still nothing. "We're running low on gas!" he yelled through the intercom plugged into the flight helmets.

"One more circle," replied Gordon and leaned out of the door for a better view of the ground below. "There!" he shouted, pointing at the tiny flash in a small clearing.

"The chopper settles to the earth," wrote Dickey, "and the ragged, bearded Lao company commander is the first to shake Gordon's hand. He is Captain Kham Sung, known in his army as Capt. Dynamite."

Between his few words of French and Lao and Kham's spattering of English, Gordon managed to ask about their tactical position.

"Good, good," said Kham.

"With his hands and his dirt-smudged map, he makes clear what he means. The enemy is on only two sides of him, not three," wrote Dickey, emphasizing his fighting spirit and the dedication of his men.

So assured, they left the company resupplied with food and ammo. Johnnie flew low since they were short of fuel and for a moment, Dickey paused to marvel at the sublime landscape of Laos's famed Plain of Jars. Then, a faint popping noise came over the chop of the rotor. Turken jumped back from the door.

"UP!" he yelled into the intercom.

"The chopper leaps like a rabbit," wrote Dickey, "banks like a roller coaster and turns as it rises." Quickly, they were out of range.

"This chopper sure can climb," said Turken.

"Empty it can," replied Johnnie.

All of these clandestine preparations culminated in the only way they could, in the act of war. Dickey witnessed the direct engagement of Special Forces troops in combat, an act that would threaten the tenuous balance of diplomacy between the United States and the Soviet Union if publicly known.

In the afternoon of one of her last days in the field the sound of an exploding mortar shell echoed down the river.

"Incoming. Eighty-two," Sigward noted laconically, estimating the size of the shell.

"Nah," said Turken. "Bigger."

In ten minutes they counted five shells, but Major Gao, who always seemed to be on the radio, said the official count held at seven. On a map, he had marked where he wanted to strike back.

Careful not to capsize, Turken, a Hmong guerrilla by the name of Lek, and four RLA soldiers climbed into a sampan. Dickey playfully waved away Turken's hand as he offered to help as she stepped in last. Another sampan followed behind with the ammo.

The men poled upstream as far as they could, pulling into a river-bank cove when the current grew too strong. They would have to walk the rest of the way. "In the cathedral light of the jungle stream, the men form a splashing serpentine," wrote Dickey, "Lek in the lead followed by Turken then the men with the mortar and finally the ammo bear-ers." It took them twenty minutes to walk half a mile up a steep path that led to a hillside clearing where the Lao soldiers, Lek, and Turken set up and fired the mortar.

As they expended their last shell, four T-6 propeller planes from the Royal Lao Air Force roared into view. Each fired two rockets into the areas where they had aimed their mortars. The deep rush of sudden conflagration reached them after bright orange flames began tearing across the mountainside. Turken, the RLA soldiers, and Lek cheered, as did Dickey.

But even with her steadfast belief in American leadership, Dickey began to sense something was not quite right. As she wrote back at the Constellation Hotel to her family, "I was helicoptered some 50 miles behind enemy lines for the purpose of covering a little handful of Americans—Americans!—working there. We lost two of them in a he-licopter crash, and between it and the considerable volume of artillery fire, refugee movement, a threatened cholera epidemic and other con-comitants of 'the cold war,' I am still more than a little numbed."

That evening, wrapped in a sarong, Dickey bathed in the rivulet run-ning beside the village while Sigward played guitar on the veranda of the thatched hut they had rented as a field command post. In the long glow of twilight, he began to pluck the notes of "America the Beautiful." Half homesick, half proud, the seven Special Forces soldiers began to sing.

This might have been the closest America ever came to such a hal-cyon dream in Laos, and it was very far indeed.

For the next fourteen years, the United States waged a shadowy war in Laos with no regard for those who had the most to lose, the Lao themselves. By the war's end in 1975, the United States had dropped more bombs on Laos, a country approximately the size of Idaho, than it did on all the European Axis Powers countries in World War II. Forty thousand Lao lost their lives during the war. Since then, another twenty thousand have been killed by unexploded bombs, at least five thousand of whom were children. In the aftermath, tens of thousands of Hmong and other highland peoples, whether or not they collaborated with the CIA, were forced to flee Laos or face imprisonment, torture, and execution under the Pathet Lao government.

Even as early as her initial stay in the summer of 1961, Dickey witnessed the first frayed threads of this unraveling and the rapidity with which the CIA was willing to abandon America's allies. In June, a temporary cease-fire had been declared. Dickey had cause to doubt its legitimacy from the outset, writing, "This is, in case the papers have not made it clear, the noisiest goddamn cease-fire I ever covered."

In the wake of the temporary armistice, the CIA and the US Special Forces pulled back while the Pathet Lao advanced on the severely weakened Hmong. The consequences were immediate and deadly.

"The last time I stayed with his battalion," she wrote of Major Gao, "some weeks later, it was to perform the grim chore of interviewing the survivors of a retreat. No American had seen it; the Red assault against him had come on a day when both Lao officers and American advisors were simply spread too thin. They were back at the rear in part to plead with the Lao controlling distribution of American military aid for better support." In retrospect, this reason for the absence of any official military personnel seems all too convenient, as did their failure to return with any sense of urgency. The Pathet Lao attacked again while she was there, sending seven medium mortar shells in their general direction, though thankfully missing.

Finally, back at the Constellation Hotel, Dickey began crafting her notes into an article. As she often portrayed freedom fighters, Dickey portrayed the RLA soldiers as revolutionaries cast from the same mold as America's own. They were brave, aggressive, and well trained. The

Hmong villagers they were billeted with were industrious while the guerrillas were grave in their endeavor to defeat the Pathet Lao.

Her terminology, however, sometimes missed the mark, particularly in her often used reference to Lao soldiers as "little." The adjective was meant to dispel the widely held racist idea that the height of a person bore some bearing on their strength, bravery, and resolve. But in hindsight many would justifiably interpret her overuse of this pointedly diminutive term as both disparaging and lazy writing.

But she listened when remonstrated for using an insensitive term or holding onto a prejudicial concept and sought to change her thinking, writing, and photography accordingly. It was a lesson she learned from the Quakers, whose belief that the Deity resides within every human necessitates a perspective of radical equality. Not without irony, this central tenet of a quintessentially nonviolent religion endeared Dickey to every fighting force she ever marched with. It also allowed her to perceive both the fallacy and national security threat posed by institutionalized racism toward Southeast Asians at the exact moment when America needed them as allies. In the months ahead, her critiques of these misconceived and counterproductive attitudes became as scathing as they were pointed.

But as she was finishing her draft on the secret war in Laos, tragic news arrived at her hotel in Saigon. George, her aunt, her most trusted confidante, her most ardent supporter, had passed away. Dickey's reaction bespoke a change in her. She would not, Dickey told her family, be returning home—not for months and not for the funeral. "I hope the story I am bringing back will in some way expiate my failure to be with you," was all she offered by way of explanation before continuing, almost mechanically. "I expect to be in Laos, untangling red tape and trying to draft my story, through this week, staying on at the Constellation. I expect to go from here directly to the Majestic in Saigon over the weekend; then I'll begin all over again."

As it would for so many, the war unfolding in Southeast Asia began to consume her, and like millions of others, she would not survive it.

PART V

. . . .

27

Guerrilla Warfare

"EVERY PHASE OF guerrilla fighting is going on here in one part of the country or another," Dickey wrote to her editor at *Reader's Digest* one week after arriving in Saigon. Though the actual state of the war eluded so many, Dickey came to this incontrovertible yet apparently elusive conclusion without having to leave the city. In a letter to Stevie, she explained how she had come to this deduction, "This country is lousy with people I knew at Fort Bragg and Camp Lejeune."

Over platonic dinner dates, her longtime contacts in the Marines and Special Forces told her "almost everything I can't print," as she phrased it in one letter home. It didn't take many bowls of pho and congee to determine things were far more critical than the press was reporting.

Though anxious to get in the field and confirm these reports with her own eyes, a more pressing assignment kept her chained to the desk in her room for the next week and a half. The Marines' Division of Information had asked her to write a memo on guerrilla warfare. Taking what she had learned in Hungary, Algeria, Lebanon, Cuba, and most recently Laos, she wrote an incisive and prescient disquisition on the tactics and strategies, means and ends of limited war that described the future trajectory of the Vietnam War with uncanny foresight.

In one of the most insightful points of her treatise, entitled "An American's Primer of Guerrilla Warfare," Dickey observed that guerrillas did not adhere to Western conceptualizations of battle maps. As she wrote, "guerrillas do not undertake at once to 'seize, occupy and defend' earth or to control air, as the maps and orders of conventional warfare require. The initial guerrilla objective is separate from real estate." Instead, she said, the initial objective of guerrillas is "to break the individual will of individual people to resist them." That is, the objective is to conquer not land, but people, one at a time if need be.

This was a much longer form of warfare, and a much more "intimate" one, to use Dickey's description. "Guerrilla warfare is more nearly the total war in a given time and place than the originator of the phrase, 'total war,' Von Clausewitz, anticipated," she explained, referencing the founding theorist of modern warfare. "He foresaw the engagement of every man, woman and child in an embattled nation at some mission contributing to military victory. But, in guerrilla action, every able human being does not just risk at work, they kill or are killed. Children of ten or twelve were Castro's main dependence as battalion runners; comely girls delivered his ammunition under their skirts."

On the other hand, those who once claimed and received noncombatant status became primary targets in guerrilla warfare. "Doctors in their operating rooms, lawyers in their courts and teachers in their classrooms were military objectives. In short," she wrote, "the more untouchable a sanctuary had been regarded, the more likely it was to become a killing ground."

Dickey argued that, contrary to this gruesome and personal form of warfare, Americans "trust machinery to do our work." But, as she cautioned, "machinery can't win a war any more than dollars can buy friends. Wars are won by men using machines; the machines can only express the will of the men." The revolutionary will always outlast an occupying force unwilling to fully commit.

What's more, as she observed, guerrillas often turned the greatest strength of conventional armies into their ultimate weakness. "An ideal of guerrilla warfare is to let the enemy pay for arms, to let him bring them freely into the battle zone—and there to capture them without having the nuisance of acquisition and transport. This is such a workaday guerrilla practice," she continued, "that the forces often train with enemy weapons, certain they will capture enough in combat to apply their training."

Drawing on her twenty years of combat reporting and five years of guerrilla warfare coverage on three continents, Dickey concluded her primer by cogently distilling the means and ends of limited warfare. "I have come to think of guerrilla fighting as decisive warfare undeclared, total, intimate, off the map and phased into infiltration, terrorism, commitment and exploitation." She had no reason to think Viet Cong strategies would diverge significantly from those of the other guerrilla forces she had covered. But with the benefit of history, she had hoped the United States Armed Forces would adapt to the new conditions of limited warfare. Her hopes were soon dashed along the Ho Chi Minh Trail.

In September, Dickey attached herself to a battalion of Vietnamese marines along with its Military Assistance Advisory Group (MAAG) unit. Their often fatal reliance on conventional warfare tactics became immediately evident when they arrived at their destination, the Ho Chi Minh Trail. With the intent of stemming traffic along this belligerent highway, MAAG had advised the Vietnamese marines to establish a series of stationary guard posts along the border of Cambodia. This proved as ineffective as it did dangerous. Designed and maintained not as a set route but as a nexus of roads, paths, and trails, this central artery of soldiers, weapons, and information shifted in real time as the war evolved. As such, stationary guard posts did little if anything to disturb its trade. And in very simple terms, it made those who defended these guard posts sitting ducks for the Viet Cong, who made their camp where they lay their heads.

"When we got out there," Dickey wrote in another strategic assessment for the military, "we discovered that there was a kind of gentlemen's agreement between fighting forces that if you didn't step out of the barbed wire, nothing happened. But if you were out of the barbed wire . . . The only way to get out was to set up your mortar and keep firing as you retreated." In effect, the Viet Cong curtailed the ability of the marines to patrol the Ho Chi Minh Trail, thereby negating the entire point of their presence.

On those occasions when they managed to get beyond the perimeter and go on patrol, they were met with nearly invisible snipers. Dickey described the inevitable result of one such patrol she accompanied, writing, "I was in the main path with the battalion command group—a wonderful marine was killed who had been hit by a single burst of fire . . . All I could think of was that getting supplies through to a guard post that probably shouldn't be held militarily speaking anyway is a heck of a way to lose an 11-year veteran fighting man."

Dickey did not lay the blame on the Vietnamese marines for these failures, writing in her analysis, "I was tremendously impressed with the degree of soldierliness that I observed," and "they are some of the most experienced soldiers on earth and thank goodness they are on our side." She added, "Over all, I feel very much at home with them, except for one technical change. They use a three-man fire team, and we use a four-man fire team. But," she went on, "it is not a real problem for a correspondent going from one to the other." The only real difference she saw between the Vietnamese and American Marines was "their attitude towards physical fitness." Whereas the Vietnamese expected themselves—and her—to walk *at least* twenty-five miles a day, American Marine recruits walked a *maximum* of twenty-five miles a day. In her estimation, which she relayed to the US Marines top brass, the Vietnamese would out-soldier the Americans were it not for bad advice and contradictory orders—given by the Americans.

Adding insult to injury, the Vietnamese marines were not even provided the basic support. As Dickey wrote, "I'm always interested in how soldiers eat, and I think I have a perfect way of checking. I go around and steal their food, and the ones that have plenty are pleased about it, but the ones that are awfully hungry cut my hand off—they all know I could eat with the command group," referencing MAAG. Going from campfire to campfire one night with a pair of chopsticks, she asked to try several of the marines' dishes. "I always got it but quite reluctantly," she wrote. "They finally put it into words, and said, 'If you ever get to see the president of our country and maybe you will, but we never will, please tell him we don't have enough to eat for the way we are working and that we have to buy our own food on the road.'" Incidentally, she did bring it up when she interviewed President Diệm in Saigon later that summer. Her words went unheeded.

She found the Vietnamese airborne no better equipped by the Vietnamese government or their supposed American advisors. In the summer of 1961, Dickey made nine jumps with the Vietnamese airborne and was the first reporter of either gender permitted to do so. Once on the ground she marched over three hundred miles with them, went on nineteen operations, and came under ambush thirteen times. For her valor, expert parachuting ability, and composure under fire, the Vietnamese airborne awarded her their wings, which she wore on the left lapel pocket of her fatigues, the right already being occupied by the wings of the 101st Airborne. So it was with a great deal of authority that she wrote, "They are jumping over water, and we haven't given them life preservers—this I think is the silliest thing I have heard of . . . These guys are jumping in the rainy season when water is a tremendous hazard."

But none of this, by her estimation, did half as much damage as the lack of meaningful interpersonal relationships between the Americans and the Vietnamese troops they were supposed to be leading. As Dickey wrote, "The majority of the several thousand foreign professional observers"—referencing MAAG personnel, the diplomatic corps, and various military attachés—"work geographically INSIDE the network of normal public communication facilities—and the communist military and paramilitary forces by enemy design fight openly only BEYOND that network." In quarantining themselves in Saigon, the American military failed to recognize the ways in which warfare had radically shifted so completely that its troops were not even sent to the actual field of battle newly and successfully defined by the Viet Cong.

As with many of Dickey's analyses of combat conditions, her initial insight came not from previous belligerent engagements, but from peacetime observations. In this case, she drew a parallel to the alienated humanitarian aid administered through the Marshall Plan that failed to produce the intended effect and instead often engendered hostility toward the United States. Wartime proved no different. Arms and money could not alone build an alliance. Human connection, empathy, understanding, and trust were required to create a bridge between nations, just as between individuals.

Summarizing America's multivariate strategic failures in a language any military man could understand, she wrote, "One of the great needs in Vietnam right now is the development of a counterinsurgency doctrine because we don't have one. We can only teach the people we help with military aid the doctrines that we ourselves have." Taking aim at the commonly held logical fallacy that Asians could not effectively fight, she continued, "Among the real experts in the world on our way of fighting is the enemy. With seven years of very bloody effort and with many, many discouragements, I am sure they have figured a pretty good way to blunt conventional tactics." In other words, the very people who were accused of lacking backbone were the same who had through trial and error, blood and sweat, figured out how to beat Western occupiers.

At last she wrote simply: "We are not winning."

Back in Saigon, Dickey was more pessimistic than ever. In a letter to her editor at the *Digest,* she tried to contextualize her gloomy pages of a draft article, citing counterproductive orders, inadequate medical care, and ill-advised tactics. "There is no lack of toughness, training, or bravery among the Marines, but they just aren't able to kill the enemy under the present set up. In short," she continued, "the Vietnamese Marines, trained by ours, are first, just as impressive and second, just as ineffective as ours would be. I'm sure this isn't all of the story in Vietnam," she concluded, "but the newspaper stories that the war here has reached a turning point find no echo in my experience."

In desperately searching for the story of South Vietnamese victory, she had neglected to keep an eye on her own autobiography, currently in the hands of her editors. On a break from the field, she sorted through a pile of edits. They were, in her mind, atrocious. She had wanted to title her book either *Trouble I've Asked For* or *With My Eyes Wide Open,* the latter in reference to her paratrooping instructor's edict. Her editors however had settled on *What's a Woman Doing Here?,* in reference to the insulting question she had been asked by armed service members at the beginning of her career during World War II. In any case, she wrote one of her editors, they'd even got the question wrong.

"I'll just comment that the real phrase of greeting I most often hear is: 'But what the <u>hell</u> are you doing here?'"

Then there was the matter of the book's dedication, which Dickey wanted to read: "To my communist interrogators, in deference to their repeated assurances that I would never live to write another line for print." Her editors nixed this.

Last and worst was the complete shift in tone. Whereas Dickey's initial draft had focused on her methodology as a journalist and the people she reported on, her editors rewrote entire sections that played into stereotypes of femininity. In Dickey's words, "My story seems to have been feminized the hell out of." Her self-deprecating humor had been contorted into buffoonery. Rather than a gritty reporter willing to risk life and limb to get the story, she came off as a ditzy dame who stumbled into the middle of things despite herself.

Recently back from her fifth jump with the Vietnamese airborne into a combat zone, Dickey did not take kindly to this distortion of her story. "Maybe the sale of this one book will somehow be better this way," she wrote of the new tone. "But my alleged future as an alleged observer . . . does not and cannot depend on my being a broad but rather on my being a story-teller of integrity."

Her protests fell on deaf ears. "Don't worry!" replied her editor. "Repeat don't worry! Your book has not been feminized!" Misunderstanding her concern completely, he went on to assure her that the men in the office didn't think it had been and therefore, with tautological reasoning, it wasn't. Dickey wasn't ameliorated. The book's poor sales only reinforced her misgivings. But at the moment, she had neither the time nor the energy to fight another front. There were too many openings in Vietnam.

THE WINDS BLEW in from the west as the summer monsoon season came to an end. Somewhere along the line, she'd ceased to cover the story of Vietnam and had become part of it. The black-and-white morality of World War II, the easily defined differences between wrong and right, between freedom and fascism, became blurred in the endless tangle of shadow governments and clandestine operations. Once, after a firefight outside of an old French fort, Dickey went into the Viet Cong enclave to photograph their dead. She focused her lens on the body of a suspected communist in one of the thatched huts. But seeing only one bullet hole, she knelt beside him and picked up his wrist to check for a pulse. There wasn't one but her soldier escort mistook the gesture for one of sympathy.

"I think he was very puzzled at the time as to how to communicate the utter contempt for what he thought I had done," she recorded in her notes. "But he solved it by pulling his .45 and fired two more bullets into the body of the soldier." On their walk back to base he caught up with her to explain. "As a child he had been forced to witness the murder of his father and mother when the communists took over Hanoi."

The last frays of the narrative thread she had tried to stretch all the way back to 1939 finally disappeared into the pit of the Cold War. There could be no morality here, only violence. Accordingly, her sole comment on the incident was that this kind of hatred bred the die-hard commitment that made Vietnamese soldiers more dependable than American MAAG personnel in the fight against communism. She had been right about the totality of this war that engulfed everyone it touched, including her.

Yet, in Dickey's analysis, the politicians and generals in Washington refused to acknowledge this raging fire of war even while they fanned it with weapons and money. In no uncertain terms, she advocated for expanded American commitment, if not with boots on the ground then through the full recognition of the Vietnamese as equals and allies. "This is a hard choice for power-habituated white Americans to make," she wrote to Hobe Lewis at the *Digest,* "our blood or our vanity?" In the end, America would lose both.

For now, Dickey cautioned once again that America and its allies had no chance of winning without a coherent counterinsurgency doctrine. But according to her Special Forces contacts, one was being hammered out in the Mekong Delta where a village of refugees had effectively beaten back the Viet Cong, turning their own tactics against them. On this note, Dickey proposed to Hobe she stay on in Vietnam, at least for the beginning of the dry season, to see this new doctrine taking shape firsthand.

Perhaps Dickey should have known she was about to walk into one of the darkest periods of American history. If she had, she may never have embarked down that path. But through her own naivete or fear or desire to believe that America could still be a beacon for freedom or some combination of them all, she did not recognize what lay ahead. Regardless of why or how she took these first steps, there was no turning back from them.

28

The Sea Swallows

SHE FIRST HEARD of Father Augustin Nguyen Lac Hoa over the dying embers of a campfire on the Ho Chi Minh Trail from a couple of MAAG advisors debating who was the toughest man they had ever met.

"Nobody is tougher than Father Hoa," said one of them, a veteran paratrooper. The rest nodded in silent agreement.

As a country priest in Canton Province (now Guangdong), China, Father Hoa had been pressed into teaching the sons of river pirates how to read. As compensation, his pupils taught him jujitsu while their fathers taught him the principles of guerrilla warfare. During World War II, the priest's unlikely military training continued when the government drafted him into the army where he learned the basics of munitions. He survived to return to his flock. But after Mao Zedong seized power, Catholics became the target of mass arrests, torture, and execution. Father Hoa and his parish fled to Cambodia until communist guerrillas began to harass them there as well.

Resettling once more, this time on the mouth of the Mekong River Delta, they established the village of Binh Hung and gained citizenship in time for the 1959 national elections. Aware of their politics, the Viet Cong, who had recently gained a foothold in the region, told the priest that his village shouldn't vote. Several communists were on the ballot and the Viet Cong knew his parish would cast their ballots against them. Undaunted, Father Hoa, along with every adult of voting age, trekked several hours to their polling place in the regional center of

Tan Hung Tay. As a reprisal, the Viet Cong hung an eleven-year-old boy named Ah Fong from a cross with a sign on his chest reading, THIS CAN HAPPEN TO ALL YOUR CHILDREN.

Already twice made refugees by communists, the parish collectively chose to stand their ground this time. Putting his military training into practice, Father Hoa formed the Sea Swallows, a counterinsurgency militia named for the nearly indestructible species of tern that migrated through the Mekong Delta each spring. Since its founding, the Sea Swallows had grown from several dozen soldiers to a force of seven hundred that included volunteers from almost every province in South Vietnam.

Eager to meet this fighting priest, as she would later dub him, Dickey arranged for them to have tea at the American embassy in August. Over their second cup of oolong, Father Hoa invited Dickey to come live with them for a while, another first for any reporter.

The chopper dropped her off in mid-October. A squadron welcomed her on the landing pad, firing a twenty-one-gun salute and raising their flag. Dickey quickly fell into the village's rhythm.

Every morning, bugles called the village to wake, soldiers to drill, and prisoners to work. Ducks and pigs and dogs and babies composed the chorus of afternoons. Stringed pipas, instruments similar to guitars, and mouth harps announced the end of the workday. Sometimes when the air was cool enough, the militia's radio picked up the Saigon jazz station that was piped through an enormous Pioneer loudspeaker, washing the village in Coleman and Coltrane, Evans and Getz, Mingus and Roach. The resounding percussive of tanggu drums called the devout to evening prayers at the Our Lady of Victory Chapel. In the dark, gongs made from flattened mortar shell tips rang out the all clear every hour on the forty-five, except when incoming Viet Cong bullets made them chime like kindergarten triangles. This music played almost every night. The Sea Swallows replied with their own refrain of artillery, mostly left over from the French Indochina War, along with psyops messages broadcast over the same loudspeaker that earlier might have played jazz.

But more than defend, the Sea Swallows went on the offensive against the Viet Cong and had so far secured a five-mile perimeter around the village. Dickey of course insisted that she accompany them. The night before her first patrol, she joined the officers for dinner in their mess beside the Sea Swallows' armory. On one side of the long table, two German shepherds, gifts from US Army Research and Development, strained at their leashes. On the other, soldiers tossed their scraps to caged boa constrictors. Dickey sat in the center beside the ranking officer, Captain Nguyen, who talked of the liberation of Vietnam while Dickey used chopsticks to feed succulent crab to the cat that had crawled on her lap. Occasionally, a soldier would interrupt, asking the captain to inspect his modifications on a 1953 French mortar or World War I bullets that had been polished back into working order. Each time, he nodded a hesitant approval. They needed new weapons, but these would have to do. After dinner, Nguyen handed her a carbine to carry the next day. "You might need it," he cautioned.

Dickey went back to her quarters to practice carrying the gun along with her cameras. "How do Marine combat correspondents do it with an M-1?" she wondered in her journal, then packed her pockets with extra film and cigarettes for tomorrow's march.

They left in a thick rain at dawn, made too much noise, and only had a captured flag to show for their mosquito bites. "I scratched like a civilian," Dickey wrote. Still, the squadron gave her the flag. She would later unfurl this keepsake from her purse on stages in the Plains states in order to drive home the necessity of supporting the Sea Swallows and groups like them.

That afternoon she photographed the demolition class in the chapel. Like her, the instructor was an outsider, a member of the Vietnamese special forces sent here both to teach and to learn. She had met him before, what seemed like a lifetime ago, on one of her first patrols in the highlands.

"Don't you get homesick?" he asked her as his students practiced inserting fuses. Then shyly added, "I think you are willing to die for your duty."

"I'm sure you are too," she replied, then added, "We might both live through our whole careers." The look on his face told her she had said the wrong thing. He expected to die defending the freedom of his country. To think otherwise was tantamount to a dereliction of duty.

A week later, Nguyen announced the next patrol mission beyond the walls of Binh Hung. The troops assembled in a portentous gray dawn. Dickey ignored the omen, instead scanning the faces of the hundred assembled regulars as Nguyen gave them their orders. "I was surprised to realize how many of the Binh Hung faces had become familiar and even a little dear to me in the ten days I have been among them," Dickey wrote in an unpublished article about the operation. But combat, she knew, always made fast friends.

Nguyen dismissed them to load into the Sea Swallows' fleet of weathered motorboats with mounted automatic rifles at the bow and stern. Amidships, soldiers clutched their American M-1s and French Lebels with shells in the chambers and their safeties off. Bathing children laughingly swam out of their way as they departed down the canal. Dickey noted with no small degree of sentimentality the woman who saluted the soldiers, then blew a kiss to her husband, blushing behind his Browning automatic.

Outside of the village, water lilies and floating buttercups swirled in the eddies of their wake. Skirting the edge, farmers on the way to market poled their sampans stacked high with bundles of watercress, bananas still on the stalk, baskets full of fish, and clinking bottles of home-brewed beer. On the banks, children played and fishermen fished, boatbuilders caulked their hulls, and housebuilders thatched a new roof. The whole scene seemed so utterly pastoral, so opposed to their actual purpose.

A stone lion and live Tommy gunners guarded a Buddhist temple just outside Tan Hung Tay where they rendezvoused with a company of Montagnard militia. "They are mountain people from central Vietnam," wrote Dickey, "the Father and the captain have been delighted with their performance . . . My first chore of the day was to help prove it by photographing a Viet Cong corpse lying in the marketplace." She then added parenthetically, "(I guess I should point out that in my experience the public exhibition of enemy dead is still considered a pretty normal part of warfare in every culture but our own.)" Inured by now to the spectacle of violence, the marketgoers hardly noticed the body as they went about their shopping. With equal nonchalance, Dickey focused her lens on metal spikes across his chest, classic Viet Cong booby traps, that he had been caught planting along the path into town.

Reports of an approaching enemy column took them farther down the canal to Van Binh, another Catholic Chinese refugee settlement where the Viet Cong had recently poisoned the drinking water and shelled its market. The village chief welcomed the Sea Swallows with a feast of pork liver soup, roast duckling, shrimp, crab, beer, and French brandy. Evening fell. Dickey slept in the same barracks as the soldiers and woke with them before dawn.

"The first firing came at 08:10 exactly," wrote Dickey, "a few rifle shots and a submachine burst of three. Then for several minutes the fire was so heavy that I couldn't count." Dickey expended a roll of film and was loading another when she saw the mortar crew run by. She followed, film in hand, and dropped to one knee as the crew assembled the mortar in three and a half minutes flat. They fired. A dud. Military protocol dictated waiting ten minutes before loading a new shell in case the old one had simply yet to explode. But there was no time for such caution under heavy fire closing in on a thousand yards. Without hesitation, the crew reloaded and fired three more times. On the fourth, incoming fire slackened and the enemy dispersed.

Whatever misgivings the Sea Swallows or any citizens of Binh Hung had about Dickey disappeared after that. Farmers' wives hosted dinners for her. The commander of Companies Six and Seven invited her to his wedding. She celebrated the Vietnamese Independence Day by setting off fireworks with the best of them, went to children's birthday parties, and attended mass on Sunday. And, whenever the Sea Swallows went on maneuvers, she went with them.

She regularly joined them on perimeter night patrols and marched out to confront reported bands of Viet Cong. She came under fire nine times, endured clouds of mosquitoes so thick they clouded her glasses, and watched deadly snakes slither by her boots as she stood motionless for fear the smallest sound might alert the enemy to their location.

She described in gripping detail the dangers and difficulties of warfare in Vietnam that confronted the Sea Swallows even before one reached the enemy—charging water buffalo, mined canals and spiked foxholes, and terrain that both the Viet Cong and MAAG personnel considered equally impossible to traverse but which the Sea Swallows crossed by the mile. She portrayed them as they were under fire, cool and collected as any soldiers she'd ever seen.

"The Reds had chosen a spot where the walkers were cut off from the two boats by a hundred yards of swamp," she wrote of her last mission with the Sea Swallows. "Suddenly there came a lone rifle shot followed by a second's pause. Then half a dozen rifles spoke at once." Among them she heard the sound of an American M-1, distinguishable by its cannon cracker sound. Dickey threw herself flat on the bilge as the rounds of fire intensified. "But it was not a mere single shot we were hearing now . . . Our own counterattack party had opened up on the Reds with burst after burst from their automatic rifles." The firefight lasted an hour until there "came the detonation of what I took to be a grenade and finally— deep, shocking silence." The enemy dispersed.

The Sea Swallows gathered their wounded and began their long trek back to Tan Hung Tay where they found a banquet laid in their honor. Word had reached Father Hoa that a battalion of three hundred heavily armed Viet Cong had surrounded the patrol, but he could not determine the outcome of the battle. "If there are survivors, we will sate them," he told the women and children as they laid out the meal. "If there are not, we will rededicate ourselves to avenging their sacrifices."

Father Hoa invited Dickey to sit at the head of the table with him. "I demurred," she wrote, "I said that was a place for a soldier."

"Sit down," intoned the priest.

After dishes of crab, sweet-and-sour pork, roast goose, and broiled shrimp, it became clear why Father Hoa had wanted her to sit next to him. In front of everyone, he asked her to stand, then pinned the insignia of the Sea Swallows on the muddied shoulder of her fatigues. When she realized what he was doing, it took all of her strength not to cry. She felt honored and unconditionally welcomed. In other words, at home.

On November 6, 1961, nearly a month after arriving, Dickey left by helicopter along with the three who had been wounded in the previous day's attacks. She lingered a long time at the porthole, watching Binh Hung fade like an island in the sea of Viet Cong territory.

Back in Saigon, a cable waited for her at the Majestic Hotel.

PLEASE FORWARD THESE WORDS TO THE FIGHTER OF BINH HUNG NAMED DICKEY CHAPELLE. WE EXTEND OUR BEST WISHES FOR YOUR SUCCESS. AS WE ARE MOVING

INTO A LARGE OPERATION WE HAVE INFORMED ALL OUR
FIGHTING MEN OF YOUR DEPARTURE. THIS AFTERNOON
TWO COMPANIES OF OUR ASSAULT GROUPS MET AND
HAD A BATTLE WITH THE ENEMY. WE HAVE HEARD VERY
HEAVY SOUNDS OF GUNFIRE SO IT IS POSSIBLE THAT
WE HAVE ENCOUNTERED THE ENEMY MAIN FORCE.
IT IS SO HEAVY THAT WE ARE SENDING TWO MORE
COMPANIES OF REINFORCEMENTS. WE HAVE NAMED
THIS BATTLE THE CHAPELLE BATTLE. DUE TO LACK OF
COMMUNICATION WE DO NOT YET KNOW THE RESULT.

In the end, the Sea Swallows won the day.

But for all the declarations of mutual respect and admiration, Dickey
had arrived at, documented, and in some ways unwittingly abetted one
of the darkest turns in the history of the Vietnam War. The first clue she
failed to decipher were the Montagnards stationed at Tan Hung Tay.
A moment's pause might have led her to question why and how these
indigenous highland men had come to be in the heart of the Mekong
River Delta. The answer, of course, was the CIA. As with the Hmong in
Laos, the CIA recruited and trained guerrillas from Vietnam's polyglot
of indigenous highland peoples only to abandon them to the communists when Saigon fell.

In coordination with the decidedly pro-Catholic and openly corrupt
government of President Diệm, the CIA had also started organizing the
many ethnic-Chinese Catholic parishes in the Mekong Delta into a cler-
ical paramilitary program that formed an archipelago of anticommunist enclaves within the delta region. But this operation remained in its
fledgling stage when Dickey was on patrol with the Sea Swallows.

However, even in their early stages, these operations were beginning
to ramp up. On October 18, 1961, Dickey wrote a letter to Hobe Lewis
at *Reader's Digest* that read, "I am not being disappointed in my stay
here. These Asians are daily and literally fighting Reds; I have been on
four operations with them so far. . . . They are heavily though not well
armed and organized as semi-regulars. . . . They are improvising the
military doctrine of the future—and so if they succeed, the whole free
world will be richer for it."

Hobe then replied to her letter on October 23, writing, "With General Van Fleet and General Taylor both concerned with guerrilla warfare, I don't need to tell you how urgently we would like to see an article on the subject. I cannot direct you since you know so much more about the subject than I do, but I do hope that you will give this top priority." As to the generals he referenced, they could not have been more consequential to the Vietnam War. General James Van Fleet had been a gunner during World War I, a hero of D-Day during World War II, and a commanding general during the Korean War. President Kennedy had recently recalled him to serve as a consultant on guerrilla warfare. General Maxwell D. Taylor had been the commanding general of the 101st Airborne during World War II, had recently become chairman of the Joint Chiefs of Staff, and in 1963 would be appointed as ambassador to South Vietnam. Whether or not the military or the CIA gave direction to the *Reader's Digest* editorial board, they were clearly the magazine's primary audience.

Five days later, on October 28, 1961, Special Forces Major Donn Fendler was welcomed on the Binh Hung helicopter pad. His presence, though possibly unrelated to Dickey's exchange with Hobe, was far from coincidental. In 1938, at the age of twelve, Fendler became famous for surviving nine days in the mountains of Maine after being separated from his family. When President Roosevelt invited him to the White House and asked him what he wanted to do when he grew up, he answered without hesitation that he wanted to join the Navy. Six years later, at eighteen, he did just that and fought in the World War II Pacific Theater with distinction. After the war, he reenlisted with the Army and trained in the 101st Airborne Division. When he arrived in Binh Hung, it was in the capacity of a military advisor, most recently and most often to the CIA's Montagnards.

Dickey did not mention his presence in any of the articles she wrote and his name appeared only once in her journal. How long he stayed, she didn't note, but an addendum to her photo captions for *The New York Times* indicated he remained long enough to go on one or more combat missions. "Publication of this photograph without prior security review by US authorities," she wrote, "would be most embarrassing to the photographer. Unfortunately both the face and name of an

American frequently on duty behind enemy lines are plain in the picture."

The backward gaze of history all too easily connects these occurrences into the causality of what happened next. In early January 1962, only weeks after Dickey helicoptered out, CIA director William Colby ordered the fourteen-man "A" detachment of the Special Forces into Binh Hung on an extended assignment. As in Laos, they organized the citizens to clear a landing strip large enough to land a twin-engine Caribou transport plane. By midsummer 1962, some fourteen hundred light and heavy weapons had been delivered and the combined American-Chinese Special Forces team approached two thousand soldiers. In the CIA's estimation, Binh Hung would serve as the nucleus of the Delta Pacification Program that in turn laid the groundwork for the expanded war that emerged in 1966 and 1967.

Though she witnessed most of these developments or was made aware of them by her contacts, Dickey failed to add these parts together into their grisly and inevitable sum. In this she was not alone. Indeed, most of her journalistic peers were content to keep quoting the Kennedy administration's line that insisted the conflict in Vietnam amounted only to petty skirmishes that Saigon-based, US-backed forces had under control.

As one of the few willing and able to spend weeks at a time embedded with armed forces; one of the only accredited to paratroop; and the only reporter who wore the wings of the Vietnamese airborne and 101st Airborne and the insignia of the Sea Swallows, Dickey had a unique and hard-won knowledge of the early days of war in Vietnam. But as a survivor of the physiological torture of solitary confinement who came out of prison only to live her life primarily in active war zones, she only saw the walls closing in on her again as America's losses mounted in Southeast Asia. As such, she searched for the only way to win she knew: fighting.

Back in the States, the Marine Corps chief of staff, Lieutenant General Wallace Greene, asked for an in-person briefing and update to her original "An American's Primer of Guerrilla Warfare." Dickey pulled no punches.

She began by characterizing the recent neutralization of Laos—meaning neither the USSR nor the US could claim it as an ally—as dangerously naive, while categorizing the half measures to contain communism with Vietnam as categorically ineffectual. "In fact," she wrote, "in both countries the pursuit of both aims is now proceeding at a rate so slow as to suggest failure of attainment of any objective in the US interest."

The solution by her estimation was an increase in commitment, if not with the number of men, then the degree to which they stood with and beside their Asian allies. MAAG personnel should be deployed to the villages where counterinsurgency militias like the Sea Swallows or regulars in the Army of the Republic of Vietnam were daily engaging the Viet Cong. They should be expected to eat the same food, live in the same quarters, walk the same distances, and take the same risks as their Asian counterparts.

Having spent five months in the field with a myriad of Lao and Vietnamese troops as well as MAAG advisors, Dickey also knew the harm caused by the racist attitudes of Americans both on a policy and personal level. She'd gained substantial insight into the stereotypes that fed these attitudes, the logical fallacies behind them, and the fallout their perpetuation catalyzed.

Dickey addressed all these points head-on in the second appendix to her primer, entitled "An American Mythology* of Asian Defense." The explanatory note to the asterisk read: "I have with difficulty resisted the temptation to substitute a forward-area term such as 'hogwash' for the word MYTHOLOGY." Anyone in any branch of the military would have understood that by "hogwash" she really meant "bullshit."

The first hogwash-myth she addressed was that Buddhism prevented Lao and Vietnamese recruits from becoming effective soldiers. This she dismissed handily, writing, "the Pathet Lao which inexorably advanced against the Royal Lao forces month after month was almost all composed of Lao apparently uninhibited by killing." The real difference, she argued, was their training, just like any other fighting force.

Dickey additionally spoke to the idea that historical animus and language barriers prevented White American military advisors from effectively training Southeast Asian troops. For the past five years Dickey had felt nothing but welcome and warmth from numerous guerrilla forces from Algeria to Cuba to Vietnam. As such, Dickey knew that this

animus, when it existed, could be overcome if Americans would only submit to the idea of a universal meritocracy. As she wrote, "This is another
BIG LIE serving communism. Why do we believe it? Because, I think, of
our distaste for thinking of any American in a situation where he is not
automatically accepted because of his mere nationality and the cash in his
wallet as a symbol of omnipotence the way we like to think Americans
should be—but must earn respect by personal merit before he gets it."

She further addressed the racist idea once famously espoused by
General Westmoreland that "Asians just don't have the high regard for
the value of human life that we Americans feel." The US military often
cited the "human waves" tactic employed by Chinese troops during
the Korean War as proof of this prejudicial concept. But Dickey easily
countered this logic, "It is western military practice as well as Asian to
employ human waves in war; what else is the classic infantry charge?"
Iwo Jima and D-Day would come to the minds of those reading her
words. "The ultimate contemplated waste of human life—the use of the
nuclear bomb—is a real factor in the security plans not of Asia but of
two non-Asian powers, Russia and the US."

Drawing from her own experience in Fö Street Prison when she
ceased to care about her own mortality, Dickey wrote, "I have never
seen any evidence that the skin color or continental origins of anyone
affects his respect for life. Scientifically, only pain (of exhaustion, injury,
disease, hunger, disappointment) can reduce that instinctive respect."

Realizing the full weight of this dangerous attitude, Dickey concluded her point with a personal experience worth quoting at length.

> I have been in the presence of death among Asians very often. I have
> never known their reactions to be very different from my own if there
> was hope we could save a life; under that condition they eagerly did
> everything humanly possible just as Americans would. But there was
> a difference when it was clearly hopeless to try to save life. Then their
> reaction was to far better control the bitterness we all felt than I was
> able to do.
>
> Once I remember there were tears in my eyes only as we loaded the
> body of a man who had just died fighting among us onto a helicopter.
> Later, the Asian sergeant told me:

"We liked you for crying. We think to show tears is unmanly. But you are a woman and we were glad you were there to cry for all of us."

In so many words, Dickey once again told the US Marine Corps to soldier up to the level of those they dared deride at the risk of losing their own life and liberty.

The military establishment listened to her on a great many topics, incorporating a number of her suggestions, such as stationing MAAG personnel in the field and maintaining constant contact with their Vietnamese counterparts. Undoubtedly, others made these same points. But it was a small chorus and Dickey had the voice of a drill instructor. In the coming months and years, Dickey would give numerous briefings to top brass at the Army, Navy, and Marines. She gave lectures to new recruits on the basics and specifics of guerrilla warfare. The Marines included her writing in their counterinsurgency manual. Her photographs were often used in briefings for President Kennedy and Defense Secretary Robert McNamara. After her presentation on "An American's Primer of Guerrilla Warfare," General Greene wrote her to say, "I think that you are a good Marine."

But they did not listen to her in any discernible way when it came to creating a culture of racial equality within their ranks.

In truth, by the time Dickey had seen what she had seen and said what she had said, America's racial bias had been so interwoven into its war plans that one voice could not have made a substantial difference. Instead, the opposite occurred.

On the same visit to Washington, DC, during which she briefed the Marine Corps, Dickey was recruited by the Human Ecology Fund. Outwardly, the fund invested millions in anthropological, psychological, and sociological research on a myriad of subjects largely pertaining to human behavior. Headquartered at the Cornell University College of Human Ecology, the fund ran satellite programs at twenty separate institutions, including George Washington University, where Dickey signed a contract for "$50 dollars a day and travel expenses" for work on unspecified "research problems in areas of your competence."

Only two clues remain as to the nature of her work: a pamphlet advertising her lecture on methods of resisting communist attempts at brainwashing, given at a Human Ecology Fund conference; and a letter indicating she submitted a treatise on the importance of supporting a free press within a democratic society. In both cases, Dickey seems to have assumed her work would be used to expand and protect the constellation of rights enshrined in the US Constitution and Bill of Rights while informing the evolving field of international law with the ultimate goal of expanding the borders of the free world. Indeed, the vast majority of those who received grants and contracts assumed similarly benign, if more banal, motives behind the fund since they were given no reason to suspect otherwise.

In reality, the Human Ecology Fund was a front for the research and development of MK-Ultra, a CIA-led interrogation enhancement program that used psychotropic drugs, electroshock, and psychological torture to illicit confessions from detainees across multiple conflicts during the Cold War. None of the researchers that received Human Ecology Fund grants or contracts, Dickey included, were told that their research would be used for these gruesome purposes. Nor would any have cause to suspect these covert and criminal intentions with Cornell University as a front. Not until an investigative report by *The New York Times* in 1977 was the scope and scale of the Human Ecology Fund revealed even in part. But by then the CIA had purposely shredded the majority of the paperwork pertaining to the development of MK-Ultra through the fund, forever concealing the extent of this program.

Washington had turned America down a dark road that Dickey would follow as far as she could.

29

No Turning Back Now

DICKEY MET 1962 in full stride. Despite her misgivings, her autobiography received positive reviews. *The New York Times, Saturday Evening Post, World Affairs, Leatherneck,* and the *Marine Corps Gazette,* among others, praised her stirring prose as well as Dickey's tenacity and grit as a reporter. *Reader's Digest* printed a condensed version, which apparently Vietnamese president Diệm very much enjoyed. After reading her book, General Greene wrote to say, "I enjoyed it very much. I congratulate you on your ability to write prose as well as you take photographs." Assistant Secretary of Defense Ed Lansdale—whom she had met through her work in Binh Hung and who was now working on Operation Mongoose, a covert CIA operation to overthrow Castro—told her, "I circulated it [your book] to a limited and select group whom I felt needed to catch a bit of your spirit." But perhaps the review she treasured most came from an acquaintance, Marine Lieutenant Colonel Philip Pierce, who wrote to say, "I read your f—ing book. It's a good f—ing book."

Success begat success. *Tonight Starring Jack Paar* booked her for a segment. Renowned journalist Mike Wallace, later of *60 Minutes,* hosted her on his radio program as did the groundbreaking commentator Betty Furness. With her voice graveled from decades of smoking Pall Malls and shouting over semiautomatics, Dickey recounted her stories of hearing the sound of bullets buzz like wasps across the sands of Iwo Jima, being imprisoned in a Hungarian jail, marching with the Algerian

National Liberation Front, and paratrooping with the Vietnamese airborne into Viet Cong territory.

Still, the title her editors had chosen always managed to overshadow her accomplishments, as she had warned it would. Wallace put it point-blank. "Your book, which has just come out and is really a fascinating book, is called 'What's a Woman Doing Here?' which seems to me a pretty good question because, Dickey, is a woman's place at the front, jumping out of airplanes the way that you've done and ending up in solitary confinement? Is that a woman's job?"

In response, Dickey simply returned to the refrain she had first used during World War II. "It is not a woman's place," Dickey began, "there's no question about it. There's only one other species on earth for whom a fighting front or any of the other situations you describe is no place, and that's men. As long as men continue to fight wars, why, I think observers of both sexes will be sent out to see what happens."

Publishers and the public alike started taking more notice of her work. In February, *The New York Times* ran her photographs of the Sea Swallows on the cover of their Sunday magazine section. From that she sold another cover photo to the *News of the Week in Review,* a full-color multipage spread to *USA-1* magazine, and a feature in *Army* magazine.

The coup de grace came in April when the Overseas Press Club gave her their highest honor, the George Polk Award for the Best Reporting Requiring Exceptional Courage and Enterprise Abroad, for her coverage of the conflict in Vietnam. She had a gown tailor-made with a floor-length skirt of gold-shot off-white and a bodice of gray-green velvet. She bought a little black bag at Saks Fifth Avenue to show off both pairs of her airborne wings and put a pair of elbow-length doeskin gloves on her charge card. The club put her up in the Waldorf Astoria, Manhattan's iconic Art Deco hotel. That night, in front of all the men who had for decades told her she couldn't because she was a woman, Dickey swept up the stairs onto the stage of Waldorf's grand ballroom, looking radiant and feeling justifiably vindicated. She beamed in the pictures with her award.

Tony's son Ron wrote to congratulate her and to say he'd recently joined the Air Force. "I'm really pleased and proud to hear that the Air Force has been doing right by our Ron, even if you feel you're missing the adventure of the generation by not being a parachute jumper like your stepmother," she wrote jokingly, then added parenthetically, "(Notice I go right on calling myself your stepmother even though I guess legally dear we are now friends only.)" Friends or family, Ron would continue to look to Dickey as a guiding figure in his life. In the PBS documentary about Dickey, *Behind the Pearl Earrings*, Ron said of Dickey, "She was my hero, yes, certainly . . . I should have worn a short sleeve shirt today so I could roll up my right sleeve, and show you the tattoo of the American flag and a quote from MacArthur that says Duty, Honor, Country. Underneath that is my Vietnam Service ribbon. This level of patriotism, I learned from her."

To Dickey, patriotism meant upholding and expanding the rights that at its best America embodies. But in the months to come, the American government itself would start to assail those very rights and specifically the freedom of the press. On the front lines of a war the Kennedy administration would rather have concealed from the public eye, Dickey also found herself one of the first to arrive on this new ideological battlefield. Through history and experience, Dickey knew attacks against the press were always a prelude to systematic repression. She never thought she'd see this opening salvo come from the White House. But when it did, she recognized it for what it was.

Her feature for *Reader's Digest* on the American Special Forces stationed in the highlands of Laos had been cleared by the MAAG censors the previous summer. That fall, she also sent it to Assistant Defense Secretary Ed Lansdale, who passed the manuscript along to his staff, "with the injunction that they can't go running out to volunteer again when they've finished reading it." As he continued, "It's a grand bit of writing you did and certainly captured the spirit of something which has eluded others. Sure did like it!" From there, both President Kennedy and Secretary of Defense McNamara requested to see her photos. Approved, welcomed, and applauded by the highest officials, it would seem her article checked all the boxes of a positive piece of journalism for America's cause.

Yet somehow, between the Oval Office and the printing press, eight hundred of her photographs disappeared in possession of the Army censorship office. At first willing to entertain the idea that it had been a bureaucratic snafu, Dickey soon suspected a more nefarious motivation when she spotted one of her photos in *Army Digest* magazine without crediting her.

One of the requested MAAG edits, which Dickey kept, foreshadowed their censorship by bureaucratic fiat. In her article, Dickey accurately placed American Special Forces engaging in combat prior to the Royal Laos Government's (RLG) request for troops. This was a blatant violation of the 1954 Geneva Agreements and could, if published, upset the delicate detente between the USSR and the US. In response, the MAAG censor, Lieutenant Colonel John T. Little, wrote, "This entire paragraph is a security compromise. Must jibe with the cover story no matter how thin it appears. Recommend rewriting to indicate that personnel here prior to spring 1961 were in USAR and were recalled to active duty in place when the RLG appealed for direct military help."

In deference to national security and her respect of the military, Dickey edited the article accordingly. Yet, apparently, this proved insufficient for whomever or whichever department wanted the story buried entirely. At the time, her photos of American Special Forces engaging in combat while wearing White Star patches were the only of their kind. Disappearing them beneath the sea of boxes in Army censorship proved easy enough.

Dickey would spend eighteen months trying to retrieve her photos, writing to the highest echelons of military leadership, including General David Shoup, the Marine Corps commandant, to no avail. Though acknowledging their receipt and proving they had them by publishing one in their flagship magazine, the Army never released her photos. This marked both the last time Dickey would trust her government wholesale as well as the beginning of her fight to protect the freedom of the press.

But for now, her campaign would have to be delayed. In May 1962, *National Geographic* commissioned her to cover the most recent addition to combat in Vietnam: American helicopters. To understate the matter, Dickey was eminently qualified to write this story. After all, she had been researching helicopter warfare from its inception in 1955 at Camp Pendleton.

Packed and ready to depart, she checked her mail one last time. In it she found a letter from Robert K. Brown, former Army captain, soon to be Green Beret, later founder of *Soldier of Fortune* magazine, and one-time vice-chair of the National Rifle Association, with whom she shared several mutual acquaintances.

"Hey Dickey," he wrote, "Another quick note. If you can get a tape recorder for a while, I'll send you the tapes I cut with the Commando L people and Orlando Bosch." His casual tone did not match the implications of his note. Orlando Bosch was a militant anti-Castro Cuban exile who would be arrested in 1968 for firing on a Polish freighter with a bazooka only to flee to Venezuela and then eventually be granted residency in the United States by President George H. W. Bush, a former CIA director. At the time however, Orlando was the leader of the Coordination of United Revolutionary Organizations (CORU), an umbrella organization for the Cuban exile militias working out of Miami that the FBI regarded as a terrorist group, the CIA funded generously, and of which Commandos L was a part. As a well-known anti-communist, Robert was acquainted with several militias and wanted Dickey to cover CORU and Commandos L's efforts to get back the weapons seized by the government in various raids under somewhat extralegal circumstances. Intrigued, Dickey nevertheless replied she would have to revisit his tip. War waits for no reporter and she had an appointment in Vietnam.

On May 27, 1962, Dickey arrived at Soc Trang Airfield in the Mekong River Delta where the Marines had started airlifting Vietnamese combat troops in April. Originally built by the Japanese in World War II, subsequently occupied by the French, and recently overhauled by the Americans, the airfield smacked of modern war. Seventy-five strong-back tents were arranged in neat rows, a state-of-the-art water purification system purred twenty-four hours a day, and the mess, she was assured, served three hot meals a day. Razor wire surrounded the entire perimeter.

Before dawn the next morning, Dickey piled her plate high with ham, eggs, and pancakes, got a cup of coffee, smoked a cigarette, then went out to photograph the troops loading onto the fleet in the day's first light. Sixteen helicopters each held eighteen Vietnamese infantrymen along with three Marine advisors. As the rotors began to whir, she jumped in the rearmost chopper and watched the ground fall away from the open loading door. When it closed, she noticed light streaming in from the bullet holes in the chopper's fuselage.

Dickey spent dozens of hours aloft with the US Marines and Vietnamese infantry. As in World War II, when reporters flying over the Allied fleet described it with a dispassionate air, journalists in Vietnam often wrote about the view from helicopters with a sense of detachment. Dickey noted this tendency in her *National Geographic* article, writing, "In the newspaper back home the reports always seemed so cool, somehow detached from life." But here too she disagreed with this attitude of distance. In her eyes, the altitude of their chopper only illustrated how omnipresent the war had become as it wound its way ever deeper into the heart of Vietnam.

From Dickey's vantage point, generals and presidents neither composed nor directed this conflict. Instead those fighting, dying, and trying to survive were once more at the center of her coverage. Dickey tried to portray this truth in her photography and writing. Painting a portrait of the landscape outside, she wrote, "The sunlit rice fields of Ba Xiuen Province seemed to sink beneath us as the formation of 16 helicopters cast dragonfly reflections on the standing water below. Oddly, the utter serenity of the mirrorlike water increased my tension. It brought home a banality that was nevertheless bedrock truth—it was too nice a day to die. Or to Kill. Or to manhunt. But that was what the men were here for, and I was going along to photograph them and write their story."

Inside the helicopter, she focused her viewfinder on the infantrymen, packed shoulder to shoulder, gun to gun. The soldier farthest to the back seems to be made of steel while the man in front of him looks into her lens with an almost boy-like fear. The soldier in the center leans deliberately forward, as if purposely framing himself as the focal point. Beside him, another prays over his gun, and finally closest to her, the soldier looking up at her lens seems to ask if everything will be okay. It is a masterful portrait of men about to go into battle and one of the first to come out of the Vietnam War.

The pilot signaled they were reaching their destination of Ap My Thanh, where there had been reports of Viet Cong activity. She felt the heat of the earth as they sank lower, the pressure mounting. Her camera and press pass offered no protection here. Her lot would be the same as those she covered. She took solace in the fact they were professionals, especially Corporal Nguyen, the squad leader whose cool demeanor calmed her.

"The Vietnamese troops smoothly shifted their weight," she wrote. "They had been sitting, now everyone was crouched, ready to spring." The door opened. The chopper hovered, its rotor and blades churning the tall grass below into hundred-mile-an-hour vortexes. Nguyen jumped. Dickey followed.

"The first firing rolled over us then," wrote Dickey. Nguyen responded like the well-trained officer he was, signaling to his men to pay no attention and keep moving. But by the time the sixteen units had made a sweep of the town, the Viet Cong had done what they did best and disappeared, leaving behind fifty camouflaged foxholes and little else. The troops made three arrests, released two, took the third in for questioning since they found a single South Vietnamese one-piastre note in his pocket, supposedly a recognition signal between operatives. Though little occurred by military standards, it struck Dickey that it had a great deal of meaning to the villagers.

"This small event in Ap My Thanh," Dickey reflected, "bespoke a shift in the winds of a war. Two years earlier, isolated villagers could have had little notion of their government's efforts to defend them. Now an outer world was being unveiled with fleets of helicopters overhead, hunting Viet Cong guerrillas, or alighting to disgorge disciplined troops, at times by the battalion." For all the times Dickey got it right, there were those when she got it completely wrong, all the more misguided for being so close to seeing the truth.

Though she accurately assessed a change in prevailing winds, she miscalculated in whose favor they blew. America based a large part of its strategy in Vietnam on the belief that helicopters would provide an antidote to the Viet Cong's confounding stealth. Many, including Dickey, bought into this theory. Yet increasing reliance on air deployment meant that American and ARVN (Army of the Republic of Vietnam) troops ceded the ground entirely to the Viet Cong. As a result, the Viet Cong were given free rein to move, organize, attack, and disperse, as well as embed themselves in villages where they recruited new guerrillas, levied taxes, and fed themselves from the fields. As counterinsurgency expert Sir Robert Thompson later wrote, helicopters proved "a fatal fascination for military commanders." Evidence of the faulty logic behind this thinking amassed throughout the war, and unknowingly, Dickey would document one of the first and most telling instances of this flawed tactic.

IT HAPPENED BY accident. The helicopter she rode in had engine trouble while on the way to another search and destroy mission like the one she had accompanied in Ap My Thanh. While Dickey waited in the briefing tent for the malfunction to be repaired, the province's governor sped into camp in his jeep with news. Vinh Quoi, a village thirty miles to the west, was under attack.

The repairs made, Dickey reboarded the chopper once more as it departed for a reconnaissance mission. The veil of morning mist cleared as they approached, revealing the horror below. Vinh Quoi was on fire. All of it. Rifles cracked at the fleeing villagers, then at their helicopter. The Marine aboard slid into position behind the Browning automatic and began to fire. Dickey pointed and clicked, capturing the first image of a Marine in combat in Vietnam.

"See them go!" he yelled over the helicopter's intercom. "I bet I can count two hundred right now!"

Dickey looked down. "Even my nearsighted eyes could spot scores of them," she wrote of the troops below. "They were exploding out of the village in a circle that widened as I watched. They were using a pattern of dispersal that marked them as trained soldiers." And even more tellingly, they wore helmets and carried military packs. "We were seeing what had been only a ghost force to most Americans here: conventional Communist forces miles from North Viet Nam."

In actuality, these troops were more likely from the National Liberation Front (NLF), composed largely of former anti-French Viet Minh fighters from South Vietnam, trained in North Vietnam, and transported back into the field of battle via the Ho Chi Minh Trail. Formed in 1960, this regular army quickly increased its numbers and strength. Six months after Dickey took this photo, the NLF's effectiveness became fatally clear.

On January 2, 1963, ARVN ground troops and their American advisors were taken by surprise by a 350-man-strong force of the NLF's best troops in the Battle of Ap Bac. In total, eighty Saigon-based forces were killed and more than a hundred were injured while five helicopters were downed over the course of a few hours. Conversely, the NLF suffered only eighteen killed and thirty-nine wounded.

In the end, the NLF won a textbook victory while American and ARVN troops suffered a crushing defeat. As a result, the NLF were emboldened and lauded as heroes, while the Americans scrambled to shift the blame onto ARVN. Succeeding in doing so, the ensuing erosion of confidence in the ability of the South Vietnamese forces to fight their own war quickly precipitated the subsequent Americanization of the conflict.

As former South Vietnamese ambassador to the United States Bui Diem observed following the disaster of Ap Bac, US leaders were "horrified by the resulting mess, took the whole ball of wax into their hands, intervening with massive military might. They did this suddenly and unilaterally, without even consulting their ally in any meaningful way. In effect, they had worked themselves into a corner from which they could only escape—or so they thought—by making the war American."

With macabre serendipity, exactly one week after the battle of Ap Bac, Dickey won her second major award, the National Press Photographers Association's Picture of the Year Award for "Helicopter War in South Viet Nam" in *National Geographic,* which pictured US advisors firing on NLF troops for the first time. By then, she had reengaged her own government over the right to a free press, the final fuse to this fight having been lit over that very article.

30

Freedom of the Press

"This is a protest against the deletions requested by government security review officers from 'Helicopter War in South Viet Nam,'" Dickey wrote to the DOD press secretary, Arthur Sylvester. The photograph in question pictured a Marine in firing position on a helicopter while communist National Liberation Front troops ransacked a village below. Their objection supposedly stemmed from a concern that such a photo would provide the Viet Cong with new intelligence as to the strategic thinking and combat practices of American troops.

As per usual, Dickey countered faulty logic with eyewitnessed facts. "I am alive to make this protest only because of such readiness, and I have witnessed it on no less than 23 flights (four times we did come under hostile fire, and returned it) in Viet Nam. Printing this photograph can give the Viet Cong no information they do not have." Without a viable rebuttal, the DOD had to remove its objection and her photo appeared in *National Geographic*.

Yet the DOD, CIA, and White House's efforts to exert control did not end here. Instead, each ratcheted up their efforts of wholesale propaganda and blackout campaigns, which Dickey witnessed first with the Bay of Pigs and now again in October 1962 as Kennedy and Nikita Khrushchev faced off over nuclear missiles in Cuba, an event Dickey planned on witnessing.

With plenty of time, she applied for and received *Reader's Digest* credentials that were subsequently acknowledged by the Marine

Corps. Proper paperwork in hand, she requested permission to land with the Marines should an invasion of Cuba occur during what came to be known as the Cuban Missile Crisis. Yet as the events unfolded, it became clear that neither she nor any reporter would be allowed to witness any of the quickly escalating situation. Pivoting, she called the assistant White House press secretary, Malcolm Kilduff, and amiably suggested she parachute into wherever the troops were stationed as she had already done in South Korea, Laos, and Vietnam.

In response, the White House denied any such troops existed and waved her off the story entirely. Months later she and Malcolm met again at the Overseas Press Club where he was the keynote speaker at an event honoring college newspaper editors. As Dickey recounted in a letter, "Mr. Kilduff recalled my visit to the White House recently when I met him at the Press Club. As we shook hands he said, smiling faintly to the meeting chairman, that he hoped he wouldn't have to 'sit next to that crazy paratrooper.' So I sat across from him instead."

Unfazed by his rudeness, she exposed his hypocrisy during the question and answer period following his speech.

"Mr. Kilduff," began Beverly Kees, one of the editors in attendance, "a reporter told me today that even if correspondents had been assigned by big publications to see armed forces during the Cuban crisis last October, they weren't allowed to go."

"That's right," he replied.

"Why was that?" Beverly followed up.

Then Dickey jumped in.

"Mac, this is all in the family—I'm the reporter Beverly is talking about, and she is referring to me coming to your office late in the crisis week last fall."

"We decided to have no eyewitnesses at this time," Malcom replied flatly.

"Can you tell us why you made that decision?" another reporter pressed.

"You can't ever expect to have an eyewitness observer when you drop an atom bomb, for Heaven's sake," he guffawed.

"There is in this building, at this moment, Mac," Dickey shot back, "a man who won the Pulitzer Prize in 1945 for being an eyewitness observer when the atom bomb was dropped, Bill Laurence of *The New York Times*."

The exchange cemented the administration's and Dickey's mutual antipathy. But more than this, Kennedy's overt attempts to suppress the media marked a shift in Dickey's willingness to take officials at their word as she had in the past, especially during World War II. Having often reported on and experienced in Fö Street Prison the end result of press censorship, the threat posed by the Kennedy administration's repressive policies toward the media were more than academic for Dickey. They were existential and would in the near future magnify her own tendency toward radical action. For now, though, she tried her best to combat these disturbing developments through nonviolent means.

Christmas and New Year's came and went. Dickey went back on the road, telling the uncensored truth to whomever would listen. At night in motel rooms, she hammered out her manifesto of a free press, then sent it to everyone she could think of. Published in the winter edition of *National Photo Journalist* magazine under the title "Is the News Controlled?," Dickey breathed into it all the fire she had, writing, "handouts and news briefings, which have all the authenticity of patent medicine ads, are replacing eye-witness accounts." From her experiences behind the Iron Curtain, Dickey knew that if such secondary news sources became the bedrock of American journalism, it would not only mean "that I and others like me will be out of jobs, but it also means we have suffered the greatest loss of freedom to occur under the American flag."

Yet for all the miles she drove, all the petitions she organized, all the articles she wrote, Dickey saw no change and no give in the Kennedy administration's policy of stonewalling the press. Instead, it became more entrenched and more resolute in withholding information from the media and the public at large.

Simultaneously, Castro clenched his iron grip around the throat of Cuba. Many of those Dickey had reported on and marched beside during the revolution were now in jail, accused of being anticommunists. All the while, the Kennedy administration did nothing to oppose this increasingly brutal regime and, what's more, were actively suppressing the

Cuban exiles in Miami who were trying to effect regime change. In a fog of disillusionment, disappointment, and most of all anger, Dickey secured an assignment from *Reader's Digest* to cover these anti-Castro militias. But somewhere along the way she abandoned any pretense of journalistic perspective and jumped into the fray with both feet.

31

Ninety Miles

THE ALARM RADIO clicked on.

"¡Buenos días!" the disc jockey shouted. "Son las seis de la mañana en Miami en otro día soleado!"

Dickey groaned, rolled over, and turned it off. There was something she had forgotten to do but could not remember what. The crimson sunrise creeping in through the leaves of the grapefruit tree outside her window reminded her of mornings at her grandparents' house, not ten miles from here, where she had lived for a while in 1939 as an itinerant teenager. Things were not so different now, with Castro taking pages from Batista's book. New boss same as the old boss.

Dickey swept her legs over the edge of the bed and pushed her feet into black tennis shoes, then remembered what she had forgotten: she had accidentally left the nitroglycerin in the refrigerator's vegetable drawer overnight.

The last straw came when the assistant secretary of defense for public affairs, Arthur Sylvester, said that "the government has the right to lie" when it came to the Cuban Missile Crisis. At that point, Dickey circled back with Robert K. Brown, who offered to introduce her to the Commandos L. Her initial point of contact came through Gerald "Gerry" Patrick Hemming, an ex-Marine who ran a military training school for anti-Castro militia members.

With her sources secured, *Reader's Digest* gave her the go-ahead with the story, along with six months' rent in advance for a duplex in Hialeah she now shared with the Commandos L. Through the wall she could hear them getting ready for their morning calisthenics. Anyway, the nitro hadn't exploded last night and it was too nice of a morning to worry about it now.

She'd been with them living under an assumed name for three months. Ostensibly, she was there to get the story. But it was more than that. It had become a way of life. She ate what they ate, a mix of canned charity food and sumptuous dinners donated by local Cuban restaurants in support of the cause. She began to learn Spanish, radio code, and knife throwing. "I now can wheel and throw a trench knife from six paces hard enough to drive it point first into the trunk of a tree forty times out of fifty," she bragged in her notes. And she made friends, as she always did, with the military men she covered.

There was Jorge, who had been a fisherman's son in Cuba and now served as the Commandos' main helmsman. In March, he drove the boat while his compatriots attacked and sank the Russian freighter, the *Baku*, in the harbor of Caibarién, Cuba. Pablo, their boatbuilder, kept alive the fierce spirit of his ancestor, who refused to renounce his beliefs in the face of Spanish conquistadors and died a martyr at the stake.

She had met Ramón Font before in Cuba when the platoon she traveled with had been cut off from the main battalion. It had been Ramón and his wife who fed and sheltered them when they straggled past his farm, hungry and exhausted. Now his wife was in a Cuban prison and Ramón built bombs in the hopes they would one day free her. The Commandos nicknamed him Act of Love for his devotion.

Roberto, aka the Bank Robber, had earned his nickname for stealing $60,000 from Castro's nationalized bank where he had been the head teller. He lived a few houses down with his wife, Dari, who, as Dickey wrote, "I will longest remember." A mother of four, she nevertheless made time to cook for twenty Commandos while they used her carport as a dry dock, and summoned the energy to clean up after her living room had been transformed into a bomb factory. All the while, she got her children to school and bed on time, every morning and night. Dickey wrote, "If there is a Valhalla for women freedom fighters, I am sure a corner beside the Hungarian women I knew in Budapest in 1956 is already reserved for Dari." There is no revolution without domestic labor.

Finally, there was Tony Questa. Tall and handsome, with eyes like Gregory Peck and a chin like Cary Grant, he exuded the kind of charm that people wanted to follow. As a teenager, he'd been an Olympic swimmer. As a young man, he'd been an officer in Castro's army. At thirty-six, he led the Commandos L, having defected when Castro cozied up to communism.

After their Marine Corps workout, as per Gerry's training, Tony held court in the duplex's sunporch that had been converted into an arms factory. Everyone worked, including Dickey.

"The bullet polishing department is in the southwest corner," Dickey wrote in her journal, and had "an electric motor with a grinding brush on an overturned broken chair. We have six thousand rounds to the wrong caliber dated 1906 to clean off the crud. It's busy work for everyone, and charmingly hazardous." In order to polish the bullets they held them barehanded against the steel brush, a process that heated exceptionally old, exceptionally volatile gunpowder. "We take turns," she deadpanned.

Across lay the station for reboring and rechambering machine guns. Dickey had personally searched for these supplies in Hialeah's hardware stores wearing hoop earrings and orange pedal pushers so as not to arouse suspicion. It worked. No one even batted an eyelash as she asked for yards of eighth-inch steel tubing.

Finally, the entire north side of the porch was taken up by the bomb-building department where Ramón and Dickey constructed what they called "Canon de Materialet."

"You take an empty #10 can (we used Hunt's tomato and catsup cans)," Dickey explained in her notes, "with the top cut off and put a quarter-inch bolt six inches long stuck up through the bottom" for the detonator. Then, they finally got the nitroglycerin out of her refrigerator, packed it into the cans with a Coke bottle, and topped it off with homemade napalm laden with scavenged shrapnel like rusty bolts and ball bearings. Lastly, they sealed it with a tri-folded *Life* magazine double-page spread and painters tape, inserted the fuse, and spray-painted the whole thing black.

"I think anyone who prepares a napalm bomb is already guilty of first-degree murder," wrote Dickey. "I remember my righteousness in 1958 when I made the pictures in Mayerí, Cuba, to prove that two lousy bombs of it had in fact been airdropped on dwellings by Batista B-26s. And here we've made dozens of those bombs! What else can I say?"

America had changed, and seeing it for what it had become, so did she. No longer in the business of exporting freedom, the United States sought instead to consolidate power—the same as the Soviets. And like the Soviets, her country had built its own secret police in the form of the CIA that operated outside the bounds of law while pursuing its own ends.

Though she had been at the center of the world's conflicts for two decades, until now her purpose in reporting had always been to bring about the end of violence, to garner support for the side fighting for freedom, to press her government to intervene before or just after fighting had begun, thereby averting or shortening the conflict. Yet now, in this new America, Dickey could not see past the shadows of the dimming light where her camera and pen seemed to lose their usefulness. Desperate to find a way to achieve her lifelong ambition of supporting those who fought for freedom, she finished spray-painting her last Canon de Materialet. Their arsenal was nearly complete.

The lights of the city flickered across the water as they passed by along the river the next night. "Aboard were the materials to set an oil refinery aflame, burn a sugar mill, explode an ammunition dump, detonate a highway bridge, destroy a Castro militia patrol, sabotage a Russian barracks, hole a Russian built Mig jet aloft with bullets," wrote Dickey of their cargo. Ahead of them were seven bridges, then the open ocean.

Dickey looked around the deck after they passed beneath the first. "The dissimilar faces had been similarly wiped clean of expression, the eyes narrowed, the lip composed. On my way with them as a reporter," she continued, "I wondered if my face had come to look like theirs, if what we shared marked me too." Undoubtedly, it did.

A police boat approached. Roberto put his arm around Dickey. "I will tell Dari later why," he whispered, "but now it must look romantic." Dickey was flattered and amused. The police boat drove by.

Another bridge and another. The harbor lights waned. Tony stood up.

"If ever we become separated, remember these orders. We are not a powerful force and perhaps it will not be possible for all of us to come back together. So no matter what has happened to your comrades in arms, you will need to pass them without halt, to pass your best friend, to pass me if I am hurt or leave my body if I am killed. Once you are committed, all that matters is that each of you do whatever you have been ordered."

The last bridge slipped above them. The ocean opened ahead. Dickey leaned back, lit a cigarette, stared into the darkness of the unknown. She too was now committed, having relinquished the protection of her nationality and profession, neither of which meant anything in the Cold War's proxy wars anyway. If shot, she would remain where she fell.

Scanning the horizon for the four other boats they were meant to rendezvous with, Dickey spotted a blinking light and recognized them as the dots and dashes of Morse code. She took out her notebook.

"Read it to me," said Roberto.

"R . . . L . . . W—" said Dickey and turned back to Roberto. But instead of him, she saw only the blinding silver-white of a Coast Guard searchlight, coming in fast.

With no chance of outrunning them and the certainty of death if the Coast Guard opened fire in pursuit, since one bullet was more than enough to start a chain reaction igniting all the bombs on board, Jorge cut the engine. A voice came over the waves. "We've got 'em!"

The Coast Guard tied the Commandos L's boat to its own and towed them back to harbor, where they found the other four militia boats and their crews waiting on the dock. Their boats and cargos were confiscated. They were all released without being arrested or written up in any official capacity. Dickey suspected the CIA was behind this mid-sea raid.

She confirmed her suspicions in later interviews with various representatives from numerous intelligence offices including the Air Force, Customs, and Department of State, all of whom spoke on the condition of anonymity. The Commandos L had been under constant surveillance. These raids were knowingly and purposefully carried out without a warrant or any other constitutional safeguards. That the militia members were not charged, said one representative, "can be interpreted as an expression of a degree of American sympathy for the frustration of Cuban exiles," and that to prosecute them would be to risk igniting a new desire by the electorate to overthrow Cuba's communist regime.

There were no heroes, not even Dickey. But she had been right. The US government was carrying out a coordinated campaign to control the narrative surrounding Cuban-US relations and in so doing, had acquiesced to the will of a dictator less than ninety miles off the coast of America. Yet once more, the reality of the situation sank so much further into the abyss.

With the Commandos L in disarray, Dickey returned to Gerry for another introduction within the Cuban exile community. By this time, they had formed a loose friendship and Dickey had helped Gerry to craft a series of letters to various journalists and government officials with the intention of drumming up support for Cuban exile militias. She did not know, or even suspect how deeply she had trodden into the murky underworld of CIA activity in 1960s Miami.

For starters, Dickey's friend and assistant secretary of state, Ed Lansdale, had instituted and led Operation Mongoose, a CIA program that helped organize, fund, and train anti-Castro militias. Gerry had been a pivotal player in Operation Mongoose, having founded its first and most successful tactical training camps for militia members. But when the Kennedy administration grew frustrated with a lack of progress and pulled the plug on Operation Mongoose's funding, multiple parties approached Gerry with offers to pay him to assassinate the president. Gerry later testified in front of a congressional hearing that he had turned such offers down, but that the same parties approached multiple Cuban exile militias with the same offer. In the end, Lee Harvey Oswald, who had visited one of Gerry's training camps on several occasions, assassinated President Kennedy in November 1963, just as Gerry was introducing Dickey to the Exiles X, another anti-Castro militia whom he had helped train.

Soon after joining them, Dickey discovered the government kept the Exiles X under constant surveillance. "Between Christmas and New Year," she wrote to her new editor at *Reader's Digest*, Andrew "Andy" Jones, "US Special Forces opposed to Exiles X were augmented by at least a dozen men described as wearing green berets and arriving at the US Customs building in the Miami River aboard a green assault boat."

Not long after, "surveillance of the Exiles X's good cruiser, a large speed boat, became continuous."

Trying to adopt a lower profile, the Exiles X substituted a stubby twenty-two-foot craft with a cabin made of orange crates for the mission Dickey planned to accompany them on. Doing her part to help them evade the authorities, Dickey rented an apartment on the river and allowed the Exiles X to use its private dock. As ever, she lent a hand, sleeping by day and spending her nights loading boats destined for Cuba's shores. But rather than weapons, they loaded their boat with food and water for those refugees lost at sea while trying to flee an increasingly repressive regime. The Exiles X regularly ran missions in search of boats adrift to the degree that their leader, Felipe Vidal Santiago, had become known as a "fisherman" among the exile community for all the people he had rescued from the sea.

But at this point, the CIA had become methodical in their campaign to stymie the efforts of anti-Castro militias, regardless of the purpose of any individual mission.

On the night they were set to depart, Felipe and Dickey found the boat, supplies and all, underwater at the dock. The man who was supposed to be guarding it had left his post for an hour and someone thought they saw Special Forces types in the area. Men immediately dove into the water, searching for pumps attached to the haul. When they found them, they pumped for hours by hand. Dickey took her turn as well. By morning they had the boat above water again. Smashed baby food jars floated on the flooded deck.

For the next five nights they salvaged what they could, repurchased what couldn't be saved, and overhauled the engine. They left just before dawn and saw Miami fading into the distance as first light broke across the horizon. Dickey thought back to her time on the Austrian-Hungarian border, of all those nights she had spent ferrying displaced persons the last few hundred yards to safety, to the free world. Here again, she thought she might have found her true calling. Yet again, her lofty ambitions were truncated by reality.

"As my eyes went back across the engine housing between the gasoline drums, I knew a second of utter disbelief. I knew what I saw could not be.

"The blue sky, the bluer water, the bright sunlight, the gray hull, the silhouette of the cabin housing, the laughing figure at the wheel—all were gone. My world in a split second had dissolved into fire. Luminous, orange, flickering, hot, terrible flame. And then I wasn't looking at it anymore either. A giant irresistible hand had pushed me back."

The concussion of exploding gasoline drums lifted her out of the boat and into the ocean. Dickey swam to the surface, the salt water stinging her burnt skin. Incredibly, everyone had been similarly blown clear. But without speaking a word, they knew they were not yet out of danger. Neither the bulk of the gasoline nor the boat's engine had exploded yet. Worse, they were surrounded by slicks of fuel. Instantaneously, they all began swimming for their lives, desperate to get out of the blast radius and away from the spilled gasoline.

Miraculously, a fishing boat started motoring toward them. They swam faster, clambering aboard to safety seconds before their boat exploded.

Dickey checked into a hospital and out of Miami. She had had enough of this maze of smoke and mirrors. Even worse, *Reader's Digest* declined to print the majority of her work. When giving her the assignment on the Commandos L, her editor had suggested she focus on the "pitiful and minute and nearly futile gesture" of the militia members whom he said were "normal unmilitary middle-aged people who have become desperate enough to engage themselves in all but hopeless action." Seeming to follow the CIA line that sought to squash the viability of this homegrown revolution, her editor continued, "These people are excitable Latins. They're not well organized or trained, their equipment is largely makeshift."

Having found no evidence that the Commandos L were pitiful, hopeless, or desperate, Dickey refused to change her copy. Instead, she described them as stalwart, committed, and well trained as well as undaunted even against the steepest of odds. *Reader's Digest* never ran the piece, despite having paid for the Commandos L's housing for six months, not to mention Dickey's salary and expenses. Her article on the Exiles X did eventually run, though by then their leader, Felipe, had been captured by the Cuban navy on one of his rescue missions.

While she was with the Exiles X, Felipe had taught her how to give the order to a Cuban firing squad to shoot if ever she found herself in front of one, as military prisoners were expected to do. When she heard on the radio that he had been captured, she couldn't help but imagine him in front of a row of rifles, shouting, "Preparen! Apunten! Fuego!," before crumpling to the ground. "He died by force for trying to rescue others from the fear of force," Dickey wrote in conclusion to her article, "Requiem for a Rebel," "and I am a little less afraid of it myself knowing that it took bullets—not the fear of them—to stop him."

As in much of the Cold War, the line between hero and villain blurred in early 1960s Miami. Collectively, the raids conducted by Cuban exile militias killed hundreds of innocent bystanders while doing little to destabilize the Castro regime. At the same time, they gave hope and pride to so many who, having suffered under the Batista regime, fought for the 26th of July Movement only to be forced to flee their homes in fear of their lives under Castro. As ever, Dickey searched for and found the idealistic heart of the matter, though ignored the corroded arteries of corruption and undue violence.

Even so, once again, she was one of the only reporters to eyewitness this time and place that few recognized as important but that, in fact, turned out to be a moment of lasting consequence. Slanted as her reports may appear, in her notes, journals, and photographs are rare shafts of light illuminating an otherwise shadowy landscape of undercover agents and black markets, clandestine operations and government cover-ups.

In the end, Dickey spent eight months embedded with Cuban exile militias, sharing every experience, danger, and disappointment with them as an equal. Among her journalistic peers, she was once again alone in her courage and commitment. But even Dickey could only stand so many double crosses and sought to get back to where things made a little more sense, or at least had. By August 1964, she secured another assignment on the Ho Chi Minh Trail.

32

Water War

HER BURNS DIDN'T scar. By February, she'd gone back out on the road for her lecture tour of freedom and democracy. Her style of dress had always had a slickness to it—cat-eye glasses, pencil skirts, and pumps. But her edges had hardened now. She added shoulder pads to her jackets, wore spike-heel boots, pulled her hair back tight. With the softness ironed out, she stepped onstage, told the stories of the Commandos L and Exiles X, Special Forces in Laos and Sea Swallows in Vietnam, of men fighting to the death in every corner of the globe, even right here at home. She had seen them all. And she could not unsee what her camera photographed or forget the stories they had told her. Every day for months, she woke up, drove, recounted their lives and deaths, drove, told them again, drove, repeated them once more, then drove to yet another motel where she inevitably collapsed into sleep.

Summer, finally. Back in New York City just in time for those June days when fireflies rise from Central Park's lawns and warm breezes sweeping along Manhattan's rivers wash the city in a collective daydream.

Dickey let her guard down, for a moment. She and Shepard Rifkin, her literary friend and sometimes lover, fell into bed together again. Stayed there longer than usual. He almost asked her to stay forever.

"In a world where many things seem similar, the perceptive eye sees fundamental differences," he wrote to her in a little booklet of poetry and prose. The next page reads, "You, for instance!" Then his booklet asked, "Aren't you tired of things like" followed by a photograph of a painting of a naval battle between Britain and France. "Wouldn't you rather?" he asked with a picture of a woman dozing in a field, book by her side.

But he knew. "I guess not," read the penultimate page, and below it, "I have unwritten a poem only for you." They both braced themselves for the end of summer when she would shed her softness again and leave.

In July, she had to admit her age in order to push it back once more. Parachuting and marching with twentysomething soldiers took a toll on her knees and she underwent surgery. It was painful. Dickey gritted her teeth, bore it, bided her time. It paid off.

National Geographic gave her an open-ended commission to cover the Ho Chi Minh Trail (HCMT) either in Laos or Vietnam, whichever proved most feasible. They agreed to pay her $1,200 a month plus expenses, with $2,500 for the article and $200 for each color page of her photographs they printed. It was a queenly sum. And frankly, a welcome relief.

Reader's Digest had recently tried to nickel-and-dime her out of proper payment for their use of her photographs from Vietnam. "I look to the Digest to pay me as they would anybody else," she wrote to the photo editor, Andy Jones. "A normal page rate for any kind of color illustration in a major magazine might run $200 each for pictures across the gutter and $100 for the others." In the end, they paid her, but it was insulting to have to insist on her worth and value after all these years. With *National Geographic,* it felt good to be appreciated without having a fight.

Ed Lansdale, who never did tell her what part he played in Operation Mongoose and had since been reassigned to Vietnam, sent her a letter a few days before she departed in September. "Saigon keeps changing fast," he wrote. Perhaps meant as words of warning, they were an understatement.

In November 1963, a CIA-backed Vietnamese army coup overthrew President Diệm, which destabilized an already fraught political landscape and opened insurmountable rifts between the Vietnamese army and navy. That same month, President Kennedy, who'd recently tended more toward diplomacy than military action, was assassinated. His vice president and successor, Lyndon B. Johnson, favored war.

But of far greater consequence than either of these violent changes in leadership was the paradigmatic shift in the United States' principal adversary from the USSR to the People's Republic of China (PRC). The Cuban Missile Crisis along with the Soviet Union's own domestic needs persuaded the USSR to pursue a policy of détente with the United States. China on the other hand had no such compunction.

Whereas the 1950s were in many ways defined by the USSR's expanding borders into Eastern Europe, the PRC took center stage in the 1960s with its mass support of "wars of liberation," particularly in Southeast Asia and especially in Vietnam. By mid-1963, Beijing had drastically increased the amount of arms supplied to North Vietnam, and by proxy the Viet Cong as well as the Pathet Lao. This stream turned into a river in 1964 when arms shipped from North Vietnam to South Vietnam exceeded the totals of 1962 and 1963 combined. Saigon was changing indeed.

Then, only a few weeks before Dickey was set to depart, the USS *Maddox* reported an attack by the North Vietnamese navy in the Gulf of Tonkin. In response, the US Congress passed the Gulf of Tonkin Resolution, granting President Johnson the authorization to deploy conventional military forces without a formal declaration of war.

So began in earnest the era of Americanization of the Vietnam War. Yet, as with so much in the Cold War, this justification of war turned out to be more fabrication than truth. Declassified documents show that top government officials contrived much of the Gulf of Tonkin incident in order to manufacture a reason to escalate the conflict. Nevertheless, President Johnson appeared on television at almost midnight on August 4, decrying this supposedly egregious act of war. This would be their Pearl Harbor, the facts be damned.

Unaware of this deceit as everyone else, Dickey dove headfirst into this morass. In October 1964, she landed in Vientiane by way of Bangkok, Thailand, where merchants and US personnel alike had informed her Laos was anything but neutral. Instead, the HCMT that ran along the border of Laos and Vietnam continued to be a thoroughfare for soldiers, arms, and supplies from North Vietnam via the PRC into South Vietnam. The merchants that she spoke to, who relied on several of the established roads utilized by the HCMT, told Dickey that their trucks were regularly destroyed by the Viet Cong. In response, according to Ron Sher, a US press officer, the Royal Lao Air Force (RLAF) had begun to surveil and bomb the HCMT almost daily in tactical planes. Then he asked her if she'd like to ride along.

Of course she booked a ticket to Laos.

Getting on an RLAF plane proved more difficult than Ron had made it seem. She made progress at first. Ron introduced her to General Thao Ma, an innovative commander whose hands-on approach was widely credited with improving morale in and tactical efficacy of the RLAF. Later in the war, General Ma would be exiled and then executed for his refusal to accept bribes to fly heroin and opium in RLAF planes.

Now, on the precipice of a new kind of war neither of them had yet dared to face, the general welcomed her cordially and "enthusiastically endorsed my idea of riding his tactical planes to photograph the Trail." In his view, coverage of Viet Cong activity on the HCMT and the RLAF's response would prove vital to the Lao cause. They agreed she should begin her coverage the following week.

But when she returned to his office in Savannakhet, she inadvertently interrupted what she immediately recognized as a tactical briefing. "US Air Force attaché, Col. Van Bibber, was talking as he held large black-and-white photographs, obviously serials made from a great height—just the kind of pictures you might expect from the reconnaissance planes of the Seventh Fleet, which the US had publicly stated were serving the Lao government," wrote Dickey in a letter to her editor at *National Geographic,* recounting the event.

Before she could entirely grasp what the photos were, Dickey continued, "the colonel stepped and bodily removed me from the room, telling me in the most unflattering language that I was an intruder." Dickey objected that she had an appointment with the general, at which point the flustered colonel replied that he would protect the general from her. She found this both ridiculous and not hardly intimidating enough to wave her off the story.

Later that evening, she happened to be walking by US ambassador to Laos Leonard S. Unger's residence in Vientiane when his Marine Corps guard recognized her and invited her in. Apparently happy to see her, the ambassador offered her a drink and listened to her plight. After she had finished, he offered to fly her on his personal plane back to Savannakhet with orders to his subordinates to council General Ma to allow her to ride in an RLAF tactical plane and photograph their operations over the HCMT. This was arranged, as were assurances from General Ma's command group in Saigon whereupon the RLAF issued her written credentials. And yet.

"I was also instructed by General Ma's adjutant to stand by in my hotel room until I was called on by some American officers," Dickey recalled. "Three days later, they showed up—crew cuts, flat guts, sport shirts—and introduced themselves as 'semi-clandestine.'" Believing they were on her side, Dickey divulged her plans to cover the HCMT, much to her later chagrin. "Once these clowns had come into the project, I NEVER again was able to see General Ma privately," she wrote her editor.

Accurately assessing the chain of command in Laos after this encounter, Dickey wrote, "it seems clear that the Royal Lao Air Force was not guided by the express will of its own commander or of the US attaches, or of the US ambassador. It is unclear whether in this matter the force was in fact guided by the wishes of the clandestine types."

Once again, history proved just how perceptive and prescient Dickey had been.

In mid-1964, President Johnson authorized Operation Barrel Roll, a clandestine bombing operation carried out by the US Air Force largely directed and informed by the CIA in support of their Hmong army waging a guerrilla war against the Pathet Lao. In interrupting the meeting between Van Bibber and General Ma, Dickey had witnessed the lead-up to this illegal operation in direct violation of the international agreement guaranteeing the neutrality of Laos. For decades, Operation Barrel Roll remained one of the most secretive components in America's strategy in the Vietnam War. It was also one of the most devastating to the civilians who were caught beneath this nine-year cataract of napalm, rockets, and bombs. In the end, the campaign failed in its objective to meaningfully stifle traffic along the HCMT.

In pursuit of the story from a different angle, Dickey left Laos for Saigon on November 13, 1964, coincidentally exactly one month before Operation Barrel Roll would commence. But where she had been turned back from getting the story from the sky, she succeeded in getting it from the water.

Once the domain of river pirates, the vast maze of lakes, streams, swamps, and islands that make up the Mekong River Delta had become an invaluable extension to the HCMT. In the delta's headwaters, North Vietnamese arms traders and the South Vietnamese navy played a deadly game of hide-and-seek in sampans through a rhizome of rivulets. Where the delta spilled into the South China Sea, the South Vietnamese Junk Force tried to stem the influx of North Vietnamese armored boats that carried more weapons than the war had seen yet.

For the sixty thousand miles of waterways that lay in between, there was the River Assault Group (RAG). This was where Dickey went first. Things were not going well, to put it mildly.

Traditionally, the navy had been aligned with President Diệm, who had recently been deposed in a violent coup by the Army of the Republic of Vietnam (ARVN). When navy commander Ho Tan Quyen refused to participate, the coup's ARVN leaders assassinated him with a macabre twist while he was on the way to his birthday party. The rift between the ARVN government and the navy never healed, and the resultant dysfunction sowed its strangling roots.

Neither navy crew members nor officers were paid a living wage, forcing almost all to work second jobs while also ensuring that their wives had to find employment in addition to their myriad responsibilities within the home. Nor did sailors receive adequate training. Graduates of Radioman School were not properly taught how to line up a transmitter or load an antenna. Enginemen were deprived of instruction on even the most basic of repairs. In the field, crewmen and officers were often assigned to areas in which they had neither expertise nor experience.

Physical conditions on board were no better with faulty equipment, a dearth of proper hygiene facilities, and a shortage of food as well as medicine. Morale neared rock bottom, then hit it with the introduction of American advisors. With no knowledge of the inadequate conditions and little interest in Vietnamese cultural customs, naval MAAG personnel often exhibited racist attitudes toward their counterparts, second-guessing their capabilities rather than taking a closer look at their impossible circumstances. Yet naval operations on the Mekong Delta were imperative to the objectives of Saigon and Washington. Perhaps aware of her penchant for presenting the armed forces in the best light and fully cognizant of their own need for good PR, the MAAG press office assigned Dickey to RAG 23, the exception that proved the rule.

Dickey met up with RAG 23 in Can Tho, a small city on the Hau River known for its intricate network of canals that had once supported a thriving community of floating markets, now shuttered by scores of mines floating just beneath the water lilies. The Jolly Roger flag flying from the command ship greeted her before she stepped on board. The ranking officer, Lieutenant Nguyen Tan Hoa, welcomed her next, followed by the group's advisor, Lieutenant Harold Dale Meyerkord.

They wasted little time in showing her the ropes and set out for a water patrol that same night. They were ambushed twice and lost a man by the time the sun came up without finding even one enemy unit. When the next few days followed the same pattern, Dickey came to the conclusion that the war on the Mekong Delta was "the loneliest war I'd known in the score of years I'd been taking pictures along bayonet borders." Units were small and isolated. There were no USO shows, no mess halls, no PX stores where service members could blow their paychecks on reminders of home. There was just the river and the wish that the sun would not set since almost the entire war was fought in the dark. As Dickey predicted in her treatise of guerrilla warfare there were no defined battle lines, no maps, and no rules of engagement. There were only night raids, the meaning of which disappeared with each dawn.

A week into her stay, RAG 23 prepared for an overland patrol. Nguyen gave Dickey a carbine. She counted her shells on the deck of their gunboat as the tropical December twilight faded into dusk. A circle of troops crouched around Nguyen as he gave clear and concise orders. Earlier in the day, a villager had informed them the canal they were on was heavily mined. Meyerkord took a unit on foot patrol for confirmation, and found it. "The mine," wrote Dickey, "had been no homemade guerrilla gadget but a modern, electrically-detonated device big enough to sheer off the body and armored gun turret of his FOM, the standard 50-foot armed craft of the river patrol force." Chinese weaponry had officially penetrated the whole of the delta.

Dickey leaned over to Meyerkord. "When will we leave?" she asked. "As soon as the light goes," he replied.

Dusk, then dark. Nguyen led half their eighty-man team on the east canal bank to search for detonating wires. Meyerkord took the remaining men up the west bank where they had found the mine wire earlier in the day. "If either patrol force of a target was too big for its own rifles to handle," wrote Dickey, "the boats would come up shooting to help them out."

Dickey followed Meyerkord's patrol into the pitch-black. The stars looked like pinpricks in velvet. The sweet-sour smell of rice permeated the air. Their boots fell into the rhythm of patrol. The moment seemed so familiar to her now, yet it was precisely this that made their mission inexplicable by her estimation. "How was it possible that human beings still got along so badly with each other that conflicts among them were settled like this, by young men betting their lives on hide-and-seek in the darkness? Who could think that sending them out to kill and be killed like this was an affirmation of the dignity of man?"

Within this incomprehensible paradox her mind called into question her own purpose. "Did I truly think I could, with the tool of the camera around my neck, help end the need for the tool of the carbine on my shoulder?" she continued. "True, poets and politicians had exalted soldiering since the dawn of time. But the furtive line of real, uneasy people here somehow did not seem to include any of them; had they known what they were talking about? Did I have the vanity to think I ever could make plain to anyone how it really was?"

But none of these questions mattered in the end. Not here, not now, already in the middle of war, when rightly or wrongly, their lives were at stake and the only way to live was to kill. "Here and now," wrote Dickey, "the sum total of virtue would be—no it is—the ability to shoot back fast."

They pressed on. No mine wires yet and they reached a hamlet where Nguyen suspected there to be an arms factory. Meyerkord released his safety with a snap that echoed down the line, even in Dickey's own carbine.

"Look for anything metal," he whispered and the troops fanned out to every hut, with him in the lead.

It soon became clear the village had been deserted, except for one hut at the edge of a field of sugarcane. In whispers, an ensign spoke to the group of women still living there. They told him they hadn't seen any mines wired on this side of the canal today, but maybe, one said, there were some from the house on the other side of the canal.

Meyerkord reached in his pocket for a wad of piastres, Vietnamese currency, and offered to pay the women for the information they had provided. The women refused.

He smiled and said to Dickey as they walked away, "Not everyone even in the Viet Cong's territory hates cố vấn người Mỹ," the Vietnamese phrase for "American advisor." In all likelihood, it was just him.

Meyerkord made it a point to visit the village councils and hamlet chiefs within his patrol area, listen to their needs and assure them that RAG could provide protection, medicine, and if need be, evacuation—and kept his promises. Meyerkord also had a deep and abiding respect for his counterpart, Nguyen, as well as the sailors who served under his command, an admiration he demonstrated by engaging in battle and submitting himself to the same dangers as the rest of the members of RAG 23.

Dickey witnessed his commitment moments later as machine-gun fire crashed through the night. Meyerkord and Dickey crouched beneath a screen of knee-high grass where they could see tracer fire directed at a half dozen men on the far side of the canal. They returned fire and Dickey could not distinguish whose gun was whose in the cacophony. A stray bullet ignited spilled fuel. A single finger of flame ran up the hut from which the Viet Cong fired. The thatched roof burst into flames and the guerrillas fled.

By the light of the burning hut, the Vietnamese ensign who had first approached them brought one of the women to their position. She said thirty Viet Cong were at their back on the landward side of the cane field.

"If they charge through the cane, we'll hear them in time," said Meyerkord. "But if they set up a machine gun and sweep the fire past us, low . . ." Without having to finish his instruction Dickey and the handful of soldiers that had gathered around spread out so they couldn't all be killed by a single burst of fire.

But the ensign and the radioman remained close, whispering furtively. "He was asking whether anybody remembered the frequency on which he could call in the boats," Dickey recorded. More than a delayed pickup or a long march home, this oversight meant they were in direct danger since in such situations RAG boats usually swept the banks with machine guns. Without the means to give the boat their location, it was entirely possible that they would be caught in the hailstorm of friendly fire.

Recognizing this oversight as the result of inadequate training, Dickey marked it as such in her article. "I knew this was not just a simple matter of remembering a fixed number, like one's own telephone number. The Viet Cong had captured many American battle radios . . . So new channels were secretly chosen by the Vietnamese just before the jump-off of each new operation and confided to only the commanders." Except, apparently, this new code had not been communicated tonight. "The Vietnamese ensign did know that in his inexperience he had made a bad mistake," she wrote, while at the same time trying to dispel the malignant belief within the American military that Vietnamese service members were intransigent. "Clearly, he was appealing to the lieutenant for help; clearly he was not saving face before his American mentor. But equally clearly," Dickey wrote to those responsible for his lack of instruction, "it was now very late to start his basic training."

Resigning herself to fate, Dickey rolled onto her knees. Then, the sound of engines and no guns. "It seemed [trung úy]," wrote Dickey, using the Vietnamese word for lieutenant, "had correctly concluded, from the end of the rifle firing and the dying hut blaze, that no Viet Cong remained to detonate mines here. He was bringing his force up the canal. In ten minutes, he had located and embarked both patrols from the banks without another shot being fired."

A seemingly anticlimactic end to an otherwise dramatic scene, Dickey's writing appealed not to the bloodlust of those who experienced war vicariously, but spoke instead to the primary goal of all soldiers: to survived, uninjured. Notably, Nguyen and not Meyerkord proved the hero of the day. Her account of Nguyen's ability to correctly read the situation and take appropriate, autonomous action refuted the American-held idea that Vietnamese officers were incapable of self-direction.

After departing RAG 23, Dickey went on to spend time with the junk and sampan forces on opposite ends of the Mekong Delta. In Camp Don Hung in the village of Don Phuc near the Cambodian border, the top sergeant gave her an AR-15 and taught her to fire a mortar. She tried to demur from both until he said, "You know how many people it takes to hold this base if we get hit? Maybe about 400. You know how many warm bodies we got here tonight? With you, 78." At a naval base where the Co Chien River met the South China Sea, she ran out to photograph a firefight in her shower sandals, after which the Vietnamese Junk Force sailors she was stationed with gave her a black beret with their silver twin-sail insignia to wear.

But no story affected her like that of Nguyen and Meyerkord, which to her embodied what a truly allied United States and South Vietnam looked like and could accomplish. So news of Meyerkord's death in March of the next year hit her hard. She ended her article for *National Geographic* with his eulogy, writing, "Shortly after I returned home, there appeared on the casualty list another name: Harold Dale Meyerkord. Audacious, ebullient, Lieutenant Meyerkord of River Assault Group 23, once of St. Louis, Dale Meyerkord, husband, father, leader and teacher of men, dead of a bullet in the brain on a muddy canal 9,000 miles from Missouri."

The circumstances surrounding his death didn't make it any easier. In January 1965, RAG 23 had come under fire from a Viet Cong ambush that critically wounded Nguyen in the leg. Meyerkord assumed command and though also injured, ordered a devastating counterattack that sent the Viet Cong into full retreat. Both Nguyen and Meyerkord recovered. No other troops were injured.

But on the day Meyerkord was scheduled to receive a Bronze Star for a heroic and meritorious achievement, he asked to be excused from the ceremony in order to accompany Nguyen on a mission against a suspected Viet Cong stronghold near Vinh Long. Later that day, RAG 23 was caught in a barrage of enemy fire. Meyerkord kept his position in the deckhouse to return fire. The first bullet struck him in the stomach. The second in the chin. He died aboard the helicopter on the way to the Vinh Long medical center. As one of Meyerkord's fellow American advisors said of him, "If you send the best over here, you're going to lose the best."

In March 1965, the same month as Meyerkord's death, the Navy initiated Operation Market Time, which significantly increased its activities off the coasts of North and South Vietnam; the Air Force began a sustained campaign of bombing North Vietnam in Operation Rolling Thunder; the first combat Marines arrived in Da Nang; and the first antiwar teach-in was announced at the University of Wisconsin.

Dickey flew to Madison to speak at the university, though not in support of the peace demonstrators. Instead, she spoke at a counter-teach-in supporting the people of South Vietnam. As ever, Dickey readily acknowledged America was losing the war, but she said it was losing "because we haven't tried." A factor of ten, she said, could turn the war around. At the time that she spoke, there were approximately 1,400 combat troops and 23,000 advisors in various capacities.

"We have developed a new doctrine in warfare in the four years we have been there," she said. "In the eleven conflicts between Communism and the Free World that I have covered, this is the first time I have seen us take the initiative and the enemy respond."

But she was wrong.

She was wrong in her belief that the United States had implemented a holistic counterinsurgency doctrine that differed significantly from past colonial practices of warfare. It would have been difficult not to have been blindsided. Back again from Vietnam, the military seemed to embrace not only the information she gathered, but also, this time, her ideas on winning the war through a policy of egalitarianism.

The Warfare Systems School located at Maxwell Air Force Base invited her to speak at a special course on counterinsurgency. Entitled "Human Factors in Counterinsurgency," Dickey's lecture focused on the basic yet overlooked concept that "our allies, associates, and enemies as well must be considered as individual human beings and treated accordingly. To know of the successes others have had with the practical application of human factors." The course instructor wrote to thank her: "Your comments were hard-hitting and to the point. Your observations clearly indicated your expertise in the field. Our students were very favorably impressed with your presentation and your panel participation."

Ed Lansdale gave her another reason to hope the tide had turned in America's strategy in Vietnam. He had spent several years as advisor to the French in their fight against the Viet Minh, a precursor to the Viet Cong. Now, assigned to the US embassy in Saigon with the title of minister, which apparently meant whatever he wanted it to mean, his thinking on what victory meant had evolved. In the spring of 1965, he sent Dickey a recent talk he gave at the prestigious Principia Conference on Vietnam that gathered political and military strategists.

At the top of his lecture copy, he wrote, "To Dickie Chapelle, a girl guerrilla, girl counter-guerrilla, and a damn fine soldier in the good fight!"

Far from a knee-jerk diatribe in favor of war, his speech addressed the complexities of the political landscape in Vietnam, admitted the draw that communism's rhetoric had for the oppressed, while also honestly assessing the failure of America's diplomatic and military strategies in creating an effective counterdoctrine. Rather than attempt to provide these solutions, he proposed a mechanism for arriving at them through conversations among journalists and diplomats, academics and politicians. Moreover, he suggested this work would require "an attitude of warm brotherhood in giving help with the honest humility which can be accepted with honor," and suggested looking to the international labor movement for a model.

His greatest insight came in his conclusion that drew from the wisdom of Vietnamese students fighting for their own peace, not with guns, but with words and actions:

> To give point to all of the foregoing, let me quote from a current Vietnamese student handbill in Saigon. It was written by student leaders to their fellow students. The young Vietnamese who wrote this want to lead 5,000 students in Saigon out into the countryside this coming summer vacation, despite the dangers and hardships they know await them in the country, to do social action work, literacy training, land rehabilitation, and construction. The student leaders make this plea to their fellow students:
>
> "You will warm up your unfortunate comrades with your humanity

and love. You will throw a bridge of communion between cities and countryside, the educated class and the uneducated one, the privileged people and the ill-treated ones. You are workers to build up Love, Understanding, Sacrifice, Confidence, and Hope. You will revive the national self-reliant spirit, the four thousand year old moral tradition of Vietnam."

There speak the Vietnamese. Surely we have a bond of brotherhood with people such as they. I trust that you feel it and understand it. Our great challenge still awaits.

The peace for which a war is waged determines its end before the first bullet is even fired. Dickey believed in the kind of peace these students were fighting for as she believed the United States, with all its might, should join them as allies and equals.

There was ample evidence this would never be the case.

The CIA had recently pulled funds from the Sea Swallows, tried to remove Father Hoa as their leader, and left them surrounded by three battalions of well-armed, well-trained Viet Cong. The first of many callous abandonments of onetime allies, the move also prefigured the American-centric military strategy swiftly being enacted. Dickey was neither unaware nor indifferent to these developments. She attempted to cover the Sea Swallows in their hour of need, pitching the story to *Reader's Digest,* which had previously published her piece on them. Perhaps for a combination of liability and policy reasons, they declined.

Painfully aware of the steep hill ahead and the precipice below, Dickey still preserved a last bit of hope, choosing to believe that the United States might yet still pursue a just peace. As always, she did what she could to help bring it about.

33

On Patrol with the Marines

I side with prisoners against guards, enlisted men against
officers, weakness against power.

—Dickey Chapelle

IN THE SPRING of 1965, Dickey had grown tired of war and violence, of
the immeasurable sadness of orphans and mothers who had lost their
children, of the never-ending hailstorms of bullets and rivers of blood
she had seen drench four continents. She searched for another way
to effect the change she wanted to see in the world. For a moment it
seemed she found it, once more through the Quakers.

Grace Perkins, assistant director of the Quaker American Friends
Service Committee, wrote to Dickey in the summer of 1965 with a proposal. Their fiftieth anniversary was coming up in 1967 and they wanted
to publish a history of the organization. Her experience with the Quakers coupled with her talents as a photographer and writer made Dickey
the ideal candidate to develop such a project. "Would you be interested
to pick up this idea on your own?" she wrote.

Dickey wrote back immediately, suggesting she photograph Quaker
programs around the world and structure the book around themes of
the "Quaker view of history" as well as the "declining prestige of violence."
But her plans to document peace would have to wait as the world raced
once again toward total war.

Only a few days after her writing to Grace, President Johnson announced a massive buildup of troops in Vietnam and increased draft calls

to thirty-five thousand every month. Simultaneously, the 82nd Airborne was deployed to help preserve the cease-fire between rebel factions in the Dominican Republic.

Dickey pitched stories on both emergent developments. *The National Observer* was the first to bite and sent her to Santo Domingo, where she landed on a hot July day after jumping out of a plane with the 82nd Airborne. More than a story, Dickey discovered how the United States Armed Forces could win the war in Vietnam and even the Cold War: not through bullets, but through compassion.

Entitled "Seize, Occupy, Defend, and Make Friends," Dickey's article drew a direct line between the 82nd Airborne's tactics and the larger US Cold War strategy, particularly as it applied to Vietnam. As she wrote, "On line through the heart of Santo Domingo are companies from the 82nd Airborne Division, tough fighters like the Special Forces in Vietnam. The two outfits share the same home base, Fort Bragg, and the same lonely hard-earned pride in being among the fiercest men alive." But when she asked to photograph one of the officers as he engaged in a normal line of duty activity, he did not raise his gun. Instead, as Dickey wrote, "he posed—willingly—dancing ring-around-a-rosy with a dozen fourth-grade girls, pupils of one of the seven schools his company had organized in an effort to keep the local children clear of lines of fire." The 82nd Airborne also provided medicine, clothes, and food to local residents, and in so doing built relationships and goodwill with those they were trying to win over.

"Perhaps, someday," she concluded, "compassion as an infantry tactic will be taught to every American soldier. He still will need to know, of course, his rifle number, his commanding general's name, and how to kill without hesitating. And, when he kills, he will ask—as soldiers have so often asked—if it was necessary. It will be that last reflex—the wondering why, the compassion for others—that will be harnessed to the purposes of foreign policy; an Idea, really, that is new to great world powers."

Dickey mailed an early draft to the article's real audience: General Wallace Greene. "I hope shortly to be able to arrange another assignment in Vietnam so I can cover the Marines in Combat," Dickey wrote in her letter enclosed with the article. "With that in mind I have reported to several publications my recent observations of compassionate tactics by American fighting men in Laos, Vietnam, and the Dominican Republic. I've called my outline, 'Love As an Infantry Tactic.'"

Instrumental in Dickey's early coverage of the Vietnam War as the Marine Corps chief of staff, Greene had since been promoted to commandant, the Marine's highest-ranking officer. In this role, he more than anyone would set the tone and tenor for the Marine Corps as the first of the US Armed Services to deploy combat units to South Vietnam, and it was his thinking that she sought to influence through her article.

Greene responded by inviting her to his office in Washington, DC. Besides, she needed a favor. *The National Observer* had commissioned her to follow the newly deployed Marines as they began their initial search-and-clear operations near Da Nang. Her increasingly critical stance on both press censorship and counterproductive military tactics had once again made her persona non grata with the Armed Services press office, which dragged its heels on approving her visa for Vietnam. But Greene knew her, knew the criticisms she leveled were in service of her lifelong patriotism, her love of country, and her admiration of the Marines.

She arrived at his office in a suit with the Australian bush hat she had taken to wearing in the field tucked beneath her arm. On it were the Vietnamese airborne and 101st Airborne wings as well as the insignias of the Sea Swallows and the Vietnamese Junk Force sailors.

General Greene took the hat from her, looked it over.

"What is it sir?" said Dickey.

"I don't see any Marine insignia there, aren't we tough enough for you?" he asked and took his own from his collar. "I don't think anybody will mind," he said, pinning it to her hat.

For a second it seemed she had caught the dream she had been chasing for so long, the one in which the United States stood for the freedom of everyone, everywhere. She thought of Iwo Jima and Okinawa, of the Marines who had inspired the trajectory of her life, marching shoulder to shoulder against a common enemy, in the service of a common good. The words she had spoken then came back to her now. "When I die I want to be on patrol with the Marines."

As always, she asked to go as far forward as they would let her. As ever, the Marines obliged by sending her to the front.

On November 2, 1965, Dickey arrived at the newly constructed Chu Lai Marine Air Base buried deep in Viet Cong territory. With the First and Third Battalions of the Seventh Marines Regiment, Dickey left the base the following day, hiking out to a nearby village where the Viet Cong maintained a stronghold. In the warm evening rain, Dickey dug her foxhole, huddled under her poncho, and smoked a cigarette. She was forty-seven years old. The smell of the earth recalled memories of other underground places, of trenches and empty canals and root cellars where people go to hide from war and where she had gone to find them. Here she was again. The silver trails of tracer shells illuminated the night sky as she drifted off to sleep.

She woke to a rainbow arcing over her foxhole. Dickey climbed out, cut her C ration can open with her Swiss Army knife, a poor replacement for the trench knife the dying Marine had given her on Iwo Jima. But at least it reminded her of him.

She found Staff Sergeant Albert P. Miville, whose patrol was set to depart soon.

"Can I go with?" she asked.

"Sure, Dickey," he said, "fall in."

They left at 0745, walking toward a cane field across which lay a sniper hill they had been tasked to take. Before they even got to the field, the Marine in front of her, just a boy, tripped an improvised explosive device with his boot. He ran. She stood. The M-26 grenade attached to an 81mm mortar shell lifted her twenty feet in the air. She died as she had always wanted, while on patrol with the Marines, marching shoulder to shoulder with those willing to fight for a better world.

Epilogue

Into That Heaven of Freedom

ON NOVEMBER 14, 1965, a cold wind gathered the fallen leaves as her family entered the First Unitarian Church on Ogden Avenue in Milwaukee. They were followed by a Marine honor guard in full dress, a distinction for those who have served. Friends entered after. Finally, the press who had come to cover her funeral as the first American female journalist to be killed in combat.

Reverend John W. Cyrus, one of the city's most respected clergymen, stepped to the pulpit beneath the church's vaulted ceiling. He cleared his throat. The cameramen snapped their lenses. He waited for them to quiet again before reading a poem by the Nobel Prize–winning poet and confidant of Mahatma Gandhi, Rabindranath Tagore.

> Where the mind is without fear and the head is held high;
> Where knowledge is free;
> Where the world has not been broken up into fragments by
>   narrow domestic walls;
> Where words come out from the depth of truth;
> Where tireless striving stretches its arms towards perfection;
> Where the clear stream of reason has not lost its way into the
>   dreary desert sand of dead habit;

Where the mind is led forward by thee into ever-widening
thought and action—
Into that heaven of freedom, my Father, let my country awake.

This, he said, embodied all that Georgette "Dickey" Meyer Chapelle
had strived to achieve through her work, which was her life, which was
her legacy.

When they arrived at her grave site, the funeral procession found
a dozen red roses from the Hungarian Freedom Fighters. The Marine
honor guard buried her with full military honors. A bugler played taps.
Two Marines folded the American flag thirteen times into a blue field of
stars and presented it to her brother, Robert Meyer.

The 82nd Airborne, whose dedication to service had inspired her
idea of love as infantry tactic, staged a mass paratroop jump over the
Dominican Republic in her honor and named their drop zone after her.
On the first anniversary of her death, the Marine Corps dedicated a
marble plaque to her at Chu Lai that reads:

**TO THE MEMORY OF DICKEY CHAPELLE,
WAR CORRESPONDENT, KILLED IN ACTION
NEAR HERE ON 4 NOVEMBER 1965.**

SHE WAS ONE OF US, AND WE WILL MISS HER.

For twenty-five years, Dickey traced the thin line between war and
peace. Her dispatches wove between aircraft carriers in the Pacific and
helicopters in Vietnam, bonfire beacons on the Austro-Hungarian border and water wells in the Middle East, secret wars in Laos and clandestine missions in Miami, traffic clerks turned revolutionaries in Cuba
and shepherds turned guerrillas in Algeria. Like no other reporter, her
body of work forms a complex tapestry of one of history's most consequential eras.

Yet what makes her work ever more relevant to our own time was
her ability to recognize and document the human element in each of the
conflicts she covered. She was never a big-picture journalist, never one
to pull back to the safe distance of dispassionate reporting, but always

on the ground, eye to eye, first to the front. She understood why those she covered were fighting and what they were risking, the freedoms they hoped to gain and those they would lose if they failed. Most of all, she understood each of the conflicts she covered not as separate or isolated, but as they were, as battles in a global struggle for the freedom of all people.

In this, she found the force that sustained her throughout her career, that kept her going after so many setbacks and hard years, through so many firefights and deaths of those she admired. She found a universal esprit de corps, a communion that cut across color and creed and geography. She devoted her life to documenting its progress. Nowhere is this idea of fierce solidarity better expressed than in the words she wrote about those who gave their lives on the sands of Iwo Jima: "My favorite image of a better world is not one without struggle, but simply one in which committed thousands move shoulder to shoulder disregarding risk and loss toward objectives of more lasting worth than a volcanic island fit only to grow white crosses."

ACKNOWLEDGMENTS

I owe a great debt of gratitude to so many. First and foremost, I want to thank the Meyer family for their extraordinary generosity and trust. For decades, the Meyer family have stewarded and preserved the legacy of their beloved family member, Georgette "Dickey" Meyer Chapelle. Without them, her stories, insights, and photographs would be lost to history. It was through them that I was able to access her archives, and though this is a debt I cannot repay, I hope this book is a start.

I am also indebted to the Wisconsin Historical Society and its capable staff. Thanks especially to Cynthia Bachhuber, who fielded my early inquiries with aplomb; to Lee Grady, whose daily expertise helped me find just what I needed; and Jennifer Barth, whose curiosity and enthusiasm never ceased to inspire me even on the longest of days elbow-deep in research. This book would not have taken shape without the professionalism and brilliance of my research assistants, Abigail Lewis and Meghan O'Donnell. Their insights into Dickey Chapelle's archives proved invaluable, as did their contributions to this book.

I am forever in the debt of Ronald Gerber, literary agent extraordinaire, who called me out of the blue, who believed in this book before even I did, and who has done so much to help shepherd it into being. Like Michelangelo, my remarkable editor, Hannah O'Grady, saw a fine-tuned sculpture in the great slab of my first draft. Her insight, passion, and patience were invaluable and immensely appreciated. Nor would these pages be what they are without Bill Warhop, who astonished me with his military expertise and profound knowledge of grammar. I am also grateful to all the proofreaders who combed this book for errant typos and incongruities. Their work was imperative and most appreciated.

To my husband and best friend, Joshua Miles Shelton: your encouragement and indefatigable positivity gave me the will to continue even after the hundred-thousandth word and the millionth edit. I love you from here to the moon and back. As a constant source of inspiration and joy, our sons, Hudson and Thoreau, have contributed more to this book than they will ever know.

I want to thank my father, whose insatiable reading habits and curiosity inspired my own and who supported my every aspiration, myriad though they have been. I am also deeply grateful for the support of my aunt, Robbie Brinton, whose belief in me as a writer has been as steadfast through the years as it has been enthusiastic. From childcare to farmers market runs to never-ending love and support, my devoted stepfather, Sandy Lejeune, is in no small part responsible for these pages.

Most of all and above all, I am grateful for the support of my mother, whose belief in my writing never failed or flagged, whose support is stronger than a cathedral buttress, and whose example is and has always been a source of wisdom and inspiration. Thank you, Mom.

SOURCES

Sources are listed in the order in which material first appears in each chapter.

INTRODUCTION

Various. *Correspondence.* 1961–1962. Box 5, Folders 1–7. Wisconsin State Historical Society, Dickey Chapelle Archives.

Ostroff, R. *Fire in the Wind: The Life of Dickey Chapelle.* Annapolis, MD: Naval Institute Press, 2001.

Behind the Pearl Earrings: The Story of Dickey Chapelle, Combat Photojournalist. PBS. November 3, 2015.

1. A WORLD ON THE BRINK OF WAR

Chapelle, D. *What's a Woman Doing Here?: A Reporter's Report on Herself.* Emeryville, CA: Franklin Classics, 2018.

Chapelle, D. "A 20-Year-Old Girl Dives 10,000 Feet in a Fighting Plane to Prove That Women Can Be Combat Pilots." 1939. Box 14, Folder 1. Wisconsin State Historical Society, Dickey Chapelle Archives.

2. TRIAL BY FIRE, REPORTING FROM PANAMA

Chapelle, D. *What's a Woman Doing Here?: A Reporter's Report on Herself.* Emeryville, CA: Franklin Classics, 2018.

Various. *Correspondence.* 1933–1950. Box 2, Folders 2–9. Wisconsin State Historical Society, Dickey Chapelle Archives.

3. THE WAY BACK

Chapelle, D. *What's a Woman Doing Here?: A Reporter's Report on Herself*. Emeryville, CA: Franklin Classics, 2018.

Ostroff, R. *Fire in the Wind: The Life of Dickey Chapelle*. Annapolis, MD: Naval Institute Press, 2001.

Chapelle, D. "Nursing in Wartime." 1945. Box 13, Folder 9. Wisconsin State Historical Society, Dickey Chapelle Archives.

Various. *Correspondence*. 1933–1950. Box 2, Folders 2–9. Wisconsin State Historical Society, Dickey Chapelle Archives.

Chapelle, D. *Notes, Drafts, and Captions, 1945, from Iwo Jima, Okinawa, and Saipan*. 1945. Box 11, Folder 4. Wisconsin State Historical Society, Dickey Chapelle Archives.

Chapelle, D. "Notes on Saipan Trip." 1945. Box 11, Folder 4. Wisconsin State Historical Society, Dickey Chapelle Archives.

Chapelle, D. "Village at the Front." 1945. Box 9. Wisconsin State Historical Society, Dickey Chapelle Archives.

4. AS FAR FORWARD

Chapelle, D. *With My Eyes Wide Open: The Autobiography of Dickey Chapelle*. 1960. Boxes 15–17. Wisconsin State Historical Society, Dickey Chapelle Archives.

Various. *Correspondence*. 1933–1950. Box 2, Folders 2–9. Wisconsin State Historical Society, Dickey Chapelle Archives.

Chapelle, D. *Blood Talk*. Edited by A. R. Cross. 1945. Box 12. Wisconsin State Historical Society, Dickey Chapelle Archives.

Chapelle, D. "Joe Coming Home." 1945. Box 13. Wisconsin State Historical Society, Dickey Chapelle Archives.

Chapelle, D. "Caption for Negatives: Pacific Ocean Theater." 1945. Box 13. Wisconsin State Historical Society, Dickey Chapelle Archives.

Chapelle, D. "The Quality of Mercy." *Reader's Digest*, October 1957, 173–76.

5. TO THE FRONT

Chapelle, D. *Iwo Jima Notebook*. 1945. Box 18, Vol. 71. Wisconsin State Historical Society, Dickey Chapelle Archives.

Chapelle, D. *With My Eyes Wide Open: The Autobiography of Dickey Chapelle*. 1960. Boxes 15–17. Wisconsin State Historical Society, Dickey Chapelle Archives.

Sherwood, J. D. *War in the Shallows: US Navy Coastal and Riverine Warfare in Vietnam, 1965–1968*. Washington, DC: Naval History and Heritage Command, Department of the Navy, 2015.

Lotring, K. "WWII Archives." Submarine Force Library & Association. April 3, 2020. https://ussnautilus.org/tag/world-war-ii.

Chapelle, D. *What's a Woman Doing Here?: A Reporter's Report on Herself*. Emeryville, CA: Franklin Classics, 2018.

Chapelle, D. "Nursing in Wartime." 1945. Box 13, Folder 9. Wisconsin State Historical Society, Dickey Chapelle Archives.

6. FLOATING CITY

Chapelle, D. *Notes, Drafts, and Captions, 1945, from Iwo Jima, Okinawa, and Saipan.* 1945. Box 11, Folder 4. Wisconsin State Historical Society, Dickey Chapelle Archives.

Chapelle, D. *With My Eyes Wide Open: The Autobiography of Dickey Chapelle.* 1960. Boxes 15–17. Wisconsin State Historical Society, Dickey Chapelle Archives.

USS Franklin CV-13 War Damage Report No. 56. Washington, DC: Naval History and Heritage Command, 1945.

Chapelle, D. *What's a Woman Doing Here?: A Reporter's Report on Herself.* Emeryville, CA: Franklin Classics, 2018.

7. OKINAWA

Various. *Correspondence.* 1933–1950. Box 2, Folders 2–9. Wisconsin State Historical Society, Dickey Chapelle Archives.

Chapelle, D. *Notes, Drafts, and Captions, 1945, from Iwo Jima, Okinawa, and Saipan.* 1945. Box 11, Folder 4. Wisconsin State Historical Society, Dickey Chapelle Archives.

Chapelle, D. *With My Eyes Wide Open: The Autobiography of Dickey Chapelle.* 1960. Boxes 15–17. Wisconsin State Historical Society, Dickey Chapelle Archives.

Chapelle, D. *What's a Woman Doing Here?: A Reporter's Report on Herself.* Emeryville, CA: Franklin Classics, 2018.

Chapelle, D. "Village at the Front." 1945. Box 9. Wisconsin State Historical Society, Dickey Chapelle Archives.

Chapelle, D. "Mission of Mercy." 1945. Box 9. Wisconsin State Historical Society, Dickey Chapelle Archives.

8. THE LIMIT OF HUMAN ENDURANCE

Chapelle, D. *What's a Woman Doing Here?: A Reporter's Report on Herself.* Emeryville, CA: Franklin Classics, 2018.

Chapelle, D. *With My Eyes Wide Open: The Autobiography of Dickey Chapelle.* 1960. Boxes 15–17. Wisconsin State Historical Society, Dickey Chapelle Archives.

Chapelle, D. "Combat Fatigue." 1945. Box 9. Wisconsin State Historical Society, Dickey Chapelle Archives.

Appleman, R. E. *Okinawa: The Last Battle.* Washington, DC: US Army, 2005.

Chapelle, D. "Kamikaze Notes." 1945. Box 9. Wisconsin State Historical Society, Dickey Chapelle Archives.

9. THE WAR AT HOME

Chapelle, D. *With My Eyes Wide Open: The Autobiography of Dickey Chapelle*. 1960. Boxes 15–17. Wisconsin State Historical Society, Dickey Chapelle Archives.

Erikson, L. "Shower Baths and Ice Cream Help War's Combat Fatigue Casualties." *Baltimore Sun,* May 23, 1943.

Various. *Correspondence*. 1933–1950. Box 2, Folders 2–9. Wisconsin State Historical Society, Dickey Chapelle Archives.

Staff. "Doctors Discuss Combat Fatigue." *The New York Times*. January 29, 1943.

Ostroff, R. *Fire in the Wind: The Life of Dickey Chapelle*. Annapolis, MD: Naval Institute Press, 2001.

Chapelle, D. "It Still Hurts." 1945. Box 11. Wisconsin State Historical Society, Dickey Chapelle Archives.

Chapelle, D. "Civilians Just Don't Get the Word." 1945. Box 11, Folder 12. Wisconsin State Historical Society, Dickey Chapelle Archives.

Various. *Correspondence*. 1951–1956. Box 3. Folders 1–7. Wisconsin State Historical Society, Dickey Chapelle Archives.

Behind the Pearl Earrings: The Story of Dickey Chapelle, Combat Photojournalist. November 3, 2015, PBS.

10. THE CRATER OF RECENT PEACE

Various. *Correspondence*. 1933–1950. Box 2, Folders 2–9. Wisconsin State Historical Society, Dickey Chapelle Archives.

Chapelle, D. "Background and Captions for AVISO." 1947–1949. Box 9, Folders 6–11. Wisconsin State Historical Society, Dickey Chapelle Archives.

Chapelle, D. *With My Eyes Wide Open: The Autobiography of Dickey Chapelle*. 1960. Boxes 15–17. Wisconsin State Historical Society, Dickey Chapelle Archives.

Chapelle, D. *What's a Woman Doing Here?: A Reporter's Report on Herself*. Emeryville, CA: Franklin Classics, 2018.

Resch, A., and D. Stiefel. "Vienna: The Eventful History of a Financial Center." In *Global Austria: Austria's Place in Europe and the World*, edited by G. Bischof and F. Plasser, 117–46. New Orleans: University of New Orleans Press, 2011.

Chapelle, D. "Are We Committing Genocide in Europe?" 1948. Box 9, Folder 11. Wisconsin State Historical Society, Dickey Chapelle Archives.

Ostroff, R. *Fire in the Wind: The Life of Dickey Chapelle*. Annapolis, MD: Naval Institute Press, 2001.

11. HOME AGAIN

Various. *Correspondence*. 1933–1950. Box 3, Folders 2–9. Wisconsin State Historical Society, Dickey Chapelle Archives.

Chapelle, D. *What's a Woman Doing Here?: A Reporter's Report on Herself*. Emeryville, CA: Franklin Classics, 2018.

12. INCREMENTALISM

Various. *Correspondence.* 1933–1950. Box 3, Folders 2–9. Wisconsin State Historical Society, Dickey Chapelle Archives.

Chapelle, D. "Background and Captions for AVISO." 1947–1949. Box 9, Folders 6–11. Wisconsin State Historical Society, Dickey Chapelle Archives.

Chapelle, D. "Notes on Foreign Aid." 1948. Box 13, Folder 11. Wisconsin State Historical Society, Dickey Chapelle Archives.

13. NAPLES

Various. *Correspondence.* 1933–1950. Box 3, Folders 2–9. Wisconsin State Historical Society, Dickey Chapelle Archives.

Chapelle, D. *With My Eyes Wide Open: The Autobiography of Dickey Chapelle.* 1960. Boxes 15–17. Wisconsin State Historical Society, Dickey Chapelle Archives.

Chapelle, D. "Are We Committing Genocide in Europe?" 1948. Box 9, Folder 11. Wisconsin State Historical Society, Dickey Chapelle Archives.

Chapelle, D. "Perspective." 1952. Box 8, Folder 10. Wisconsin State Historical Society, Dickey Chapelle Archives.

Chapelle, D. "Mud Hut." 1956. Box 13, Folder 14. Wisconsin State Historical Society, Dickey Chapelle Archives.

14. IRAQ

Various. *Correspondence.* 1951–1956. Box 3, Folders 1–7. Wisconsin State Historical Society, Dickey Chapelle Archives.

Various. *Correspondence.* 1933–1950. Box 2, Folders 2–9. Wisconsin State Historical Society, Dickey Chapelle Archives.

Chapelle, D. *Basra Diary.* 1952. Box 11, Folder 2. Wisconsin State Historical Society, Dickey Chapelle Archives.

Chapelle, D. "Locust Wars Draft." 1952. Box 8, Folder 10. Wisconsin State Historical Society, Dickey Chapelle Archives.

Chapelle, D. "Report from the Locust Wars." *National Geographic*, April 1953.

Chapelle, D. "Khidr Al-Ma'a Notes." 1952. Box 11, Folder 2. Wisconsin State Historical Society, Dickey Chapelle Archives.

Chapelle, D. "Top Locust Fighter." 1952. Box 8, Folder 10. Wisconsin State Historical Society, Dickey Chapelle Archives.

Chapelle, D. "Mabee Anecdotes." 1952. Box 8, Folder 10. Wisconsin State Historical Society, Dickey Chapelle Archives.

Chapelle, D. "Borrowed Easter." 1952. Box 11, Folder 2. Wisconsin State Historical Society, Dickey Chapelle Archives.

Chapelle, D. "Easter Sunday." 1952. Box 11, Folder 2. Wisconsin State Historical Society, Dickey Chapelle Archives.

15. IRAN

Various. *Correspondence.* 1951–1956. Box 3, Folders 1–7. Wisconsin State Historical Society, Dickey Chapelle Archives.

Gasiorowski, M. J. "The 1953 Coup d'État Against Mosaddeq." In *Mohammad Mosaddeq and the 1953 Coup in Iran*, edited by M. J. Gasiorowski and M. Byrne, 227–60. Syracuse, NY: Syracuse University Press, 2004.

Chapelle, D. *With My Eyes Wide Open: The Autobiography of Dickey Chapelle.* 1960. Boxes 15–17. Wisconsin State Historical Society, Dickey Chapelle Archives.

16. INDIA

Various. *Correspondence.* 1951–1956. Box 3, Folders 1–7. Wisconsin State Historical Society, Dickey Chapelle Archives.

Various. *Correspondence.* 1933–1950. Box 2, Folders 2–9. Wisconsin State Historical Society, Dickey Chapelle Archives.

Sackley, N. "Village Models: Etawah, India, and the Making and Remaking of Development in the Early Cold War." *Diplomatic History* 37, no. 4 (2013): 749–78.

Chapelle, D. "The Community Development Experiment in India." 1953. Box 10, Folder 10. Wisconsin State Historical Society, Dickey Chapelle Archives.

Chapelle, D. "Plumb to the Punjab." 1953. Box 8, Folder 10. Wisconsin State Historical Society, Dickey Chapelle Archives.

Bhattacharyya, R., Birendra Ghosh, Prasanta Mishra, Biswapati Mandal, Cherukumalli Rao, Dibyendu Sarkar, Krishnendu Das, et al. "Soil Degradation in India: Challenges and Potential Solutions." *Sustainability* 7, no. 4 (2015): 3528–70.

Chapelle, D. "Master Race." 1952. Box 8, Folder 10. Wisconsin State Historical Society, Dickey Chapelle Archives.

Chapelle, D. "Tiger Hunt." 1952. Box 8, Folder 10. Wisconsin State Historical Society, Dickey Chapelle Archives.

Chapelle, D. "Changing Life for the Mudia Gond." 1953. Box 8, Folder 10. Wisconsin State Historical Society, Dickey Chapelle Archives.

Chapelle, D. "New Life Photo Captions." 1952. Box 8, Folder 10. Wisconsin State Historical Society, Dickey Chapelle Archives.

Chapelle, D. "New Life for India's Villagers." *National Geographic,* April 1956, 572–88.

Chapelle, D. "Mud Hut." 1956. Box 13, Folder 14. Wisconsin State Historical Society, Dickey Chapelle Archives.

17. LEAVING

Various. *Correspondence.* 1951–1956. Box 3, Folders 1–7. Wisconsin State Historical Society, Dickey Chapelle Archives.

Barron, J. "When New York Baked for 12 Sweltering Days." *The New York Times*, July 19, 2013.

"Reader's Digest." St. James Encyclopedia of Popular Culture. Encylopedia.com. June 21,

2022. https://www.encyclopedia.com/media/encyclopedias-almanacs-transcripts
-and-maps/readers-digest.

Staff. "Rodell, Marie Freid." The Martin Luther King Jr. Research and Education Institute. June 5, 2018. https://kinginstitute.stanford.edu/encyclopedia/rodell-marie
-freid.

Chapelle, D. *What's a Woman Doing Here?: A Reporter's Report on Herself.* Emeryville, CA: Franklin Classics, 2018.

Higgs, R. *US Military Spending in the Cold War Era: Opportunity Costs, Foreign Crises, and Domestic Constraints.* Cato Institute Policy Analysis, 1988.

Rawlins, E. W., and W. J. Sambito. *Marines and Helicopters: 1946–1962.* Washington, DC: History and Museums Division, Headquarters, US Marine Corps, 1976, 40–57.

18. STARTING AGAIN

Various. *Correspondence.* 1951–1956. Box 3, Folders 1–7. Wisconsin State Historical Society, Dickey Chapelle Archives.

Chapelle, D. "Test Unit Number One." 1955. Box 13, Folder 14. Wisconsin State Historical Society, Dickey Chapelle Archives.

Chapelle, D. "How Rough Does It Need to Be." 1955. Box 13, Folder 14. Wisconsin State Historical Society, Dickey Chapelle Archives.

U.S. Marine Corps. *Battalion Training Order 73–55.* 1955. Box 12, Folder 6. Wisconsin State Historical Society, Dickey Chapelle Archives.

Price, D. H. *Cold War Anthropology: The CIA, the Pentagon, and the Growth of Dual Use Anthropology.* Durham, NC: Duke University Press, 2016, 195–220.

Ostroff, R. *Fire in the Wind: The Life of Dickey Chapelle.* Annapolis, MD: Naval Institute Press, 2001.

"History of the International Rescue Committee." International Rescue Committee (IRC), February 28, 2022. https://rescue.org/page/history-international-rescue
-committee.

19. THE IRON CURTAIN IS A CORNFIELD

Various. *Correspondence.* 1951–1956. Box 3, Folders 1–7. Wisconsin State Historical Society, Dickey Chapelle Archives.

Chapelle, D. *With My Eyes Wide Open: The Autobiography of Dickey Chapelle.* 1960. Boxes 15–17. Wisconsin State Historical Society, Dickey Chapelle Archives.

Chapelle, D. "Nobody Owes Me a Christmas." *Reader's Digest,* December 1957, 37–41.

Society for the Investigation of Human Ecology. New York, 1955. [Brochure.] Box 3. Wisconsin State Historical Society, Dickey Chapelle Archives.

Chapelle, D. "An Anguished Exodus to Liberty." *Life,* December 3, 1956.

Williams, J. "Soviet Steps Up Revolt Charges." *The New York Times,* December 4, 1956.

20. IMPRISONMENT

Chapelle, D. *With My Eyes Wide Open: The Autobiography of Dickey Chapelle*. 1960. Boxes 15–17. Wisconsin State Historical Society, Dickey Chapelle Archives.

Chapelle, D. "Red Terror." 1957. Box 10, Folder 8. Wisconsin State Historical Society, Dickey Chapelle Archives.

Chapelle, D. *What's a Woman Doing Here?: A Reporter's Report on Herself*. Emeryville, CA: Franklin Classics, 2018.

Chapelle, D. "Red Dungeon." 1957. Box 10, Folder 8. Wisconsin State Historical Society, Dickey Chapelle Archives.

Chapelle, D. "You Can't Be Brainwashed." 1957. Box 10, Folder 8. Wisconsin State Historical Society, Dickey Chapelle Archives.

Chapelle, D. "Nobody Owes Me a Christmas," draft. 1957. Box 10, Folder 8. Wisconsin State Historical Society, Dickey Chapelle Archives.

Chapelle, D. "The Limit of Human Endurance." 1957. Box 10, Folder 8. Wisconsin State Historical Society, Dickey Chapelle Archives.

21. SCAR TISSUE

Chapelle, D. *What's a Woman Doing Here?: A Reporter's Report on Herself*. Emeryville, CA: Franklin Classics, 2018.

Chapelle, D. "Red Dungeon." 1957. Box 10, Folder 8. Wisconsin State Historical Society, Dickey Chapelle Archives.

Chapelle, D. "Proof of God." 1957. Box 10, Folder 8. Wisconsin State Historical Society, Dickey Chapelle Archives.

Chapelle, D. *With My Eyes Wide Open: The Autobiography of Dickey Chapelle*. 1960. Boxes 15–17. Wisconsin State Historical Society, Dickey Chapelle Archives.

Various. *Correspondence*. 1957–1958. Box 4, Folders 1–7. Wisconsin State Historical Society, Dickey Chapelle Archives.

22. THE ALGERIAN NATIONAL LIBERATION FRONT

Chapelle, D. *With My Eyes Wide Open: The Autobiography of Dickey Chapelle*. 1960. Boxes 15–17. Wisconsin State Historical Society, Dickey Chapelle Archives.

Chapelle, D. *Notebook 22*. 1957. Box 18, Vol. 22. Wisconsin State Historical Society, Dickey Chapelle Archives.

Chapelle, D. "My Harem Family." 1957. Box 10, Folder 1. Wisconsin State Historical Society, Dickey Chapelle Archives.

Chapelle, D. "A Hill Is to Climb." 1957. Box 10, Folder 1. Wisconsin State Historical Society, Dickey Chapelle Archives.

Chapelle, D. "Now I Know Why the Algerians Fight." *Pageant,* April 1958, 113–17.

Chapelle, D. "The Moral Issue and One Hostage." 1957. Box 10, Folder 1. Wisconsin State Historical Society, Dickey Chapelle Archives.

23. BECOMING A PERPETUAL MOTION MACHINE

Chapelle, D. "Nobody Owes Me a Christmas." *Reader's Digest,* December 1957, 37–41.
Various. *Correspondence.* 1957–1958. Box 4, Folders 1–7. Wisconsin State Historical Society, Dickey Chapelle Archives.
Chapelle, D. *With My Eyes Wide Open: The Autobiography of Dickey Chapelle.* 1960. Box 15–17. Wisconsin State Historical Society, Dickey Chapelle Archives.
Chapelle, D. "Raw Notes 6th Fleet." 1958. Box 12, Folder 7. Wisconsin State Historical Society, Dickey Chapelle Archives.
Chapelle, D. "Turkey: The Land Where Russia Stops." *Reader's Digest,* June 1958, 63–69.
Chapelle, D. "Now I Know Why the Algerians Fight." *Pageant,* April 1958, 113–17.

24. CUBA

Chapelle, D. "Remember the 26th of July." *Reader's Digest,* April 1959, 50–56.
Chapelle, D. *What's a Woman Doing Here?: A Reporter's Report on Herself.* Emeryville, CA: Franklin Classics, 2018.
Chapelle, D. "How Castro Won." *Marine Corps Gazette,* February 1960, 36–44.
Chapelle, D. "Cuba Draft 1/19." 1958. Box 10, Folder 4. Wisconsin State Historical Society, Dickey Chapelle Archives.
Chapelle, D. "Cuban Marine." 1958. Box 10, Folder 4. Wisconsin State Historical Society, Dickey Chapelle Archives.
Chapelle, D. "Day and Night with Castro's Forces." 1959. Box 10, Folder 4. Wisconsin State Historical Society, Dickey Chapelle Archives.
Chapelle, D. "You Must Know That You Have Become a Legend." *National Observer,* vol. 4, no. 25, 1965, 1, 12–13.
Chapelle, D. "Cuba One Year After." *Reader's Digest,* January 1960, 67–74.

25. WITH HER EYES WIDE OPEN

Various. *Correspondence.* 1959–1961. Box 4, Folders 1–7. Wisconsin State Historical Society, Dickey Chapelle Archives.
Ostroff, R. *Fire in the Wind: The Life of Dickey Chapelle.* Annapolis, MD: Naval Institute Press, 2001.
Chapelle, D. *What's a Woman Doing Here?: A Reporter's Report on Herself.* Emeryville, CA: Franklin Classics, 2018.
Clymer, K. "Cambodia and Laos in the Vietnam War." In *The Columbia History of the Vietnam War,* edited by D. L. Anderson, 357–81. New York: Columbia University Press, 2002.
Chapelle, D. "Our Secret Weapon in the Far East." *Reader's Digest,* June 1960, 189–99.

26. LAOS

Various. *Correspondence*. 1959–1961. Box 4, Folders 1–7. Wisconsin State Historical Society, Dickey Chapelle Archives.

Chapelle, D. "I Roam the Edge of Freedom." *Coronet*, February 1962.

Various. *Correspondence*. 1963–1964. Box 7, Folders 1–5. Wisconsin State Historical Society, Dickey Chapelle Archives.

Leary, W. "CIA Air Operations in Laos, 1955–1974." *Studies of Intelligence*, vol. 3, no. 25 (1999): 71–89.

Head, W. P. "Dirty Little Secret in the Land of a Million Elephants." *Air Power History* 64, no. 7 (2017): 7–28.

Chapelle, D. "The Men Who Didn't Give Up Laos." 1961. Box 11. Wisconsin State Historical Society, Dickey Chapelle Archives.

Various. *Correspondence*. 1961–1962. Box 6, Folders 1–7. Wisconsin State Historical Society, Dickey Chapelle Archives.

Staff. "Clearing Cluster Bombs in Laos." The HALO Trust, http:www.halotrust.org /where-we-work/south-asia/laos/.

Chapelle, D. "The War We Have Just Begun to Fight." 1962. Box 13, Folder 5. Wisconsin State Historical Society, Dickey Chapelle Archives.

27. GUERRILLA WARFARE

Various. *Correspondence*. 1959–1961. Box 5, Folders 1–7. Wisconsin State Historical Society, Dickey Chapelle Archives.

Various. *Correspondence*. 1961–1962. Box 6, Folders 1–7. Wisconsin State Historical Society, Dickey Chapelle Archives.

Chapelle, D. "An American's Primer of Guerrilla Warfare." 1961. Box 12, Folder 9. Wisconsin State Historical Society, Dickey Chapelle Archives.

Chapelle, D. "Notes; Untitled; Laos, Vietnam." 1961–1962. Box 13, Folder 7. Wisconsin State Historical Society, Dickey Chapelle Archives.

28. THE SEA SWALLOWS

Various. *Correspondence*. 1961–1962. Box 6, Folders 1–7. Wisconsin State Historical Society, Dickey Chapelle Archives.

Chapelle, D. "The Fighting Priest of Vietnam." *Reader's Digest*, July 1963, 194–200.

Chapelle, D. *Binh Hung Diary*. 1962. Box 12, Folder 10. Wisconsin State Historical Society, Dickey Chapelle Archives.

Chapelle, D. "Three Day Operation." 1961. Box 12, Folder 10. Wisconsin State Historical Society, Dickey Chapelle Archives.

British Pathé. "Kennedy Speaks on Vietnam." 1962. Reuters. Video.

Grimes, W. "Donn Fendler, Who Was Lost in Wilds of Maine as a Boy, Dies at 90." *The New York Times*, October 11, 2016.

Chapelle, D. "Caption Data: Laos." 1962. Box 9, Folder 13. Wisconsin State Historical Society, Dickey Chapelle Archives.

Ahern, T. L. *In Vietnam Declassified: The CIA and Counterinsurgency*. Lexington: University Press of Kentucky, 2012, 71–90.

Chapelle, D. "An American's Primer of Guerrilla Warfare." 1961. Box 12, Folder 9. Wisconsin State Historical Society, Dickey Chapelle Archives.

Hofmann, G. R. *The Path to War: US Marine Corps Operations in Southeast Asia 1961 to 1965*. Quantico, VA: History Division, Marine Corps University, 2014.

Various. *Correspondence*. 1963–1964. Box 7, Folders 1–5. Wisconsin State Historical Society, Dickey Chapelle Archives.

Horrock, N. "Private Institutions Used in CIA Effort to Control Behavior." *The New York Times,* August 2, 1977.

Thomas, J. "Extent of University Work for CIA Is Hard to Pin Down." *The New York Times,* October 8, 1977.

29. NO TURNING BACK NOW

Ellis, F. R. "Dickey Chapelle: A Reporter and Her Work." Master's thesis, journalism, University of Wisconsin, 1968.

Various. *Correspondence*. 1961–1962. Box 6, Folders 1–7. Wisconsin State Historical Society, Dickey Chapelle Archives.

"Mike Wallace Interview of Dickey Chapelle." *PM Starring Mike Wallace*, edited by M. Wallace. Westinghouse TV, February 15, 1962.

Behind the Pearl Earrings: The Story of Dickey Chapelle, Combat Photojournalist. November 3, 2015, PBS.

Various. *Correspondence*. 1963–1964. Box 7, Folders 1–5. Wisconsin State Historical Society, Dickey Chapelle Archives.

Chapelle, D. "Caption Data: Laos." 1962. Box 9, Folder 13. Wisconsin State Historical Society, Dickey Chapelle Archives.

Hofmann, G. R. *The Path to War: US Marine Corps Operations in Southeast Asia 1961 to 1965*. Quantico, VA: History Division, Marine Corps University, 2014.

Chapelle, D. "Caption Data Helicopter War." 1962. Box 9, Folder 13. Wisconsin State Historical Society, Dickey Chapelle Archives.

Chapelle, D. "Helicopter War in South Viet Nam." *National Geographic,* November 1962, 723–54.

Keever, B. D. *Death Zones and Darling Spies: Seven Years of Vietnam War Reporting*. Lincoln: University of Nebraska Press, 2013.

Head, W. "The March to Oblivion: The Defeat at Ap Bac Hamlet and the Americanization of the Vietnam War." *Journal of Third World Studies* 31, no. 2 (2014): 57–81.

30. FREEDOM OF THE PRESS

Various. *Correspondence*. 1961–1962. Box 6, Folders 1–7. Wisconsin State Historical Society, Dickey Chapelle Archives.

Chapelle, D. "Memo: Recent Personal Experience with Attempted Management of News." 1963. Box 7. Wisconsin State Historical Society, Dickey Chapelle Archives.

Chapelle, D. "Is the News Controlled?" *National Photo Journalist,* 1963.

31. NINETY MILES

Chapelle, D. "Day Underground." 1963. Box 10, Folder 4. Wisconsin State Historical Society, Dickey Chapelle Archives.

Staff. "Arthur Sylvester, 78." Obituary, *The Washington Post,* December 30, 1979.

Various. *Correspondence.* 1963–1964. Box 7, Folders 1–5. Wisconsin State Historical Society, Dickey Chapelle Archives.

Chapelle, D. *Untitled: Miami Journal.* 1963. Box 10, Folder 5. Wisconsin State Historical Society, Dickey Chapelle Archives.

Chapelle, D. "Report from Miami: The Commandos and the Company." 1963. Box 10, Folder 4. Wisconsin State Historical Society, Dickey Chapelle Archives.

Chapelle, D. "Bridges to Nowhere." 1964. Box 10, Folder 3. Wisconsin State Historical Society, Dickey Chapelle Archives.

Russell, R. "An Ex-CIA Man's Stunning Revelations on 'The Company,' JFK's Murder, and the Plot to Kill Richard Nixon." *Argosy,* April 1976.

Chapelle, D. "Underground Letters." 1962. Box 10, Folder 5. Wisconsin State Historical Society, Dickey Chapelle Archives.

Final Report of the Select Committee on Assassinations. US House of Representatives, Ninety-Fifth Congress, Second Session. Washington, DC: US House of Representatives, 1979.

Chapelle, D. "Requiem for a Rebel." 1964. Box 10, Folder 3. Wisconsin State Historical Society, Dickey Chapelle Archives.

32. WATER WAR

Various. *Correspondence.* 1963–1964. Box 7, Folders 1–5. Wisconsin State Historical Society, Dickey Chapelle Archives.

Sherwood, J. D. *War in the Shallows: US Navy Coastal and Riverine Warfare in Vietnam, 1965–1968.* Washington, DC: Naval History and Heritage Command, Department of the Navy, 2015.

Lin, M. "China and the Escalation of the Vietnam War: The First Years of the Johnson Administration." *Journal of Cold War Studies* 11, no. 2 (2009): 35–69.

Peterson, L. C. P. "The Truth About Tonkin." *Naval History Magazine* 22, no. 1 (2008).

Various. *Correspondence.* 1965–1967. Box 8, Folders 1–3. Wisconsin State Historical Society, Dickey Chapelle Archives.

McCoy, A. W. *The Politics of Heroin: CIA Complicity in the Global Drug Trade.* Brooklyn, NY: Lawrence Hill Books, 1991, 283–386.

Head, W. P. "Dirty Little Secret in the Land of a Million Elephants." *Air Power History* 64, no. 7 (2017): 7–28.

Carson, A. *Secret Wars: Covert Conflict in International Politics.* Princeton, NJ: Princeton University Press, 2020, 187–237.

Chapelle, D. "Water War in Vietnam." 1965. Box 13, Folder 6. Wisconsin State Historical Society, Dickey Chapelle Archives.

Chapelle, D. "Water War in Vietnam." *National Geographic,* February 1966, 270–96.

Staff. "'Teach-in' at University." (Madison, WI) *Capital Times,* April 3, 1965, 1, 4.

33. ON PATROL WITH THE MARINES

Various. *Correspondence.* 1963–1964. Box 7, Folders 1–5. Wisconsin State Historical Society, Dickey Chapelle Archives.

Various. *Correspondence.* 1965–1967. Box 8, Folders 1–3. Wisconsin State Historical Society, Dickey Chapelle Archives.

Chapelle, D. "Seize, Occupy, and Defend—and Make Friends." *National Observer,* August 2, 1965.

Haines, D. "One Helluva Woman." *Combat Magazine,* July 2006.

INDEX

Chiang Kai-shek, 57
China (People's Republic of China),
 23, 57, 295
 Indian policies of, 155
 Indochina War and, 276
 Korean War and, 305
 Vietnam policies of, 332, 336
Chu Lai Marine Air Base,
 Vietnam, 347
CIA, 149
 Bay of Pigs invasion and,
 274–75, 317
 Cuba covert operations by, 274–75,
 308, 312, 317
 Cuban exile group operations by,
 274–75, 312, 324–27, 331
 Iran covert operations by, 153
 Laos operations by, 267–68, 276–79,
 282, 301, 333–35
 MK-Ultra interrogation program by,
 306–7
 Operation Barrel Roll and, 333–34
 Operation Erawan by, 267–68, 276
 Vietnam covert operations by, 276,
 301–3, 331, 333–34
Civil Air Transport (CAT), 276
Cohn, Sol H., 181–82
Colby, William, 303
Cold War, ix–xv, 105, 131, 142, 183,
 232–33, 236–37
 arms race in, 118, 234
 China's role in, 155, 332
 Cuba and, 260–61, 317–20, 321–29,
 332
 Hungarian Revolution in, xi,
 188–94, 195–219, 231, 241,
 262, 273, 350
 Iran and, 152–53
 Laos and, 267–68
 military training scenarios for,
 176–80
 proxy wars/conflicts in, 262–63,
 267–68, 274–78, 280, 303, 308,
 312, 317, 324–27, 332
 Red Scare/McCarthyism in,
 120, 137, 165
 Turkey-USSR conflicts in, 235
combat fatigue, 82–83. *See also*
 post-traumatic stress disorder
Commando L (anti-Castro Cuban
 exile group), 311–12,
 321–26, 328

communism, 228–29, 274, 306, 341
 in China, 57, 155, 295, 332
 in Cuba, 260–61, 312, 319–20,
 323, 326
 in Hungary, 188–216, 218–19, 222,
 231, 235–36, 241
 Laotian Civil War and, 262–63,
 267–68, 276–83, 332
 Red Scare/McCarthyism and,
 120, 137, 165
 in USSR, x–xi, 94, 100, 130, 155,
 188–216, 234, 261, 267, 277, 280,
 324, 332
 of Viet Cong, 263, 273, 276–77,
 291, 293–94, 295–96, 301, 304,
 315, 317, 342
Community Development Program,
 India (CDP), 159–61, 164
concentration camps, 102–3
Congressional Record, 264
Converse, Earl T., 8–9
Coordination of United Revolutionary
 Organizations (CORU), 312
Cople, Johnnie, 279–80
Cornell University College of Human
 Ecology, 306–7
Coronet, 273
Cosmopolitan, Chapelle articles
 in, 83, 85
Cowan, John, 65–68, 70–71, 75–76
Cuba
 air shows in, 5–6, 10
 anti-Castro exile groups and, 170, 274,
 311–12, 320, 321–29
 Bay of Pigs invasion in, 275, 317
 Castro-led oppression in, 319–20
 Chapelle's reports from, xii, xiv, 5–6,
 10, 216, 237, 241–63, 273
 CIA covert operations targeting,
 274–75, 308, 312, 317,
 324–27, 331
 missile crisis in, 317–20, 321, 332
 revolution in, xii, xiv, 216, 237–63,
 273, 275, 287–88, 308, 322,
 324, 329
Cuban Missile Crisis, 332
 censorship of, 317–19, 321
Cuban Revolutionary Army, xii, xiv.
 See also 26th of July Army
Cuban Revolutionary Council (CRC),
 274–75
Cyrus, John W., 349